GOVERNMENTS, NON-STA'
AND TRADE POLICY-M

One of the most pressing issues confronting the multilateral trade system is the challenge posed by the rapid proliferation of preferential trade agreements. Much has been written about why governments might choose to negotiate preferentially or multilaterally, but until now it has been written almost exclusively from the perspective of governments. We know very little about how non-state actors view this issue of 'forum choice', or how they position themselves to influence choices by governments about whether to emphasize PTAs or the WTO.

This book addresses that issue squarely through case studies of trade policy-making and forum choice in eight developing countries: Chile; Colombia; Mexico; South Africa; Kenya; Jordan; Indonesia; and Thailand. The case studies are based on original research by the authors, including interviews with state and non-state actors involved in the trade policy-making process in the eight countries of this study.

ANN CAPLING is Professor of Political Science at the University of Melbourne.

PATRICK LOW is Director of Economic Research and Statistics, WTO Secretariat and Adjunct Professor at the Graduate Institute of International and Development Studies, Geneva.

GOVERNMENTS, NON-STATE ACTORS AND TRADE POLICY-MAKING

Negotiating Preferentially or Multilaterally

Co-edited by
ANN CAPLING AND PATRICK LOW

CAMBRIDGE UNIVERSITY PRESS

CAMBRIDGE UNIVERSITY PRESS
Cambridge, New York, Melbourne, Madrid, Cape Town, Singapore,
São Paulo, Delhi, Dubai, Tokyo, Mexico City

Cambridge University Press
The Edinburgh Building, Cambridge CB2 8RU, UK

Published in the United States of America by Cambridge University Press, New York

www.cambridge.org
Information on this title: www.cambridge.org/9781107000186

First published 2010

Printed in the United Kingdom at the University Press, Cambridge

A catalogue record for this publication is available from the British Library

Library of Congress Cataloguing in Publication data
Governments, non-state actors and trade policy-making : negotiating
preferentially or multilaterally / [edited by] Ann Capling, Patrick Low.
p.   cm.
Includes index.
ISBN 978-1-107-00018-6 – ISBN 978-0-521-16561-7 (pbk.)
1. Tariff preferences – Developing countries.   2. Trade blocs – Developing
countries.   3. Non-governmental organizations – Developing countries.
I. Capling, Ann, 1959–   II. Low, Patrick, 1949–   III. Title.
HF2580.9.G68 2010
382′.9091724–dc22
2010029995

ISBN 978-1-107-00018-6 Hardback
ISBN 978-0-521-16561-7 Paperback

CONTENTS

LIST OF FIGURES AND TABLES

Figures

Tables

vii

CONTRIBUTORS

Co-editors (and project directors)

ANN CAPLING,
Professor of Political Science, University of Melbourne, Australia.

PATRICK LOW,
Director of Economic Research and Statistics, WTO, Switzerland and
Adjunct Professor, Graduate Institute of International and Development
Studies, Geneva, Switzerland.

Authors

GILBERTO BIACUANA,
Economist, Development Through Trade Project, South African
Institute of International Affairs.

ANN CAPLING,
Professor of Political Science, University of Melbourne, Australia.

ALEXANDER C. CHANDRA,
Southeast Asian Coordinator, Trade Knowledge Network, Jakarta,
Indonesia.

TSIDISO DISENYANA,
Deputy Head, Development Through Trade Project, South African
Institute of International Affairs.

PETER DRAPER,
Head, Trade Programme, South African Institute of International
Affairs.

JAVIER GAMBOA,
Executive Vice President, Colombian Council of Competitiveness,
Bogotá.

HERNANDO JOSÉ GOMEZ,
President, Colombian Council of Competitiveness, Bogotá.

LUTFIYAH HANIM,
Research Associate, Third World Network, Jakarta, Indonesia.

SEBASTIÁN HERREROS,
Regional Expert, International Trade and Integration Division, United
Nations Economic Commission for Latin America and the Caribbean,
Santiago, Chile.

RIAD AL KHOURI,
Dean of Business School, Lebanese French University, Erbil, Iraq.

PATRICK LOW,
Director of Research and Statistics, WTO, Switzerland and Adjunct
Professor, Graduate Institute of International and Development Studies,
Geneva, Switzerland.

NJUGUNA NG'ETHE,
Institute for Development Studies, University of Nairobi, Kenya.

JACOB OMOLO,
Institute of Policy Analysis and Research, Nairobi, Kenya.

LINDA PASQUEL,
Counsel, IQOM Inteligencia Comercial, S. A. de C. V.

MARÍA PÉREZ-ESTEVE,
Counsellor, Information and External Affairs Division, WTO
Secretariat, Geneva, Switzerland.

THITINAN PONGSUDHIRAK,
Director, Institute of Security and International Studies, Chulalongkorn
University, Bangkok, Thailand.

JAIME ZABLUDOVSKY,
Executive President, Mexican Council for Industry and Consumer
Products, Mexico City, Mexico.

ACKNOWLEDGEMENTS

First and foremost, the editors would like to thank the chapter authors for their patience, fortitude and commitment to making this project a success. The bulk of this volume is theirs and we have found it a great pleasure to work with them.

The volume is the product of research collaboration between the University of Melbourne and the World Trade Organization Secretariat, and was made possible by financial and/or in-kind contributions from a number of sources. First, we should like to express our gratitude to the Australian Research Council (Grant DP0772790) and the WTO for their valuable support, without which the project would not have come to fruition.

We wish to thank all the following individuals and institutions for their generous support: Ms Wendy Ruffles of the School of Social and Political Sciences, University of Melbourne for her administrative assistance throughout the course of the project; Paulette Planchette of the Economic Research and Statistics Division of the WTO, who has also provided assistance in preparing the manuscript for publication; Alvaro Baillet of El Colegio de México and El Colegio itself provided generous support for the first project meeting in Mexico City. Thitinan Pongsudhirak and the Institute of Security and International Studies of Chulalongkorn University did the same for our second project meeting; and Alejandro Jara was a valuable source of support and advice throughout the project.

DISCLAIMER

Opinions expressed in this volume and any errors or omissions therein are the responsibility of the authors concerned, and not of the editors. Opinions expressed by the editors are their own and should not in any way be attributed to the institutions with which they are associated.

Introduction

ANN CAPLING AND PATRICK LOW

Gone are the days when trade policy decisions were settled by one or two government ministries and conveyed with little ceremony to parliament and the public. Evolving views and practices on participatory decision-making, along with a policy-making environment that continues to grow in complexity, have changed the manner in which national trade policy is formulated. The number of governmental authorities and agencies implicated in national trade policy dialogues has multiplied, and so too has the number and diversity of non-state actors (NSAs) laying claim to a say in policy deliberations.[1] This array of parties, including both business and civil society organizations (CSOs), will frequently be pulling governments in different directions. They will also make greater efforts in some policy contexts than others.

The transformation of trade policy-making has attracted considerable attention from scholars and practitioners alike, and there have been many studies that explore the broadening of the trade policy agenda, the emergence of new actors seeking to influence that agenda and the need for governments to manage the growing complexity and politicization of trade policy. However, most of this work has focused on the impact of these changes at the global level, particularly in relation to the workings of the World Trade Organization (WTO), rather than at the domestic level where trade policy-making actually begins. And while there is growing interest in measures taken by governments to 'democratize' trade policy development by making it more open, inclusive and participatory, this literature is largely descriptive, with little analysis of the impact of these processes and interactions on the decisions ultimately taken by governments.

Even less is known about the relationship between these interactions and the preferences of both governments and NSAs on alternative

---

[1] When we refer to NSAs we include both 'economic' and socially-motivated non-state actors. In some contexts we distinguish between the two, and often refer to the latter group as CSOs.

instruments for trade cooperation – that is, preferential (bilateral and plurilateral) versus multilateral negotiations. To be sure, there is a burgeoning literature on the political and economic motives that spur governments to enter into these arrangements (WTO 2007; Ravenhill 2005). By contrast, literature on societal preferences for regional versus multilateral trade negotiations and the impact of these preferences on government policy and the choice of negotiating forum is scant (Mansfield and Milner 1999). Given the rapid proliferation of preferential trade agreements (PTAs) in recent years, and the accompanying debates about whether PTAs are trade-creating or trade-diverting, and their consequences for the multilateral trade system, this is a particularly striking gap in our knowledge and understanding of domestic trade policy-making.

This book presents the findings of an international research project that was aimed at gaining a better understanding of how NSAs see their interests and seek to influence government policy in relation to PTAs and the WTO as alternative venues for international trade cooperation. The project has explored these issues through case studies of eight developing countries from three continents. The case studies address several related questions. What is the role of NSAs in the development of national approaches to policy formulation in relation to PTAs and multilateral negotiations through the WTO? Do governments and NSAs come to the table with their preferences fully formed, or are they shaped and influenced by their interactions with each other? What are the implications of the interactions between NSAs and governments in terms of preferred instruments for trade cooperation? What then are the 'optimum' modes of cooperation? And for whom? What does this tell us about the drivers of multilateralism and regionalism/preferentialism in terms of domestic political and economic interests? Does this offer us any lessons about government choices vis-à-vis multilateralism versus regionalism? Does this offer us any lessons about the multilateralism versus regionalism debate more generally?

The volume begins with a conceptual chapter examining the theory of trade policy-making and issues influencing preferences in relation to the negotiating forum – that is, the choice between a preferential and a multilateral setting. Chapters 2 to 9 contain the case studies on Chile, Colombia, Mexico, Indonesia, Thailand, Jordan, Kenya and South Africa. These chapters broadly follow the same structure. They start with background analysis of the economic, trade and trade policy context of the country. Subsequent sections discuss the major governmental and non-governmental actors in the trade policy-making process, their aims and their interests. This sets the scene for an analysis of the interaction between different actors, followed by a summary and findings. Chapter 10 complements the country case studies by examining the role of NSAs in the WTO. The chapter analyses how NSAs try to influence WTO decision-making and how, if at all, this international activity is linked to the domestic context in the case study countries. Chapter 11 contains the findings and conclusions of the study.

References

Mansfield, E. D. and Milner, H. V. 1999. 'The New Wave of Regionalism', *International Organization* **53**: 3.

Ravenhill, J. R. 2005., 'Regionalism', in J. R. Ravenhill (ed.), *Global Political Economy*. Oxford University Press, pp. 116–47.

World Trade Organization 2007. *World Trade Report 2007: Six Decades of Multilateral Trade Cooperation: What Have we Learnt?* Geneva: World Trade Organization.

The domestic politics of trade policy-making: state and non-state actor interactions and forum choice

ANN CAPLING AND PATRICK LOW

This chapter outlines the conceptual framework and surveys the existing literature underpinning the case studies that follow. This survey is as important for some of the gaps it reveals as it is as a stock-taking of previous conceptual and empirical work. The first section explores the literature on the evolution of trade policy-making in domestic settings and, in particular, the imperatives that are driving trade ministries to engage much more closely with non-state actors (NSAs) in the formulation of trade policy. Most of this research has focused on government-initiated consultation exercises and it has been largely descriptive rather than analytical. Nonetheless, these studies have yielded some preliminary findings that are relevant to this project, and these are briefly discussed. Section 2 outlines the major theories of trade policy-making more generally, with a view to shedding light on the competing explanations of preference formation and how governmental and NSA preferences are translated into policy choices. While each group of theories offers illuminating insights, we suggest that none alone can adequately explain the complexity of trade policy-making in the real world, and we argue for a synthetic approach that is attuned to the role of interests, ideas and institutions in understanding the policy process. The third section discusses the issue of forum choice. Compared with the growing literature seeking to explain why governments might prefer regional to multilateral approaches to trade cooperation, there is very little analysis of NSA preferences in relation to forum choice, let alone any research that seeks to investigate this through the prism of government–NSA interactions. This section lays out some of the issues that may influence forum choice among decision-makers, but has little to say as to whether these same factors will influence NSA attitudes to forum selection. That, indeed, is one of the key questions to be addressed in this project.

1   The changing nature of trade policy-making

The trade policy-making process has evolved in ways that would have been unimaginable only twenty years ago. Once a closed and technocratic process, dominated by officials in one or two ministries and largely insulated from political debate and public scrutiny, the formulation of trade policy now demands the participation of a broad and diverse range of government and non-governmental actors, including business interests, civil society organizations, think tanks, consultants and academic experts. In many countries, these developments have also been complemented by a range of government-initiated measures to promote greater public education about trade issues and the benefits of trade liberalization, greater access to information about government policies and greater transparency in policy development processes at every step of the way.

The reasons for this transformation are well understood. First, as measured by the ratio of trade to GDP, virtually all countries have become increasingly trade-dependent in terms of their overall economic activity. Trade policy-making has therefore grown in importance to both government and private sector actors. But most governments lack the internal research capacity and commercial intelligence that is crucial for the identification of negotiating positions for trade agreements and they are dependent on the private sector for information on barriers to trade and investment posed by trade measures, systems of regulation, standards, public procurement policies and so on. Hence, governments are compelled to engage directly with business actors through a broad range of formal and informal consultative mechanisms aimed at eliciting this information. The converse is equally true: in order to achieve some of their goals, private sector organizations rely on the authority of the state, through the unique ability of governments to negotiate, implement and enforce international trade agreements. Hence, many NSAs are increasingly inclined to pursue their agendas through 'partnership' with government (Shaffer 2003).

A second reason for this transformation is the growing breadth and complexity of the contemporary trade policy agenda. While it is not strictly true to assert, as many do, that the inclusion of 'behind the border' issues in trade negotiations is a recent phenomenon,[1] it is fair to say that by the mid-1990s, the Uruguay Round outcomes, in tandem with the conclusion

---

[1] Although early GATT negotiations focused on tariff reductions, later negotiating rounds addressed a broad range of 'behind the border' issues.

of a number of comprehensive preferential trade agreements (PTAs), represented the extension of international trade rules into domestic regulatory and legal systems in an unprecedented way. The impingement of trade rules on policy domains once considered to be 'domestic' and in policy spheres that had been previously insulated from trade policy, such as the environment, have had several consequences for the policy process. Within the confines of government, the expansion of the trade agenda has greatly complicated the policy development process, requiring the active involvement of multiple ministries and agencies. This process is further complicated in federal states where sub-national governments must also be involved in trade policy formulation, as responsibility for some regulatory issues resides at the sub-national level. Thus, trade policy officials must engage a far greater number of governmental actors, because of the need for information, expert advice and cooperation.

The expansion of the trade policy agenda has also prompted a broad range of civil society organizations (CSOs) to demand greater involvement in the trade policy process. Prior to the mid-1980s, there was very little civil society interest in the arcane world of trade agreements, but a number of major negotiations – including the North American Free Trade Agreement (NAFTA) and the Uruguay Round of the General Agreement on Tariffs and Trade (GATT) – began to attract their attention. This attention was not always favourable: in addition to expressing substantive concerns about the provisions of these agreements, CSOs were also critical of their inability to participate directly in bilateral and multilateral trade negotiations, of the privileged access that governments afforded to business interests and of the general lack of transparency surrounding every stage of the trade policy-making process (e.g., Wallach and Sforza 1999; Barton et al. 2006, 182–203).

These criticisms were coupled with a more general and growing concern in many countries about the impact of trade agreements on domestic economies, on domestic policy autonomy and even on local culture and identities. Part of this unease stemmed from the view that important decisions affecting local communities were being made by secretive and unaccountable international bodies – the so-called 'democratic deficit' in global governance (O'Brien et al. 2000). But these concerns were also played out in many national jurisdictions where disaffected publics and CSOs began to demand greater opportunities for participation in all stages of trade policy development from the broad determination of trade policy objectives to all stages of a trade negotiation, beginning with the initial decision to negotiate, through to the establishment of negotiating objectives, the negotiation itself and the legislative processes that accompany ratification and/or implementation of a trade agreement. Similar pressures have come from parliamentarians: with the notable exception of the United States, legislatures have traditionally been sidelined from the trade policy-making process, in part because constitutions vested treaty-making power, and therefore the power to make trade agreements, with the executive branch of government. In recent years, a number of developed and developing countries have sought to address that anachronism through the introduction of a variety of institutional innovations aimed at giving parliamentarians a greater say in trade policy-making (Capling 2005a).

Governments have responded to the civil society challenge in a number of ways. Mirroring initiatives taken by the WTO (WTO 2007, 333–42), many governments have established mechanisms designed to facilitate greater access to trade policy information and to promote dialogue and interaction between state and civil society actors. In some cases, governments have established entirely new processes for consulting CSOs on trade policy matters, whereas in others, CSOs have been invited to participate in multi-stakeholder consultations alongside business groups. Such initiatives have drawn mixed reviews to date. For instance, Stairs (2000) is wary of bureaucratic exercises that deflect fundamentally political issues away from ministers and parliamentarians. Draper (2007) suggests that multi-stakeholder forums that encompass business, trade unions and CSOs are not an appropriate place for governments to source commercial intelligence. And Weston (2005) cautions that consultative processes that become bogged down by demands from CSOs that do not share the interests or goals of business organizations could be counter-productive. Notwithstanding these reservations, there is a consensus among trade experts (Ostry 2002; Hocking 2004; Wolfe and Helmer 2007) that efforts by governments to increase transparency and to promote greater participation in trade policy-making are crucial to enhancing the legitimacy of these processes which, in turn, is a necessary condition for maintaining social cohesion and broad support for trade liberalization.

There are now a number of studies that have explored the transformation of trade policy-making in a number of developed and middle income developing countries (e.g., INTAL-ITD-STA 2002; Hocking 2004; Gallagher, Low and Stoler 2006; Halle and Wolfe 2007). In common these case studies describe the consultative mechanisms that governments have developed for the purpose of engaging non-governmental stakeholders in trade policy, and a number offer some assessment of the impact of these consultations on the transparency and legitimacy of the policy process. Although their findings are limited, for the purpose of our study, they yield several interesting observations.

(i) Approaches to government–NSA consultations differ widely among countries; in some cases they are formal and institutionalized and in others they remain less formal.

(ii) In most developing countries, only business actors possess the resources and capabilities that are essential to effective policy participation. Non-business actors, including in many cases governmental actors, lack technical, analytical and financial resources, and thus have a limited capacity to influence trade policy.

(iii) Consultative mechanisms tend to privilege business actors above CSOs.

(iv) Developing countries are lagging well behind developed countries in providing basic public information on trade flows, progress in trade negotiations and general research and analysis on trade-related matters. This in turn inhibits meaningful engagement in the trade policy process.

(v) Increasingly NSAs are engaging directly with their relevant ministries (e.g., industry, agriculture, the environment, etc.) in the expectation that they will act to represent and defend their interests in inter-governmental decision-making.

(vi) In most instances, these consultative processes first arose in relation to PTA rather than WTO negotiations. This was true, for example, in the cases of Argentina, Brazil, Canada, Chile and Uruguay, either because the regional integration process is deeper and more demanding or/and because there is more organized opposition to regional trade agreements, especially bilateral agreements involving a much stronger partner (often the United States).

(vii) Finally, the trade agenda is far more diverse and difficult as a result of the involvement of these new actors. Traditional protectionist coalitions which once dominated the process have been replaced by export-oriented business organizations, who perceive that there are greater opportunities available in PTAs than in the WTO, by CSOs advocating variants of protectionism for societal reasons, and by expanded government players (da Motta Veiga 2007, 177).

The findings from these case studies enrich our understanding of the growing complexity of trade policy-making and, in particular, the pressures on governments to engage with NSAs. They also generate some important questions for this project in relation to capacity and access. More important perhaps are the questions that arise from point (vi) above – namely, that because much of the government–NSA consultation activity first arose in the context of PTA negotiations, is it possible that these interactions have served to institutionalize NSA preferences for PTA rather than WTO negotiations?

While the existing literature is helpful in the way it describes the various ways that governments seek to engage and channel their interactions with NSA stakeholders, it does not tell us the whole story. One problem is that the focus on government-initiated consultations necessarily excludes analysis of the other ways in which NSAs might interact with and seek to influence government. These might include lobbying and political donations, clientelistic relations with particular government departments or agencies; the mobilization of potential electoral influence in specific regions (e.g., farmers), the mobilization of public opinion more broadly (e.g., environmental NSAs); or appeals based on ethical or moral persuasion (e.g., development NSAs, church groups, etc.). A second shortcoming of the literature is that it stops short of offering theoretical insights into how government–NSA interactions influence trade policy preferences and decision-making, including decisions to negotiate a particular PTA, resourcing decisions for particular trade negotiations, the establishment of negotiating positions, etc. Much of the literature seems to assume implicitly that governments have fixed preferences and that they seek to mobilize NSA participation in a way that supports those preferences; in other words, state preferences are assumed to be fixed and not influenced by NSAs. Similarly, it assumes that NSAs have fixed preferences that are not influenced by their interactions with government. This project seeks to interrogate these assumptions, with a view to developing an empirically-grounded understanding of how these government–NSA interactions influence trade policy decision-making.

2 Theories of trade policy-making

One of the primary aims of this project is to gain a better understanding of how non-governmental actors see their interests and seek to influence government policy in relation to trade agreements. There is a rich literature in economics and political science that seeks to explain how governments and NSAs form their trade policy preferences; it is widely agreed that no single theory provides an adequate explanation of this complex process. Thus, the purpose of this section is to provide a brief overview of each of the main theoretical approaches and to argue that each provides useful insights for our understanding of the development of trade policy preferences.

2.1   State-centric approaches

In seeking to explain the trade policy choices of governments, the literature on international relations begins with the state as its primary unit of analysis and it conceives of the government as a unitary rational actor. Within this literature, there are conflicting explanations as to what drives state behaviour. For instance, realist and structuralist theories emphasize relative power capabilities and argue that states are concerned above all to maximize their power in relation to other states. Thus, trade policies are secondary to other considerations, such as military power and security, and are used as instruments to support the goal of power maximization or strategic alliances (Krasner 1976; Lake 1988; Grieco 1990; Gowa 1994). By contrast, neoliberal institutionalist theory argues that states are primarily concerned with wealth and efficiency rather than power. However, its focus is not on how trade policies are determined *per se*, but on how governments can overcome collective action problems that prevent international trade cooperation (e.g., Keohane 1984).

State-centric approaches in international relations remind us that trade policy-making may be deeply influenced by international conditions, including the global distribution of wealth and power. In that sense, trade policy cannot necessarily be separated easily from other aspects of a country's foreign relations, and economic goals may be intertwined with strategic or other foreign policy considerations. But state-centric theories of trade policy have been widely criticized for their failure to explain how systemic constraints or considerations are transformed into policy preferences, for their inability to shed light on the complexities of decision-making processes and for their silence in relation to the political pressures faced by governments when making trade policy decisions. Indeed, these theories seem too far removed from the more detailed reality of trade policy-making where governments are confronted with a broad range of competing interests at home, and where trade policy decisions have consequences for the distribution of resources within national communities.

State-centric approaches in economics do not offer us much help either. Neoclassical economic theory also conceives of the state as a unitary rational actor, but extrapolates its interests from those of the individual consumer. Thus, the state's utility function is assumed to be economic welfare, and from this, its sole interest is the pursuit of the greatest income possible for its society, which in most cases is through the pursuit of free trade.[2] However, given the propensity of governments to use protectionist measures, this generates an obvious puzzle, which most economists have tried to answer by looking at the role of societal interests.

2.2   Societal approaches

In theorizing how governments make trade policy decisions, and why these decisions vary among countries and across time, societal accounts focus on the role of domestic pressure groups that seek to influence policy decisions. Societal accounts of trade policy-making generally begin with the assumption that domestic economic actors – firms, producers groups, trade unions, consumers – are rational decision-makers and that their interests are pre-determined and materially-derived. Within this political economy literature, there are competing theories that predict which groups will support free trade or protection, depending on their factor endowments (e.g., capital, land, labour). The Heckscher–Ohlin model predicts that within nations the owners of locally abundant factors of production will support trade liberalization, while the owners of scarce factors will oppose openness. Thus, trade policy preferences will follow factor or class lines. The Ricardo–Viner model predicts that individuals who own or work in export industries are more likely to favour trade liberalization than those who are invested in or employed by import-competing industries.

Closely linked to the Heckscher–Ohlin model, the Stolper–Samuelson theorem shows that when the relative price of a good rises, so too do the returns to the factor of production used intensively in the production of that good. What this predicts in practical terms is that unskilled workers producing traded goods in an industrial country will be worse off from trade because an unskilled worker in an industrial country is a less abundant factor of production than capital. This often becomes an argument in rich countries for eschewing trade in manufactures with poorer countries. Other theories reject these endowments-based models of trade preferences and instead focus on economies of scale, intra-industry trade, or the impact of the international economic structure (Milner 1988; Frieden and Rogowski 1996) as predictors of firm preferences.

---

[2]   Some studies have shown that in cases where a country possesses significant market power, government can use tariffs to manipulate the terms of trade in order to raise national income to the detriment of other countries (Johnson 1965; Bagwell and Staiger 2002).

As there is partial and contradictory evidence for each of these theories, political economists are generally in agreement that none in itself provides a sufficient understanding of societal trade policy preferences (Alt *et al.* 1996). For our purposes, it is sufficient to note that the political economy models are all premised on the assumption that the preferences of economic actors are driven by material interests, and therefore the lobbying behaviour of economic actors can be predicted by specific factors and the distributional consequences of liberalization.

So how are these societal interests translated into policy? In societal accounts, there is a presumption that individuals and firms demand policy and governments supply it in response to these demands. But economists and political scientists part ways when it comes to explaining how societal demands are translated into policy outcomes. As economists see it, governments are concerned with maximizing national economic welfare but not at the cost of losing office. Thus, there is a political market for certain trade policies and governments feel obliged to balance the power of rent-seekers (that may influence blocks of votes or provide campaign contributions) against the broader welfare interests of voters/consumers (see Magee and Young 1987; Grossman and Helpman 1994).

The value of this approach is that it draws attention to the broad array of domestic constituencies that influence policy considerations and it reminds us that governments have multiple and competing objectives, thus exposing the limitations of an assumed 'national interest'. However, most political scientists reject the notion that the political process is comparable to an auction. As Odell (1990, 148) notes, 'treating politics as analogous to a market of individuals obscures the society's institutionalized structures of authority and their effects'. Thus, in seeking to explain how societal groups influence trade policy-making, political scientists are interested in the role of political institutions and the way that they structure interactions between societal groups and government and influence policy outcomes.

2.3 The role of institutions

Institutionalist theory is premised on the idea that the organization of the political system has a direct bearing on the power that different sets of actors can exercise over policy outcomes (March and Olsen 1989). While the preferences of non-state and state actors remain important considerations, in order to explain variations in trade policy, institutionalist theory focuses on the way in which different institutions aggregate these preferences in different ways. For instance, many American scholars have argued that the Reciprocal Trade Act of 1934, which loosened the grip of Congress over trade policy while giving the executive greater control, reduced the ability of protectionist pressure groups to influence Congress (e.g., Haggard 1988; Destler 1992; Goldstein 1993).

In seeking to explain why governments adopt particular trade policies, and how trade policies change over time, institutionalists focus on the formal structures and procedures of government – such as regime type, electoral systems, party support and bureaucratic structures – and the way in which these structure the interactions between societal actors and policy-makers, and empower one set of actors over another. For instance, there is a large literature on the way in which different types of electoral institutions – the franchise, voting systems and the size of electoral districts – shape trade policy outcomes (for an overview see Hiscox 2005). The constitutional rules that determine which branch of government has authority over trade policy, the nature of legislative processes, and the extent to which they include formal mechanisms that provide societal groups with routine access to legislators are all said to have an impact on trade policy processes and outcomes. Institutionalist theory is also attentive to the role of bureaucratic agencies and the extent to which they have independent preferences or are 'captured' by the sectors that they are meant to be regulating.[3]

Much of this literature focuses on the extent to which political institutions insulate key policy-makers from domestic pressures, although there is little agreement as to whether relative state autonomy produces protectionist or liberalizing outcomes (Milner 1999). Other research has focused on the degree to which state power is fragmented, either between national ministries or between levels of government, as an explanation for trade policy outcomes. One recent study of economic policy-making in sixty countries found that the greater the number of independent institutional actors whose agreement is necessary to make trade policy (e.g., political parties, branches of government, bureaucratic actors) the more difficult it is for societal groups to press their demands effectively (Henisz and Mansfield 2006). In a similar vein, Tsebelis (1995) has argued that the more 'veto players' in the political system and the greater the conflict in their preferences, the less likely it is that policy change can be effected.

---

[3] Economists have borrowed from political scientists in developing public choice theory. Public choice theory models politicians and government officials as largely self-interested agents pursuing their own objectives rather than those of the society they are supposed to serve.

The emphasis on the central role of political institutions in structur-
ing the interactions between society and state helps to explain why governments may be relatively more or less responsive to societal pressures.
However, a second wave of institutional theory – sociological institutionalism – views these interactions as having transformative as well as
strategic effects. In this view, institutions not only structure the interactions between interests, these interactions also affect the way in which
problems are perceived and solutions are sought. In other words, institutional interactions can produce sets of shared understandings, which
in turn influence the preferences of both state and societal actors. Thus,
rather than being pre-determined and endogenous, preferences themselves may be shaped by institutions. While sociological institutionalism
has informed theories of international cooperation through the multilateral trade system (e.g., Ruggie 1982), few researchers have sought to apply
these insights to the domestic processes of trade policy-making (though
Woll 2008 is an exception).

2.4   The role of ideas

Another criticism that has been levelled at both state-centric and societal
accounts of trade policy is their shared assumption that preferences are
rationally determined to the exclusion of any consideration of the influence of ideas, values, norms and identities in preference formation. This
could be seen as a surprising black spot given the significant body of work
by trade scholars on the influence of ideologies and ideas on trade policy-
making over many centuries (e.g., Bhagwati 1988; Irwin 1996). However,
the sociological turn in recent thinking about trade policy development
reminds us that interests can be socially constructed, formed and transformed by the social environment which is specific to culture, place and
time (Trentmann 1998; Ford 2003).

'Constructivist' theory argues that ideas matter and that they play
a powerful role in shaping the interests and, therefore, the behaviour of
state actors. It is not difficult to identify different ideologies, ideas and theories that have had a great impact on trade policy in different countries
and across time. For example, theories of the 'developmental state' and
the belief in the importance of protection for infant and strategic industries were once deeply influential in many countries, but they now enjoy
less currency in theory and practice. The world view of policy-makers will
also influence governmental preferences; hence, mercantilist practices
were common in an age when the benefits of trade were seen in zero-sum

terms. Similarly, the behaviour of governments is conditioned by their self-identification and the image they wish to project to the world; for instance, a country that is seeking to act as a 'good international citizen' may be more inclined to support international institutions for trade cooperation, and less inclined to pursue predatory or discriminatory trade policies.

Similarly, constructivists argue that the preferences of societal actors are not only driven by rational calculations of material interests. For instance, in her study of trade in services liberalization, Woll (2008) found that the preferences of firms were 'socially embedded', influenced by regulatory and political arrangements, their self-identities, their beliefs about their international operations and their interactions with policy-makers. In addition, in thinking about contemporary trade policy-making, it is important to take account of societal groups that are motivated primarily by values rather than by calculations of economic self-interest, for example, environmental organizations, development agencies and human rights advocacy groups. Notwithstanding these examples, there are also cases where ideas have been mobilized for strategic purposes, as a camouflage for vested interests that seek to influence trade policy outcomes (Sell and Prakash 2004).

While ideas, norms and values are undeniably important influences in trade policy-making, we are not aware of any studies that argue convincingly that these are the only thing that matter. Ignoring completely the interests of actors, as either subjectively or objectively defined, and the constraining role of institutions, is simply too far removed from the real world of trade policy-making. Finally, researching the influence of ideas, disembodied from interests and institutions, is methodologically fraught.

2.5   Argument for a synthetic approach

As is evident from this discussion, no single theory or level of analysis can explain adequately the complexity of contemporary trade policy-making. Instead, a synthetic approach is required, one that is attentive to the role of interests, ideas and institutions, as well as to the international and the domestic dimensions of a negotiation and the interactions between them.[4] This has implications for our study: in seeking to develop a better understanding of why governments choose to negotiate a PTA or negotiate multilaterally, our case study writers have had to give careful

---

[4] Putnam (1988) developed the idea that trade negotiations are 'two-level' games between negotiators constrained by domestic constituencies. Thus, negotiators could use these

consideration to all of these approaches. As we shall see in section 3 on forum selection, this has been no easy task as the existing literature on forum choice is heavily state-centric (e.g., Elsig 2007). We know very little about the attitudes of non-state actors to questions of forum choice, or about how non-state actors seek to influence decision-makers.

3   Forum selection: alternative modes for trade cooperation

Much of the early literature that seeks to explain the motivations for trade cooperation is indifferent to forum choice – that is, it does not seek to distinguish between multilateral trade agreements and preferential (bilateral and regional) trade agreements (Yarbrough and Yarbrough 1992 is an exception). From about the early 1980s and particularly the 1990s onwards, however, preferences among most governments for multilateral trade liberalization and rule-making under the auspices of the GATT/WTO weakened. These developments have generated a voluminous literature on whether PTAs are trade-creating or trade-diverting and, more generally, their impact on the multilateral trade system. However, with very few exceptions, these debates have tended to treat governments as unitary actors, with little consideration of the role of non-state actors that seek to influence forum choice. Thus, our understanding of what drives decision-makers to choose one venue for trade cooperation over another is incomplete.

Forum selection may refer either to the choice of venue for negotiating specific issues or to the choice of forum for more broadly-based international trade negotiations. In the former case the question has generally been whether a particular topic should be negotiated in one international institution or another. Such debates have raged, for example, on whether intellectual property rights should be negotiated in the WTO or in the World Intellectual Property Organization, or whether labour issues belong in the WTO or the International Labour Organization. These are not the questions that concern us here.

Rather, our forum selection issue is about whether governments choose to negotiate a PTA or to negotiate multilaterally. One problem with posing the question thus is that it may be taken to assume that governments choose one or the other – in other words that these venues are mutually exclusive and a choice must be made between the two. This used to be the

domestic constraints while bargaining internationally, but also use the international negotiation as a bargaining tool at home. However, this study is not primarily concerned with understanding negotiating tactics and outcomes, but rather understanding the formation of negotiating preferences.

case for the United States, which until the beginning of the 1980s eschewed all reciprocal preferential trade agreements.[5] But today virtually no WTO member is not party to at least one PTA. Governments routinely operate in both domains to achieve comparable or sometimes very different trade cooperation objectives. It is not the objective of this project to reach normative conclusions on the relative merits of regional and multilateral forums for trade or trade-related negotiations. But neither can we be entirely blind to perceptions of the relative utility of the alternative venues when comparing the attitudes and behaviour of non-state actors towards government-led negotiations in regional and multilateral settings.

It may be useful to note here that while most of the discussion has been about negotiating trade rules or trade liberalization within one or other of these two settings, we would be taking too partial a view if we limited the analysis to these kinds of negotiation only. Another important aspect of forum choice relates to the enforcement of trade contracts through dispute settlement – a different kind of negotiation, but a negotiation nevertheless. The WTO has a well developed and largely successful dispute settlement mechanism. Some regional agreements do as well. When parties to a PTA contemplate dispute settlement proceedings to rectify a perceived infringement of a legal obligation, they are often in a position of choosing between the WTO or the PTA machinery for this purpose. There is growing interest in forum shopping for dispute settlement (Busch 2007), but relatively little literature on the role of NSAs in this process (for an exception see Davis 2006). We consider that factors underlying such a choice, and the role that is subsequently played by non-state actors in the dispute settlement process, are as important as the broader forum selection choice. Where appropriate, therefore, episodes of dispute settlement will be incorporated into the analysis.

A good deal has been written about the contrasts and similarities between regional and multilateral approaches to trade negotiations, but almost exclusively from the perspective of governments (de Melo and Panagariya 1993; Frankel 1997; Pomfret 1997; Bhagwati, Greenaway and Panagariya 1998; World Bank 2005; Baldwin 2006; Bhagwati 2008; Baldwin and Low 2009; Estevadeordal, Suominen and Teh, 2009). We know very little about how non-state actors view this issue, or how they position themselves to influence choices by governments about whether to emphasize PTAs or the WTO. As Mansfield and Milner (1999, 604) argue:

---

[5] The first foray by the United States into PTAs was the agreement with Israel, followed by the agreement with Canada and eventually NAFTA.

Though research stressing the effects of societal factors on regionalism offers various useful insights, it also suffers from at least two drawbacks. First, there is a lack of empirical evidence indicating which domestic groups support regional trade agreements, whose interests these agreements serve, and why particular groups prefer regional to multilateral liberalization ... Second, we know little about whether, once in place, regional arrangements foster domestic support for broader multilateral trade liberalization or whether they undermine such support. These issues offer promising avenues for future research.

In what follows we shall first attempt to contrast multilateral and regional venues in terms of a set of functions that we attribute to trade agreements. This will be followed by a non-exhaustive list of factors that might influence the choice of venue made by decision-makers. We do not claim that this list is exhaustive, nor that it is original, but we believe an attempt to systematize thinking about venue choice will facilitate systematic analysis of outcomes. As already noted, little has been written about non-state actor preferences in this context and how they may affect outcomes. Some of the same factors influencing forum choice within a government may well apply to NSAs. This is something we hope the present research will clarify. It is also worth noting here that we are likely to know much more about non-state economic actors and their attempts to influence governments, and rather less about the non-economic interests and what outcomes they have attempted to obtain.

3.1   The functions of trade agreements and the choice of venue

A typical characterization of the functions of a trade agreement would include the promotion of trade liberalization, rule-writing, dispute settlement and a deliberative or learning role arising from trade cooperation. We shall consider briefly each of these functions in relation to multilateral and regional agreements.

3.1.1   Trade liberalization

A significant difference with a multilateral approach under the GATT/WTO is that it extends the benefits of liberalization on a non-discriminatory basis to all members,[6] which is a much greater number of countries than under a regional agreement. The multilateral setting

---

[6] The WTO has 153 members and most non-members are seeking to join. It is not unreasonable for our purposes, therefore, to characterize the WTO as universalist, at least in intent.

does not throw up discriminatory privileges that favour a narrow group of insiders over outsiders. A first factor to consider, then, is how far-reaching and how economically and politically damaging the fragmentation implicit in a preferential or regional approach is in terms of the global trading community. This is largely an empirical question, and the problems are likely to be more acute in the case of some regional accords than others.

On the other hand, PTAs generally aspire to attain free trade among their members, whereas GATT/WTO negotiations have generally focused only on reducing some tariffs. But not all PTAs go to free trade among themselves. Again, an empirical question arises as to whether the GATT/WTO delivers more liberalization with its shallower but geographically diverse tariff reductions, or whether PTAs do better because cuts are deeper. Obviously a comparison between a WTO negotiation and a single PTA would reveal that the former yielded a far higher degree of liberalization. But taking the population of PTAs as the point of comparison over a given period of time may well reverse that finding.

A third point to bear in mind in a comparison between the two venues is that a world of PTAs will entail higher trade costs than non-discriminatory trade relations because of rules of origin. Much has been written about the cost burdens and distortions that can be hidden within complex systems of origin rules under free trade agreements. This factor reduces the attractiveness of PTA-based liberalization compared with a non-discriminatory approach. The severity of the problem will be strongly influenced by the size of the discriminatory margin that is being protected.

More generally, we should not forget that multilateral and regional venues are not the only ones for trade liberalization – dozens of countries have undertaken unilateral (non-discriminatory) trade liberalization on a unilateral basis over the past two or three decades.

3.1.2   Rule-making

The structure and content of GATT/WTO rules have arguably played an important role over the years in influencing the architecture and content of rules within PTAs. At the same time, some PTAs in recent years have been rather like laboratories for experimenting with rules, which later influence the WTO negotiating agenda. As traditional trade barriers such as tariffs and quantitative trade restrictions have fallen away, we have become much more aware of the role of non-tariff measures and trade-related policy areas in determining trade flows and the conditions of competition. This is what has led to growing concern with rule-making in international trade negotiations. A number of PTAs go further than the WTO in their coverage of rules relating to trade.

Just as with trade liberalization, the difference between PTAs and a multilateral focus on rule-making is important because of the discrimination embodied in the former and the supposed universality of coverage implied by the latter. Strictly speaking, discriminating variations in regulatory approaches fashioned within a PTA could hurt the trade prospects of PTA members in relation to third parties as well as countries outside the PTA. This would depend very much on the nature of the regulatory intervention and the degree of differentiation embodied in more locally specified regulation. On the other hand, some PTA-based regulatory reform or redesign could actually carry an 'MFN dividend' (Baldwin, Evenett and Low 2009). This would happen where it became impractical for a policy improvement (e.g., more trade facilitation) to be applied in a discriminatory fashion among trading partners.

A final related point to bear in mind is that PTA members have their WTO rights and, therefore, any regulatory changes within a PTA that enhance competition may be considered 'WTO-plus'. The same could be said of tariff reductions. But this still leaves the question of how much harm has been done to the trade interests of outsiders.

3.1.3   Dispute settlement

Not all PTAs have dispute settlement provisions. In these cases a cross-reference is sometimes made in the agreement to WTO dispute settlement rights. This does not raise any problems if the policy area concerned is covered by the WTO and does not involve additional obligations in other domains.

Some have argued that parties to PTAs often prefer the WTO dispute settlement machinery to the PTA option. Such a choice would be influenced primarily by credibility considerations. The PTA machinery may be considered to be weaker and more politicized, whereas the WTO dispute settlement system has a reputation for effectiveness and carries the weight of the entire WTO membership behind it. We are not aware of literature that has systematically analysed the political economy of forum choice in relation to dispute settlement.

3.1.4   Deliberative and learning functions

Trade agreements, whether they are preferential or multilateral, can be thought of as instruments for trade cooperation. As such, they serve important beneficial purposes such as promoting predictability and transparency in trade relations. However, one important difference between PTAs and multilateral agreements as instruments for trade cooperation is their degree of institutionalization. Whereas multilateral trade agreements are embedded within the World Trade Organization, very few PTAs are strongly institutionalized.

This difference may be important in relation to the opportunities for deliberation and learning that accompany trade negotiations. Most PTAs involve a one-off set of negotiations, which present opportunities for governments and stakeholders to exchange information and ideas in ways that foster mutual understanding. But beyond the negotiation, PTAs are relatively rigid and static, lacking in provisions that would foster on-going dialogue and deliberation. In that sense, the learning opportunities are limited.

By contrast, multilateral trade negotiations occur in a larger institutional setting, under the auspices of an international organization that serves a large membership for a broad range of purposes related to the goal of overcoming collective action problems in international trade. Moreover, the WTO presents opportunities for on-going dialogue and discussion beyond that which occurs in the context of a specific negotiation. In this way, the WTO can be said to promote learning, shape norms and expectations and influence behaviour in a way that is thought to be conducive to the broader goals of international trade cooperation. Relatively few PTAs afford these opportunities.

3.2   Some factors affecting choice of venue by decision-makers

In the following discussion we seek to explain a preference for PTAs and not a preference for the WTO (Warwick Commission 2007). The risk in choosing this default is that we may omit consideration of economic, social or political reasons why there may be a preference for a non-discriminatory, multilateral setting. Some reasons for this may be apparent from the previous section which compared the two venues in terms of the set of functions we attributed to trade agreements. PTAs, for example, carry trade costs that do not afflict non-discriminatory trade arrangements. Political considerations may simply dictate a preference for the WTO, just as they might dictate the opposite. The list below also includes some factors from which it is possible to see an argument in favour of the alternative non-discriminatory WTO venue. For example, an efficiency counter-argument could apply where the preference for a PTA is based on protectionism.

We have divided the list of factors into two categories. The first category explicitly seeks discrimination for an economic advantage or because a political motivation is involved which renders the multilateral venue irrelevant. The second category of factors identifies considerations where the preference for a PTA is a reflection of a reality that could change if the WTO was regarded as more effective or as more complete.

3.2.1   Discrimination intrinsic to an objective involving trade policy

(i) **Protection from foreign competition**: this reflects an economic interest in enlarging the geographical base for import substitution (Chase 2003).

(ii) **Smaller regional agreements as a stepping stone**: governments may be attracted to the idea that PTAs can act as laboratories for reform, with lessons learned serving to inform multilateral negotiations.

(iii) **Political consolidation at the regional level**: governments often have bilateral or regional political or strategic objectives that cannot be served in a multilateral setting. A separate question is whether preferential trade policy is required to meet such objectives, or whether they could be attained in other policy or political domains.[7]

(iv) **Enhancing bargaining power**: governments within a region may perceive an interest in consolidating their policy cooperation in order to constitute a larger bargaining entity in multilateral negotiations (Mansfield and Reinhardt 2003).

3.2.2   Objectives regarded as less effectively attainable in a multilateral setting

(i) **More efficient negotiations with fewer parties**: negotiating in large groups may be less efficient and render issues less tractable. If subsets of nations at the regional level were able to make common cause and negotiate as one, this would obviate the numbers problem at the multilateral level.

(ii) **Absent subject matter at the multilateral level**: because the membership of the WTO is more numerous than any PTA and variance across many dimensions of preferences among countries much

---

[7] See, for instance, Capling (2005b) for an argument against the use of PTAs for the pursuit of foreign policy, strategic and geo-political objectives.

higher, issues that some countries wish to address may not be easily included on the WTO agenda.

(iii) **Speed of negotiations**: it is often argued that WTO negotiations take far longer than PTAs. This is likely to occur for the sort of reasons mentioned above, but it may not always be true that complex PTAs have been completed in much less time than some earlier GATT/ WTO negotiations.

(iv) **Domestic policy lock-in**: a government may see value in locking-in a domestic policy position through an international commitment (Ethier 1998). This may also be feasible in the WTO, but may not be as effective because of WTO escape clause provisions or because the issue upon which lock-in is sought is treated differently or not at all.

(v) **Reducing policy uncertainty**: in some PTAs the agreement is valued as a guarantor of greater certainty and policy continuity on the part of major trading partners.

(vi) **Fear of exclusion**: governments will be wary of finding themselves excluded from other countries' preferential trade arrangements, particularly if such arrangements involve significant trading partners (Lloyd 2002). This motivation for entering into PTAs is sometimes referred to as the domino effect (Baldwin 1997) and has also been characterized as competitive liberalization.

4   Summary and key questions

In the absence of a body of theoretical or empirical work that analyses the attitude of NSAs towards questions of forum selection, our preceding discussion has by necessity focused almost exclusively on the perspective of decision-makers. Such a state-centric account is adequate only if we accept that governments make trade policy decisions in isolation from NSAs. However, we have argued in this chapter that strictly state-centric accounts are inadequate to explain contemporary trade policy-making; hence, our understanding of why governments choose to negotiate a PTA rather than negotiate multilaterally is incomplete in the absence of a much better understanding of the role of NSAs, institutions, ideas, norms and values in these processes, and the impact of interactions between state and non-state actors in shaping preferences and policy.

In opening up the 'black box' of decision-making in relation to forum selection, the case studies have been informed by the following questions: who are the non-state actors that seek to influence forum choice? What interests do they represent? How do they perceive their interests in relation to the question of forum choice? More specifically, do they have a preference for PTAs over multilateral trade negotiations, and if so, why? By what means do they seek to influence decision-makers? Are the non-state actors who seek to influence decisions at the national level also active internationally? If so, how effectively coordinated are their actions and positions? If they are only local NSAs, are they influenced in any way by the existence of interest groups active at the multilateral level?

Similar questions apply to decision-makers in governments: who are the key political and bureaucratic actors that influence forum choice? Whose interests do they represent? Do different government agencies or ministries vie for influence against a background of diverse interests and priorities, and, if so, how does this work through the decision-making process? Do such differences influence interaction with NSAs? Do governments have a preference for PTAs over multilateral trade negotiations, and if so, why? By what means do they seek to engage with NSAs in decision-making in relation to forum selection?

Issues on the table are not necessarily the same, or addressed in the same manner, in PTAs and multilateral negotiations. In the cases you consider, do differences in the content of, or approach to, the negotiating agenda play a significant role in influencing the degree and content of non-state actor engagement?

In what way do institutional configurations – including the shape of political and bureaucratic structures – structure the interactions between policy-makers and NSAs? To what extent do these institutions make governments more or less responsive to societal pressures, privilege certain interests and/or promote transparency or hide information? More specifically, does the way in which institutions are structured, including government-driven consultation processes, influence preference formation? In other words, do the institutional arrangements for PTA policy-making differ to those for WTO policy-making, and, if so, what is the impact?

To what extent do ideas, values and norms play a role in shaping preferences for PTAs over multilateral negotiations? Or are these preferences rationally and endogenously determined?

Finally, to what extent do the interactions between state and non-state actors affect the way in which interests are determined, problems are perceived and solutions sought? Do these interactions influence preferences, and/or produce learning and shared understandings?

References

Alt, J. E., Frieden, J., Gilligan, M. J., Rodrik, D. and Rogowski, R. 1996. 'The Political Economy of International Trade: Enduring Puzzles and an Agenda for Inquiry', *Comparative Political Studies* **29**, 6: 689–717.

Bagwell, K. and Staiger, R. W. 2002., *The Economics of the World Trading System*. Cambridge, MA: MIT Press.

Baldwin, R. E. 1997. 'The Causes of Regionalism', *World Economy* **20**, 7: 865–88.

Baldwin, R. 2006. 'Multilateralizing Regionalism: Spaghetti Bowls as Building Blocs on the Road to Global Free Trade', *World Economy* **29**, 11: 1451–518.

Baldwin, R., Evenett, S. and Low, P. 2009. 'Beyond Tariffs: Multilateralizing Deeper RTA Commitments', in R. Baldwin and P. Low (eds.), *Multilateralizing Regionalism*. Cambridge University Press.

Baldwin, R. and Low, P. (eds.) 2009. *Multilateralizing Regionalism*. Cambridge University Press.

Barton, J. H., Goldstein, J. L., Josling, T. E. and Steinberg, R. H. 2006. *The Evolution of the Trade Regime: Politics, Law, and Economics of the GATT and the WTO*. Princeton University Press.

Bhagwati, J. 1988, *Protectionism*. Cambridge, MA: MIT Press.
    2008. *Termites in the Trading System: How Preferential Agreements Undermine Free Trade*. Oxford University Press.

Bhagwati, J., Greenaway, D. and Panagariya, A. 1998. 'Trading Preferentially: Theory and Policy', *Economic Journal* **108**, 449: 1128–48.

Busch, M. L. 2007. 'Overlapping Institutions, Forum Shopping, and Dispute Settlement in International Trade', *International Organization* **61**, 4: 735–61.

Capling, A. 2005a. 'Can the Democratic Deficit in Treaty-Making be Overcome? Parliament and the Australia–United States Free Trade Agreement', in H. Charlesworth, M. Chaim, D. Hovell and G. Williams (eds.), *The Fluid State: International Law and Legal Systems*. Sydney: The Federation Press, pp. 57–81.
    2005b. *All the Way with the USA: Australia, the US and Free Trade*. Sydney: University of New South Wales Press.

Chase, K. 2003, 'Economic Interests and Regional Trading Arrangements: The Case of NAFTA', *International Organization* **57**, 1: 137–74.

da Motta Veiga, P. 2007. 'Trade Policy-making in Brazil: Changing Patterns in State–Civil Society Relationship', M. Halle and R. Wolfe. (eds.), *Process Matters: Sustainable Development and Domestic Trade Transparency*, pp. 143–82.

Davis, C. L. 2006. '*The Politics of Forum Choice in Trade Disputes: Evidence from U.S. Trade Policy*', paper presented at the annual meeting of the American Political Science Association, September 2006.

de Melo, J. and Panagariya, A. (eds.) 1993. *New Dimensions in Regional Integration*. Cambridge University Press.

Destler, I. M. 1992. *American Trade Politics*, 2nd edn. Washington: Institute for
    International Economics and New York: The Twentieth Century Fund.
Draper, P. 2007. 'Consultation Dilemmas: Transparency Versus Effectiveness
    in South Africa's Trade Policy', in M. Halle and R. Wolfe (eds.), *Process
    Matters: Sustainable Development and Domestic Trade Transparency*,
    pp. 241–64.
Elsig, M. 2007. 'The EU's Choice of Regulatory Venues for Trade Negotiations: A
    Tale of Agency Power?', *Journal of Common Market Studies* **45**, 4: 927–48.
Estevadeordal, A., Suominen. K. and Teh, R. 2009. *Regional Rules in the Global
    Trading System*. Cambridge University Press.
Ethier, W. J. 1998. 'The New Regionalism', *Economic Journal* **108**, 449: 1149–61.
Ford, J. 2003. *A Social Theory of the WTO: Trading Cultures*. Basingstoke: Palgrave
    Macmillan.
Frankel, J. A. 1997. *Regional Trading Blocs in the World Economic System*.
    Washington, DC: Institute for International Economics.
Frieden, J. and Rogowski, R. 1996. 'The Impacts of the International Economy on
    National Policies', in R. Keohane and H. Milner (eds.), *Internationalization
    and Domestic Politics*. New York: Cambridge University Press, pp. 25–47.
Gallagher, P., Low, P. and Stoler, A. 2006. *Managing the Challenges of WTO
    Participation*. Cambridge University Press.
Goldstein, J. 1993. *Ideas, Interests and American Trade Policy*, Ithaca, NY: Cornell
    University Press.
Gowa, J. 1994. *Allies, Adversaries, and International Trade*. Princeton University
    Press.
Grieco, J. M. 1990., *Cooperation among Nations: Europe, America and Non-Tariff
    Barriers to Trade*. Ithaca, NY: Cornell University Press.
Grossman, G. M. and Helpman, E. 1994. 'Protection for Sale', *American Economic
    Review* **84**: 833–50.
Haggard, S. 1988. 'The Institutional Foundations of Hegemony: Explaining the
    Reciprocal Trade Agreements Act of 1934', *International Organization*
    42: 91–120.
Halle, M. and Wolfe, R. (eds.) 2007. *Process Matters: Sustainable Development
    and Domestic Trade Transparency*. Winnipeg: International Institute for
    Sustainable Development.
Henisz, W. J. and Mansfield, E. D. 2006. 'Votes and Vetos: The Political
    Determinants of Commercial Openness', *International Studies Quarterly*
    50, 1: 189–212.
Hiscox, M. J. 2005. 'The Domestic Sources of Foreign Economic Policies', in
    J. Ravenhill (ed.), *Global Political Economy*. Oxford University Press,
    pp. 51–83.
Hocking, B. 2004. 'Changing the Terms of Trade Policy-making: From the "Club"
    to the "Multistakeholder" Model', *World Trade Review* **3**, 1: 3–26.
Hocking, B. and McGuire, S. (eds.). 2004. *Trade Politics*. London: Routledge.

Irwin, D. A. 1996. *Against the Tide: An Intellectual History of Free Trade*. Princeton University Press.

Johnson, H. G. 1965. 'An Economic Theory of Protectionism, Tariff Bargaining, and the Formation of Customs Unions', *Journal of Political Economy* **73**: 256–83.

Keohane, R. O. 1984. *After Hegemony: Cooperation and Discord in the World Political Economy*. Princeton University Press.

Krasner, S. 1976. 'State Power and the Structure of International Trade', *World Politics* **28**, 2: 317–47.

Lake, D. A. 1988., *Power, Protectionism, and Free Trade: International Sources of U.S. Commercial Strategy, 1887–1939*. Ithaca, NY: Cornell University Press.

Lloyd, P. J. 2002. 'New Bilateralism in the Asia Pacific', *World Economy* **25**, 9.

Magee, S. P. and Young, L. 1987. 'Endogenous Protection in the United States, 1900–1984', in R. M. Stern (ed.), *U.S. Trade Policies in a Changing World Economy*. Cambridge, MA: MIT Press, pp. 145–95.

Mansfield, E. D. and Milner, H. V. 1999. 'The New Wave of Regionalism', *International Organization* **53**, 3.

Mansfield, E. D. and Reinhardt, E. 2003. 'Multilateral Determinants of Regionalism: The Effects of GATT/WTO on the Formation of Preferential Trading Arrangements', *International Organization* **56**, 3: 477–513.

March, J. G. and Olsen, J. P. 1989. *Rediscovering Institutions: The Organizational Basis of Politics*. New York: Free Press.

Milner, H. 1988. *Resisting Protectionism: Global Industries and the Politics of International Trade*. Princeton University Press.

1999. 'The Political Economy of International Trade', *Annual Review of Political Science* **2**: 91–114.

O'Brien, R., Goetz, A. M., Scholte, J. A. and Williams, M. 2000. *Contesting Global Governance: Multilateral Institutions and Global Social Movements*. Cambridge University Press.

Odell, J. S. 1990. 'Understanding International Trade Policies: An Emerging Synthesis', *World Politics* **43**, 1: 139–67.

Ostry, S. 2002. 'Preface', in *The Trade Policy-Making Process: Level One of the Two Level Game: Country Studies in the Western Hemisphere*, INTAL-ITD-STA (Inter-American Development Bank), Occasional Paper 13, Buenos Aires: Institute for the Integration of Latin America and the Caribbean and the Inter-American Developmental Bank, pp. i–iv.

Pomfret, R. 1997. *The Economics of Regional Trading Arrangements*. Oxford University Press.

Putnam, R. D. 1988. 'Diplomacy and Domestic Politics: The Logic of Two-Level Games', *International Organization* **42**, 3: 427–60.

Ravenhill, J. R. 2005. 'Regionalism', in J. R. Ravenhill (ed.), *Global Political Economy*. Oxford University Press, pp. 116–47.

Ruggie, J. G. 1982. 'International Regimes, Transactions, and Change: Embedded Liberalism in the Postwar Economic Order', *International Organization* **36**, 2: 379–415.

Sell, S. K. and Prakash, A. 2004. 'Using Ideas Strategically: the Contest between Business and NSA Networks in Intellectual Property Rights', *International Studies Quarterly* **48**, 1: 143–75.

Shaffer, G. C. 2003. *Defending Interests; Public–Private Partnerships in WTO Litigation*. Washington DC: Brookings Institution Press.

Skocpol, T. 1985. 'Bringing the State Back In: Strategies of Analysis in Current Research', in P. Evans, D. Rueschemeyer and T. Skocpol (eds.), *Bringing the State Back In*. Cambridge University Press.

Stairs, D. 2000. 'Foreign Policy Consultations in a Globalizing World: The Case of Canada, the WTO, and the Shenanigans in Seattle', *Policy Matters* **1**, 8.

Trentmann, F. 1998. 'Political Culture and Political Economy: Interest, Ideology and Free Trade', *Review of International Political Economy* **5**, 2: 217–51.

Tsebelis, G. 1995. 'Decision-Making in Political Systems: Veto Players in Presidentialism, Parliamentarism, Multicameralism and Multipartyism', *British Journal of Political Science* **25**, 3: 289–325.

Wallach, L. and Sforza, M. 1999. *Whose Trade Organization? Corporate Globalization and the Erosion of Democracy*. Washington, DC: Public Citizen.

Warwick Commission 2007. *The Multilateral Trade Regime: Which Way Forward?* Coventry: University of Warwick.

Weston, A. 2005. *The 'Canadian Model' for Public Participation in Trade Policy Formulation*. Ottawa: The North–South Institute.

Wolfe, R. 2007. 'Transparency and Public Participation in the Canadian Trade Policy Process', in M. Halle and R. Wolfe (eds.), *Process Matters: Sustainable Development and Domestic Trade Transparency*. Winnipeg: International Institute for Sustainable Development, pp. 21–72.

Wolfe, R. and Helmer, J. 2007. 'Trade Policy Begins at Home: Information and Consultation in the Trade Policy Process', in M. Halle and R. Wolfe (eds.), *Process Matters: Sustainable Development and Domestic Trade Transparency*. Winnipeg: International Institute for Sustainable Development, pp. 1–19.

Woll, C. 2008. *Firm Interests: How Governments Shape Business Lobbying on Global Trade*. Ithaca. NY: Cornell University Press.

World Bank 2005. *Global Economic Prospects: Trade, Regionalism, and Development*. Washington, DC: World Bank.

World Trade Organization 2007. *World Trade Report 2007: Six Decades of Multilateral Trade Cooperation: What Have we Learnt?* Geneva: World Trade Organization.

Yarbrough, B. V. and Yarbrough, R. M. 1992. *Cooperation and Governance in International Trade: The Strategic Organizational Approach*. Princeton University Press.

2

Chile

SEBASTIÁN HERREROS[1]

This chapter reviews the participation of non-state actors (NSAs) in trade policy and negotiations in Chile over the last two decades, following democratic restoration in 1990. The analysis focuses on three main types of NSAs: business associations; labour organizations; and civil society organizations (CSOs). Most information has been gathered through structured interviews with NSA representatives and current and former government officials (see the list in the Annex below). The existing literature has been used as a secondary source.

The chapter is structured as follows: section 1 presents an overview of Chilean trade policy since the 1930s and a description of the country's trade patterns; section 2 describes Chile's main actors in trade policy; section 3 contains an analysis of NSA participation in a number of specific trade negotiations; and section 4 presents the study's main findings and conclusions.

The main findings that emerge from the chapter are the following. First, the intensive process of trade negotiations which started in 1990 has been dominated from the outset by the executive branch of government. Second, the business sector is by far the most influential constituency among NSAs. Third, NSA participation in trade debates (with the exception of the business sector) has been rather sporadic, and decreased significantly after major negotiations with the United States and the European Union were completed in 2003. Fourth, the relatively strong support for 'free trade' that exists within business and political elites as well as among the Chilean population at large means that those NSAs critical of trade negotiations have played a mostly marginal role.

Concerning forum choice, no clear conceptual preference between the multilateral and the preferential level is discernible among Chilean NSAs. However, in practice they have privileged preferential negotiations

[1] International Trade and Integration Division, United Nations Economic Commission for Latin America and the Caribbean (ECLAC). The views expressed here are exclusively those of the author and do not reflect necessarily those of ECLAC.

to pursue their goals, as they perceive that Chile has a greater leverage to influence their agenda, timing and outcome than is the case at the WTO.

1 Background and context

1.1 Evolution of Chile's trade policy since the 1930s[2]

From the 1930s until the mid-1970s, Chile's development strategy was based on industrialization by import substitution. Chile's embrace of import substitution was the result of the dramatic impact that the Great Depression had on its economy,[3] and of the scarcity of imported goods caused by the Second World War. During this period, Chile promoted industrialization through the use of exchange controls, multiple exchange rates, high import tariffs, export taxes, import licences, import quotas and prohibitions, credit rationing and different types of subsidies. The distortions in Chile's trade regime became especially pronounced under President Salvador Allende's left-wing administration (1970–3).

Throughout this period, import substitution delivered modest growth: GDP grew at an average of 3.8% a year between 1940 and 1970 (Meller 1996). This period was also characterized by high inflation, chronic fiscal deficits, frequent balance of payments crises and an overgrown public sector. While the share of manufacturing in GDP climbed from 13% in 1925 to about 25% in 1970, large segments of Chilean industry were internationally uncompetitive.

Following the coup of September 1973, the military junta headed by General Augusto Pinochet led the country into a radical process of deregulation and privatization. Its blueprint was provided by the 'Chicago Boys', a group of Chilean economists most of whom had pursued graduate studies at the University of Chicago. Trade liberalization was an essential component of the new strategy. By the time the first trade reform was completed in 1979, Chile had a uniform 10% tariff for all imports (except automobiles), a level that was at the time unusually low among economies at a similar development stage. There were no quantitative restrictions, no prohibitions, no anti-dumping or countervailing duties and no export subsidies. Essentially all selectivity was removed from trade policy. In 1976 Chile withdrew from the Andean Pact,[4] both due to discrepancies

---

[2] This section draws on Herreros (2009).
[3] Compared with its average for the 1927–9 period, in 1932 Chile's per capita GDP had fallen by 42% (Meller 1996).
[4] The Andean Pact (now Andean Community) is an integration scheme created in 1969. Its other members in 1976 were Peru, Bolivia, Colombia, Ecuador and Venezuela.

with that bloc's restrictive treatment of foreign investment and to Chile's unwillingness to maintain the high protection levels demanded by the bloc's common external tariff.

Chile bound its entire tariff schedule during the GATT's Tokyo Round of 1973–9, the first GATT member to do so. All tariffs were bound at a flat 35%. The Chilean example of a ceiling binding for the whole tariff universe would be followed by a number of developing countries, especially in Latin America, during the Uruguay Round.

Following the outbreak of the debt crisis in 1982, there was a partial reversal of previous trade reforms. Tariffs were raised to 20% in March 1983 and to 35% in September 1984. Temporary tariff surcharges were authorized in 1982 for sectors in particular difficulty (mostly industrial ones), and a mechanism to compensate for external price instability – the price band system – was introduced in 1984 for wheat, sugar and vegetable oil. However, the flat tariff policy remained in place (with the exception of the price band system), and there was no recourse to quantitative restrictions.

Once the external disequilibrium was reduced, a second trade reform was launched. Tariffs were reduced from 35% to 20% in 1985 and then to 15% in 1988. This second reform was accompanied by a strong economic recovery and an export boom, helped by a favourable real exchange rate, the use of several export-promotion mechanisms and a high price for copper, which was then – and continues to be – Chile's main export product.

Since 1990 Chile has been governed by a centre-left coalition, the Concertación, which has won four consecutive presidential elections. Trade policy under the Concertación has followed a 'multi-track' or 'lateral' approach (Sáez and Valdés 1999). Unilateral opening has continued,[5] while the country has been an active player at the multilateral level, both during the Uruguay Round and in the current Doha Round. Most notably, preferential trade agreements (PTAs) have become a prominent feature of Chile's trade policy.

Chile's 'lateral' strategy is based on the concept of 'open regionalism', made popular in the 1990s by the United Nations Economic Commission for Latin America and the Caribbean (ECLAC),[6] and the Asia Pacific Economic Cooperation forum (APEC). According to Chilean authorities, open regionalism 'seeks to ensure that no trade agreement limits the freedom [of Chile] to negotiate further agreements or creates more obstacles vis-à-vis other trading partners' (WTO 1997).

---

[5] The general MFN import tariff was reduced from 15% to 11% in 1991, and to the current 6% between 1999 and 2003.

[6] See ECLAC (1994).

Chile's move into PTAs is a response to several factors. First, democratic restoration made it an eligible partner for many countries once again. Second, its open trade regime meant that additional efficiency gains from further unilateral opening would be relatively small (and that PTAs should not create significant trade diversion). Third, the authorities' interest in increasing the value-added of Chilean exports required improved access to foreign markets, which could not be achieved via unilateral opening. Fourth, the emergence of regionalism as a key feature of the world economy since the late 1980s provided a defensive rationale for a small country like Chile to either join or negotiate PTAs with the main blocs. The substantial geographical diversification of Chilean exports made this argument especially compelling. An additional argument was uncertainty about the outcome of the Uruguay Round and subsequently some disappointment about the Round's results in areas of interest to Chile, such as agricultural market access.

Chile has followed a gradualist approach to PTAs. It started in the early 1990s negotiating 'economic complementation' agreements (ECAs) with other Latin American countries, which covered only trade in goods. From the mid-1990s, it began negotiating more comprehensive trade agreements with its major partners outside Latin America. Today, Chile has twenty PTAs with fifty-eight countries in force (see Table 2.7).[7] The majority of them cover trade in goods and services, investment, intellectual property, public procurement and other trade-related areas. Some of them also cover labour and environment, either directly or through side cooperation agreements.[8]

Chile's achievements in terms of PTAs have been made possible by its decision not to become a full member of either of South America's two main integration schemes: the Andean Community – successor of the Andean Pact – and the Common Market of the South (MERCOSUR).[9] Joining either group would have meant surrendering Chile's autonomy in trade and other economic policies, including trade negotiations.[10] Instead, Chile obtained 'associated member' status in both groups.

---

[7] In July 2009 an FTA was signed with Turkey. At the time of writing, there are PTA negotiations underway with Malaysia and Vietnam.

[8] For greater clarity, henceforward all these agreements will be referred to as PTAs, except where distinguishing between the different categories is relevant.

[9] Created in 1991, its full members are Argentina, Brazil, Paraguay and Uruguay. Venezuela is negotiating its accession.

[10] The argument can be summed up as 'the advantage of being single (and small)'. Chile is an economy small enough not to threaten the viability of any productive sectors in its

Chile's bound tariff since the end of the Uruguay Round is a flat 25%, with a handful of exceptions in agriculture.[11] Its applied most favoured nation (MFN) tariff has been a flat 6% since 2003, with roughly the same exceptions as for the bound rate. Taking into account PTAs, its average applied tariff was 1.1% in August 2009, according to a study by the Santiago Chamber of Commerce.[12] Trade remedies are seldom used. Chile is considered to have generally very open regimes concerning foreign investment, services and government procurement.

Chile's approach to trade negotiations is informed by its open trade and investment regimes. First, it follows a general policy of no product exclusions in its PTAs. Sensitivities are dealt with through longer tariff phase-out periods, and the only exclusions respond to reciprocity considerations. Second, Chile maintains the policy that its PTAs must have the widest coverage possible, including trade in services, investment, government procurement and other 'second generation' areas. Accordingly, it has been upgrading its 'first generation' ECAs within Latin America, usually by replacing them with free trade agreements (FTAs).

Chile applies its 'wide coverage' policy towards PTAs with some pragmatism, and has been willing to accommodate the negotiating positions of some partners, especially if they represent attractive markets. For example, in the agreement with India each country grants tariff preferences (not elimination) to a list of products of interest to the other country. Similarly, the PTA with China originally covered trade in goods only, since at the time China was not prepared to negotiate other areas.[13]

1.2   Chile's trade patterns

Chile's total merchandise trade reached a record US$126,547 million in 2008, with exports of US$69,821 million and imports of US$56,726 million. Copper alone accounted for 52% of total exports. Other main export products – all of them with individual shares below 3% – correspond also to mining (molybdenum, gold), forestry (wood pulp, sawn coniferous

---

PTA partners. This is not the case with MERCOSUR, for example, which contains agricultural powerhouses such as Brazil and Argentina.

[11] Wheat, wheat flour, edible vegetable oils and dairy (bound at 31.5%) and sugar (bound at 98%).

[12] The study (in Spanish) is available at: www.ccs.cl/html/informe_Economico_files/11%20 Arancel%2003-11-09.doc.

[13] Subsequently, the agreement was expanded to include trade in services, and negotiations on investment are currently underway.

Table 2.1 *Chile's main export and import products, 2008*

	No.	Product	Amount exported/ imported (US$ million)	Share of total (%)
Exports	1	Refined copper: cathodes and sections of cathodes	20,243	29.0
	2	Copper ores and concentrates	13,005	18.6
	3	Unrefined copper; copper anodes for electrolytic refining	2,477	3.5
	4	Molybdenum ores and concentrates (roasted)	2,027	2.9
	5	Fuels and other merchandise for ships, aircraft and other vehicles engaged in international transport	1,329	1.9
	6	Chemical wood pulp (coniferous)	1,249	1.8
	7	Chemical wood pulp (eucalyptus)	1,208	1.7
	8	Services considered exports	881	1.3
	9	Ferromolybdenum	839	1.2
	10	Gold in other unwrought forms	732	1.0
		Total 10 top export products	43,990	63.0
		Rest	25,831	37.0
		Total exports	**69,821**	**100.0**
Imports	1	Petroleum oils and oils obtained from bituminous minerals (crude)	7,175	12.6
	2	Distilled fuel oils (gas oil, diesel oil)	5,092	9.0
	3	Motor cars and vehicles for transporting persons	1,542	
	4	Molybdenum ores and concentrates (other than roasted)	845	1.5
	5	Telephone sets	743	1.3
	6	Bituminous coal	625	1.1
	7	Propane (liquefied)	486	0.9
	8	Motor vehicles for the transport of goods	469	0.8
	9	Natural gas	452	0.8
	10	Sulphuric acid	447	0.8
		Total 10 top import products	17,876	31.5
		Rest	38,850	68.5
		Total imports	**56,726**	**100.0**

Source: General Directorate for International Economic Relations, Ministry of Foreign Affairs.

Table 2.2 *Composition of Chile's trade by main partners, 2008*

Partner	Exports		Imports	
	Amount (US$ million)	Share of total (%)	Amount (US$ million)	Share of total (%)
NAFTA	11,794	16.9	13,697	24.2
United States	*8,131*	*11.6*	*10,982*	*19.4*
Latin America	10,674	15.3	16,887	29.8
MERCOSUR	*6,747*	*9.7*	*11,089*	*19.5*
European Union (27)	17,235	24.7	7,204	12.7
Asia (4)[a]	22,816	32.7	13,097	23.1
China	*9,873*	*14.1*	*6,800*	*12.0*
Main four partner regions	62,519	89.6	50,885	89.7
Rest	7,302	10.4	5,841	10.3
Total	69,821	100.0	56,726	100.0

[a] China, Japan, Korea and India.

wood), the chemical sector (methanol) and agriculture and agro-industry (salmon, wine, grapes). Chile's main import items correspond to petroleum and related products such as gasoline, gas oil and diesel oil, followed by vehicles, molybdenum, telephone sets and natural gas (see Table 2.1).

In 2008, 90% of Chilean exports were sent to countries with which Chile had PTAs in force. These countries also accounted for 90% of Chilean imports in the same year. Chile's trade is geographically well diversified. Asia has emerged in recent years as its main export region, and in 2008 China became its top individual export destination. Latin America is Chile's main supplier of imports (especially of energy products), although in 2008 the United States was the top individual origin of Chilean imports (see Table 2.2).

2   Main actors in Chilean trade policy

2.1   State actors

2.1.1   The executive branch

Chile has a strongly presidential political regime. According to the country's constitution, the conducting of foreign policy (including trade negotiations) is a special prerogative of the president.[14] Consequently, its approach to trade negotiations is led by the executive branch of government.

Since its creation in 1979, responsibility for conducting trade negotiations has been entrusted by law to the General Directorate for International Economic Relations (DIRECON), a specialized agency within the Ministry of Foreign Affairs. DIRECON oversees the whole range of trade negotiations in which Chile participates, at the bilateral, sub-regional and multilateral levels. It also coordinates the implementation of trade agreements. This role has consolidated over time: in the early 1990s, overall responsibility for trade negotiations was in practice less clearly defined, with the ministries of Economy and Finance competing to some extent with DIRECON for the leading role (Silva 2000; Jara 2001; Porras 2003).

The formal institutional setting for inter-agency coordination dates from 1995, when the Inter Ministerial Committee on International Economic Negotiations (IMCIEN) and the Committee of Negotiators were created. The role of the IMCIEN is to advise the president on international economic negotiations. It is composed of the Minister of Foreign Affairs, who chairs it, and the ministers of Finance, Economy and the Secretary General of the Presidency, plus other ministers depending on the issues to be discussed. The Committee of Negotiators prepares the agenda for the meetings of the IMCIEN, including proposals for action. It is chaired by the director general of DIRECON and includes representatives of the ministries of Finance, Economy, Agriculture, the Secretariat General of the Presidency and the Secretariat General of Government.

The IMCIEN met extensively over the 2000–3 period, while Chile was simultaneously negotiating PTAs with the United States and the European Union. Thereafter the frequency of its meetings decreased, the last one being held in 2006. According to several interviewees, those two large negotiations essentially 'set the terms' for further negotiation processes. Therefore, no further ministerial-level meetings have been considered necessary.

Today, formal inter-agency coordination rests with the technical-level Committee of Negotiators, which meets two or three times a year. In practice, however, inter-agency coordination takes place on a daily basis. As the negotiations agenda has become ever wider and more complex,

---

[14] The constitution currently in force dates from 1980, in the middle of the military rule period (during the whole duration of which Congress was suspended). It therefore reflects a strong presidential bias, which persists despite several amendments.

DIRECON constantly coordinates with a wide range of ministries and agencies. The interaction with the Ministry of Finance is particularly important. Finance leads negotiations on financial services, has a prominent role in those about other services, investment and government procurement, and otherwise has a general overview role.[15]

Other ministries involved in trade negotiations are those of Economy, Agriculture, Labour, Education, Transport and Telecommunications and Health, as well as the Central Bank, the Foreign Investment Committee and a large number of specialized agencies. These include the National Customs Service, the Internal Revenue Service, and agencies overseeing sanitary and phytosanitary regulations, intellectual property, government procurement, immigration and the regulation of several services sectors.

Reflecting the emergence of intellectual property in the trade agenda since the Uruguay Round, an Inter Ministerial Committee on Intellectual Property was established in 2005. Its goals are to coordinate the implementation of commitments adopted in trade negotiations and in international bodies such as WIPO and WHO, and to establish national positions in those forums. It is composed of the ministries of Agriculture, Culture, Economy, Education, Health and Foreign Affairs (through DIRECON, which serves as secretariat).

2.1.2   The legislative branch

Congress plays a relatively passive role in trade negotiations. It does not participate in either the selection of negotiating partners or the definition of negotiating mandates. As defined in the constitution, the main role of Congress in trade policy is to either approve or reject those international treaties (including trade agreements) already signed. It is not entitled to amend them.

Nonetheless, Congress has gradually assumed a more prominent role in trade policy in general, and in trade negotiations in particular, due to their increased public visibility. For example, during the first half of the 1990s, the PTAs negotiated with countries such as Mexico, Colombia, Ecuador and Venezuela were not sent to Congress for ratification, and instead were put into force by Executive Decree. This practice was based on the notion that those PTAs were implementing agreements of the Treaty of Montevideo of 1980, which established the Latin American Integration

---

[15] By law, the appointment of the director general of DIRECON must be explicitly approved by the ministers of Foreign Affairs and Finance.

Association (ALADI).[16] This changed with the PTA between Chile and
MERCOSUR, signed in 1996. Although this agreement enjoyed the support of a majority of the business sector, it faced the active opposition of
the import-competing segment of Chilean agriculture and their allies in
Congress. In this context, the executive decided to submit the agreement
for parliamentary ratification, a practice which has been followed with all
subsequent trade agreements.

2.1.3   Channels for participation of non-state actors

Participation by NSAs in trade negotiations is a relatively new phenomenon in Chile. During the period of military rule, civil society involvement
in the formulation of public policies in general was almost non-existent,
apart from well-connected business interests. Moreover, during that
period Chile did not participate much in trade negotiations (other than in
the GATT and some minor ones within the framework of ALADI). It was,
therefore, only after 1990 that this issue became relevant, coinciding with
the first PTA negotiations. Non-state actor involvement was essentially
confined to business associations for most of that decade. Other actors,
such as the labour movement, academic institutions and CSOs, showed
little interest in and knowledge of trade negotiations. It is only since the
late 1990s that some of these actors became more actively involved in negotiation processes.

The evolution of channels for NSA participation in trade negotiations
reflects the trend described above. During the first half of the 1990s consultations were mostly informal, given the limited range of interested
actors. The first attempt to create a formal structure came in 1995 with
the creation of the Committee for the Participation of the Private Sector
(CPPS). This body, which ceased meeting in 2000, had the role of inform-
ing the private sector about developments in trade negotiations, getting
its feedback and transmitting it to the IMCIEN.

The CPPS was composed, on the government side, by the Minister of
Economy, who chaired it, plus the ministers of Foreign Affairs, Finance
and Agriculture, the Secretary General of the Presidency, and the director
general of DIRECON. On the private side, it was composed of two representatives of the Confederation of Production and Commerce (CPC, the
main umbrella organization for the business sector), two of the Workers'

---

[16] The Treaty of Montevideo allows two or more ALADI members to negotiate 'Economic
Complementation' Agreements among themselves. It was thus considered that, since the
Treaty of Montevideo was already in force in Chile, the subsequent ECAs did not need
parliamentary ratification.

Unitary Central (CUT, the main umbrella organization for organized labour), plus three individuals with experience in international economic negotiations, appointed by the president. Other individuals could be invited to participate depending on the agenda.

Because of its composition, the CPPS provided opportunities for expressing views only to the highest level entities representing organized business and labour. Besides, it usually met no more than twice a year, so it was therefore of limited value as a forum for NSA participation in trade negotiations. But this was a reflection of the incipient state of NSA involvement in trade at the time.

The situation evolved in a more participatory direction in the second half of the 1990s as a result of the negotiations with MERCOSUR and Canada. The importance of the agreement with MERCOSUR in fostering parliamentary involvement in trade has been already mentioned. The PTA with Canada was Chile's first with a developed country, and marked a watershed in several respects. On the one hand, it involved negotiations on areas that were at the time essentially new for Chile, such as services and investment. On the other hand, it involved the negotiation of cooperation agreements on labour and environment.[17] For Chilean negotiators, the negotiation and implementation of commitments in all these areas meant having to expand the scope of internal consultations beyond traditional stakeholders in the business sector. It also set in motion a learning process for Chilean NSAs, such as environmental CSOs and labour unions, which until then were not familiar with the world of trade negotiations.

Non-state actor participation in trade negotiations peaked in the first half of the current decade, when Chile was simultaneously negotiating PTAs with the United States and the European Union, as well as participating in the Free Trade Area of the Americas (FTAA) negotiations. A number of channels were consequently opened for negotiators to interact with organized civil society (see section 3, below).

The issue of mechanisms to engage NSAs in trade policy and negotiations cannot be looked at in isolation from the broader trends in civil society participation in public policies. This is a fairly recent development in Chile: the first explicit instructions to open channels for public participation in the formulation and implementation of public policies came only in 2000 through a decree issued by then President Ricardo Lagos.

---

[17] This PTA was seen by both Canada and Chile as an interim agreement towards eventual Chilean membership of NAFTA (which ultimately did not materialize).

New directives on citizens' participation in public administration were subsequently issued by President Michelle Bachelet in August 2008. They required all state agencies, as of 1 April 2009, to: (1) establish a mechanism for public participation in the development of public policies within the competencies of each agency; (2) provide a yearly public report on their overall (including budgetary) performance; (3) establish consultative civil society councils; and (4) make available to the public, in a timely, complete and widely accessible fashion, relevant information on their policies, plans, programmes, actions and budget.

In parallel with the above changes, Law 20,285 on transparency of the public function and access to information on the state's administration entered into force on 20 April 2009. It requires the vast majority of state agencies to make publicly available through their websites a wide range of information, including their applicable laws, budget, personnel, internal organization, procurement practices, etc.

The presidential directives and the new transparency law should have profound implications for relations between Chile's state institutions and the public. This process is unfolding at the time of writing, as both the directives and the law have been in force for only six months. Therefore, it is still too early to predict how the new requirements will affect NSA participation in trade policy. However, it seems clear that the overall trend is towards greater transparency and accountability, which should facilitate NSA involvement.

2.2   Non-state actors

In Chile, the most relevant types of NSAs in trade negotiations are: (a) business associations; (b) labour organizations; (c) CSOs; and (d) professional associations. NSAs are also organized in broader coalitions encompassing entities belonging to two or more of these categories. Other categories, such as think tanks or academic institutions, participate sporadically in trade discussions. There is little NSA participation in trade policy discussions outside the context of trade negotiations, with the exception of directly interested business actors. Table 2.3 briefly describes the NSAs involved in trade policy-making.

2.2.1   The business sector

The business sector is by far the most active and influential NSA in Chile's trade policy and negotiations. Its main umbrella organization is the CPC, which groups six associations representing mining, commerce, services and tourism, industry, agriculture, the building sector and the banking and financial services sector. Both the CPC itself and two of its member associations have been traditionally very active in trade negotiations. These are the Federation of Chilean Industry (Sociedad de Fomento Fabril, SOFOFA) and the National Agriculture Society (Sociedad Nacional de Agricultura, SNA).

Below the CPC's main six associations, there are other, smaller ones which represent specific export interests. This is the case with the Manufactures' Exporters Association (Asociación de Exportadores de Manufacturas, ASEXMA), which groups small- to medium-sized industrial exporters, and the Association of Exporters (Asociación de Exportadores, ASOEX), which represents the exporters of fruits and vegetables.

As the trade policy agenda has enlarged, so has the range of consulted business interests. For example, the Services Exporters' Committee (later renamed Services Exporters' Coalition) was created in 1996 following the launch of PTA negotiations with Canada. Unlike the organizations mentioned above, the Coalition is an informal platform, grouping over forty entities spanning a wide range of sectors (banking, transport, pensions, audiovisual, health insurance, etc.) and professional associations (lawyers, engineers, journalists, medical doctors, dentists, etc.). Its secretariat functions are performed by the Santiago Chamber of Commerce.

As Chile started negotiating intellectual property issues in its PTAs with the United States and the European Union, other organizations have become involved in trade negotiations. This is the case with the Industrial Property Association of Chile (Asociación Chilena de la Propiedad Industrial, ACHIPI), the Chilean Copyright Society (Sociedad Chilena del Derecho de Autor, SCD) and the Industrial Association of Pharmaceutical Laboratories (Asociación Industrial de Laboratorios Farmacéuticos, ASILFA), among others.

2.2.2 Labour organizations

The government's main counterpart in this area is the country's biggest labour coalition, the CUT, founded in September 1988 (see Table 2.3).[18] There was little participation by the labour union movement in Chile's trade negotiations for most of the 1990s. This was caused by a combination of factors, including more pressing domestic priorities within a movement that was just being reconstructed, the relatively low public visibility of Chile's first trade negotiations and the lack of technical expertise

---

[18] The CUT is the successor organization of the Central Única de Trabajadores, created in 1953 and outlawed by the military in 1973.

Table 2.3 *Some NSAs involved in trade policy-making in Chile since 1990*

Business sector

Name	Policy interest (trade-related)	Constituencies served	Source of funding	Local affiliates	International affiliates	Negotiations active in
ASEXMA	Representing associates' interests before authorities and negotiators	Associated companies (exporters of manufactures and services)	Membership fees	Associated companies	None	All PTAs since 1990
Services Exporters' Coalition	Representing associates' interests before authorities and negotiators	Associated business organizations and professional associations	Santiago Chamber of Commerce	Associated members	Part of the Global Services Network (GSN)	All PTAs since the FTA with Canada, plus Doha Round at the WTO
SOFOFA	Representing associates' interests before authorities and negotiators	Associated business organizations (mostly industrial)[19]	Membership fees	Associated business organizations		All PTAs since 1990

Civil Society Organizations (CSOs)

Oxfam International	Promotion of fair trade through changes in trade rules in the WTO and PTAs	Had a national office in Chile until early 2009		Oxfam International network	PTAs with USA, EU, FTAA
OCEANA	Support the adoption of new WTO rules to combat subsidies that promote over-fishing	Has its headquarters for South America in Chile		OCEANA international network	Fisheries subsidies' negotiations at the WTO
Chilean Alliance for Fair and Responsible Trade	To foster civil society's participation in (and surveillance of) trade negotiations, and to promote an integration agenda based on fair trade and on the strict respect of economic, social and cultural rights	See 'Local affiliates'	• Institute of Political Ecology • Consumers International (Chile) • International Gender and Trade Network • Human Rights' Continental Platform (Chilean Chapter) • Etc.	Alianza Social Continental (Hemispheric Social Alliance)	PTAs with USA, EU, FTAA

Table 2.3 (*cont.*)

Name	Policy interest (trade-related)	Constituencies served	Source of funding	Local affiliates	International affiliates	Negotiations active in
Labour organizations						
CUT	Promote the respect of workers' rights in trade agreements	Its 670,000 members (see 'Local affiliates')	Membership fees	28 confederations, 64 federations, 20 associations and 132 labour unions	Member of the International Trade Union Confederation (ITUC)	PTAs with USA, EU
Other						
Chilean Coalition for Cultural Diversity	Representing associates' interests before authorities and negotiators	See 'Local affiliates'	N/A	• Audiovisual Platform • Association of independent publishers • Actors' union (SIDARTE) • Music workers' union	Member of the International Federation of Coalitions for Cultural Diversity (IFCCD)	PTAs with USA, EU, FTAA

Source: Author's interviews with representatives of the different NSAs during 2009. N/A: Not available.

[19] Includes agro-industry organizations.

on trade within the labour movement. For example, the CUT was not actively involved in the negotiation of the Chile–Canada Agreement on Labour Cooperation (CCALC) that entered into force in 1997. The situation changed only during the Chile–US PTA negotiations (see section 3). However, after their completion the labour movement has largely retreated back into its domestic agenda.

2.2.3   Civil society organizations

CSOs were largely absent from trade negotiations during most of the 1990s, for similar reasons to those of labour organizations. The situation started to change gradually in the second half of the 1990s, with CSO participation reaching its peak between 2000 and 2003. Since then, and again similar to the labour movement, they have mostly turned their attention to domestic concerns.

The launch of the FTAA project at the first Summit of the Americas in December 1994 catalysed the involvement of CSOs in trade debates in Chile. In 1998 the first Summit of the Peoples of America (Cumbre de los Pueblos de América) took place in Santiago de Chile, in parallel with the second Summit of the Americas. The former was organized by the Hemispheric Social Alliance (Alianza Social Continental), a CSO network created in 1997 to confront the FTAA project and which groups CSOs from the whole American continent.

In 1999 the Chilean Alliance for Fair and Responsible Trade (Alianza Chilena por un Comercio Justo y Responsible, ACJR) was created. During its brief existence,[20] it was Chile's most influential CSO network active in trade debates, becoming the Chilean Chapter of the Hemispheric Social Alliance. It was very active in the first years of the FTAA process, as well as during the negotiations of the Chile–US PTA, adopting a critical view of both (see section 3).

Environmental CSOs have generally not been very active in trade discussions, partly due to lack of technical knowledge. However, on discrete occasions they have resorted to mechanisms created by trade agreements to pursue their goals. For example, the Chile–Canada Agreement on Environmental Cooperation (CCAEC) established a process by which individuals and CSOs can claim that either country is failing to effectively enforce one or more of its environmental laws. This mechanism has been used by several Chilean CSOs to denounce alleged violations by the Chilean government. The CCAEC also created mechanisms for

---

[20] It ceased to exist in 2006 due to funding problems.

civil society to participate in the implementation of the agreement, for example, by suggesting areas of cooperation. These channels have been used by CSOs and other actors such as academic institutions.

As to the local branches of 'multinational' CSOs, the most active ones have been Oxfam (during the PTA negotiations with the United States and the European Union and those within the FTAA) and, to a lesser extent, OCEANA (concerning the negotiations on fisheries subsidies which are part of the Doha Round at the WTO). Their respective positions are elaborated in section 3.

2.2.4   Professional organizations

The emergence of professional organizations as relevant actors in trade negotiations is closely related to the incorporation of services to the negotiating agenda. A large number of them are actually members of the Services Exporters' Coalition.

An interesting case is that of the cultural industries. In 2001 the Audiovisual Platform, created in 1997 and which groups several entities active in that sector, joined forces with the association of independent publishers, the actors' union and the music workers' union to form the Chilean Coalition for Cultural Diversity (CCCD). The Coalition actively lobbied for the complete exclusion of cultural industries from the Chile–US PTA, as had been the case in the Chile–Canada PTA (due to Canadian sensitivities). According to Bruno Bettati, then secretary general of the Audiovisual Platform, the Coalition did not fit into any of the typical NSA categories as it encompassed elements of both a business association and a CSO. Therefore, Chilean negotiators initially had some difficulty in deciding how to interact with it.[21]

During the Chile–US PTA negotiations and afterwards, the CCCD worked actively with similar movements from other countries, such as Canada's Coalition for Cultural Diversity. The First International Meeting of Professional Associations from the Cultural Milieu took place in Montreal in September 2001, with the attendance of representatives from twelve countries (among them Chile). The meeting's Final Declaration called on governments to refrain from undertaking any commitments on cultural industries or policies, be it in bilateral, regional or multilateral negotiations.[22]

---

[21] Eventually the Coalition's representatives participated in the same 'adjacent rooms' as business organizations (see section 3).

[22] For the full text, see www.cdc-ccd.org/main_pages_En/Publications_En/Declaration_1stmeeting_montreal_En.pdf.

Table 2.4 *State actors, main reason to engage with NSAs in trade policy-making*

Main reason for engaging NSAs	Number of responses	Share of total (%)
Satisfying public policy (including statutory) requirements	3	60
Promoting transparency	1	20
Seeking technical advice and commercial intelligence	0	0
Gauging potential views in relation to potential points of opposition to negotiating positions	0	0
Creating coalitions to support negotiating positions and outcomes	1	20
Other	0	0
Total	5	100

Source: Questionnaires administered to current and former government officials.

After the PTA negotiations with the United States were concluded, the CCCD continued working with groups from other countries that lobbied against the inclusion of cultural industries in trade agreements. They campaigned for the negotiation within the framework of UNESCO of what would become the Convention on the Protection and Promotion of the Diversity of Cultural Expressions. In their view, this convention, which entered into force in March 2007, was a necessary counterweight to the purely commercial approach to cultural activities inherent to trade negotiations (including in the WTO).

2.3   Findings about the interaction between state and non-state actors

Tables 2.4, 2.5 and 2.6 summarize the answers provided by representatives of both state and non-state actors to questionnaires administered

Table 2.5 *NSAs' preferred way of influencing trade negotiations*

Preferred way of influencing negotiations	Number of responses	Share of total (%)
Participating in meetings or committees organized by government	3	37.5
Self-initiated interaction with government or other lobbying activity	3	37.5
Publishing or broadcasting material	0	0
Conducting public campaigns	2	25.0
Other	0	0
Total	8	100.0

Source: Questionnaires administered to NSA representatives.

Table 2.6 *NSAs' preferred target to influence trade negotiations*

Preferred target	Number of responses	Share of total (%)
Ministers and vice ministers	2	22.2
Government officials	6	66.7
Legislators	0	0.0
Public opinion	1	11.1
Other	0	0
Total	9	100.0

Source: Questionnaires administered to NSA representatives.

in the course of this research project. It should be noted that the majority of the replies by both groups, while in principle not specific to any particular negotiation, relate mostly to Chile's PTA negotiations with the United States and the European Union, and to a lesser degree to those of the FTAA and the Doha Round. The main findings stemming from them are presented below.[23]

Government officials' main reason to engage NSAs has been to satisfy public policy requirements, and, to a lesser extent, to promote transparency and create support coalitions (see Table 2.4). Interviewed officials agreed that seeking technical advice and commercial intelligence was not a relevant motivation to engage NSAs, including business interests, as negotiators usually handled better information than the business sector and were familiar with the latter's demands from previous negotiations.

Non-state actors prefer direct interaction with government as a means of influencing negotiations. This is the case with all business NSAs, as well as with the labour movement and local CSOs. Participation in government organized meetings and self-initiated interaction were mentioned by the same number of respondents as their preferred option (see Table 2.5). Unsurprisingly, the option of conducting public campaigns as the main vehicle for influencing negotiations was mentioned only by the local representatives of Oxfam and OCEANA, two 'multinational' CSOs that operate to a large extent on the basis of global public campaigns.

Two-thirds of NSA representatives interviewed for this research considered government officials (more specifically, negotiators from DIRECON) as their main target in trying to influence negotiations (see Table 2.6). As several interviewees mentioned, this reflects the fact that both the technical expertise and the decision-making power are heavily concentrated in DIRECON. Ministers and vice-ministers come a distant second place, as they do not often get involved in the handling of negotiations (with the already noted exception of the PTAs with the European Union and the United States). Legislators were not mentioned at all, in recognition of the relatively passive role of Congress in trade negotiations.

3   Non-state actors and Chile's PTAs

Chile's current network of PTAs is shown in Table 2.7. Out of these twenty agreements, the analysis in this chapter focuses on the following:

- The Chile–Mexico PTA of 1991 (replaced in 1999 by the one currently in force) was Chile's first free trade negotiation ever, and its first major bilateral trade negotiation since recovering democracy. It was therefore conducted in an environment of no previous experience in such negotiations.

---

[23] These findings should be treated with some caution, due to the small sample of persons interviewed.

Table 2.7 *Chile's network of PTAs, September 2009*

Country/group	Type of agreement[a]	Signing date	Entry into force
(1) Latin America			
Bolivia	ECA/PSA[b]	6 April 1993	7 July 1993
Central America[c]	FTA	18 October 1999	14 February 2002
Cuba	PSA	21 August 1998	28 August 2008
Colombia	FTA	27 November 2006	8 May 2009
Ecuador	ECA	20 December 1994	1 January 1995
MERCOSUR	ECA	25 June 1996	1 October 1996
Panama	FTA	27 June 1996	7 March 2008
Peru	FTA	22 August 2006	1 March 2009
Venezuela	ECA	2 April 1993	1 July 1993
(2) North America			
Canada	FTA	5 December 1996	5 July 1997
Mexico	FTA	17 April 1998	1 August 1999
United States	FTA	6 June 2003	1 January 2004
(3) Europe			
EFTA[d]	FTA	26 June 2003	1 December 2004
European Union	AA	18 November 2002	1 February 2003
(4) Asia Pacific			
Australia	FTA	30 July 2008	6 March 2009
China	FTA	18 November 2005	1 October 2006
India	PSA	8 March 2006	17 August 2007
Japan	FTA	27 March 2007	3 September 2007
Korea	FTA	15 February 2003	1 April 2004
P4[e]	AA	18 July 2005	8 November 2006

[a] *Source*: General Directorate for International Economic Relations, Ministry of Foreign Affairs.
[b] ECA: Economic Complementation Agreement; FTA: Free Trade Agreement; AA: Association Agreement (including an FTA); PSA: Partial Scope Agreement.
[c] Comprises Costa Rica, El Salvador, Guatemala, Honduras and Nicaragua.
[d] Comprises Iceland, Lichtenstein, Norway and Switzerland.
[e] Comprises Brunei Darussalam, New Zealand and Singapore (plus Chile).

- The Chile–MERCOSUR PTA, as previously noted, was Chile's first PTA to meet significant opposition from segments of both the private sector and Congress.
- The Chile–Canada PTA had a much wider coverage than Chile's previous agreements, forcing Chilean negotiators to expand the scope of NSA consultations.
- The Chile–US and Chile–EU PTAs represent the high mark in civil society participation in Chile's trade negotiations.
- The Chile–China PTA involved negotiating the complete liberalization of trade in goods with a country that has come to be seen as the world's industrial powerhouse and whose exporting potential is a source of concern in countries across the world.
- The now defunct FTAA negotiations (1998–2005) and the ongoing Doha Round negotiations have also been selected for analysis. This allows comparison between the dynamics of NSA participation in bilateral, plurilateral and multilateral negotiations.

This list also provides a representative cross-section of the trade agreements and negotiations Chile has entered into since 1990. It includes: agreements with other developing countries (Mexico, MERCOSUR and China), as well as with developed countries (Canada, the United States and the European Union); bilateral agreements as well as plurilateral and multilateral negotiations; agreements with fellow Latin American countries, as well as with countries in North America, Europe and Asia; 'first generation' agreements (ECAs) and 'second generation' ones (FTAs and an Association Agreement). Moreover, the list includes agreements and negotiations spanning the whole period since 1990, which allows the tracking of changes in civil society participation over time.

3.1 State–non-state actor interactions in trade negotiations

3.1.1 Chile–Mexico PTA

This negotiation is a typical example of Chile's first generation of PTAs. Participation by NSAs was confined to the business sector, and more specifically, to associations representing firms engaged in trade in goods. They were mainly consulted about their defensive and offensive interests (for the purposes of drafting tariff offers and requests, respectively), and their preferences on rules of origin (especially in the industrial sector).

3.1.2   Chile–MERCOSUR PTA

As was the case in Chile's previous PTAs, participation by NSAs was limited to those associations representing firms engaged in trade in goods. However, unlike previous negotiations, Chilean negotiators had considerable difficulty reconciling the conflicting interests of associations interested in expanding export opportunities and those concerned about import competition. This was especially clear in the agricultural sector, where export-oriented interests in wine, fruits and vegetables and agro-industry clashed with those of 'traditional', import-competing farming in sugar beet, wheat, vegetable oils and dairy. The politically well-connected sectors opposing liberalization in sensitive crops mobilized rural communities and Congress members from the affected constituencies to oppose the agreement (and afterwards to demand compensation for it). This episode sparked parliamentary interest in trade negotiations, which peaked at the time of those with the United States and the European Union.

3.1.3   Chile–Canada PTA

The expanded scope of these negotiations vis-à-vis those of all previous PTAs posed technical challenges to Chilean negotiators. For example, their only experience of negotiating services (the Uruguay Round) was of limited value, as the negotiating model was very different from the 'NAFTA type' proposed by Canada. Moreover, during the Uruguay Round Chile assumed very limited commitments on services, in contrast to the substantially wider coverage that was expected in the negotiations with Canada. Similarly, Chilean firms and associations engaged in the provision of services were not organized as exporters. This changed with the creation of the Services Exporters' Committee. The PTA negotiations thus set in motion a process of constant interaction and mutual learning for both negotiators and services firms which continues to the present today.

While CSOs and labour organizations did not participate in the negotiations of the side agreements on labour and environmental cooperation, these agreements opened the way for them to participate in their implementation. In general, the negotiations with Canada first exposed Chilean negotiators to that country's culture of civil society participation in trade and other public policies (Rojas and Pey 2002).

3.1.4   Chile–US PTA

The negotiations towards a PTA with the United States represented the highest point in the process of increasing NSA participation started in the late 1990s. There was unprecedented interest among a great diversity of CSOs to express their views on the negotiations. This responded to a number of factors. First, the sheer size of the US economy, much larger than any of the economies with which Chile had hitherto negotiated trade agreements. Second, the aggressive stance taken by the United States – or was perceived to take – on highly sensitive topics such as pharmaceutical patents, investment and some services. Third, the negotiations took place during an extremely turbulent period in international relations, spanning the 11 September 2001 terrorist attacks, the US operations against the Taliban in Afghanistan and the run up to the US invasion of Iraq. Accordingly, some groups in Chile were worried that through the PTA Chile could be 'turning its back' to Latin America and associating itself with what they perceived as an aggressive and unilateralist US approach in foreign policy.[24]

Chilean negotiators were acutely aware of the high economic and political stakes involved in the negotiations and of the need to publicly legitimize them. Several channels were therefore established to receive inputs from NSAs:

- At the launch of negotiations, an open invitation for submissions from all interested parties was extended through announcements in newspapers nationwide.
- An advisory council was created, composed, *inter alia*, of former ambassadors to the United States, businessmen, members of Congress, other politicians and academics.
- During the whole period of negotiations, there were direct consultations with the business sector and with labour organizations. They included the participation of representatives from both business associations and the CUT in several negotiating rounds. To that effect, three 'adjacent rooms' ('cuartos de al lado') were set up: one for associations representing large businesses; one for those representing small- and medium-sized enterprises;, and one for labour representatives. This mechanism allowed Chilean negotiators to report to and receive feedback from those actors during the rounds.
- Specific consultations were also held with CSOs to explain the contents of the negotiations and to collect their views. These consultations took

[24] As it turned out, Chile declined to support the draft resolution presented in February 2003 by the United States, the United Kingdom and Spain to the UN Security Council and which would have amounted to the latter's approval of the Iraq invasion. This decision was made in spite of implied warnings that the US Congress might react by not approving the implementing legislation for the Chile–US PTA. At the time the negotiations had concluded, but the agreement was only signed in June 2003.

place mostly in the early part of the negotiations and were not as systematic as those with the business and labour organizations.
• Also during the negotiations several information seminars and presentations were jointly organized with all the above groups.

For its part, and in order to interact more effectively with Chilean negotiators, the CPC set up 'mirror working groups' replicating each of the negotiating groups. This illustrates the unprecedented level of interest generated by these negotiations within Chile's business sector.

The CUT had an ambivalent attitude towards the PTA. Publicly it adopted a critical stance towards it, which was motivated at least as much by political considerations as by substantive concerns. Chile's Communist Party, which has historically been strongly anti-American, at that time exercised (and continues to exercise) great influence within the CUT. Therefore, the CUT leadership was not prepared to speak up in favour of the PTA for fear of being accused of 'selling out to the United States'.

While publicly adopting a critical stance towards the PTA, the CUT presented concrete demands to Chilean negotiators as to the content of the agreement. Specifically, it demanded and obtained the inclusion in its text (not in a side agreement as was the case with the Chile–Canada PTA) of provisions ensuring the enforcement of each party's own labour legislation and of the fundamental workers' rights established by the ILO. This position was even articulated through a public joint declaration with the AFL–CIO from the United States in August 2002.[25] Moreover, CUT representatives participated in several negotiating rounds, and its leadership did not lobby against passage of the PTA in Congress. Summing up, their opposition was more formal than real. This point was made by at least two interviewees directly involved in the talks.

As for the CCCD, it argued that opening up Chile's cultural industries to competition from their world-dominant US competitors could threaten the former's viability. However, wholesale exclusion of cultural industries from the PTA was unacceptable to the United States. Eventually, Chilean negotiators secured a reservation in this sector allowing Chile the right to accord differential treatment to countries under existing or future bilateral or multilateral agreements, such as audiovisual cooperation agreements, as well as to subsidize its cultural industries. Although this achievement was at the time recognized by the CCCD, it fell short of its demands for a complete carve-out of the cultural sector.

[25] For the text (in Spanish) see www.union-network.org/uniflashes.nsf/0/16ee1b423da38a 28c1256c210058521d?OpenDocument.

Both Oxfam and the ACJR were critical of the agreement on several counts.[26] On investment, they criticized its investor–state dispute settlement mechanism (modelled after NAFTA), arguing that it put at risk the ability of the host state to regulate in the public interest. They also expressed apprehensions about the potentially negative impact of Chilean commitments in education and health on the universal provision of those basic services. On intellectual property, they opposed US demands for protection of pharmaceutical patents beyond that granted by the WTO's TRIPs Agreement, on the ground that it put at risk the Chilean population's access to generic medicaments. Both Oxfam and the ACJR criticized the labour chapter, claiming that it did not sufficiently protect workers' rights. The ACJR also disapproved the PTA's provisions (or lack thereof) on issues such as gender, the environment and public procurement.

3.1.5   FTAA negotiations

These negotiations aroused considerable interest among Chilean NSAs, particularly the ACJR. This interest responded to the very ambitious nature of the FTAA project, in terms of the agreement's potential scope and geographical coverage, and to anxieties about its potential to become an instrument for the promotion of US economic and political hegemony in the region. NSA participation was encouraged by the invitation made by participating governments to civil society to express its views on the FTAA process and to submit contributions.

The overall approach of local CSOs to the FTAA was largely informed by their critical view of globalization. As was the case in the Chile–US PTA negotiations, they opposed the US stance on services, investment and intellectual property. They were also critical of the US refusal to discuss agricultural subsidies in the FTAA context. The most decisive part of the FTAA negotiations took place within the difficult political context that followed the 9/11 attacks, further strengthening the opposition by local CSOs.

The negotiations soon ran into difficulties, mainly due to disagreements between the United States and Brazil on the negotiating agenda. Progress slowed down and the negotiations were eventually suspended in February 2004. Despite some efforts to break the deadlock, the process is now considered over. As negotiations languished, NSA interest and participation diminished.

---

[26] Oxfam has articulated similar concerns about the other PTAs and PTA negotiations between the United States and the European Union, on one side, and Latin American countries, on the other.

3.1.6   Chile–EU PTA

All interviewees who were involved in these negotiations agreed that they were much less controversial than those with the United States. This was due to several factors. First, the European Union's generally gentler negotiating style (even if its substantive demands were sometimes not very different from those of the United States, for example, on issues such as intellectual property).[27] Second, its more comprehensive approach to negotiations; Chile and the European Union negotiated an Association Agreement, spanning not just trade but also cooperation and the establishment of a political dialogue mechanism. Third, the European Union's larger 'goodwill capital' and its more favourable perception among Chilean members of parliament, political parties in government, CSOs, labour movement and society at large. This was reinforced by the absence of the difficult geopolitical context that surrounded the negotiations with the United States. Several interviewees made the point that CSOs and the labour movement were never openly critical of the negotiations with the European Union, in spite of their similar content to those with the United States. This underscores the importance of the political factor in the latter.

3.1.7   Doha Round

Almost all interviewees concurred in stating that the Doha Round negotiations, while important, seem very remote and complex, making them difficult to follow. Moreover, they agreed that the Round has a clear credibility problem after many years of seemingly intractable problems. Interviewees were also mostly of the view that a small country like Chile, despite its good reputation in the area of international trade, has very little leverage with which to influence the outcome of the Round. Besides, multilateral negotiations are seen as removed from the concerns of Chilean public opinion.

All interviewees from the business sector pointed out that Chile has – unilaterally and through PTAs – both opened up its economy and obtained improved access to foreign markets beyond any likely outcome in Doha. In their view, this has had the effect of discouraging stronger involvement in the Round by the business sector. This assessment was shared by representatives of both goods and services interests. As a result of all the above factors, as well as of resource constraints (especially among non-business

---

[27] One important substantive difference was that, unlike the United States, the European Union asked for the exclusion of the audiovisual sector from the agreement. However, the European Union was not prepared to exclude the other cultural industries.

organizations), NSAs in Chile have not attached a high priority to the Round to date.

The one exception to the above assessment is OCEANA, whose main goal is the conservation of the word's oceans and whose headquarters for Latin America are in Santiago. OCEANA has gained recognition in trade policy circles because of its 'Cut the Bait' campaign, aimed at banning subsidies that promote over-fishing in the context of the Doha Round's negotiations on rules. When interviewed, its vice president for South America indicated that there was an almost complete correspondence of views between OCEANA's goals for these negotiations and those of the Chilean government.[28]

3.1.8   Chile–China PTA

Contrary to what might be expected, these negotiations proved to be largely uncontroversial. Despite the anxiety that China's huge export potential tends to provoke across both developed and developing countries alike, the negotiations did not face strong opposition, either from import-competing interests or from CSOs. On the contrary, they were strongly supported by those segments of the private sector that saw the enormous potential of the Chinese market for Chilean exports. The PTA was also approved unanimously by Congress.

Probably a large part of the explanation as to why this PTA faced so little opposition from the private sector is that by the start of negotiations in 2004 Chile was already a very open economy, whose low MFN tariff did not impede the access of Chinese imports. Moreover, Chile has a small industrial sector and therefore there was little prospect of direct competition with Chinese manufactures. Summing up, the benefits to be reaped in terms of increased access to the Chinese market were perceived to outweigh any potential costs.

4   State–non-state actor interactions and forum choice

Less than twenty years old, civil society participation in trade negotiations is a relatively new phenomenon in Chile. Thus, there is not a large body of experience on the basis of which to identify trends. However, some findings emerge from the interviews conducted for this project, as well as from a review of the existing literature and from this author's experience

---

[28] Chile, along with Australia, Ecuador, Iceland, New Zealand, Peru, the Philippines and the United States is a member of the 'Friends of Fish' alliance, whose goal is to eliminate, or at least reduce substantially, those subsidies that promote over-fishing.

of thirteen years as a trade official in DIRECON. They are summed up below.

First, for several reasons it is necessary to distinguish between business actors and other types of NSAs. The interaction between negotiators and the business sector started earlier and has been much more systematic than with any other NSAs. Today the business sector remains engaged in trade negotiations long after other groups shifted their attention elsewhere. This is only logical: business associations have a direct commercial stake in negotiations, whereas other groups (even trade unions) do not see the interests they represent as so directly affected by them.

Differences between business interests and other NSAs also relate to their capacity to interact with government. Business associations, especially the larger ones such as CPC and SOFOFA, have the financial resources, technical expertise and internal organization required to deal with complex trade negotiations. This stands in sharp contrast to the limited financial and technical capabilities of local CSOs and labour organizations.[29]

The interviews also revealed that business associations have a very positive assessment of their interaction with negotiators, whereas other NSAs have a more mixed evaluation. This reflects the fact that negotiators have been more able to deliver on business demands (almost always revolving around market access issues) than on those from CSOs or labour groups. The latter often involve issues which either are not in the agenda of negotiations (for example, gender issues, or very specific environmental demands), or are unacceptable to the counterpart (such as the rejection of investor–state dispute settlement and TRIPs-plus protection of pharmaceutical patents during the Chile–US PTA negotiations). Put differently, business demands (which are based on commercial interest) tend to be more amenable to negotiated solutions than demands from other NSAs (which are often based on principles).

Within the business sector, goods exporters have a more positive assessment of their experience in trade negotiations than do services exporters. This has to do with the fact that barriers to trade in goods are relatively easier to identify and negotiate away than those affecting trade in services, which tend to be more opaque.

A second finding is that the participation of non-business NSAs in debates concerning trade negotiations has not proceeded in a linear

---

[29] By contrast, one interviewee made the point that Brazilian labour organizations even develop formal positions on issues within the Doha Round, thanks to their vastly superior resources.

fashion. It was very limited during the first half of the 1990s, increased gradually during the second half of that decade, peaked in the 2000–3 period and has receded substantially since 2004. As the negotiations with the main players have been completed, the attention of many NSAs has shifted towards domestic, non-trade related issues. For example, environmentalist CSOs have turned their attention to issues such as deforestation, sustainability problems in the salmon industry and the environmental risks of dam construction projects in southern Chile.

The low intensity of NSA participation in trade debates in Chile, compared with other countries in this study, is arguably explained in large part by the fact that the main economic and social costs of trade liberalization were incurred during the military rule period. By the time the country regained democracy, the open economy model had already been showing positive results for half a decade, both in terms of growth and employment. While the majority of the business sector had come to support 'free trade' by the end of the 1980s, the open economy model became quickly legitimized among the Chilean population at large during the first years of democracy.

A third finding is that the labour movement enjoys better access to government in trade debates than is the case with most CSOs. This responds to several factors. First, the CUT formally represents a much larger constituency, made up of workers who have (at least in principle) a direct stake in trade negotiations. Second, its capacity to mobilize its base is vastly superior to that of any CSO. Third, it has been a member in its own right, along with business organizations, of all tripartite dialogue schemes since being set up in 1990. Finally, there is an historical connection between the political parties within the Concertación and the CUT which dates back to the opposition movement to the military regime in the 1980s. Although today the CUT is often critical of government decisions, several CUT leaders are members of the different political parties that form the Concertación.

A fourth finding, and one of the most robust in this study, is the remoteness of the Doha Round from the everyday agenda of Chilean NSAs. This is the case across the business sector as well as for labour organizations and CSOs, with the already noted exception of OCEANA. This situation partly responds to factors inherent to Chile, such as its limited capacity to influence outcomes due to its small size, and the perception that the country's network of PTAs makes it less dependent on the outcome of Doha. However, it is undeniable that another part of the explanation lies with the WTO itself, as the continued setbacks in the Doha Round have reduced its credibility as a negotiating forum. Moreover, negotiations in Geneva (as well as the everyday business of the WTO) are often perceived as arcane and difficult to follow.

The role of WTO rules in providing a more stable trading environment and containing protectionist pressures did not emerge in the interviews. This important aspect of the WTO should perhaps be stressed more, as it appears that in the case of Chile these rules are somewhat taken for granted even by business interests which directly benefit from them.

Fifth, on forum selection, it emerged from the interviews that Chilean NSAs do not perceive multilateral and preferential negotiations as mutually exclusive. Neither did they express a clear conceptual preference for one or the other. Their approach to this issue is a pragmatic one, reflecting the fact that a small country like Chile has very little influence on the timing and agenda of multilateral negotiations, so these are essentially assumed as exogenous. Consequently, bilateral negotiations appear in practice as the preferred forum, because they can produce concrete results within a shorter timeframe.

Sixth, although NSA participation in trade negotiations has receded in the last five years, state institutions (including those dealing with trade policy) are heading towards greater openness and accountability to the public. This move should encourage civil society's involvement in future debates on trade. This is desirable, given the ever-expanding agenda of trade negotiations, which now has direct implications on a wide range of public policies. But while open channels are a necessary condition for informed NSA participation, they are not sufficient by themselves. Overcoming the severe limitations that non-business NSAs face in Chile in terms of resources and technical expertise on trade will be as important.

Finally, beyond the issue of their financial and technical limitations, some non-business NSAs should re-examine their general attitude towards trade. In many cases, that attitude reflects an ideological rejection of concepts such as 'neoliberalism' and 'globalization', as well as a 'presumption of unfairness' about trade negotiations.[30] While during negotiations non-business NSAs have expressed a number of valid concerns on issues such as intellectual property and investment, their demands have often been unrealistic, thereby hurting their credibility and ultimately

---

[30] To be sure, asymmetries of power do influence the outcome of trade negotiations, especially those between developing and developed countries. However, assuming that only because of this fact developing countries should refrain from entering those negotiations is questionable.

their relevance. More importantly, the evidence suggests that they have failed to connect with the concerns of the wider population. The relatively strong support for 'free trade' that exists among the Chilean population means that opposition to trade agreements on principle grounds has so far been (and is likely to remain) a minority cause.

References

ECLAC 1994. *'Open Regionalism in Latin America and the Caribbean'*, Santiago de Chile.

Herreros, S. 2009. 'Chile', in P. Draper, P. Alves and R. Sally (eds.), *The Political Economy of Trade Reform in Emerging Markets. Crisis or Opportunity?* Cheltenham: Edward Elgar.

Jara, A. 2001. 'Aspectos institucionales y económicos en las negociaciones comerciales de Chile. Parte I: Aspectos institucionales', in A. Estevadeordal and C. Robert (eds.), *Las Américas sin barreras. Negociaciones comerciales de acceso a mercados.* Washington, DC: Inter American Development Bank..

Meller, P. 1996. *Un siglo de economía política chilena (1890–1990).* Santiago de Chile: Editorial Andrés Bello.

Porras, J. 2003. *'La estrategia chilena de acuerdos comerciales: un análisis político'*, Serie Comercio Internacional, No. 36, CEPAL, Santiago de Chile.

Rojas, F. and Pey, C. 2002. *'Participación de la Sociedad Civil en el ALCA'*, Caso Chile, Facultad Latinoamericana de Ciencias Sociales (FLACSO), Santiago de Chile.

Sáez, S. and Valdés, J. 1999. 'Chile and its "Lateral" Trade Policy', *CEPAL Review* **67**, April 1999, Santiago de Chile.

Silva, V. 2000. 'Política comercial y la relación público – privada en Chile durante los noventa', in O. Muñoz Gomá *et al.* (eds.), *El Estado y el sector privado. Construyendo una nueva economía en los años 90'*, Facultad Latinoamericana de Ciencias Sociales (FLACSO), Santiago de Chile.

World Trade Organization 1997. *Trade Policy Review. Chile.* WTO: Geneva.

ANNEX

List of interviewees

Hugo Baierlein, Head of the Foreign Trade Department, Federation of Chilean Industry (SOFOFA) (www.sofofa.cl).

Bruno Bettati, President, Association of Film and Television Producers (APCT). Former Secretary General (March 2001–March 2003), Audiovisual Platform (www.plataforma-audiovisual.blogspot.com).

Alicia Frohmann, Director, Export Promotion Directorate (ProChile), Ministry of Foreign Affairs. Head of the North America and FTAA Department, General Directorate for International Economic Relations, Ministry of Foreign Affairs (1999–2003).[31]

Pablo Lazo, adviser on labour issues, General Directorate for International Economic Relations, Ministry of Foreign Affairs (www.direcon.cl).

Cecilia Millán, regional programme manager, Economic Justice, Latin America and the Caribbean Oxfam International. Formerly country director, Chile Office, Oxfam International.

Alex Muñoz, Vice President, Office for South America, OCEANA (www.oceana.org/america-del-sur/quienes-somos/oficina-oceana-chile).

Coral Pey, former Executive Secretary (1999–2006), Chilean Alliance for Fair and Responsible Trade.

Joaquín Piña, Executive Secretary, Services Exporters' Coalition (www.chilexportaservicios.cl).

Osvaldo Rosales, Director, International Trade and Integration Division, United Nations Economic Commission for Latin America and the Caribbean.

General Director for International Economic Relations at the Ministry of Foreign Affairs (2000–4). Chief negotiator of Chile's free trade agreements with the United States, the European Union, EFTA and Korea.

Edda Rossi, Head, Trade and Sustainable Development Department, General Directorate for International Economic Relations, Ministry of Foreign Affairs (www.direcon.cl).

Paulina Vásquez, Vice Manager for International Affairs, Association of Manufactures' Exporters ASEXMA) (www.asexma.cl).

Valentín Vega, President, Confederation of Graphic Workers of Chile (CONAGRA) (www.conagra.cl). Counsellor, Unitary Workers' Central Union (Central Unitaria de Trabajadores) (www.cutchile.cl).

---

[31] Among her responsibilities was liaising with civil society groups during the Chile–US and FTAA negotiations.

3

Colombia

HERNANDO J. GÓMEZ[1] AND JAVIER GAMBOA

It is usual for both governments and organizations from the private and civil society sector of developing countries to dedicate more time and resources to bilateral and regional negotiations than to multilateral negotiations. In principle, this contradicts the classic theory of trade in which the greatest welfare gains are to be found in the multilateral field and in which preferential trade agreements (PTAs) can lead to trade diversion and welfare losses.

In popular defence of PTAs, it is pointed out that multilateral negotiations are slow, uncertain and, given the veto power of members of the WTO, it is very difficult to obtain the required consensus, in contrast to bilateral negotiations where there is greater control of the negotiating agenda, process and timeframe. Hence, developing countries confront situations typical of the 'prisoners' dilemma' when they decide to carry out bilateral or regional negotiations and simultaneously carry on with multilateral negotiations.

In this chapter, based largely on interviews with government officials, business association managers and civil society organizations (CSOs), the intention is to interrogate this hypothesis. Furthermore, the attitudes and strategies of different types of non-state actors (NSAs) are scrutinized in relation to the question of forum choice – preferential or multilateral – in order to determine whether there are underlying explanations that could explain their preferences; for instance, in relation to their particular interests or to their winning or losing position in specific negotiations.

Section 1 provides an overview of the evolution of Colombia's trade policy, its composition of trade and trade partners. Section 2 provides an overview and analysis of the principal state and non-state actors involved

---

[1] Mr Gómez is president of the Colombian Private Council on Competitiveness and former chief negotiator of the FTA with the United States. Mr Gamboa is Executive Vice President of the Colombian Private Council on Competitiveness and was the head negotiator on intellectual property rights in the FTA negotiations with the United States.

in the trade policy-making process. Section 3 outlines Colombia's principal trade agreements. Section 4 describes and analyses the interactions between state and non-state actors. Section 5 explores the question of forum choice and section 6 concludes.

1   Colombia's trade policy and patterns of trade

In general terms, the Colombian commercial policy followed the patterns of the rest of Latin America. At the end of the nineteenth and beginning of the twentieth centuries, Colombia had an open economy and with productive structures oriented towards world markets. Based on the accumulation of capital, and exports of cinchona bark and subsequently of coffee and petroleum, the first banking institutions and some industrial institutions were created in this period.

The worldwide depression of the 1930s led to the adoption of protectionist policies, which were subsequently reinforced with the impact of the Second World War and, even more, with the influence of the development theories led by the Economic Commission for Latin America (ECLA) in the 1950s and 1960s. At that time, the country embarked upon a strategy of import-institution industrialization, reinforced with complementary policies such as subsidized credit. At the end of the 1980s, Colombia began a trade opening process which has generally been maintained up to the present day.

Colombia's trade evolution has had some peculiarities. At the beginning of the twentieth century, Colombia had a more open economy than other similar countries. But from that point until the mid-1990s, it retreated almost continuously from this openness. After exporting 25% of its GDP in the 1920s, this gradually fell to an average of 15% by the 1980s. Likewise, when world commerce was reduced during the Great Depression and the Second World War, Colombia closed down faster than expected. And when world trade was reactivated in the post-war period, Colombia remained closed until the end of the 1980s.[2]

This development policy created a very fragile foreign trade structure, which led to great instability in the balance of payments. Raw materials and basic goods were exported and intermediate goods and machinery and equipment were imported. This led to a boom and bust cycle, with

---

[2] National Planning Department 1990, 'Decisions Regarding the Economic Opening Program, in the Pacific Revolution, Modernization and Opening of the Economy'. National Planning Department, Bogotá, p. 20.

the economy booming when international prices went up, but then pass-
ing to situations of great shortage of foreign currency and abrupt and
pronounced devaluations in the periods of low international prices of
basic goods. Fiscal policy was also fragile as government revenues were
dependent on high import tariffs, which would follow the cycle of the balance of payments as well. This generated economic 'stop and go' policies
that discouraged long-term investment; especially foreign investment.

Throughout the twentieth century, the main instruments of Colombian
commercial policy were tariffs and quantitative import restrictions,
exchange controls and a great variety of instruments for the promotion of
exports. With regard to the latter, the import–export system known as the
'Plan Vallejo' is notable. It was a tariff and tax exemption system for the
importation of raw materials and capital goods destined to produce goods
for export, and was one of the key mechanisms used from the end of the
1960s for the promotion of non-traditional exports. The Plan Vallejo was
intended to reduce the anti-exporting bias of Colombia's commercial policy and allowed for the export of a few manufactured goods. This scheme
was not abolished until the expiry in 2002 of the WTO waiver, which then
required Colombia to come into conformity with its WTO obligations.

Another key decision at the end of the 1960s was the transition from a
fixed exchange rate system to a crawling-peg devaluation system administered by the Central Bank. This decision was prompted by the realization that inflation in Colombia was higher than world inflation due to the
indexation to the consumer price index of mortgages and the minimum
wage among other prices in the economy, which led the over-valuation
of the real exchange rate over time. This affected the competitiveness
of the productive sector, generating imbalances in the current account.
Likewise, due to the continued fluctuations in the country's terms of
trade, an administered exchange rate system permitted exchange adjustments in a progressive and less traumatic manner, noticeably reducing
the political dimension in exchange rate management.

With regard to international commercial negotiations, it is worth indicating that Colombia participated in the failed negotiations of the Havana
Conference between 1947 and 1948. However, Colombia's membership of
the General Agreement of Tariffs and Trade (GATT) was pursued only at
the beginning of the 1970s, and once the mechanisms for regional integration within the Andean Pact were established.

At that time, because of their growing share in world trade of manufactured goods, mining and agricultural products, developing countries were invited to participate in the Tokyo Round of negotiations of

the GATT, which commenced in 1973. In 1975 the contracting parties of the GATT granted Colombia provisional membership, which made it eligible for most favoured nation (MFN) treatment but ineligible to participate in the decision-making processes or in the dispute settlement mechanisms. It was only in October 1981 that Colombia acquired the category of contracting party with full rights in the GATT.[3] Subsequently, Colombia participated fully in the Uruguay Round of the GATT negotiations, which ended on 15 April 1994 with the establishment of the World Trade Organization (WTO). Colombia was an original member of the WTO, joining on 30 April 1995.

At the regional level, in May 1969 Colombia, together with Bolivia, Chile, Ecuador and Peru, signed the Cartagena Agreement which established the Andean Group. In February 1973, Venezuela joined this organization and in October 1976 Chile withdrew from it. During the 1970s and 1980s, the Andean Group operated under the import-substitution industrialization model. Its objective was to protect the national industries of its members through an extended market sheltered by high tariff barriers and other types of commercial restrictions. Thus, for example, there was an intention to develop certain strategic manufacturing sectors sheltered by protectionist measures and the extended Andean market with limited tariff preferences. The automobile sector was outstanding among these sectors, and was the only industry sector that was successfully developed under this model in the region.

In 1989 the Andean Group members decided to abandon the closed development model and give way to the open model. They eliminated the tariffs among themselves and formed a free trade zone in 1993. In 1997 the Andean Group became the Andean Community of Nations (CAN) with a stronger institutional structure and a scope beyond commercial matters. In April 2006, Venezuela abandoned the CAN, arguing that the free trade agreements of Colombia and Peru with the United States undermined the CAN, even though the General Secretariat of the Community had endorsed the compatibility of the two commercial agreements.[4]

Colombia also negotiated the Free Trade Agreement of the Group of the Three (G-3) with Mexico and Venezuela in 1994 (Venezuela withdrew from this in 2006). It also participated in the negotiation of the Free Trade

[3] Ministry of Commerce 1996, 'World Trade Organization II', Collection of International Commercial Agreements, No. 4, Ministry of Commerce, Bogotá.

[4] Andean Community of Nations 2006, 'Elements for an Evaluation of the Free Trade Agreement of Colombia and Peru with the United States, with Regard to the Judicial Regulation of the Andean Community', General Secretariat of the CAN, Lima.

Area of the Americas (FTAA) which did not materialize and whose suspension occurred in 2004.

In the last few years there has been a renewed effort towards the negotiation of reciprocal market liberalization. In October 2004 Colombia, together with Venezuela and Ecuador, negotiated an Economic Complementation Agreement with the Common Market of the South (MERCOSUR). In November 2006, it concluded free trade agreements (FTA) with the United States and Chile. In August 2007, an FTA was signed with the North Central American Triangle (El Salvador, Guatemala and Honduras). In mid-2008, PTAs were concluded with Canada and with the European Free Trade Association (EFTA). At the time of writing, Colombia is negotiating, together with Peru and Ecuador, an FTA with the European Union, which is due to be completed in 2010.

To date the agreements with MERCOSUR, Chile and the North Central American Triangle have come into force. The rest of the treaties have not yet come into force, since they are in different stages of their approval and ratification process in Colombia, or with the corresponding commercial partner.

1.1 Colombia's trade patterns

During most of the twentieth century Colombian exports were dominated by coffee. According to Villar and Esguerra (2005), between 1910 and 1940 coffee exports grew at annual average rates of 7.4%. This rapid growth resulted in coffee accounting for more than 70% of the total value of Colombian exports by the mid-1920s. Declining coffee prices in the 1930s caused this share to decrease somewhat, but it remained above 50%. Subsequent to the coffee bonanza of the 1960s, a sharp fall in international prices occurred, especially after the breaking of the International Coffee Pact in 1989. The importance of coffee in Colombia's export mix has since declined markedly, due to the diversification of export production in mining (petroleum, coal and nickel), agriculture (flowers, bananas and beef) and manufacturing for the Andean markets.

Mining exports have also been important, and during the colonial period and throughout the nineteenth century gold was Colombia's main export. Its importance decreased with the rise in coffee sales, but, together with platinum, represented 20% of exports in the early twentieth century.

Petroleum began to be produced at the end of the 1920s, and the share of mining products in the total goods exported increased to 25% in the

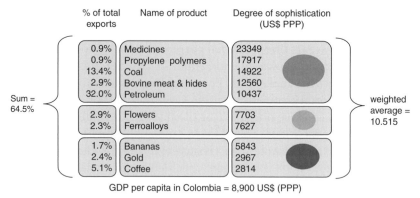

Figure 3.1   Degree of sophistication of Colombia's ten most exported products, 2008

1930s and 1940s. However, this share began to reduce gradually, until 1970 when it almost disappeared and Colombia became a net importer of crude oil. In 1985 petroleum and coal exports surged again, and in the 1990s they became Colombia's major exports, representing more than 45% of the country's foreign sales at the time of writing.

Apart from coffee, exports of bananas, sugar, beef, tobacco and flowers have been important at various times. Trade in manufactured goods truly developed only after the 1960s, a period in which the exports of these products represented 40% of the country's total exports. The growth of these exports has been linked to the integration processes with the Andean region, especially with Venezuela and Ecuador.

At present, Colombia's top ten exports, representing 64.5% of total exports (figures are for 2008) are: petroleum, coal, coffee, flowers, bovine meat and hides, gold, ferroalloys, propylene polymers and medicines.

Figure 3.1 is organized according to the degree of sophistication of the ten products most exported by Colombia. The degree of sophistication of the product refers to the average weighted income of the countries that export said product, according to calculations made by Hausmann, Hwang and Rodrick (2006).

Bearing in mind that the per capita income of Colombia in 2008 is approximately US$8,510 (World Bank 2009) (in terms of purchasing power parity), at first sight it would appear that there are five products (medicines, propylene polymers, coal, bovine meat and petroleum) in which Colombia still has a vast margin to compete by way of less relative costs. However, it is clear that in the case of petroleum and coal they are primary exports that depend on international prices.

Parallel to this, medicines are found in the table, more as a matter of classification than of relevance, due to the fact that the type of products manufactured in Colombia, mainly generics, do not correspond to the degree of sophistication assigned to the general category of medicines.

The case of bovine meat is really a phenomenon of trade diversion, since 92% of the total heading of exports is to Venezuela. Likewise, in the case of flowers and apparel (not even included in the ten most exported products), the figure shows how they are beginning to face competitive pressures, which is reflected in the sensitivity of these two sectors to any adverse fluctuation in the exchange rate. Finally, the low degree of sophistication of products such as coffee, banana and gold, in comparison with Colombia's average present income, shows the urgent necessity of generating a productive transformation process in order to add value to them or find a product niche if it is desired that they continue being relevant as exported products in the future and not be displaced by competitors with much lower relative costs.

With regard to the destination of exports, for Colombia, the main destination is the United States, with 38% of the total exports (figures for 2008), of which the great majority is made up of primary products or manufactured goods based on natural resources (such as petrochemicals). Latin America and the Caribbean are the second most important export destination with 33.9%, mainly to Venezuela (16.2%) and Ecuador (4%). In contrast to exports to the United States, the bulk of the exports to these countries are manufactured goods of a low and medium technological content. In the case of Venezuela, 2007 showed an exceptional increase, accounting for 17.4% of Colombia's total exports. Other export destinations are the European Union (12.8%), China (1.2%), Japan (1%) and the rest of Asia (1.6%). In the case of China, 2007 also showed an important rise accounting for 3% of Colombia's exports.

As far as imports are concerned, the great majority are in the industrial sector (93.3% in 2008), especially machinery and equipment (12.8%), basic industry (metallurgic, basic chemistry and paper) (28.8%) and the automotive industry (8.2%). With regard to the farming and animal husbandry sector (5.6%), the bulk corresponds to cereals, especially corn, wheat and soybean.

The United States is also the main origin of Colombian imports with 29.2% of the total (2008). The European Union represents 13.5% and, climbing rapidly, China is the third source of Colombia's imports with 11.5% in 2008. Other important sources of foreign purchases are made up of Mexico (7.9%), Brazil (5.9%) and Venezuela (3.0%).

Table 3.1 *Share of foreign commerce, by destination*

	Exports (%)			Imports (%)		
	1995–8	2001–4	2005–8	1995–8	2001–4	2005–8
United States	38.0	44.2	38.6	34.2	30.6	27.6
European Union (27)	23.7	14.2	13.9	19.8	16.2	13.2
Latin America and the Caribbean	28.2	32.4	34.2	24.8	27.2	30.0
Asia	3.5	2.3	3.2	9.2	11.2	15.0
China	0.2	0.5	1.7	1.1	5.2	9.8
Japan	3.1	1.5	1.3	7.2	4.4	3.4
Others Asia	0.2	0.2	0.3	0.8	1.7	1.8
Rest of the World	6.6	7.0	10.1	12.1	14.8	14.3
World	100.0	100.0	100.0	100.0	100.0	100.0

Source: Osvaldo Rosales, 2009. *Colombia: An Insertion Strategy in Pacific Asia*, based on CEPAL, COMTRADE database and official figures from the National Administrative Department of Statistics (DANE), Santiago, Chile. Percentages calculated on the basis of annual averages for each four-year period.

Table 3.1 shows the dynamics of Colombia's main commercial partners between 1995 and 2008.

2   State and non-state actors in trade policy-making

In 1991 as a fundamental part of the commercial opening strategy and the internationalization of the economy, the Ministry of Commerce was established with the mandate of coordinating this strategy. Under the model of import-substitution industrialization which had prevailed until then, the functions associated with the administration of foreign trade were performed by the Ministry of Economic Development, while representation in international commercial negotiations corresponded to the Ministry of Foreign Relations.

In effect, the establishment of the Ministry of Commerce meant that Colombia had opted for the institutional 'foreign trade' model for the handling of its commercial policy, as opposed to the institutional 'foreign affairs' model which continued to prevail in other Latin American countries, such as Brazil, Argentina and Chile. The idea was that the new ministry would specialize in carrying out a very active search for new markets, in which the initial objective was to have improved access to the United States market.

However, after an initial period of activity in which Colombia negotiated the Free Trade Agreement of the G-3 (which imitated the North American Free Trade Agreement (NAFTA)), as an intermediate step towards access to the United States' market, Colombia's search for PTAs lost impetus between 1995 and 2002 with the exception of the Andean integration process, a partial agreement with Chile and participation in the failed FTAA negotiations.

In 2002 the new administration of President Álvaro Uribe established new institutional arrangements for Colombian commercial policy, which saw the merging of the ministries of Economic Development and Foreign Trade and the creation of a new Ministry of Commerce, Industry and Tourism. While responsibility for international trade negotiations remained with this new ministry (except that it was now the responsibility of the Vice Minister of Commerce), in the opinion of some of the persons interviewed for this research, it implied a disfigurement of the 'foreign trade model', as the new ministry also took on sectoral responsibilities for the industrial sector. This has generated concerns in the agricultural sector that the interests of industry will take precedence over agriculture in the context of trade policy and trade negotiations.

Another important institutional change was constituted by the structure of the negotiating team itself. Since the beginning of the 1990s, the country's 'technical' representation had been headed by the Vice Minister of Foreign Trade, acting as head of the negotiating team. Prior to the negotiations for an FTA with the United States, the participation of other ministries was very limited, with the exception (above all, in the negotiations of the FTAA) of the ministries of Foreign Relations, Treasury and Agriculture and the National Planning Department.

The importance of the FTA with the United States, and the concomitant need for significant resources, required a new institutional arrangement with regard to the negotiating team, greater inter-institutional coordination, consultations with the territorial entities (departments, municipalities and capital district) and with NSAs in business, producers and civil society. Decree 2314 of 2004 was issued for the purpose of regulating these procedural aspects of the FTA negotiations with the

United States. Subsequently, by means of Decree 4712 of 2007, with some minor changes, these new procedural arrangements were converted into the general applicable rule for all Colombia's international commercial negotiations.

With regard to the negotiating team, Decree 2314 of 2004 formalized the existence of a Head of the Negotiating Team of Colombia, different from the Vice Minister of Foreign Trade. The Head of the Negotiating Team became the visible head of the negotiations and was authorized to remove any member of the different negotiating teams made up of functionaries from different governmental entities. Furthermore, this position was responsible for achieving the overall balance of the negotiation from the point of view of the national interest. This way, despite formally belonging to the Ministry of Commerce, the head of the negotiating team was given wide-ranging and substantial faculties and responsibilities in every negotiation.

Thus, the Ministry of Commerce was given clear leadership in the trade negotiations, with responsibility for control of the negotiation strategy and its overall balance. However, in the negotiation of the FTA with the United States, the different ministries assumed their corresponding thematic responsibilities within the negotiation; for example, Agriculture, Treasury, Communications, Social Protection (on matters concerning labour and health), Interior (on intellectual property rights), and began to take an active part in the negotiating teams. This situation required that specific sensitive subjects had to be referred to the President of the Republic for ultimate decision.

With respect to the formulation of the national negotiating objectives, the different thematic committees (one for each chapter of the corresponding Agreement) were supposed to act in consensus, in accordance with legislative decrees. In the case of the FTA negotiation with the United States, the negotiating team ultimately came to be composed of more than a hundred officials belonging to more than twenty ministries and agencies. In case no consensus was reached with regard to the negotiating interests and positions, the matter had to be referred to the Head of the Negotiating Team. If consensus could not be reached at that level, then it was referred to the Vice Minister of Foreign Trade, who was required to consult with other vice ministers and officials with relevant portfolio responsibilities. Matters not resolved at that level were to be resolved at the ministerial level, or considered by the Superior Council for Foreign Trade, or, as a last resort, by the Cabinet of Ministers, headed by the President of the Republic.

2.1 Mechanisms for consultation with non-state actors

With regard to the procedure for consultations with NSAs, it was established that the ministers, relevant vice ministers, the Head of the Negotiating Team and the heads of the thematic committees would be the national government's spokespersons with NSAs. In order to guarantee the consistency of the country's negotiating position, under Decree 4712 (and formerly Decree 2314) consultations with NSAs were to be coordinated by the Minister of Commerce, Industry and Tourism. All communications from NSAs to government regarding international trade negotiations had to be sent to the Head of the Negotiating Team for consideration.

Generally, this inter-institutional coordination plan has functioned quite well. The only important tensions that have been registered since the negotiation of the FTA with the United States have been with the ministries of Agriculture and of Social Protection. In the case of Agriculture, due to distortions in international agricultural markets created by huge internal support given to the farmers in most rich countries, the objective of making the agricultural negotiation as 'self-contained' and independent as possible generated frictions with regard to the responsibilities of strategic management and global balance entrusted to the Ministry of Commerce. There were also tensions with the Ministry of Social Protection due to the public sensitivity on the issue of drug patents and their potential impact on access to medicines.

On the other hand, the standards in force point out the Ministry of Commerce's obligation to promote the participation of the NSAs in the negotiating process and, in that sense, establishing suitable mechanisms to receive and analyse their contributions keep them properly informed of the progress being made in the course of the negotiations.

The mechanisms established for the FTA negotiation with the United States provided for a broad range of public inputs. During the preparatory phase of the negotiation, the Government defined clear rules on the procedures in order to inform citizens and share information with the private sector. In this phase, Colombia's negotiating position was constructed and some matrixes of interest of the parties involved were drawn up, as well as list of requests, which were made public.

As the negotiating process advanced and drafts texts were drawn up highlighting the areas of discussion or disagreement, they were shared with the private sector and discussed in depth with the negotiating team. This work was carried out in special detail for each one of the thematic negotiating texts after each round, in the official reports that the

Government submitted to the public in events carried out in public auditorium in Bogotá, each with a duration of two to three days and attended by more than 5,000 persons. Complementary to these, the negotiating team summoned the private sector each time a detailed discussion of specific points of the negotiation was considered necessary.

Furthermore, the draft texts of the negotiations were made available for the public at 'reading rooms' which operated in Bogotá, Medellín, Cali and Barranquilla. At the conclusion of the negotiation, the government published the text it called the 'negotiation's white book', a database published on the Internet with more than 8,000 documents which gathered all the reports of the interaction process between the negotiating team and NSAs. This database is evidence of the extent of the consultation process carried out by the Government of Colombia with the business sector, producer groups, civil society organizations and the general public.

The 'room next door' was another participation mechanism which was very important, serving as the main consultation forum with the private sector during the individual rounds of the negotiations. In the case of the FTA with the United States, on some occasions this forum was attended by more than 600 persons, mainly promoters and business association leaders, but also by CSOs, unions and even ethnic minorities. The 'room next door' permitted consultation in 'real time' with the interested parties regarding the dynamics that occurred in the development of each round of the negotiation.

A special socialization exercise was carried out with regard to the ethnic minorities (native people and Afro-American communities), in which approximately fifty encounters were developed exclusively with these groups. There were also special spaces in order to hold dialogues with the unions and other groups that opposed the agreement. However, they were hardly used by opponents who feared that this mechanism could be used as a strategy for legitimizing the agreement and consequently for weakening their opposition.

In this context, it is important to point out that in Colombia a very important part of labour organizations consists of government employees, who were among the most belligerent opponents. Their view is that trade agreements have little or no effect on their employment, hence, their position is more ideological and political than derived from specific economic interests. This ideological bias is confirmed as their opposition was stronger to the PTA negotiation with the United States than the one that is being negotiated with the European Union, even though the content of both PTAs is essentially the same.

With regard to the role of the legislative power, under the terms of the political constitution, it has the function of approving or disapproving the treaties that the Government enters into with other states (Article 150(16)). Therefore, its formal competence appears only once the corresponding commercial agreement is negotiated. Even if the treaty is approved by the Congress of the Republic, the President of the Republic, in his capacity as head of state, has the discretional power of whether or not to ratify.

However, bearing in mind the importance for the country of the negotiation of the FTA with the United States, Congress was actively involved during the negotiating stage itself, albeit indirectly. The Government actually had a 'room for the accompaniment of Congress' available during the negotiation rounds. According to the statistics of the Ministry of Commerce, an average of twenty-five Congress members and fourteen Counsels for the Congress members attended each one of the rounds, as well as more than thirty summonses to the Congress, attended by the Head of the Negotiating Team and by the Minister of Commerce.[5]

2.2   Non-state actors

2.2.1   Business and farmers' associations

The main NSAs who participate in the commercial negotiations are the representatives of business associations and CSOs dedicated to specific causes (see Table 3.2). NSAs that were especially active in the negotiation of the PTA with the United States were interviewed for this research and they include the president of the National Business Association (ANDI), who is also acting president of the National Business Union Council; the president of the Farmers' Society of Colombia (SAC), who is also vice president of the National Business Union Council; the president of the National Federation of Cattle Breeders (FEDEGAN); the director of the Agriculture National Salvation Association and member of the Colombian Network against the FTAA and the FTA (RECALCA); the technical coordinator of the National Trade Union Council for the FTA with the United States; the president of the National Federation of Poultry Breeders of Colombia (ENAVI); and the director of the Health Mission NGO.

---

[5] Government of Colombia 2006, Exposition of Motives of Law Project 178 of November 30, 2006, by means of which the Commercial Promotion Agreement is approved between the Republic of Colombia and the United States of America, its Enclosed Letters and its Amendments, Ministry of Trade, Industry and Tourism of the Government of Colombia, Bogotá.

Table 3.2 *NSAs involved in trade policy-making*

NSA	Policy interest	Constituencies served	International affiliation
National Business Association (ANDI)	All topics, especially non-agricultural market access	Business association	
Farmers Society of Colombia (SAC)	Agriculture	Business association	
National Federation of Cattle Breeders (FEDEGAN)	Agriculture	Business association	
Agriculture National Salvation Association	Agriculture	CSO	
National Trade Union Council for the FTA with the US	All topics	Coordination of business associations	
National Federation of Poultry Breeders of Colombia	Agriculture	Business association	
Health Mission Foundation	Public health, intellectual property	CSO	International Alliance for the Defence of Health
Colombia Trade Agreements			
Andean Community (CAN)**			
CAN – MERCOSUR**			
United States*			
Canada**			
European Free Trade Area			
North Central American Triangle			

* Analysed in detail
** Served as reference

With regard to private sector representatives (producer and business associations), their roles and strategies usually differ, depending on whether they view a particular trade negotiation as an opportunity or as a threat. Likewise, it would be necessary to differentiate between those managers of business associations who represent a specific sectoral activity and those who act in representation of 'umbrella' business associations which include different sectoral interests. In this sense, it is important to understand how the Colombian private sector has been generally organized in recent times.

The majority of the most important business associations belong to the National Business Association Council. This council acts as a forum for the articulation of the different sectoral interests of the private sector. The president of the National Business Association (ANDI) has been acting for several years as the president of the Business Association Council, and the president of the Farmers' Society of Colombia (SAC) acts as vice president of the Council. ANDI and SAC are the country's most important production trade unions and they act as umbrella business associations; in the case of SAC for most of the agricultural trade unions and, in the case of ANDI, through the sectoral chambers affiliated to trade unions on the subjects of manufacturing and services.

As can be expected, the actions of an umbrella business association in international trade negotiations are different to those of a sectoral business association. For the FTA with the United States, the private sector was organized through an *ad hoc* committee for the negotiation, headed by a technical coordinator from the National Business Association Council. Actually, it is an 'extended' Business Association Council, because as well as the sixteen business associations that make it up traditionally, nine more sectoral business associations were added exclusively for matters relating to the negotiations.

The technical coordinator of the *ad hoc* committee for the commercial negotiations acts as the facilitator of the private sector's internal negotiation. It must be kept in mind that in a commercial negotiation having the scope of the FTA with the United States there were conflicting interests: on the one hand, the net exporters who considered the negotiation to be an extraordinary opportunity; and on the other hand, those sectors that produce goods that compete with US imports. The same thing was true within production chains. Thus, it is important to remember that the negotiation at home is as important as the negotiation abroad, and it is crucial that governments have effective means for conducting these internal negotiations.

In the case of ANDI and its sectoral associations, it is generally a busi-ness association which is clearly pro-trade (although in some associations, particular sensibilities exist). For ANDI, the existing formal mechanisms are very important and are perceived as adequate. ANDI's technical cap-acity and its pro-trade position facilitate dialogue with the Government and enhance its capacity to influence. In the case of ANDI, this dialogue is closer with the Ministry of Commerce, as would be expected, although it also takes place with the National Planning Department, the Ministry of Social Protection and the Treasury Department. By contrast, the dia-logue between ANDI and the Ministry of Agriculture is more difficult,

In the case of SAC, an umbrella for several organizations, its position with regard to the commercial negotiations is more complex because there are sectoral business associations within it which feel that they are clearly winners and others that, on the contrary, consider themselves los-ers in trade agreements. However, the role of SAC has been fundamen-tal in the efforts to legitimize and make the trade negotiations feasible, especially with developed countries (e.g., the United States, the European Union and Canada), in managing to balance the two types of interests of all its members, offensive and defensive. For those agriculture actors with export interests (an offensive position) it was achieved through rapid access (chronograms for the removal of tariffs), and real access (with regard to commitments mainly on the subject of non-tariff barriers as sanitary and phytosanitary measures) to the United States. On the other hand, for the other agriculture actors with defensive positions towards more trade competition, slow chronograms for the removal of tariffs, as well as the creation of internal assistance in Colombia, were crucial to winning their acceptance of the PTA with the United States and other developed countries.

In order to achieve its objectives, SAC has exercised influence not only on the Ministry of Agriculture, where it is natural that it should have active dialogue, but also on the Ministry of Commerce, where it under-stands that many of the key decisions of the negotiation are made. On many occasions, SAC has even acted as a 'bridge' between the two min-istries. We can assert that the upper echelons of SAC decided in favour of a long-term strategy, where the government had to commit to providing ample resources to support a structural transformation of the agriculture sector.

In contrast to these examples, FENAVI and FEDEGAN are strictly sec-toral business associations: the former being an 'opponent' of the treaty and the latter being one of its defenders. These two business associations are the only ones in the farming and animal husbandry sector that do not form part of SAC.

In the case of FENAVI, which groups together the egg and poultry producers and the incubators, a difference in the pattern of consumption of chicken in the United States and Colombia generated very high sensitivity to the negotiation of the FTA. In Colombia the so-called 'hind quarters' are the parts of the chicken preferred by the consumers, whereas in the United States the 'white' parts (breasts) are practically the only ones that are consumed. This way, the United States can export the so-called 'hind quarters' at strongly discounted prices.

Although, in theory, that situation would imply that Colombia would also have an offensive interest in exporting chicken breasts to the United States, in practice, it is not possible due to sanitary reasons that will need a decade of hard work to resolve. (Colombia has not been declared free from 'Newcastle disease' which affects chickens, and is a condition for being able to export to the US market.) In such a setting, for a business association such as FENAVI its interests in the negotiation fundamentally centred on impeding or delaying as much as possible the entrance of chicken hind quarters originating from the United States.

Opponents of the FTA with the United States focus their strategies on positioning their interests before public opinion and politicians, rather than seeking to take advantage of and 'winning' the technical debate directly with the government of Colombia, or with the US negotiators. Thus, FENAVI carried out an intense sensitizing task with the Congress of the Republic and through the media in order to raise the profile of its interests publicly, and in this way increase the political cost of making concessions for the government.

In the case of FEDEGAN, its interests are mainly in the beef and milk sectors. Although, in theory, it could have adopted a protectionist attitude with regard to the commercial negotiations, as of the negotiation of the FTA with the United States, it has adopted a position in favour of free trade, trying to capitalize on the opportunities resulting from the access to markets. The challenge for FEDEGAN, especially in the beef sector, is non-tariff barriers, mainly the sanitary and phytosanitary ones. That is why obtaining real access is the fundamental interest of this business association in the negotiation. Of course, obtaining real access is a matter that implies much more than the negotiation of some 'rules of the game' in the text of the trade agreement. It requires Colombian producers to meet sanitary and phytosanitary requirements determined by trade partners and international organizations. For this purpose, the Ministry of Agriculture is clearly the preferred channel and where it exercises the most influence. Evidently, having sub-sectors considering themselves as 'winners' within its sector in the commercial negotiations is sufficient motivation for the Ministry of Agriculture to attend to their interests in the best way possible.

2.2.2   Civil society organizations

With regard to NSAs that are representative of civil society's 'causes', the two most vocal organizations in the commercial negotiations, especially with the United States, have been the 'Agriculture Salvation' organization and Health Mission. In the case of Agriculture Salvation, as well as the set of organizations grouped together in connection with the Colombian network against the FTAA and the FTA – RECALCA – their main interests are directed towards the defence of small farmers, with a decidedly protectionist vision (an extreme food security view) and important ideological and political dimensions. In addition to contributing inputs of a technical nature, this organization's participation was directed towards causing political impact. To that end, the formation of coalitions with related organizations in other Latin American countries is an important action strategy. Likewise, coalitions with different groups that opposed the trade agreements, including trade unions and political parties, are a central element of its strategy. Raising public awareness and the potential political cost to the Government are fundamental elements of the strategy of the opponents to trade agreements.

In the case of Health Mission, which coordinates the network of institutions called Alliance for the Defence of Health, its fundamental interest is to prevent the creation of barriers to the access to medicines in trade agreements. Patents and protection of test data specifically are the subjects that concentrated its attention and management. However, unlike RECALCA, Health Mission's opposition to the PTA with the United States is more 'technical' than political, in the sense that it is not an opposition in itself, but rather it is the search for the best result possible for its interests. In that sense, its actions are more similar to those of a trade union with defensive interests, than to those of a typical anti-trade CSO. Indeed, the coincidence of specific interests within the negotiation with the business association that represents the manufacturers of generic medicines (ASINFAR) is practically total.

However, unlike business, including that of the Association of Pharmaceutical Industries of Colombia, Health Mission could mount a 'public interest' argument without the problem of being perceived as the defence of a particular vested economic interest. Hence, Health Mission used all available mechanisms to influence the result of the negotiation, from technical arguments favoured by business through to public campaigns, media campaigns and lobbying of Congress members.

3 Colombia's trade agreements

The negotiation of the FTA with the United States is the main source of analysis carried out in this work. It is probably the most debated economic policy decision in Colombia's recent history, and for this reason is the most relevant for the purposes of this study.

The importance for Colombia of the FTA with the United States is due to different factors: on the one hand, the United States has the largest economy in the world and is the main destination for Colombia's exports. On the other hand, the political importance of the negotiation resulting from the United States being the main world power and the complex framework of relationships between the two countries gave this a significance that exceeded economic matters and involved many political and ideological elements, both for opponents and allies of the negotiation.

The negotiation began in May 2004 and ended in February 2006, even though it was possible to sign the agreement only on 22 November 2006 (after the legal revision and overcoming new differences between the parties). However, after a relatively easy passage through the Congress and Constitutional Court of Colombia, it has not been approved by the US Congress or even submitted to Congress, for internal political reasons and the rise of protectionist sentiment.

Other regional agreements served as reference for this research, though to a lesser degree. In particular, prior to the FTA with the United States, the great regional experience of commercial negotiations is made up of the Agreement of Cartagena and its later developments coming from the framework of the Andean Community of Nations. The negotiations of the CAN–MERCOSUR Agreement, with the EFTA, Canada and the negotiations underway with the European Union will be taken as reference, to a lesser degree, given that their political and economic impact as well as the participation of NSAs was smaller.

In the multilateral field, the Doha Round of Negotiations of the WTO, initiated in November 2001 is the reference point.

4 Interactions between state and non-state actors

From the interviews held with state and non-state actors, different conclusions can be drawn with regard to the way each has sought to

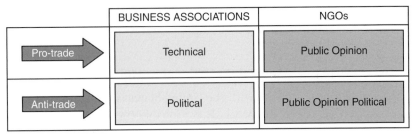

Figure 3.2   Type of interaction channel preferred by NSAs

influence the decision-making process and the results of negotiations. It is clear that the mechanisms used vary, depending on the nature and type of interest in the negotiation (see Figure 3.2). Two classifications can be established: groups that defend public and social interests; and those that have a vested commercial interest, either offensive or defensive.

A business association that supports the trade negotiations will normally privilege technical mechanisms to make sure that its interests will be reflected adequately in the final text of the agreement. In this case, the need to use political or public mechanisms is not present, as the interests of the business association and government coincide. As stated by one private sector representative interviewed for the project: 'when the particular interest coincides with general interests, the leverages are greater'. Indeed, the search for technical information and advice was usually the main reason for consultations put forward by governmental officials.

By contrast, for business or producer interests that believe they will be a net loser in the negotiation, political channels and 'appealing' to public opinion through the communications media and public events become important strategic instruments. This may have little traction with the public if it comes across as rent-seeking at the cost of consumers. However, to the extent that for electoral and political reasons Congress needs to be receptive to specific sectoral interests, public campaigns could have some effect.

In the case of the CSOs dedicated to public or social causes, efforts to influence government are more directed towards political and public opinion channels and much less towards the use of government-initiated consultative mechanisms. Most of the CSOs involved in the recent trade negotiations were opposed to them, especially those CSOs in the agricultural and pharmaceutical fields, although in some cases the CSOs were

motivated by environmental or labour concerns, and had a clear political hue. More than trying to achieve a specific result, in many cases their
objective is to postpone or delay the negotiation, or at least obtain political
benefits. For this type of NSA, more than for any other, the use of local and
international coalitions is an important part of their strategy. In addition,
the vast consultation spaces established by the Government of Colombia
are usually perceived as a weakening strategy in the way that participation
is seen to bestow legitimacy on an agreement that they oppose.

Generally, the influence of the NSAs is mixed. The technical inputs
are clearly fundamental for the Government, especially in relation to
issues of market access (including rules of origin) where a good or bad
negotiation will certainly be the consequence of having had an adequate
flow of information from the private sector to the negotiators and vice
versa. In the Colombian case, our interviews found that the private sector (even for some opponents of the negotiation) generally considers that
the consultation mechanisms established are adequate. Of course, foreign
governments are also party to the negotiation, and the fact that there is
consensus between the private sector and the Government in a negotiating position does not mean that their preferred position will be reflected
in the final agreement.

In some cases (e.g., such as on the subject of chicken hind quarters) the
effective use of a political leverage strategy enabled business to draw government's attention to sensitivities in a more effective way than technical
analyses alone would have done. Indeed, concerns about political sensitivities and public opinion with regard to potential points of opposition
to the negotiating positions was the second most important reason for
consultations put forward by governmental officials. For the same reason,
in seeking to evaluate the capacity of the CSOs to influence trade policy
and negotiating agenda, the FTA with the United States presents a good
case. Arguably, the drawing out of the negotiations due to CSO opposition ultimately prevented the agreement from being ratified by the US
Congress, with the delays in the negotiation having thus lost the window
of political opportunity to have the agreement ratified. The perception of
several CSOs is that their actions contributed to the delays and, in that
sense, to the non-passage of the deal.

It is interesting to note the lack of interest among those sectors that are
likely to gain from PTAs, and are therefore supportive of them in trying to
influence public opinion in favour of these agreements. Should opponents
of an agreement gain political traction, having limited themselves to providing technical inputs, this would only be detrimental to the interests of

those business interests that support an agreement. Perhaps these interests believe that the strategy of 'defeating' a negotiation is generally not too effective in the face of a government which has made the decision to carry it out.

Indeed, one private sector representative suggested that it could well be that PTA negotiations (especially with the United States) and the magnitude of the consultation processes designed by the Government would have influenced business associations views, rather than the other way around. Thus, for example, SAC and the Colombian Association of Small Companies (ACOPI), historically characterized by their opposition to liberalization, are now inclined to favour PTAs.

Finally, it is important to indicate that the level of influence of NSAs (especially business associations) is much greater in the definition of the schedules of market access (which, by definition, imply decisions specific to each sector) than in the definition of commercial disciplines (e.g., investment, competition, government procurement, services) in which the government usually has considerations of public interest, and are of general application which are not susceptible to adjustment because of particular interests.

5   Forum choice

In the debate regarding multilateral negotiations versus preferential regional and bilateral negotiations, there was a strong consensus among the state and non-state actors interviewed for this research. First, and confirming economic theory, there was strong agreement that the ideal setting is multilateral, as its non-discriminatory effects avoid the phenomena of trade diversion. However, in general, because of their very nature, multilateral negotiations are slow and costly as manifested in the Doha Round, and their future in the short to medium term is uncertain. This view is shared by non-state and state actors. Ironically, the slowness of the multilateral forum also makes it the preferred setting of opponents to trade liberalization.

Second, the different actors do not necessarily perceive the bilateral/regional negotiations as mutually exclusive to the WTO. For example, they understand that in a bilateral negotiation matters such as tariff barriers can be addressed but not internal support that distorts agricultural markets, which can be addressed only in multilateral settings.

Third, in the case of Colombia, the selection of the negotiating forum is a decision exogenous to the country, determined by its relative size and institutional reality. The truth is that both state and non-state actors acknowledge that the relative weight of Colombia and, therefore, its capacity to exercise influence in the multilateral forum, is limited. Thus, as a means of securing improved market access in the short to medium term, WTO negotiations are not a viable alternative to bilateral and regional PTAs. Indeed, at present more than 90% of Colombian exports are covered by existing PTAs (although in some cases, such as the United States, they are not yet in force).

A similar situation arises in relation to dispute settlement. As a general rule, if a certain action by a trade partner violates both a regional/bilateral and a multilateral agreement, Colombia prefers to turn to the regional/bilateral dispute settlement mechanism, which is assumed to be less costly due to elements such as distance, language barriers and the use of local consultants among others. Moreover, a PTA, unlike a WTO agreement, should be tailor-made for the relationship between the parties involved.

A possible exception to that general rule would be the case in which there is a potential interest in setting a precedent beyond the particular dispute regarding the matter or the commercial partner. However, this type of strategy has more relevance for those WTO actors with a global frame of reference (such as the United States, the European Union, Brazil, China and India) and not for countries with a smaller relative weight such as Colombia.

For the same reasons, NSAs (both from the private sector and civil society) understand that at the bilateral and regional level they have the capacity to influence, while in the WTO they do not. In the particular case of CSOs which are politically or ideologically motivated, the multilateral forum is even less relevant and is perceived as distant and having little impact on public opinion. Non-state actors are conscious that the use of international coalitions is the only road they have in order to be able to wield significant leverage in multilateral matters. However, the costs resulting from the distance where the negotiations take place is another obstacle repeatedly pointed out for the actions in multilateral negotiations.

Notwithstanding these findings, some of the persons interviewed for this research were critical of the perceived lack of interest by the private sector in the multilateral forum, attributing it to a 'short-term' vision of the business associations. Here the example of tariff bindings is instructive: there is a large gap between applied tariffs and tariffs bound as a result of WTO commitments, and if there are moves in the future to bind tariffs at the applied rate, WTO negotiations will possibly acquire much more interest for NSAs in Colombia.

6   Conclusion

This study has found that NSAs perceive multilateral negotiations as slow, distant and costly. This perception is shared by the national government, which dedicates the bulk of its technical resources to preferential negotiations. While the government has reasonable control over the duration of PTAs, in the multilateral field the dynamics of the negotiations are controlled by a few actors (the United States, the European Union, China, India, Brazil) with very dissimilar interests. Even if they could come to an agreement, they would have to seek consensus with the rest of the members of the WTO.

It is clear that for state and non-state actors the optimum scenario is to reach multilateral trade agreements within the framework of the WTO. The subject of distorting trade agricultural subsidies and support in particular has the WTO as the only possible forum for discussion. Nevertheless, all countries seek to position themselves, especially in the markets of their interest, by means of bilateral or regional trade agreements. Even if the trade diversion that these agreements generate reduces the level of welfare in some sectors, the losses can be greater if neighbours achieve preferential access to markets in which they compete with the country's exports. All of this leads to the well-known trend towards PTAs. The question that remains to be answered is whether this phenomenon will make it more or less difficult to reach agreements in the WTO.

As for NSAs, we find differences in their behaviour with regard to preferential negotiations and, in general, a great lack of interest in following the course of the multilateral negotiations. Non-state actors can be divided into business associations and the rest of the social actors (CSOs, labour unions). As far as business associations are concerned, if they support the negotiation, they fundamentally seek to participate at a technical level, basically interacting with the negotiating team. If the business association feels that it is going to be a net loser in a PTA, it privileges the political channels, such as Congress and the communications media. At the same time, it tries to reach the highest levels of executive power (ministers and the president) to demand compensatory measures from them, especially connected with replacing frontier protection with government subsidies.

The trade unions and CSOs have very limited technical participation and privilege political channels and communications media. Particularly when these social actors feel that they are winners in the negotiation (labour unions from the exporting sectors or political parties favourable to the negotiation), they demonstrate a preference for obtaining public acknowledgement from the executive and use the communications media to make their position known. When these CSOs and trade unions are opposed to a particular negotiation, they privilege the use of communications media, street protests and seek allies in the legislative power.

In conclusion, the means of participation in the negotiations are very different depending on the nature of the interests of NSAs and if, *a priori*, they feel that they are going to benefit or not from the negotiations. That is why the officials responsible for handling these negotiations must define different interaction strategies with each group and facilitate the participation and receipt of information from the legislature and communications media.

Finally, with regard to multilateral negotiations, the lack of relative interest in their course should not be understood as lack of concern for their eventual results, or as lack of credibility in the same. On the contrary, most social groups in Colombia generally favour multilateral negotiations, even though they know that they imply making some concessions. Nevertheless, they know that they are slow and that the responsibility for solving the main obstacles of the negotiation corresponds to the heavyweights in the WTO, who have multiple internal political obstacles to evade before reaching an acceptable package for their own nongovernmental actors. Until this occurs, countries will seek to position themselves in the markets of their interest; this is a sub-optimal strategy, but if it is not followed it could lead them to even higher costs than those that could result from a moderate trade diversion. That is why, in the case of Colombia, the strategy includes negotiating free trade agreements with all the partners who have some significant weight in their trade flows.

References

Andean Community of Nations 2006. *Elements for an Evaluation of the Free Trade Agreement of Colombia and Peru with the United States, with Regard to the Judicial Regulation of the Andean Community*, General Secretariat of CAN, Lima.

Government of Colombia 2006. *Exposition of Motives of Law Project 178 of November 30, 2006, by means of which the Commercial Promotion Agreement is Approved between the Republic of Colombia and the United States of America, its Enclosed Letters and its Amendments*, Ministry of Trade, Industry and Tourism of the Government of Colombia, Bogotá.

Hausmann, R., Hwang, J. and Rodrick, D. 2006. 'What you Export Matters', *NBER Working Paper 11905*, National Bureau of Economic Research, Cambridge, MA.

Ministry of Commerce 1996. 'World Trade Organization II', *Collection of International Commercial Agreements No. 4*, Ministry of Commerce, Bogotá.

National Planning Department 1990. 'Decisions Regarding the Economic Opening Program, in the Pacific Revolution, Modernization and Opening of the Economy', National Planning Department, Bogotá, p. 20.

Rosales, O. 2009. '*Colombia: An Insertion Strategy in Pacific Asia*', based on CEPAL, COMTRADE database and official figures from the National Administrative Department of Statistics (DANE), Santiago, Chile.

Villar, L. and Esguerra, P. 2005. 'Colombian Foreign Commerce in the 20th Century', *Economy Drafts # 358*, November 2005, Bank of the Republic, Bogotá.

World Bank 2009. *World Development Indicators Database*. Washington, DC: The World Bank.

4

Mexico

JAIME ZABLUDOVSKY AND LINDA PASQUEL

In the last quarter of a century, trade policy in Mexico has undergone dramatic changes. After more than three decades dominated by an import substitution industrialization (ISI) strategy based on high trade barriers to protect the domestic market, in the early 1980s Mexico launched an ambitious process of trade liberalization. The levels of protection were reduced, first unilaterally, as part of the process of economic reform, and subsequently, through the negotiation of bilateral and regional preferential trade agreements (PTAs) with countries in North America, South America, Europe and Asia.

This chapter recounts the Mexican experience with trade liberalization and the role of non-state actors (NSAs) in influencing Mexican policy at the World Trade Organization (WTO) and in its PTAs. The chapter is structured as follows. Section 1 contains a brief overview of Mexico's trade policy between 1982 and 2008 and a summary of Mexico's trade patterns. Section 2 describes the main government and non-governmental institutions and actors involved in Mexico's trade policy development. Section 3 summarizes the interaction between state and NSAs during the negotiating process of the North American Free Trade Agreement (NAFTA), the EU–Mexico Free Trade Agreement and the WTO. Section 4 contains an analysis of the perception by Mexican authorities and NSAs of trade policy developments based on interviews undertaken by the authors. Section 5 provides a brief overview of the core features of the dispute settlement mechanisms established under NAFTA, with a discussion of forum choice and an analysis of how these mechanisms have contributed to the interest and participation of NSAs in the development of trade policy. Section 6 concludes.

1 Mexico's trade policy evolution

During the 1980s the Mexican economy went through a process of radical change through a series of economic reforms involving the liberalization of trade, investment and capital markets; the privatization of state-owned enterprises; the reduction of agricultural price supports; and tax reform. As a result of these changes, by 1990 Mexico had been transformed from one of the most protected to one of the most open economies in the developing world (Thacker 2000; Pastor and Wise 2004). The reversal of Mexico's ISI development model was a central part of the reform process, beginning with a period of unilateral and dramatic liberalization in the wake of the macro-economic crisis of 1982. The second phase of trade liberalization occurred in the 1990s, and was anchored in a network of free trade agreements. The third stage began in 2005 and represents a combination of both unilateralism and open regionalism.

1.1   The unilateral liberalization of the 1980s

The unilateral liberalization of the 1980s was instigated by the administration of President Miguel de la Madrid (1982–8), which came to power at a time of serious economic crisis prompting a major re-thinking of Mexico's economic model. President de la Madrid's economic advisers included a core group of reformers who advocated trade liberalization as part of a broader package of free market reforms and structural adjustment. These reformers were trained in the United States and formed a tight and committed network with a strong sense of their own mission. Initially the reform position was a minority voice in government; however, in the face of a renewed economic crisis in 1985 – brought about by a collapse in the international price in oil and a major earthquake in Mexico City – it seized its moment (Teichman 2001). What had begun as tentative and gradual economic reform in 1982 was accelerated and deepened, and trade liberalization was an important part of this effort.

As part of this process, the Mexican Government relaunched the accession process to the General Agreement on Tariffs and Trade (GATT), which had been suspended in 1979 due to opposition from some sectors of Mexican society. As a result of its GATT accession, Mexico reformed its export subsidy practices, eliminated import licensing on 90% of its imports and bound its tariffs (Lusztig 2004, 86–9). Under GATT, Mexico committed itself to a maximum most favoured nation (MFN) bound tariff of 50%. In these initial stages of liberalization, however, the level of protection was always below the bound rate. In this sense, the accession to GATT did not imply an opening effort beyond the one already undertaken as part of the macro-stabilization and economic reform programmes of the second part of the 1980s. Nevertheless, the accession to GATT sent a very strong message about Mexico's commitment to trade liberalization.

The next step of the liberalization process was taken as a part of the macro-economic stabilization plan in the context of an inflationary crisis in 1987. The Pacto de Solidaridad Económica was a heterodox macro-economic programme between government, business, trade unions and agricultural producers to stabilize the economy through wage and price controls and fiscal and monetary restraints. As part of this plan, tariffs and quantitative import restrictions were further reduced, so that imports would help to impose discipline on domestic prices and induce greater efficiency among domestic producers. Thus, the strongest impulse behind the unilateral liberalization process came from anti-inflationary policies. By the end of 1987, the levels of protection within the Mexican economy had been significantly reduced. The average tariff was reduced to an historical minimum of 10%, while only 27.5% of imports remained subject to permit requirements. To put this into context, in the six years between 1985 and 1991, Mexico liberalized as rapidly as did the United States in the period between 1930 and 1970 (Lusztig 2004, 90).

1.2   NAFTA and the end of unilateralism

President Carlos Salinas de Gortarí's administration (1988–1994) marked the intensification of the reform process, but the end of unilateral liberalization efforts.

During the first year of Salinas de Gortarí's mandate, trade policy had the explicit goal of 'getting recognition for the unilateral liberalization of the 1980s' and taking advantage of the accession to GATT in order to expand Mexico's export markets in North America, Europe and East Asia. At the outset, President Salinas was not keen to pursue a comprehensive PTA with the United States, and looked instead for a closer relationship through sectoral agreements (Garciadiego 1994, 16). This approach changed rapidly as a result of President Salinas' visit to Europe in early 1990. Cognisant of the impact that the fall of the Berlin Wall was producing in the international investors´ community, as well as the challenges that the new international order posed for Mexico, Salinas concluded that if Mexico wanted to be an attractive destination for foreign investment, the economic reforms would have to be accelerated. Moreover, the country would have to take advantage of its geographic proximity to the largest economy in the world and become part of a trading bloc. Such thinking prompted Mexico's proposal to the United States to negotiate a free trade agreement in early 1990 (Salinas 2002, 47–8). These negotiations were subsequently trilateralized to include Canada, which was concerned that the negotiation of a Mexico–US PTA would jeopardize its 'special relationship' with the United States.

After four years of preparations, negotiations and legislative processes in Mexico, the United States and Canada, the NAFTA entered into force on 1 January 1994. At that time, it was the largest free trade zone in the world and the most ambitious one. The agreement included topics that had not been part of previous negotiations: the full elimination of tariffs and non-tariff barriers for apparel, textile and agricultural goods; disciplines on trade in services, investment, intellectual property rights; government procurement; and dispute settlement mechanisms to protect the rights of the member parties, as well as those of investors and exporters (Vega Cánovas 1993).[1]

NAFTA was a turning point in Mexico's foreign trade policy and created the opportunities for negotiating similar agreements with other Latin American nations, the European Union, the European Free Trade Agreement (EFTA) countries, Israel and Japan (see de Mateo Veiga 2003). NAFTA also strengthened Mexico's presence in other multilateral and regional forums. Thus, between 1992 and 2005 Mexico negotiated twelve PTAs with forty-five countries, joined the Organization for Economic Cooperation and Development (OECD), and the Asia Pacific Economic Cooperation (APEC) forum (see Figure 4.1).

The network of PTAs that followed NAFTA allowed the Mexican authorities to continue with the liberalization process on a reciprocal basis. However, at the same time that these PTAs were being negotiated, Mexico's MFN tariff levels were raised. There were several reasons for this. In some cases, such as that of the textile and footwear industries, the tariff increase was an integral part of an emergency programme designed to cope with Mexico's 1994–5 economic crises. In other cases, it was the result of the protectionist pressure exercised by the private sector faced with the emergence of China as a new export powerhouse. Last, but not least, in 1998, as had happened ten years before, the Mexican authorities resorted to an MFN tariff increase to strengthen public finances: 3% on all imports except for 'luxury articles' which were subjected to an increase of 10% on the MFN rate.

The increase of the MFN rates affected the level of protection applicable to imports from countries with no PTAs and created additional

---

[1] NAFTA Chapter 20 establishes an innovative state to state dispute settlement mechanism; Chapter 11 contains an investor–state mechanism; Chapter 14 contains a similar one that applies to disputes arising from the financial services provisions. Finally, the one provided for in Chapter 19 establishes an international review mechanism of the domestic adoption of anti-dumping and countervailing duties.

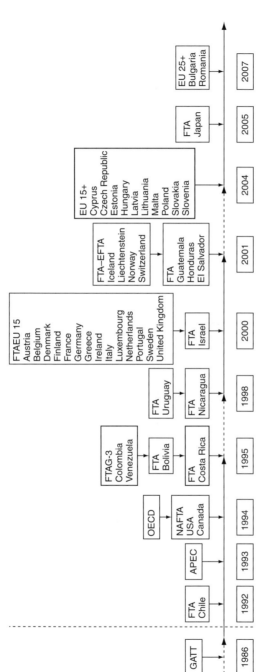

Figure 4.1 Mexico's trade agreements

complexities for the Mexican customs authorities. By 2003 imports of non-agricultural goods from non-PTA countries were subject to sixteen different tariff rates, ranging from 0% to 50%, with an average tariff of 16% – one of the world's highest.

Mexico has a highly complex tariff regime as authorities have to deal with twelve free trade agreements, the preferential agreements signed under the Asociación Latinoamericana de Integración (Latin American Integration Association or ALADI), several sectoral programmes (PROSECs), temporary imports, in-bond programmes, anti-dumping and countervailing measures and import permits. This has taken a toll on the competitiveness of the country.

1.3   Back to unilateralism

In recent years Mexico has adopted policies to reverse the increase of MFN rates. In January 2005, MFN tariffs were restored to the 1998 levels. A year later, in September 2006, 6,089 MFN rates were further reduced. Finally, in December 2008 the Mexican authorities announced the most ambitious unilateral tariff reform of the past twenty years. This reform will have an impact on 69% of the 12,119 tariff lines of the Mexican tariff; MFN rates applicable to imports of nearly all industrial goods will be eliminated or significantly reduced, although agricultural goods, art objects, antiques and other products are excluded from this initiative. The reform will be implemented in different stages, beginning in 2009 and ending in 2013. Once completed, Mexico's average import tariff is expected to drop from 10.4% to 4.3%.

1.4   Summary of trade patterns

As a result of the economic reforms, and particularly of trade liberalization, the Mexican economy has been radically transformed over the last twenty-six years. The ratio of foreign trade (imports plus exports of goods) to the gross domestic product (GDP), that was only 17% in 1982 jumped to 55% and the value of exports (in current US dollars) increased eightfold over the same period. As Figure 4.2 shows, the composition of Mexican exports has also changed substantially. In 1982, oil exports represented almost 70% of all foreign sales, while manufactured exports amounted to only 24%. In 2008 these figures had reversed themselves: manufactures represented 80%, while oil exports made up only 16%.

1982

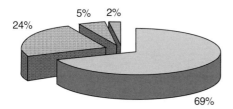

24%   5%   2%

69%

◧ Oil ▢ Manufacture ▢ Agricultural ▢ Extractive Industry

1993

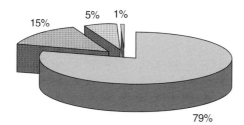

15%   5%   1%

79%

◼ Manufacture ▢ Oil ▦ Agricultural ▢ Extractive Industry

2008

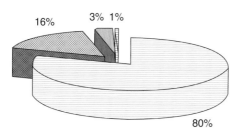

16%   3% 1%

80%

▢ Manufacture ▦ Oil ▢ Agricultural ▤ Extractive Industry

Figure 4.2   Composition of Mexican exports

Table 4.1 *Main Mexican exports, 2008 (HS Chapter's – million dollars)*

Chapter	Description	Amount (US$ million)	Share (%)
85	Electrical machinery and equipment	75,505	26
27	Mineral fuels, mineral oils and products of their distillation	50,777	17
87	Vehicles other than railway or tramway rolling stock, parts and accessories	42,851	15
84	Nuclear reactors, boilers, machinery and mechanical appliances	33,735	12
90	Optical, photographic, cinematographic, medical or surgical instruments and apparatus	9,347	3
39	Plastic articles	5,378	2
94	Furniture	5,307	2
71	Natural or cultured pearls, precious or semi-precious stones and precious metals	5,265	2
72	Iron and steel	4,839	2
73	Iron or steel products	4,455	2
	Sub-total	237,458	81
	Other	55,178	19
	Total	292,637	100

Source: IQOM with data from ProMéxico.

In 2008 Mexico's total trade in goods was US$603 billion, with US$293 billion in exports and US$310 billion in imports. Table 4.1 shows that of the export bill, 70% was from four sectors: electrical machinery; mineral fuels and oils; motor vehicles and auto parts; and machinery and mechanical appliances. An important part of Mexico's foreign trade is intra-industry and intra-firm. Table 4.2 shows that 45% of Mexican imports came from the same three manufacturing sectors that constitute the main exports.

Table 4.2 *Main Mexican imports, 2008 (HS Chapter's – Million dollars)*

Chapter	Description	Amount US$ million)	Share (%)
85	Electrical machinery and equipment	64,943	21
84	Boilers, machinery and mechanical appliances	46,642	15
27	Mineral fuels, mineral oils and products of their distillation	29,197	9
87	Vehicles, parts and accessories	26,475	9
39	Plastic articles	16,197	5
90	Optical, photographic, cinematographic, medical or surgical instruments and apparatus	12,413	4
72	Iron and steel	8,778	3
29	Organic chemicals	7,945	3
73	Iron or steel products	6,867	2
48	Paper and paperboard	4,787	2
10	Cereals	4,528	1
76	Aluminium and articles thereof	4,193	1
40	Rubber and articles thereof	4,080	1
30	Pharmaceutical products	4,069	1
12	Oil seeds and oleaginous fruits	3,503	1
	Sub-total	244,616	79
	Other	65,516	21
	Total	310,132	100

Source: IQOM with data from ProMéxico.

Historically the United States has been the main destination for Mexican exports. As shown in Table 4.3, in 2008 80% of Mexico's foreign sales were sent to the US market. However, this figure may be overestimated since it includes goods that enter US territory in transit to Canada

Table 4.3 *Mexican exports by main regions, 2008*

Region	Exports		
	Amount (US$ million)	Regional share (%)	Total share (%)
North America	241,687		83
United States	234,557	97	80
Latin America	22,081		8
Brazil	3,371	15	1
Colombia	3,037	14	1
Venezuela	2,314	10	1
Chile	1,589	7	1
Other	11,771	53	4
Europe	18,121		6
European Union	17,113	94	6
Germany	5,013	28	2
Spain	4,447	25	2
EFTA	644	4	0
Switzerland	602	3	0
Norway	37	0.2	0
Asia	8,681		3
Japan	2,068	24	1
China	2,047	24	1
India	1,588	18	1
South Korea	538	6	0
Rest	1,751		1
Total	292,321		100

Source: IQOM with data from ProMéxico

or other countries, as well as Mexican inputs imported by American manufacturers to be incorporated in final goods that are later re-exported.

While the destination of Mexican exports has remained constant, the origin of Mexican imports has shifted dramatically during the last eight years: Mexican imports coming from the United States have decreased from around 70% in 2000 to close to 50% in 2008. The most important factor behind this change has been the growing presence of Chinese imports into the Mexican economy, as shown in Figure 4.3. and Table 4.4.

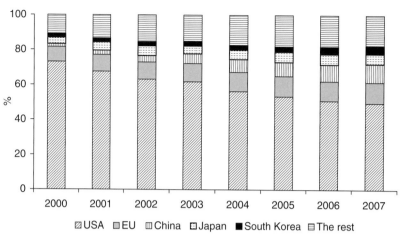

☑USA ☐EU ▥China ☐Japan ■South Korea ▤The rest

Figure 4.3   Origin of Mexican imports

2   Actors involved in the development of Mexico's trade policy

The negotiation of NAFTA and Mexico's other PTAs posed an enormous challenge, entailing the creation of a special unit for the negotiations and also extensive and unprecedented consultation processes with Congress and the rest of society.

2.1   State actors

The participation of state actors in the development of international trade policy and, thus, in the negotiation of international trade agreements is regulated in the Mexican constitution and other federal laws. The constitution establishes that any legislation that emanates from an international agreement entered into by the president and approved by the Senate becomes supreme law of the land and is, therefore, part of Mexican domestic law.

2.1.1   The executive power

The constitution vests executive power in the President of the United Mexican States. The executive is therefore unitary: the president is both head of state and head of government. In order to fulfil his/her duties, the president is aided by a number of agencies. The Organic Law of the Federal Public Administration (Ley Orgánica de la Administración Pública Federal) establishes the jurisdiction of each agency of the executive. Thus, in accordance with their jurisdiction a number of agencies of the executive are involved in the negotiation and implementation of international trade agreements.

Table 4.4 *Mexican imports by main regions, 2008*

Region	Imports		
	Amount (US$ million)	Regional share (%)	Total share (%)
North America	162,065		52
United States	152,615	94	49
Canada	9,450	6	3
Latin America	15,900		5
Brazil	5,191	33	2
Chile	2,592	16	1
Argentina	1,437	9	0
Other	6,680	42	2
Europe	42,401		14
European Union	39,277	93	13
Germany	12,623	30	4
Italy	5,222	12	2
EFTA	1,721	4	1
Switzerland	1,414	3	0
Norway	274	1	0
Other	1,403	3	0
Asia	86,458		28
China	34,754	40	11
Japan	16,326	19	5
South Korea	13,571	16	4
Other	21,807	25	7
Rest of the World	310,132		100
Total	310,132		100

Source: IQOM with data from ProMéxico.

The Ministry of Economy (Secretaría de Economía, Secretaría de Comercio y Fomento Industrial until 2000) is the federal agency in charge of the negotiating process. In particular, this ministry negotiates the provisions that regulate market access for industrial and agricultural goods, including disciplines on anti-dumping, safeguards, technical barriers to trade, sanitary and phytosanitary measures, intellectual property rights, investment, trade in services, government procurement and dispute settlement. During negotiations the Ministry of Economy is aided by the following ministries:

The Ministry of Agriculture (Secretaría de Agricultura, Ganadería, Desarrollo Rural, Pesca y Alimentación) is responsible for negotiating market access conditions for agricultural goods and sanitary and phytosanitary provisions.

The Ministry of Foreign Affairs (Secretaría de Relaciones Exteriores) is the agency responsible for Mexico's foreign relations, and during a negotiating process its officials participate to ensure that the provisions contained in the agreement do not contradict or violate other international agreements.

The Ministry of Finance (Secretaría de Hacienda y Crédito Público) participates in the negotiation of customs provisions, verification of origin, taxation matters and balance of payments provisions.

The Ministry of the Interior (Secretaría de Gobernación) regulates and implements Mexico's immigration policy. During a negotiating process this ministry participates in the development of the disciplines that regulate the entry and temporary stay of business persons.

Finally, officials of the Central Bank of Mexico (Banco de México) participate in the negotiations of investment and cross-border trade in services and balance of payments provisions.

Once a PTA is concluded, the Mexican Constitution provides that it must be signed by the president and afterwards approved by the Senate in order to become part of Mexico's legislation.

2.1.2   The Senate

The participation of the Senate in the development of Mexico's trade policy has an increasingly important role, though limited in nature. Although the selection of negotiating partners or the definition of negotiating mandates is up to the discretion of the executive, the Senate has to approve any international agreement before it is implemented and becomes domestic law. The Senate has been increasingly exercising this veto power to influence the negotiating agenda.

In September 2004, a federal law that regulates the approval of international agreements dealing with economic matters entered into force: Ley sobre la Aprobación de Tratados Internacionales en Materia Económica. The main objective of this legislation is to regulate the attributions granted by the constitution to the Mexican Senate, through which this chamber requires information from the agencies of the executive regarding the negotiation of free trade agreements.

The Ley sobre la Aprobación de Tratados Internacionales en Materia Económica provides that at the beginning of each legislative period, the Senate, through its competent committees, shall require the federal agencies of the executive to provide it with a report regarding the initiation of international trade negotiations. This report shall include a summary of the benefits and advantages expected from the negotiations. Once the appropriate Senate committees receive the report, they may establish a special sub-committee to oversee the development of the negotiations. Furthermore, the legislation obliges the executive to maintain a permanent dialogue with the Senate during all negotiating processes.

Once a PTA has been concluded and prior to its signature by the president, the executive shall submit to the Senate a detailed report regarding the scope and coverage of its provisions.

2.2   Non-state actors

The involvement of NSAs in the development of Mexico's trade policy is not a new phenomenon. During the accession process of Mexico to GATT, the business sector was consulted through its representatives at the Confederation of Industrial Chambers of Mexico (Confederación de Cámaras Industriales de México (CONCAMIN)). However, the negotiations of NAFTA, Mexico's first PTA, required a more formal consultation mechanism that would allow the Government to receive constant feedback from the Mexican business sector.

During the negotiation of NAFTA and the PTAs that followed, the main NSAs that participated in these processes were representatives of the Mexican business sector. Other NSAs, such as the environmental and labour movement or academia, have shown some interest in trade negotiations and Mexico's trade policy development; however, in recent years their interest has diminished and shifted to other areas. The non-state organizations that have been more involved in Mexico's trade policy development are:

The Coordinator for Foreign Trade Business Organizations (Coordinadora de Organismos Empresariales de Comercio Exterior (COECE)), was established prior to the negotiations of NAFTA for the purpose of coordinating the efforts of the business sector so that there would be a single, unified business position. The Coordinator is composed of representatives of all Mexican productive sectors. During each round of negotiations, officials from the Ministry of Economy consulted on a constant basis with COECE through a scheme that was known as 'the room next door' ('el cuarto de al lado'). Through this mechanism representatives of each productive sector were informed and consulted on any new offer or request while negotiations were taking place. The business sector, represented in COECE, is by far the most active, effective and influential NSA in the development of Mexico's trade policy, and it is characterized by high levels of mutual trust between state and business officials (see Zabludovsky 1994; Thacker 2000).

The Mexican Institute for Competitiveness (Instituto Mexicano de la Competitividad (IMCO)), is a non-profit research centre with the mandate to evaluate the competitiveness of the Mexican economy, develop indicators to measure it and recommend actions to enhance it. Since its establishment in 2003, IMCO has played a key role in several forums such as the Mexican Congress, the North American Competitiveness Council (NACC), the World Economic Forum, the World Bank, the Inter-American Development Bank (IADB) and the OECD.

The Mexican Action Network Facing Free Trade (Red Mexicana de Acción Frente al Libre Comercio) is a coalition of Mexican citizens composed of several agriculture, civil, social and environmental organizations, labour unions, and academia. Established in April 1991, it became the single most important organization opposing the NAFTA negotiations. During the second half of the 1990s it also participated actively in the consultation process for the Free Trade Area of the Americas (FTAA). The 'Red' has argued that all the PTAs that Mexico has negotiated lack the social provisions that would allow Mexico to fully develop (Somunano 2006). Table 4.5 provides further information on the NSAs that were approached during this study.

3   Interactions between state and non-state actors

3.1   NAFTA

The NAFTA negotiation demanded unprecedented consultation processes between the Government and the Mexican private sector. The consultations were carried on through COECE. To impose discipline on the process, the Mexican Government adopted a stand that 'everything was on the table'. Thus, the request to the Mexican productive sector was presented in terms of 'how' they wanted to participate, rather than 'if' they wished to be included in the agreement.

During the preparatory stages of the NAFTA negotiations (1990–June 1991), COECE created six separate units for industry, cross-border trade in services (except financial services), financial services, agriculture, insurance and banking. Within these six 'umbrella' groups, close to 150 sectoral committees were established. Each of these groups prepared an analysis of its sector that included a trade liberalization proposal that was further discussed with the negotiators as part of the preparatory agenda.

Table 4.5 *Key NSAs involved in trade policy-making in Mexico since 1990*

Name	Policy interest (trade-related)	Constituencies served	Source of funding	Local affiliates	International affiliates	Negotiations in which they have participated or are active in
Business sector						
Mexican Chamber of the Iron and Steel Industry	Negotiations on the following areas: • Market access • Customs regimes • Anti-dumping and countervailing duties • Government procurement	Members of the Chamber	Membership fees	56 local affiliates. 6 of them have foreign capital	The Chamber coordinates its works with international organizations: • Latin American Iron and Steel Institute • World Steel Association • Eurofer	• All PTAs and preferential agreements since the NAFTA negotiations • WTO Doha Round • FTAA
Mexican Association of the Automotive Industry		Members of the Chamber	Membership fees	All members are enterprises of foreign capital		• All PTAs and preferential agreements since the NAFTA negotiations. • WTO Doha Round • FTAA

Civil Society Organizations (CSOs)

Mexican Action Network Facing Free Trade	• Negotiations of investment and free trade agreements	Labour, Environmental, small- and medium-size entrepreneurs and agricultural producers	• Grants from international organizations • *Pro bono* work	• Latin-American Association of Small and Medium Size Entrepreneurs • Labour Action and Consulting Centre • Agriculture Democratic Front	The Mexican Action Network is a member of the: • Hemispheric Social Alliance • *Our World is not For Sale* Network • *Enlazando Alternativas* Bi-regional Network *Europe – Latin America and the Caribbean*	• All PTAs and preferential agreements since the NAFTA negotiations • WTO Doha Round • FTAA

Academia

El Colegio de México	• Negotiation of investment and free trade agreements • Analysis of Mexico's trade policies	Academia	• Tuition fees	No local affiliates	No international affiliates	• All PTAs and preferential agreements since the NAFTA negotiations • WTO Doha Round • FTAA

The NAFTA negotiations were officially launched in June 1991. The negotiating areas were grouped in six categories – trade in goods, rules of origin, investment, intellectual property, services and dispute settlement – which in turn were divided into nineteen different negotiating groups dealing with specific issues in these areas.

From this moment onward, COECE was restructured into nineteen 'shadow' groups that replicated the actual negotiating groups. It was agreed that the COECE groups would accompany the Mexican Government during all negotiating sessions in order to be available for consultation before, during or after each round. The 'room next door' system constituted the most important element of the consultation process, contributing to a trust-based relationship between the authorities and the economic sectors. This mechanism, which was later adopted by several Latin American countries, allowed the authorities to obtain constant feedback from the business sector on every area of the negotiations and helped them to adopt tough decisions when necessary. Ultimately, the consultation process that had been implemented contributed to legitimize the outcome of the negotiation.

In addition to the consultation mechanism with the Mexican business sector established under COECE, during the NAFTA negotiations the authorities sought to create a permanent forum of consultation and information exchange with other sectors of Mexican civil society, such as the academic, labour and trade experts sectors. The Advisory Council for International Trade Negotiations met on a monthly basis and provided the negotiators with opinions and analysis. It also organized several seminars on the content of the negotiations.

Furthermore, the broad spectrum of areas and disciplines that were negotiated under NAFTA made it necessary for the Mexican authorities to establish a mechanism at the highest level to coordinate the actions of the different federal agencies that participated in the negotiations. In order to coordinate the works and to guarantee an expeditious decision-making process, the Economic Cabinet, composed of the ministers of the major economic departments and the Governor of the Central Bank, and presided over by the president met periodically. During these meetings the status of the negotiations was reviewed, alternative positions were evaluated, guidelines were agreed and instructions to the negotiating team were given. To prepare these meetings and follow-up on the agreements reached at the Economic Cabinet, an Interagency Commission (Comisión Intersecretarial) was also established at the deputy secretary level.

3.2   The EU–Mexico FTA

Mexico had three reasons to negotiate the EU–Mexico Free Trade Agreement (EUMFTA). The most important of these was to continue the processes of liberalization and economic reform that Mexico undertook unilaterally in the second half of the 1980s, and that was deepened with the signing of NAFTA. The negotiation of an ambitious agreement with the European Union, Mexico's second most important trade partner, would make it possible to continue to eliminate tariffs and non-tariff barriers with the reciprocity demanded by the Mexican private sector following the signing of NAFTA.

The second reason for the negotiation of EUMFTA was to continue fostering flows of foreign investment into Mexico. The agreement would eliminate the bias, introduced by NAFTA, against users of European inputs and European investors in the Mexican market. As in any preferential agreement, NAFTA's provisions of trade in goods, investment, services and government procurement entailed discrimination against investors and exporters who were not part of the North American Free Trade Area.

The third reason for the negotiation of EUMFTA was to improve Mexican exporters' access to Europe. The European integration process, the proliferation of trade agreements that the European Union had concluded with some of its former colonies and with the East European countries, as well as the unilateral preferences granted through the generalized system of preferences (GSP), the Lomé Convention and other similar accords, implied a growing discrimination against Mexican exports. Mexican producers had to pay tariffs to enter the European market that did not apply to the then fifteen members of the Customs Union, nor to the members of EFTA[2] or several countries in Eastern Europe, the Caribbean and North Africa.

Notwithstanding the fact that Mexican exporters enjoyed some degree of preferential access under the European GSP, this was limited and subject to possible unilateral modifications by the European Union, as became evident in 1995. The new system that entered into force that year obliged Mexico to pay a significant part of the MFN tariff for most of the exports that had benefited from the GSP, a situation that made preferences practically irrelevant.

---

[2] Iceland, Liechtenstein, Norway and Switzerland.

In spite of the importance of the European market, there was no great enthusiasm for the negotiations within the Mexican private sector. Several reasons can explain this lack of interest. First, tackling the macro-economic crisis of late 1994 was understandably the main priority for the Mexican business sector. This situation, combined with the challenges arising from NAFTA's recent entry into force, demanded all its attention and resources. Nonetheless, a small but influential group of entrepreneurs recognized the strategic significance of the negotiations and the need for Mexico to continue its reform process. This group took the leadership and reactivated the consultation mechanism implemented during the negotiations of NAFTA through COECE.

The consultation mechanism of COECE and its 'room next door' scheme was active in the negotiations of EUMFTA. The constant feedback from the business sector allowed the Mexican authorities to present viable solutions to most of the complex problems that were presented during the negotiations, such as rules of origin and access to agricultural goods.

The negotiation of EUMFTA's rules of origin posed greater difficulties than those normally encountered. On the one hand, the European negotiators had an explicit mandate to replicate, in all preferential trade negotiations, the same rules of origin, irrespective of the partner at hand. This mandate substantially reduced the European negotiators' manoeuvring room. The second difficulty concerned the nature of trade relations between Mexico and the European Union. Mexico's productive structure was different from that of most of the European Union's preferential trading partners — mainly Eastern Europe or North African countries that have a high integration level with the Union. Consequently, the 'single list' rules called for a level of regional content or a degree of transformation that was unduly high. Mexican products (and even occasionally some European goods) could not comply with the rules, hence, there was a risk that they would not benefit from the tariff elimination established under the agreement. The information received by the Mexican authorities from COECE contributed to the design of a new set of permanent and transitional rules of origin that were part of a package allowing the conclusion of the negotiations.

Another area of the negotiations that greatly benefited from COECE's expert opinion was market access for agricultural goods. In any trade negotiation the agricultural sector is one of the most delicate, and the EUMFTA process was no exception. The first obstacle was the European Common Agricultural Policy (CAP). The European Union's use of export subsidies regulated under CAP made it very difficult for Mexico to accept the dismantling of tariffs on the most sensitive agricultural products, mainly cereals, dairy goods and meat products. For its part, the European authorities faced resistance in granting free access to some products that were of interest to Mexican exporters, including citrus fruits, honey, sugar, avocados and flowers. However, during the negotiations the two sides were able to reach a compromise on their offensive and defensive interests. First, they agreed on a special category that would apply to extremely sensitive agricultural products, mainly cereals, dairy goods and meat products that benefited from export subsidies under CAP. Products under this category are excluded from the liberalization schedule and are subject to a 'review clause' through which the parties shall determine their inclusion under EUMFTA.

Second, to accommodate Mexican export interests while securing an agreement acceptable to the European Union, the two sides agreed to establish permanent preferential quotas and seasonal windows for Mexican exports. This approach served Mexico's export potential, while at the same time guaranteeing European producers no market disruption as a result of EUMFTA. From the Mexican perspective, the fact that a large portion of cereals, dairy goods and meat products are excluded meant that Mexico's authorities did not have to address the sensitivities of those sectors.

3.3   The WTO

For Mexico, the Uruguay Round that led to the establishment of the WTO in 1995 did not demand a stronger effort towards liberalization than the one already undertaken under NAFTA. The texts of the agreements negotiated during the Uruguay Round have very similar disciplines to those established under the various chapters of NAFTA. For example, the elimination of quantitative restrictions for trade in agricultural products was negotiated under NAFTA before the conclusion of the Uruguay Round. During the Uruguay Round negotiations the Mexican authorities consulted with the business community through COECE and its 'room next door' scheme, but the thrust of the liberalization commitments had already been agreed upon at the regional level. Therefore, the level of interest in multilateral negotiations on the part of the private sector and civil society never reached that attained during the NAFTA negotiations.

3.4   Recent developments

The recent reversion to unilateralism on the part of the Mexican Government has coincided with an increasing resistance by the private sector against any additional trade liberalization. The business sector has exercised its pressure both publicly and directly, as well as utilizing the increasingly important role of Congress in the definition of the public agenda. Over recent years, the private sector has been able to stall the conclusion of PTA agreements with Peru and South Korea, and has opposed very vocally the recent announcement by the governments of Mexico and Brazil of their intention to negotiate a PTA. Last, but not least, during the last fiscal package adopted by Congress, the private sector pushed for an amendment that would have suspended the unilateral liberalization announced in December 2008. This amendment, after being approved by the lower house, was finally withdrawn from the legislative package in the Senate.

4   Key findings on the interaction between state and non-state actors

The development of Mexico's trade policy during the last eighteen years has been undertaken through a consultation and participation process with both state and non-state actors. In order to better understand how the Mexican business sector has influenced, and seeks to continue influencing, the development of trade policy in Mexico, and, in particular, trade negotiations at a bilateral or multilateral level, we interviewed key governmental and civil society actors. This section contains a summary of the results of these interviews. The first part reflects our findings regarding the view of state actors, while the second section summarizes the perspective of key NSAs.

4.1   State actors

During our research we contacted officials from several federal agencies of the executive that are involved in the development and implementation of Mexico's trade policy; however, most of them showed little interest in providing meaningful information and those we were able to meet with – officials from the Ministry of Economy and the Ministry of Agriculture – limited themselves to 'politically correct comments' that do not necessarily reflect their strenuous relationship: the Ministry of

Economy has traditionally promoted and enforced liberalization policies, while Agriculture supports protectionist measures.

Since the negotiation of NAFTA a specialized unit within the Ministry of Economy has been established with the objective of preparing and developing expertise in different areas of trade. We interviewed officials from this unit, formerly known as the Under-secretariat for International Trade Negotiations (Subsecretaría de Negociaciones Comerciales Internacionales), now Under-secretary for Trade (Subsecretaría de Comercio Exterior), to provide us with their views on the existing alternative negotiating forums for trade cooperation (preferential and multilateral); their interaction with the Mexican business sector, other federal agencies or the legislative branch during any negotiating process; and the level of influence that NSAs have exercised or seek to exercise in these processes and the development of Mexico's trade policy. In particular, six officials of the Ministry of Economy who are responsible for the agenda on trade in goods; trade in services; investment; Europe; and the WTO participated in the interviews. In the Ministry of Agriculture we met with officials from Apoyos y Servicios a la Comercialización Agropecuaria, the unit responsible for trade negotiations. Additionally, we interviewed the president of the Trade Commission of the Mexican Senate.

On the issue of choice of forum there is a consensus among the Ministry of Economy and the Ministry of Agriculture that the existence of alternative negotiating forums has been beneficial for Mexico's interests. In their opinion, the decision of whether an issue should be discussed at a multilateral or bilateral level is in some cases determined by external factors; for example, certain disciplines of trade liberalization by their nature cannot be negotiated bilaterally, such as the elimination of agricultural export subsidies, thus, the importance of the WTO. In other cases, it can be the result of a consultation process or the need to further advance the liberalization of the economy through the negotiation of bilateral or regional agreements.

During the last fifteen years, officials from both agencies have worked together to develop Mexico's position on twelve different trade agreements, and at a multilateral level during the WTO's Uruguay and Doha Rounds. When questioned about the interaction among agencies during a negotiating process, officials from both ministries agreed that while the Ministry of Economy is responsible for leading the negotiations, every decision that may affect agricultural products is discussed with the Ministry of Agriculture. Furthermore, since Mexico's legislation forces both agencies to report to the Senate any new initiatives for negotiations, these reports are jointly prepared. On this issue, the president of the Senate's Trade Commission stated that, in accordance with its powers, during a negotiating process the Trade Commission requires information from the executive branch regarding the status of the negotiations. In parallel, it maintains a constant dialogue with the business community in order to have a better understanding of its needs.

Regarding the extent of participation of NSAs in the development of Mexico's trade policy and international trade negotiations, officials from both ministries considered that the 'the room next door' consultation mechanism established under COECE has allowed them to develop an ongoing dialogue with the Mexican business sector. According to the officials who were interviewed, this consultation mechanism has helped them to define Mexico's position on many disciplines and instances. The authorities have used this consultation scheme regardless of the venue or forums of the negotiations (bilateral, regional or multilateral).

From the legislative perspective, the president of the Senate's Trade Commission clarified that in accordance with Mexican legislation (Ley sobre la Aprobación de Tratados Internacionales en Materia Económica) during a trade negotiating process any citizen, union, association or interested party may submit its views to the Senate with regard to any area of the negotiations. Once received, the opinions shall be analysed by the Trade Commission and, if the Commission deems it appropriate, they may send an official petition to the executive branch requesting that the opinions expressed by the private sector be taken into account.

Officials from the ministries of Economy and Agriculture indicated that they consult with NSAs during the development of Mexico's trade policy primarily to obtain technical advice and commercial intelligence from them. This consultation scheme also helps them to promote transparency and satisfy public policy requirements, and allows them to obtain public views with regard to potential points of opposition to negotiating positions. Table 4.6 summarizes the answers provided by representatives of state actors to questions about their reasons for consultation with non-state actors.

Officials from both ministries agreed that throughout the last eighteen years the Mexican business sector has played a key role in the liberalization process. Through its participation in the 'room next door' it has helped the Mexican authorities define their positions. In particular, during the NAFTA negotiations, the feedback received from the economic sectors became an essential factor in determining the liberalization schedules and rules of origin that needed to be included in the agreement.

Table 4.6 *Main reasons for state actors to engage with NSAs in trade policy development*

Main reason for engaging NSAs	Number of responses
Satisfying public policy (including statutory) requirements	1
Promoting transparency	2
Seeking technical advice and commercial intelligence	3
Gauging views in relation to potential points of opposition to negotiating positions	1
Creating coalitions to support negotiating positions and outcomes	0
Other	0
Total	7

Finally, the president of the Senate's Trade Commission considers that NSAs have certainly influenced the development of trade policy in Mexico and most definitely the outcome of trade agreements. Once an agreement has been concluded and sent to the Senate for approval, this chamber requests the opinion of the economic sectors involved and only after receiving a positive response is the agreement approved and can enter into force.

4.2 Non-state actors

In contacting these players we faced some of the same difficulties we had experienced with the Mexican authorities, and many organizations were not interested in sharing their views. This lack of interest and response from NSAs is not new in Mexico. After the conclusion of the negotiations of NAFTA, the degree of involvement of NSAs in trade policy discussions, other than in the context of trade negotiations, diminished significantly, with the exception of some sectors of the business community that remain involved in the implementation process of the commitments established under the PTAs or other trade agreements, and, as will be explained in section 5 below, those who actively engage in the defence of their interests under the various dispute settlement mechanisms provided for on those agreements. Another factor that may contribute to this lack of participation from NSAs is related to the fact that most of the industries' representatives change constantly and there is a lack of institutional memory in these organizations.

The NSAs from the Mexican industrial sector that provided us with their views were: the Mexican Chamber of the Iron and Steel Industry (Cámara Nacional de la Industria del Hierro y del Acero) and the Mexican Association of the Automotive Industry (Asociación Mexicana de la Industria Automotriz). From academia, we received feedback from one of Mexico's most prestigious research institutions, El Colegio de Mexico, which, as a member of the Advisory Council for International Trade Negotiations, provides the Ministry of Economy with permanent studies and analyses on different areas of trade. Finally, we interviewed members of one of Mexico's strongest associations against free trade: the Mexican Action Network Facing Free Trade (Red Mexicana de Acción Frente al Libre Comercio).

The participants that were interviewed indicated that they have participated in the negotiating processes of all PTAs to which Mexico has subscribed, the failed initiative of FTAA and the WTO's Uruguay and Doha Round negotiations. On the choice of forum issue, some industries indicated that their preferences are determined by the forums that they consider might provide a better position for their sector. In other cases, the industries grant more importance to those forums in which a complete liberalization of their economic sectors can be achieved. From the academic perspective, the negotiating forum is selected after thorough deliberations of the authorities in consultation with the business and civil community.

While the representatives of industry and academia who were interviewed consider that the Mexican authorities have allowed them to participate equally in the decision-making process of multilateral, bilateral or regional trade negotiations, members of the Mexican Action Network Facing Free Trade indicated that the participation process is discriminatory. In their opinion, the Mexican authorities do not take into account, or do not grant equal consideration to, opinions expressed by associations or organizations that do not share their views or goals. Furthermore, officials from the Action Network were of the opinion that the authorities always provide them with irrelevant information and consult them only to 'comply with transparency requirements'.

With regard to the means used by NSAs to influence trade negotiations, the Mexican industries expressed their preference for the interaction with

Table 4.7 *NSAs' preferred way of influencing trade negotiations*

Preferred way of influencing negotiations	Number of responses	Share of total (%)
Participating in meetings or committees organized by government	1	25
Self-initiated interaction with government or other lobbying activity	2	50
Publishing or broadcasting material	1	25
Conducting public campaigns	0	
Other	0	
Total	4	100

authorities through lobbying or other activities. Their second choice was to participate in meetings or committees organized by the Government. Launching public campaigns, publishing or broadcasting materials were the least preferred options. On the other hand, representatives from the Mexican Action Network Facing Free Trade indicated their preference for public campaigns, publication of materials or the organizing of rallies.

When seeking to influence trade negotiations the industrial sector first sought to contact ministers and vice-ministers, followed by governmental officials and legislators. Exercising influence on public opinion was the least popular option. On the contrary, the Mexican Action Network places great importance on public opinion and contacting legislators. Table 4.7 summarizes the answers provided by representatives of NSAs to the questionnaires administered in the course of this research project.

The Mexican industries and academic sector that were part of this survey consider that the authorities have listened to their opinions and that, in general, they have been able to influence governmental decisions regarding trade liberalization in their sectors at a multilateral or regional level. However, some sectors, such as iron and steel, have expressed some concerns that in certain instances their opinions have not been taken into account. This has been particularly important during the recent unilateral liberalization measures, to which the steel sector has been opposed.

From the Mexican Action Network's perspective the authorities have never taken their opinions into account. In their view, the only reason they have been consulted is to fulfil a transparency requirement. Thus, they have not been able to influence trade policy decisions in Mexico. However, as members of the Hemispheric Social Alliance, the Our World is not For Sale Network and the Enlazando Alternativas Bi-regional Network Europe – Latin America and the Caribbean they have had a deep impact on the development of trade policies at a regional and multilateral level. In particular, they indicated that they contributed to the failure of the FTAA negotiations, are partly responsible for the stalling of the WTO Doha Round talks and have helped the authorities of Bolivia and Ecuador abandon the free trade talks with the United States and the European Union.

The industry representatives suggested that the Mexican consultation scheme could be improved if the authorities were more open to working jointly with each sector in establishing programmes that could be evaluated in the short term. On this issue, the Mexican Action Network considers that the consultation process could be enhanced by the establishment of an inclusive mechanism that allows the participation of all representatives of civil society, regardless of their ideology, that will contribute to the development of Mexico's trade policy. Additionally, they propose to hold referenda prior to the signature and approval of any PTA.

5   Dispute settlement mechanisms and non-state actors

NAFTA and its two side agreements on the environment and labour contain a wide variety of dispute settlement mechanisms (DSMs) of both a traditional and highly innovative kind. Along with many new trilateral institutions and processes for dispute avoidance and management, the NAFTA regime establishes six DSMs. Three provide a right of action that, similar to the WTO dispute settlement procedure, can be exercised only by the state parties to the agreements. The remaining three establish, for the first time in a PTA and its side agreements, a right of action for members of civil society to challenge specific actions of the state parties that have not been replicated in other Mexican PTAs.

The right of private action established under three of the DSMs of the NAFTA regime constitutes a big incentive for the business community and civil society to privilege the bilateral forum over the multilateral one.

5.1   State to state DSMs

5.1.1   NAFTA Chapter 20

Chapter 20 of NAFTA contains the agreement's general dispute settlement mechanism. It provides recourse for the states parties to the agreement to a mechanism applicable to all disputes regarding the interpretation or application of NAFTA. The inter-state nature of the mechanism obliges importers, exporters, enterprises or state or provincial governments of the NAFTA region that are affected by a measure adopted by another party to convince their own governments to initiate a DSM proceeding against that other party.

Since some of the NAFTA provisions are similar in scope and jurisdiction to those established under GATT[3] and the General Agreement on Trade in Services (GATS), NAFTA Article 2005 includes a provision on choice of forum. As a general rule, this Article grants the complaining party the right to choose a forum whenever a dispute may be settled under both GATT and NAFTA. Once chosen, the dispute shall be resolved in that forum to the exclusion of the other. However, if a complaining party wants to take a dispute to a GATT panel, it must notify third parties of its intentions. If a third party wishes to have the dispute resolved under NAFTA, the disputing parties are obliged to consult and to try to reach an agreement as to a single forum. If no agreement is reached, the NAFTA mechanism will supersede. The only disputes in which the parties of NAFTA are not faced with a choice of forum decision are those relating to the adoption of subsidies and countervailing duties, since NAFTA's lack of disciplines on this matter make it necessary to use the WTO state to state DSM.

In the fifteen years since NAFTA entered into force, only three cases have been litigated under Chapter 20: Mexico's complaints against the United States over brooms and trucking, both of which were resolved in favour of Mexico; and the US complaint against Canada's Tariffs Applied to Certain US Origin Agricultural Products. Meanwhile, during that same period, several disputes among NAFTA parties that could have been litigated at a bilateral level, such as the fructose and telecom US cases against Mexico, have been analysed by a WTO panel.

The low number of state to state disputes that have been litigated by a NAFTA panel can be explained by the fact that for nearly a decade there

---

[3] Both agreements contain similar provisions on trade in goods (industrial and agricultural), safeguards, technical barriers to trade, sanitary and phytosanitary measures and general and national security exceptions.

was no agreement on a panel roster, allowing the parties to block the process and, thus, preclude any action under the DSM of the agreement. On the other hand, in many cases the NAFTA parties have preferred to settle disputes under the WTO, because of participation of third parties and the opportunity that the multilateral forum offers to publicize the alleged violation of trade commitments to other members of the international community.

5.1.2   DSM under the North American Agreement on Labor Cooperation

NAFTA was the first trade agreement linked to worker rights provisions. Its 'side agreement', the North American Agreement on Labor Cooperation (NAALC), establishes provisions through which each country agrees to enforce its own labour laws and standards while promoting worker's rights over the long run. These rights include freedom of association and protection of the right to organize; the right to bargain collectively; the right to strike; prohibition of forced labour; labour protections for children and young persons; minimum employment standards; elimination of employment discrimination; equal pay for women and men; prevention of occupational injuries and illnesses; compensation in cases of occupational injuries and illnesses; and protection of migrant workers. However, under NAALC only the persistent breach of three of the aforementioned principles – minimum wages, child labour and occupational safety and health – could be subject to monetary sanctions or to the suspension of that party's benefits under NAFTA, after a panel has issued a determination on that regard. The high threshold established under NAALC to impose trade sanctions is the result of Mexico's and Canada's request to prevent the DSM mechanism from becoming a harassment tool against the adoption of otherwise sound domestic policies. To this date, the DSM of NAALC has not been invoked.

5.1.3   DSM under the North American Agreement on Environmental Cooperation

The North American Agreement on Environmental Cooperation (NAAEC), negotiated and implemented in parallel to NAFTA, requires that each party ensures that its laws provide for high levels of environmental protection without lowering standards to attract investment. To this end, each party agreed to effectively enforce its environmental laws through the use of inspectors, monitoring compliance and pursuing the necessary legal means to seek appropriate remedies for violations. The NAAEC establishes a state to state DSM that allows for the establishment of an independent arbitral panel of experts with the authority to determine whether environmental legislation is being enforced appropriately. The end result of this process can be the adoption of trade sanctions or fines against the NAFTA country found in violation. Similarly to NAALC, the DSM of NAAEC can be enforced only after high thresholds are met. To this date the mechanism has never been used.

5.2   DSMs that grant recourse to non-state actors

5.2.1   NAFTA Chapter 11

NAFTA Chapter 11 contains provisions designed to protect cross-border investors and facilitate the settlement of investment disputes regarding a party's violation of the protection that it is entitled to grant to investments and investors of the other parties. The investor–state DSM allows a NAFTA investor who alleges that a host NAFTA party has violated the investment disciplines established under the agreement to seek, before an impartial arbitral tribunal, monetary damages.

This innovative mechanism grants civil society members direct access to international dispute settlement procedures, regardless of their national government position on the matter. Since 1994, thirty-six cases have been taken to the investor–state DSM. The majority of the disputes have been initiated by US investors against measures adopted by Mexico or Canada. To date, Mexican investors have never submitted a claim to arbitration under the investor–state mechanism.

5.2.2   Chapter 19

NAFTA Chapter 19 establishes an innovative DSM that allows for the replacement of judicial review of final anti-dumping and countervailing duty determinations with independent bi-national panel review. The request for the establishment of a panel may be initiated by a state party to the agreement or by an industry or a producer of goods affected by an anti-dumping or countervailing duty. The mandate of a Chapter 19 panel is to determine whether the decision of the investigative authority was made in accordance with the anti-dumping or countervailing duty law of that importing party.

This bi-national panel review has allowed industries, producers, exporters or importers of the NAFTA region to challenge directly, and without the need to obtain the consent of their respective authorities, the anti-dumping or countervailing duties final determinations that affect their trade interests. The mechanism has been successfully invoked by Mexican industry. Since 1994, Mexican industries or exporters have requested forty-one bi-national panels to review the final determinations issued by US authorities, and two more to review decisions adopted by the Canadian Government. See Table 4.8 for details.

Thus far, the DSM established under Chapter 19 has made officials in the United States, Canada and Mexico act within the boundaries of their own law, reducing the protectionist pressures industries can mount on their administrative tribunals at home. In doing so, it has brought more principled, less political dispute resolution, even in the high profile cases it has taken up.

5.2.3   NAAEC's citizen submission process

In addition to the state to state DSM, NAAEC established for the first time a citizen submission process that allows any member of civil society to trigger an official international investigation into a NAFTA party's failure to enforce its environmental laws effectively. The request must be submitted to the Secretariat of the Trilateral Commission for Environmental Cooperation, which was created in 1994 by NAAEC to enhance environmental cooperation, reduce potential trade and environmental conflicts and promote the effective enforcement of environmental law in the North America region. If the Secretariat deems it appropriate, it may request a response from the party in question and, ultimately, it can elaborate a factual record of the matter. This process remains one of the most advanced institutional mechanisms aimed at addressing international environmental issues related to trade liberalization, and it has been widely used by members of civil society in Mexico, the United States and Canada.

Table 4.9 summarizes the main elements of the NAFTA DSMs that grant members of the civil society a right of action to challenge measures adopted by the state parties to the Agreement.

6   Conclusion

The involvement of NSAs in the development of Mexico's trade policy is not new. However, after the unprecedented consultation process carried out for the NAFTA negotiations, the interaction between the authorities

Table 4.8 *Status of the cases established pursuant to NAFTA Chapter 19*

Statistics			
125 cases	117 resolved	77 cases vs. US	35 cases of Mexican industries vs. US
			42 cases of Canadian industries vs. US
			One case of a US corporation vs. the US Government relating to an anti-dumping investigation against Mexican products
		22 cases vs. Canada	2 cases of Mexican industries vs. Canada
			13 cases of US industries vs. Canada
			7 cases of Canadian industries vs. Canadian Government relating to six anti-dumping investigations against US products and one investigation against Mexican products
		18 cases vs. Mexico	3 cases of Mexican industries vs. the Mexican Government relating to US products.
			12 cases of US industries vs. Mexico.
			3 cases of Canadian industries vs. Mexico.
	8 pending	8 cases vs. US	6 cases of Mexican industries vs. US
			2 cases Canadian industries vs. US

Table 4.9 *NAFTA DSMs that grant a right of action to members of civil society*

DSM	Recourse to the DSM	Measure challenged	Panel decision
Chapter 11 Investor–state	Investor or an investment of a party to NAFTA	Any measure adopted by a host party to the investment that is believed to be inconsistent with NAFTA's investment disciplines	Award of monetary damages
Chapter 19 AD/CD review	Industry, producer or importer of goods that has been affected by the anti-dumping or countervailing duty final determination	Review of an anti-dumping or countervailing duty final determination by an investigative authority to determine if such decision was issued in accordance with its domestic law	Confirmation or recommendation to amend or remand investigation
Citizen submission Environmental side agreement	Any member of civil society	Failure of a NAFTA party to effectively enforce its environmental laws	Issue of a factual report

and NSAs has been declining both in intensity and awareness. This reflects the fact that after NAFTA, there has not been any other process, unilateral or bilateral, as ambitious and deep as the trilateral agreement in terms of the liberalization implied for the Mexican economy. Although the business sector remains actively engaged in the development of Mexico's trade policy, its main objective has been to stop, or at least slow down, any new liberalization attempt on the part of the Mexican Government.

One of the most important reasons for NAFTA's acceptance by the Mexican productive sector was that it offered preferential access to the United States and Canada. From a Mexican perspective, reciprocity became the biggest selling pitch of the agreement. This, however, came back with a vengeance, since any further attempt to unilaterally open up the Mexican economy became hostage of the reciprocity argument.

In recent years, however, the reciprocity criteria that made NAFTA and the additional eleven PTAs acceptable to the Mexican business sector has not succeeded in promoting further liberalization of Mexico's economy. Mexican industry has shown no interest in opening new markets. In its view, the access that has been negotiated under NAFTA, EUMFTA and the other PTAs is enough and it is not willing to face new competitors in the domestic market. Thus, in the past four years, in particular, since the conclusion of the Mexico–Japan Free Trade Agreement in 2005, representatives of the productive sectors in Mexico have opposed the launch of new free trade initiatives. Their main argument is that before entering into new agreements, the Mexican Government needs to implement policies that allow Mexican enterprises and exporters to take more advantages of the existing free trade agreements.

As for other types of NSAs, such as the labour and environmental movements, in the past decade their participation in the development of Mexico's trade policy has diminished. This lack of interest can be explained by the fact that after the NAFTA negotiation, the Mexican authorities have constantly opposed the inclusion of labour and environmental provisions in PTAs in order to avoid the establishment of new trade barriers. Thus, these groups have shifted their attention to other areas, such as the improvement of Mexico's domestic environmental policy.

Despite the fact that the Mexican business sector does not support new trade initiatives, the interviews revealed that it has a very positive assessment of its interaction with negotiators, whereas other NSAs, such as the Mexican Action Network Facing Free Trade, have a more negative view. This reflects the fact that the authorities have been more able to deliver on business demands (almost always revolving around market access issues) than on those from environmental, labour or opposing trade groups. The latter often involve issues which are either not on the agenda of negotiations (e.g., gender issues or very specific environmental demands) or are unacceptable to their counterparts. In other words, the demands of the business community (which are based on commercial interest) tend to be more amenable to negotiated solutions than demands from other NSAs.

The challenge that Mexican authorities face with regards to trade policy is to promote and adopt initiatives that could contribute to the improvement of the country's competitiveness. Today, Mexico has one of the world's most complex customs regimes, including preferential access under twelve different PTAs, preferential unilateral programmes established by the authorities and the MFN tariffs. This has taken a toll on the competitiveness of the country. Thus, in recent years the authorities have implemented policies to simplify the customs regime; among others, by unilaterally reducing the MFN rates such as the tariff reform that was announced in December 2008. However, these initiatives have not been received well by the business community, allegedly because of the lack of reciprocity.

References

De Mateo Veiga, F. 2003. 'La política comercial de México con América Latina', in R. F. de Castro (ed.), *En la frontera del imperio*. México: Planeta.

Garciadiego, J. 1994. *El TLC Día a Día: Crónica de una Negociación*. Mexico: Miguel Angel Porrúa.

Lusztig, M. 2004. *The Limits of Protectionism: Building Coalitions for Free Trade*. University of Pittsburgh Press.

Pastor, M. and Wise, C. 2004. 'The Origins and Sustainability of Mexico's Free Trade Policy', *International Organization* **48**, 3: 459–89.

Salinas de Gortarí, C. 2002. *México: The Policy and Politics of Modernization*, 1st edn. Mexico: Plaza and Janés.

Somunano, F. 2006. 'Non-governmental Organizations and the Changing Structure of Mexican Politics: The Cases of Environmental and Human Rights Policy', in L. Randall (ed.), *Changing Structure of Mexico: Political, Social and Economic Prospects*, 2nd edn. New York: M. E. Sharpe, pp. 489–500.

Teichman, J. A. 2001. *The Politics of Freeing Markets in Latin America: Chile, Argentina and Mexico*. Chapel Hill, NC: University of North Carolina Press.

Thacker, S. C. 2000. *Big Business, The State and Free Trade: Constructing Coalitions in Mexico*. Cambridge University Press.

Vega Cánovas, G. 1993, *Liberación económica y libre comercio en América del Norte: consideraciones políticas, sociales y culturales*. Mexico: El Colegio de México.

Zabludovsky, J. 1994. 'El proceso de negociación del Tratado de Libre Comercio de Américo del Norte', in C. Arriola (ed.), *Testimonios sobre el TLC*. Mexico: Diana, Miguel Angel Porrúa, pp. 107–25.

5

Indonesia

ALEXANDER C. CHANDRA AND LUTFIYAH HANIM[1]

1 Introduction

The emergence of democracy in Indonesia as a result of the economic crisis in the late 1990s has brought significant changes to the policy-making process in the country. The reform advocates who emerged following the downfall of the authoritarian Suharto regime saw liberalization and engagement with the global economy as key to advancing economic reform in Indonesia. While recognizing the importance of concluding the global trade negotiations under the auspices of the World Trade Organization (WTO), Indonesia also remains committed to pursuing liberalization at the regional level through its membership of the Association of Southeast Asian Nations (ASEAN). Recently, Indonesia has also engaged in bilateral preferential trade agreements (PTAs), in part due to the stalling of the Doha Round negotiations, but also because the pursuit of PTAs by Indonesia's immediate neighbours has generated fear among government and economic actors about the possible loss of competitiveness in key export markets.

The emergence of democracy and the increasing integration of the country into the international economy present the Indonesian government with a host of significant challenges in establishing an effective trade policy that reflects the wider interests of its domestic stakeholders. This chapter explores these challenges, focusing on two issues in particular: (i) the dynamics of the interactions between state and non-state actors (NSAs) in the country's trade policy-making structure; and (ii) the relationship between these interactions and the question of forum choice – whether to negotiate preferentially or multilaterally. The chapter opens with a brief historical overview of Indonesia's trade policy and

[1] The conduct of the field research interviews was assisted by Ainan Nuran. The views and opinions expressed in this chapter are solely those of the authors and do not represent the positions of either the Trade Knowledge Network or the Third World Network.

trade patterns, before proceeding to an analysis of the institutional structure of trade policy-making and the state and non-state actors involved in trade policy-making. It then explores the way in which NSAs attempt to influence government and the question of forum choice. The final section concludes.

2   Historical evolution of Indonesian trade policy evolution

Since independence in 1945, Indonesian trade policy has undergone multiple transformations. Successive Indonesian administrations have pursued different trade policies, ranging from protectionism to liberal open trade strategies. Under the Sukarno administration (1945–66), Indonesia adopted a strongly nationalistic economic policy with a leftist orientation (Chandra 2008, 93), but poor economic management during this period left the country in ruins. By the end of Sukarno's presidency, Indonesia's roads, shipping and infrastructure were run down; manufacturing industry was working at less than 20% of capacity; and foreign trade was throttled by complex regulations and multiple exchange rates (Coleman, Cornish and Drake 2007).

In 1957, President Sukarno launched the so-called 'Guided Democracy' principle, which strengthened the power of the executive branch of government. The effect was to give Sukarno absolute power in both domestic and international affairs of the government, including trade policy. Trade and economic policies were inward-looking, reflecting the view among Indonesia's policy elites that trade and investment were means by which industrialized nations subjugated developing countries (Weinstein 2007).

The subsequent Suharto administration (1967–98) was similarly authoritarian, but its economic reform agenda lifted Indonesia out of the economic ruin left by its predecessors. Although governing Indonesia with an iron fist, Suharto listened closely to the advice of a group of influential technocrats, known as the 'Berkeley Mafia', a group of US-trained Indonesian economists, and he led the country into an unprecedented period of growth over nearly three decades. Authoritarian rule gave the Suharto administration and the ruling party, Golkar (Golongan Karya), latitude to pursue a well-coordinated foreign economic policy, with virtually no interference from domestic pressure groups.

Suharto's 'New Order' regime adopted a *laissez-faire* approach to promoting economic growth and attracting foreign investment, with inducements to attract foreign investment. Import licensing was abolished and various export promotion schemes were developed. Other reforms followed in the 1970s and 1980s, including the elimination of capital controls and the simplification of export and import procedures. From the late 1980s until the East Asian financial crisis of 1997–8, Indonesia undertook significant unilateral trade liberalization in order to increase competitiveness, encourage investment and promote exports and export diversification (so as to reduce Indonesia's reliance on oil exports).

The economic reforms of the 1980s greatly reduced the role of the state and increased the size and importance of the private sector. However, these reforms simply transformed state-owned monopolies into private corporations controlled by President Suharto's family and cronies. In 1998 the World Bank estimated that as much as 30% of the country's development budget over the prior two decades had disappeared, while the Suharto family holdings were estimated at anywhere from US$12 billion to US$40 billion (Zabriskie 2008). Such corruption took place with the full knowledge of the private sector and a civil society that remained voiceless.

With the demise of the New Order regime following the economic crisis of 1997–8, Indonesia was transformed into one of the largest democracies in the world. While regarded by most Indonesians as a positive development, the introduction of democracy has brought the country a set of new challenges, including in relation to trade policy-making. For instance, during his first term, President Susilo Bambang Yudhoyono often had difficulty pursuing his economic agendas due to opposition from within his cabinet and parliament.

Democracy also brought Indonesian trade policy into greater public scrutiny. While public pressure was virtually absent during the tenure of President Suharto, there are now numerous NSAs, usually, although not always, driven by a nationalist economic agenda, working to influence the government's economic policy. Although this represents a sign of a healthy functioning democratic society, it also makes it more challenging for the government to pursue a consistent trade policy in line with its domestic and international priorities. For example, government's efforts to pursue active liberalization initiatives are often undermined by pressure groups calling for trade protection. Resistance to market reform from protectionist interests, which hold key positions both in the government and in the business sector, was reflected in rising protectionism from 2001 to 2004 in agricultural products (Basri and Patunru 2009, 2).

Despite the advent of democracy, Indonesian trade policy-making remains non-transparent and lacks informed dialogue among all stakeholders. Creating conditions consistent with democratic principles in trade policy-making processes is not only expensive but also difficult to pursue. As will be shown in the discussion that follows, the lack of coordination among economic-related ministries, the inability of NSAs to grasp the complexity of trade issues and, sometimes, their unwillingness to engage in meaningful discussion with the government are the most prominent challenges that the country faces today. Moreover, in the face of these deficiencies and the inability of the government to generate an effective trade policy, the forum choices of the government are still determined primarily by external factors.

3   Indonesia's trade patterns

As with nearly all the member countries of ASEAN, Indonesia's trade pattern is predominantly North–South, with a low proportion flowing South–South (Vanzetti, McGuire and Prabowo 2005, 8). This is shifting, however, particularly given the greater integration between Indonesia and its neighbouring countries in ASEAN and the wider East Asian region. Between 1999 and 2008, Japan, the European Union and the United States remained the key trading partners of Indonesia outside ASEAN. Within this period, Indonesia's exports to Japan, the United States and the European Union accounted for about 21.86%, 12.4% and 13%, respectively, of Indonesia's total exports (see Table 5.1). Meanwhile, imports from Japan, the United States and the European Union accounted for 12.59%, 8.42% and 11.9%, respectively, of total Indonesian imports. In total, the trade between Indonesia and Japan almost tripled between 2003 and 2008, from US$17.8 billion to US$42.7 billion, respectively. Meanwhile, within the same period, Indonesia's total trade with the European Union rose from US$11.9 billion to US$26 billion, while its trade with the United States rose from US$10 billion to US$20 billion.

Of increasing significance, however, is Indonesia's trade with northeast Asia. The country's total trade with the three main economies of the region – China, Japan and South Korea – rose significantly from US$37.4 billion in 2004 to US$85.6 billion in 2008. Japan took the bulk of Indonesia's trade with the region, or an average of 29.8% within the same period. But among the newcomers, Indonesia's most important trade partner is China. The total trade between the two countries tripled between 2004 and 2008, from US$ 8.7billion to US$26.8 billion. The eventual implementation of the Indonesia–Japan Economic Partnership Agreement (IJEPA), the ASEAN–China Free Trade Agreement (ACFTA)

Table 5.1 *Indonesia's total trade with major partners, 2003–8 (in US$ thousand)*

Countries	2004	2005	2006	2007	2008
Japan					
Total trade	22,043,717.3	24,955,394.9	27,247,896.7	30,159,470.7	42,871,871.4
Export	15,962,109.6	18,049,139.7	21,732,123.0	23,632,796.8	27,743,856.2
Import	6,081,607.7	6,906,255.2	5,515,773.7	6,526,673.9	15,128,015.3
European Union					
Total trade	14,456,281.4	16,184,078.9	18,080,362.0	21,024,467.0	26,014,513.9
Export	9,093,160.2	10,326,463.0	12,029,822.3	13,344,546.1	15,454,538.5
Import	5,363,121.4	5,857,615.9	6,050,539.7	7,679,920.9	10,559,975.4
United States					
Total trade	11,992,536.0	13,747,395.5	15,288,636.1	16,401,404.1	20,916,939.2
Export	8,767,140.2	9,868,476.5	11,232,103.8	11,614,229.7	13,036,866.9
Import	3,225,395.8	3,878,919.1	4,056,532.3	4,787,174.4	7,880,072.3
China					
Total trade	8,706,064.2	12,505,216.3	14,980,466.4	18,233,389.8	26,883,672.6
Export	4,604,733.1	6,662,353.8	8,343,571.3	9,675,512.7	11,636,503.7
Import	4,101,331.1	5,842,862.5	6,636,895.1	8,557,877.1	15,247,168.9
South Korea					
Total trade	6,772,760.1	9,954,730.0	10,569,393.4	10,779,421.0	16,036,882.1
Export	4,830,180.4	7,085,635.8	7,693,540.9	7,582,734.4	9,116,819.2
Import	1,942,579.7	2,869,094.2	2,875,852.5	3,196,686.6	6,920,062.9
Australia					
Total trade	4,102,276.2	4,794,748.7	5,757,541.9	6,398,569.3	8,108,503.6
Export	1,887,359.2	2,227,608.3	2,771,277.0	3,394,557.3	4,110,969.6
Import	2,214,917.0	2,567,140.5	2,986,264.9	3,004,012.0	3,997,534.0
India					
Total trade	3,272,938.5	3,930,507.7	4,798,214.1	6,553,512.8	10,065,188.5
Export	2,170,506.8	2,878,347.7	3,390,790.2	4,943,906.0	7,163,336.2
Import	1,102,431.8	1,052,160.0	1,407,423.8	1,609,606.8	2,901,852.2
ASEAN					
Total trade	24,488,649.8	32,863,633.7	37,453,707.3	46,084,248.4	68,138,577.6
Export	12,994,204.0	15,823,719.8	18,483,087.5	22,292,114.8	27,170,819.7
Import	11,494,445.8	17,039,913.9	18,970,619.8	23,792,133.6	40,967,757.9
Singapore					
Total trade	12,080,670.4	17,306,103.1	18,964,384.0	20,341,412.1	34,651,531.5
Export	5,997,898.3	7,835,385.1	8,929,849.2	10,501,617.3	12,862,045.2
Import	6,082,772.1	9,470,718.0	10,034,534.8	9,839,794.8	21,789,486.3

Table 5.1 (*cont.*)

Countries	2004	2005	2006	2007	2008
Malaysia					
Total trade	4,697,993.5	5,579,825.7	7,304,091.1	11,507,990.8	15,354,841.1
Export	3,016,048.0	3,431,299.7	4,110,757.5	5,096,063.5	6,432,551.9
Import	1,681,945.6	2,148,526.0	3,193,333.6	6,411,927.3	8,922,289.2
Thailand					
Total trade	4,747,819.6	5,693,418.1	5,685,031.5	7,341,341.4	9,995,515.6
Export	1,976,236.3	2,246,458.7	2,701,548.7	3,054,276.0	3,661,251.9
Import	2,771,583.3	3,446,959.4	2,983,482.8	4,287,065.4	6,334,263.7
Philippines					
Total trade	1,466,169.3	1,741,352.3	1,690,314.6	2,213,533.1	2,809,150.4
Export	1,237,593.8	1,419,120.4	1,405,668.8	1,853,683.1	2,053,611.3
Import	228,575.5	322,231.8	284,645.8	359,850.0	755,539.1
Vietnam					
Total trade	1,016,788.1	1,117,473.5	1,898,806.8	2,349,353.1	2,390,571.1
Export	600,989.5	678,444.9	1,052,004.3	1,355,156.1	1,672,903.4
Import	415,798.6	439,028.6	846,802.6	994,197.1	717,667.7
Brunei Darussalam					
Total trade	327,005.4	1,236,830.3	1,644,490.8	1,908,088.2	2,476,288.5
Export	31,761.8	39,332.0	37,557.9	43,367.4	59,671.0
Import	295,243.6	1,197,498.4	1,606,932.9	1,864,720.8	2,416,617.5
Cambodia					
Total trade	72,928.7	94,668.7	104,706.1	123,104.3	176,033.0
Export	71,824.7	93,936.0	103,648.2	121,853.2	174,027.3
Import	1,104.0	732.6	1,057.9	1,251.1	2,005.7
Myanmar					
Total trade	77,700.6	92,144.8	157,370.9	292,779.0	280,443.0
Export	60,281.6	77,990.0	137,708.0	262,387.3	250,765.2
Import	17,419.0	14,154.7	19,662.8	30,391.7	29,677.9
Lao PDR					
Total trade	1,574.2	1,817.2	4,511.5	6,646.4	4,203.4
Export	1,570.1	1,752.8	4,344.9	3,711.0	3,992.5
Import	4.1	64.4	166.6	2,935.4	210.8

Source: Depdag (n.d.).

Table 5.2 *Indonesia's export and import composition, 2004–8 (in US$ billion)*

Sectors	2004	2005	2006	2007	2008
Exports					
Agriculture	2.5	2.8	3.3	3.6	4.5
Industry	48.6	55.5	65.0	76.4	88.9
Mining	4.7	7.9	11.1	11.8	14.9
Others	0.4	0.7	0.8	0.8	0.9
Total exports	55.93	66.42	79.58	92.01	107.89
Imports					
Consumption goods	3.7	4.6	4.5	6.5	8.3
Raw material components	36.2	44.7	47.2	56.4	99.4
Capital goods	6.5	8.2	9.2	11.4	21.4
Total imports	46.5	57.7	61.0	74.4	129.1

Source: Depdag (n.d.).

and the ASEAN–South Korea Free Trade Agreement (ASKFTA) are likely to facilitate further trade between Indonesia and these three countries.

An interesting development has emerged around trade between Indonesia and its neighbouring countries in ASEAN. Although economic cooperation has been one of the foci of ASEAN cooperation, Indonesia's trade with its immediate neighbours has been relatively modest. Recent trade data between Indonesia and the rest of ASEAN, however, show a different picture emerging. From 2003 to 2008, Indonesia's trade with the grouping rose significantly from US$18.4 billion to US$67.4 billion. Although ASEAN economic integration initiatives have helped to facilitate greater economic linkages among all its members, trade between Indonesia and other ASEAN members was predominantly with Singapore. However, developing countries and other regions of the world are now becoming increasingly important trading partners for Indonesia.

The industrial sector remains one of the key contributors to the Indonesian non-oil and gas exports composition (see Table 5.2). From 2004 to 2008, this sector contributed an average of 83.45% of total Indonesian non-gas and oil exports abroad. The export value of Indonesian industrial export goods has increased at a constant pace, from US$48.6 billion in 2004 to US$88.9 billion in 2008. Key industrial exports are electronic goods, vegetable oil and fats, paper, textiles and garments. In terms of imports, raw materials, particularly in the form of processed industrial raw material components and unprocessed fuel and lubricants, account for a considerable proportion of Indonesia's non-oil and gas imports. In 2004, for example, the value of raw material components accounted for 77.8% of Indonesia's total imports. The value of raw material consumption increased considerably by 36.9% in 2008 to US$99.4 billion, though its share contribution relative to the country's total imports fell to 76.9%.

4   State and non-state actors in trade policy-making

4.1   State actors: structure and roles

As in many other countries, the Ministry of Trade (Depdag – Departemen Perdagangan) plays a central role in the formulation and deliberation of trade policy-making in Indonesia. Depdag deals with international and domestic trade matters and assists the president in the formulation, implementation, administration and monitoring of the country's trade policy. It has three directorate generals working on international trade, domestic trade and international trade cooperation, respectively, and three agencies, namely, the National Agency for Export Development, the Commodity Futures Trading Supervisory Agency and the Trade Research and Development Agency, to support its activities (see Figure 5.1). Depdag is also responsible for overseeing the work of its trade attachés, trade promotion centres and thirty-one local offices at the provincial level (Soesastro and Soejachmoen 2007, 7).

In matters specific to international trade, the Ministry of Foreign Affairs (Deplu – Departemen Luar Negeri) also plays an active role in supporting Depdag in preparation for trade negotiations. Other ministries involved in the formulation of the country's international trade policy include the Coordinating Ministry for Economy, Ministry of Finance (Depkeu – Departemen Keuangan), the National Development Planning Board (Bappenas – Badan Perencanaan Pembangunan Nasional), as well as a host of other sectoral ministries (e.g., agriculture, natural resources, labour). Coordination of international trade policy-making also involves various state agencies, such as the Investment Coordinating Board (BKPM – Badan Koordinasi Penanaman Modal), and many other sub-agencies within Depdag (e.g., the Anti Dumping Commission and the Indonesian Committee for Trade Security) and Depkeu (e.g., the Tariff Team and the

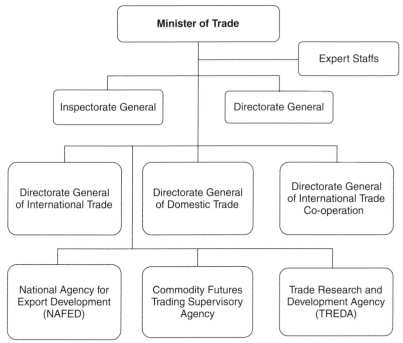

Figure 5.1   Organizational structure of the Ministry of Trade
Source: Ministry of Trade official website, accessed 11 June 2009, www. depdag.go/id/
index.php?option=organisasi&task=bagan&itemid=0101.

Board of Economic, Finance and International Cooperation, Bappeki –
Badan Pengkajian Kerjasama Ekonomi dan Keuangan Internasional).

Despite its supposed leadership in trade policy-making, Depdag is often
faced with significant setbacks in its policy-making function (Soesastro
and Soejachmoen 2007, 7–13). First, the ministry is still characterized by
some outmoded organizational features, and is more inclined to perform
many obsolete regulatory functions, such as the issue of import licensing
instead of conducting trade policy or building up efforts to facilitate the
expansion of the private sector. Second, Depdag is not given the authority to deal with non-tariff barriers (NTBs), most of which are issued by
sectoral or technical ministries, such as the ministries of Agriculture and
Forestry. Third, internal capacity is particularly weak within Depdag.
Although it is committed to improving its human resources and the use of
information technology throughout its network of offices, poor communication, even among its officials in Jakarta, is prevalent. Fourth, given the
poor human resources within the ministry, impact assessment analyses

are rarely done. Consequently, Depdag is often incapable of communicating effectively to the public and securing the essential public support for its policies. Fifth, in the area of international trade, Depdag lacks credible individuals capable of conducting good trade diplomacy.

Given the increasing scope and complexity of international trade issues and negotiations, coordination remains an important aspect for the making of an effective trade policy in Indonesia. Despite this policy-makers often find it difficult to reach consensus on key trade issues.[2] As Bird, Hill and Cuthbertson (2007, 16) argue, the crux of Indonesia's trade policy challenge is the absence of a single minister or agency able 'to take control over the full array of trade policy instruments and to adopt an economy-wide public interest viewpoint'. The multiple state ministries and/or agencies involved in trade policy-making, as well as other internal structural deficiencies within Depdag have considerably impaired effective coordination in policy-making.

Efforts to address the issue of coordination and to increase the effectiveness of trade policy-making have been pursued by Depdag and other economic ministries. For example, in 2005 the government launched the so-called National Team on International Trade Negotiations (TimNas PPI – Tim Nasional Perundingan Perdagangan Internasional), which was given the task of formulating the position and strategy of the Indonesian government in international trade negotiations. The Indonesian government also has a host of institutional mechanisms that are aimed at improving coordination on trade-related policy issues, such as the Tariff Team, the Anti-Dumping Committee and the Food Security Council. Among these non-ministerial trade-related institutions, the Tariff Team has been central in maintaining the economic openness of Indonesia. However, the Tariff Team is an *ad hoc* interdepartmental body that performs its work informally, often lacking reference to clear objectives and rigorous analytical research and in a largely non-transparent manner (Bird, Hill and Cuthbertson 2007, 32). In most instances, the Tariff Team has little control over other forms of trade barriers, such as NTBs which are determined by other sectoral ministries. Indeed, despite the inclination of post-Suharto era governments to opt for an open economic policy, some government ministries continue to favour more nationalistic and populist policies that promote the interests of their 'client' base. In their study of the political-economy of trade policy in Indonesia, Soesastro and Basri (2005, 12–13) have found evidence of 'creeping protectionism' in

---

[2] See, for example, Pangestu *et al.* (2002) and Soesastro and Soejachmoen (2007).

several agricultural and non-agricultural sectors, such as flour, textiles, sugar and cloves, which undermines the government's commitment to an open economy.

4.2 The role and interests of parliament

The Indonesian parliament, or the People's Representatives' Assembly (DPR–Dewan Perwakilan Rakyat), plays an important role in the democratic governance of the country. The DPR has three key functions: legislative, budgeting and oversight. It has the power to draw up and pass laws, debate and approve government policy proposals and question the president and government officials on the policies they introduce and implement. Despite its importance in democratic governance, the participation of the DPR in trade policy formulation and deliberation has been minimal. This is confirmed by a member of parliament,[3] who pointed out that the DPR is rarely involved in any trade policy development pursued by the government. An official from Deplu, however, defended the government's approach to parliament.[4] According to this official, there has to be clarity in the roles and functions of the DPR. Parliament, after all, is mandated, *inter alia*, to approve or disapprove policy propositions from government. Matters concerning the pursuit of trade negotiations between Indonesia and its trade partners are matters of executive prerogative. The government is also concerned that the involvement of too many parties at the policy formulation stage might jeopardize the speed of trade negotiations. In reality, it is not uncommon for the DPR to refuse to ratify government proposals.

4.3 Government mechanisms for engaging non-state actors

In its efforts to reform Indonesia's trade policy, the government needs to build supportive constituencies of key domestic actors and the public more generally. Indeed, the participation of non-state actors has been very much encouraged by the government, and its official line is that consultation of NSAs is a necessary part of the process of formulating Indonesian trade policy. In a keynote address at one of the national consultations in 2006, Dr Mari Pangestu, the Indonesian Trade Minister, stated that the key element

---

[3] Interview with Dradjat Wibowo, Member of Parliament from the National Mandate Party (PAN–Partai Amanat Nasional), Commission XI, 21 April 2009, Jakarta.
[4] Interview with Edi Yusuf, director of ASEAN Economic Cooperation, Deplu, 14 May 2009, Jakarta.

in Indonesia's free trade strategy was to have 'adequate preparations of our national position, [which would include] … a process of dialogue and inputs from all stakeholders in society ranging from the private sector, NGOs, parliamentary members and society at large' (Pangestu 2006).

As a result of the overall commitment of the government to strengthen democracy in Indonesia, policy-makers are relatively more confident in pursuing engagement with NSAs in the policy-making process. Indeed, the field research interviews that were carried out for this study found that officials from government institutions involved in trade policy-making, particularly Depdag and Deplu, consider engagement with NSAs in trade policy-making as important (see Table 5.3). Reasons such as satisfying public policy requirements and the promotion of transparency are particularly important for officials from these government institutions. However, when asked whether the involvement of NSAs in trade policy-making is important in providing technical advice and commercial intelligence, officials from Deplu and Depdag gave different feedback. Officials from Deplu, acknowledged to be one of the most reformed government institutions under the current administration, consider technical inputs and commercial intelligence from the NSAs as 'extremely important', whereas representatives from Depdag consider the role of NSAs in this regard as 'somewhat important'. This divergence of views was also apparent when asked whether the engagement with NSAs is useful as a means to, first, gauge potential public views on certain trade policy of the government and, second, to create possible coalitions to support the negotiating positions and outcomes of certain trade agreements that the government is pursuing. On both questions, officials from Deplu ranked the role of NSAs as 'important', whereas their counterparts in Depdag considered the role of NSAs in this respect as 'somewhat important'.

As part of the government's efforts to promote openness and transparency in trade policy-making, there are now several formal and informal mechanisms in which NSAs can channel their aspirations and concerns to the government. One such mechanism is the Indonesian WTO Forum, which was established in 2003 under the initiative of the then Indonesian Foreign Minister, Dr Hassan Wirajuda. The WTO Forum is presided over by three ministers (Coordinating Minister for Economy, Minister of Foreign Affairs and the Minister of Trade) and is composed of twenty-three members from various ministries, business associations, academia and CSOs. The WTO Forum often organizes and facilitates dialogues and consultancies among various interest groups in the country. There have also been instances where NSAs have been allowed access to sit in as

Table 5.3 *State actors' reasons for pursuing consultations with NSAs*

Government institutions/agencies	Reasons for pursuing consultations with NSAs					
	Satisfying public policy requirements	Promoting transparency	Seeking technical advice and commercial intelligence	Gauging potential public views	Creating coalition to support negotiating positions and outcome	Other reasons
Deplu (Directorate General Multilateral Cooperation)	2	1	1	2	2	n/a
Deplu (Directorate General ASEAN Cooperation)	2	1	1	2	2	n/a
Depdag (Directorate General Multilateral Cooperation)	1	2	3	3	3	n/a
DPR (Commission XI)	1	1	1	1	3	n/a

observers on trade negotiations with the country's trading partners. This was the case during the negotiations of Economic Partnership Agreement (EPA) between Japan and Indonesia which came into force in July 2008. The Indonesian government had actually taken a positive initiative when it decided to include as many NSAs as possible, including some civil society organizations (CSOs), during the so-called Joint Study Group (JSG) process and some of the initial phases of the negotiations (Chandra 2007, 61). However, the government was incapable of resisting the pressure from its Japanese counterparts when the latter insisted that the negotiations should be carried out at government-to-government level only.

Overall, the pursuit of democratic governance in trade policy-making is easier said than done. In the case of Indonesia, there are at least two key problems that emerge from the existing configuration of state–non-state actor relations on trade policy. First, most of the existing mechanisms to ensure civil society participation have to date been *ad hoc* in nature. To a large extent, the government has generally consulted only a narrow set of industrial and political interests (Soesastro and Soejachmoen 2007, 25), and has failed to generate enough information available to a broad range of domestic stakeholders. For instance, among the twenty-three members of the WTO Forum, only two represent CSOs (the Jakarta-based Institute for Global Justice and the Third World Network, which is an international organization). Broad-based representation of CSOs is also absent in the policy-making structure of the government. Similarly, the composition of the National Team on International Trade Negotiations consists mainly of senior government officials. The only NSA included in the Team is the Indonesian Chamber of Commerce and Industry (KADIN – Kamar Dagang dan Industri Indonesia), and a handful of academic experts who make up the Advisory Group. Precisely because of this, many trade advocacy groups in the country remain sceptical about the government's willingness to democratize trade policy-making processes in the country.

The second challenge to the implementation of democratic governance in Indonesian trade policy-making is the attractiveness of trade issues for the public (Chandra 2007, 61–2). Although international trade plays a significant role in the economic development of Indonesia, transformation of trade policy is more difficult to advocate at the national than at the regional and international levels. In the case of the former, a trade-related issue may not necessarily be attractive to either state or non-state actors, despite the growing use of trade agreements to promote partnerships with other countries. The relatively limited participation of NSAs, apart from a few of members of the academic community, business community and CSOs, in

Indonesia is due not only to the failure of the government to initiate openness and transparency, but also because of the increased complexity of the nature and substance of international trade negotiations. Such complexity has rendered it difficult for trade advocacy groups to disseminate trade-related information in layperson's terms at the grassroots level.

Even if invited, the low level of participation by NSAs in various discussion fora or events also reflects the general lack of interest among grassroots level actors towards trade issues. Indeed, it has been observed that in most of the conferences and workshops held by the Indonesian WTO Forum it is common to find more government officials than NSAs, except those from the business community. The participation of CSO representatives is relatively small considering the diverse issues that are covered in the realm of international trade. CSO activists who manage to attend the policy discussions at the Forum are normally very reluctant to make their voices heard or unable to attend the events fully, thereby limiting their ability to influence the government's policy. Moreover, there is also a tendency to lack of participation by the academic community. To date, there are really only a handful of trade experts who have traditionally been very active in trade policy-making. In response to such a low turnout of NSAs, Deplu and Depdag, two of the ministries leading the trade policy-making process, have often consulted some of the most active trade advocacy groups on how to further reach out to NSAs and expand their participation in the trade policy discussion fora.

4.4   Non-state actors: roles and interests

To date, there are only a few NSAs capable of pursuing effective engagement with the government. Apart from a handful of academic experts (e.g., the Centre of Strategic and International Studies (CSIS) and the Institute for Economic and Social Research (LPEM) of the University of Indonesia) and business communities (e.g., KADIN and the Indonesian Entrepreneurs Association (APINDO), other NSAs, particularly those from the civil society circle, either have minimum interest in engaging themselves or are lacking the capacity to participate effectively in trade policy debates. Civil society organizations that have the capacity to pursue constructive engagement with the government, such as the Institute for Global Justice (IGJ), tend to favour nationalist agendas advocating protectionism. Instead of discussing the substance of the international trade policy and agreements in question, these organizations are more interested in engaging themselves in ideological debates with the government questioning the merit of trade liberalization. While these reflect the relative health of the Indonesian democracy, these dynamics also hinder effective trade policy-making. Table 5.4 provides an overview of the key NSAs involved in trade policy-making, their role and interests, their membership base and their affiliations where relevant.

5   Trade forum choice and the influence of Indonesian non-state actors

Indonesia has been active in multilateral, regional and, to a lesser extent, bilateral trade negotiations. To date, Indonesia's involvement in PTAs has been primarily through its membership of ASEAN and the ASEAN Free Trade Agreement (AFTA), and has come as a result of ASEAN's negotiation of PTAs with China, Japan, South Korea, India, Australia and New Zealand (see Table 5.5). There are also ongoing discussions with other key trading partners, including the United States, the European Union and the European Free Trade Association (EFTA). However, according to an official from Deplu, due to resource constraints Indonesia would prefer to focus on the implementation of the four existing 'ASEAN Plus One' agreements prior to engaging in further discussion and negotiation with other trading partners.[5]

5.1   Indonesia and forum choice

In general, our research has found that Indonesian NSAs see multilateral, regional and bilateral trade forums as equally important and driven by the need for Indonesia to expand and diversify its export markets, as well as demand from its trade partners to open its market. While seeing these fora as equally important, Indonesia's NSAs have a clear preference for multilateral and then regional negotiations.

Several factors explain the NSAs' preference for multilateral trade negotiations. First, Indonesia has a long history of engagement in the multilateral trade system, having become a contracting party to the General Agreement on Tariffs and Trade (GATT) in 1950 and having joined the WTO upon its establishment at the end of 1994. Second, although ASEAN is considered to be the central pillar of Indonesia's foreign policy, trade liberalization through ASEAN has been modest. Third,

---

[5] Interview with Asianto Sinambela, Director of the Directorate of Trade, Industry, Investment and IPR, 3 April 2009, Jakarta.

bilateral PTAs are still considered to be a recent phenomenon, and there remains uncertainty among state and non-state actors alike as to how best to approach PTAs. Fourth, global civil society movements, spurred by the agendas of development agencies and other donors, have played a role in encouraging Indonesia's CSOs to pursue their agendas through the WTO.[6] Together, these points help to explain Indonesia's inclination to pursue active engagement in multilateral trade issues.

Indonesia's engagement with GATT and then the WTO has been elite-driven. While scepticism towards the WTO has been relatively minimal, political leaders and the intellectual elite have harboured suspicions about the way in which WTO rules and regulations may affect the national economic affairs of Indonesia, and the extent to which these rules have been tilted in favour of the interests of developed countries. Indeed, following the failed WTO Ministerial Meeting in Seattle in 1999, in the eyes of many state and non-state actors in Indonesia the WTO assumed the role of international villain along with the IMF and the World Bank.

More recently, however, the attitude of Indonesian NSAs towards the WTO has become more favourable. Our field research has revealed a growing inclination among Indonesian NSAs to favour multilateralism instead of bilateralism. According to NSAs, one key concern about bilateral PTAs, in comparison with the WTO, and, to a certain extent, ASEAN regional economic integration initiatives, is that they tend to accelerate the process of domestic liberalization, impacting on the development of local industries. Indeed, there is a view that WTO negotiations, unlike preferential negotiations, give Indonesia the necessary space and time to cope with the process of liberalization.

Second in importance in the eyes of Indonesia NSAs are regional agreements, particularly those pursued as a result of Indonesia's membership of ASEAN. ASEAN regional economic integration serves as both a learning ground and a stepping stone for Indonesia to participate more effectively in multilateral negotiations and world markets. By contrast, for many Indonesian NSAs, ASEAN is also preferred to bilateral PTAs because the slow progress of economic liberalization under ASEAN economic integration initiatives has had only modest impacts on the Indonesian economy. More importantly, ASEAN cooperation goes beyond trade-specific concerns, and, given the stated objectives of the ASEAN Community and the ASEAN Charter to become a more 'people-oriented' organization, it

---

[6] Interview with David Ardhian, Policy Adviser of the People's Coalition for Food Sovereignty (KRKP–Koalisi Rakyat untuk Kedaulatan Pangan), 27 April 2009, Bogor.

Table 5.4 NSAs in Indonesian trade policy-making

NSAs	Policy interests	Constituencies served	Source of funding	Local affiliates	International affiliates	Negotiations active in
Business associations						
Indonesian Chambers of Commerce and Industry (KADIN)	Trade and industrial policies	Other smaller business associations and the wider business community	Membership subscription and donors	Various economic-related government agencies and parliament	ASEAN Chambers of Commerce and Industry International Chambers of Commerce Jakarta–Japan Club Foundation Japan External Trade Organization and various chambers of commerce from key trading partners in Asia and Europe	All key trade negotiations
Indonesian Entrepreneur Associations (APINDO)	Trade and industrial policies	Entrepreneurs	ditto	ditto	n/a	All key trade negotiations
Other general and sectoral business associations	General and sectoral trade and industrial policies	Business community	Varies, but mostly membership subscription and donors	Varies, but mostly Ministry of Trade, Ministry of Industry, Board of Investment	n/a	All bilateral trade negotiations

Academic think-tanks

Centre for Strategic and International Studies (CSIS)	Foreign and domestic economic policies	The academic community, the government and the public	Consultancies and donors (international organizations and Indonesian business community)	Agency (BKPM), and district-level government agencies	ASEAN Institute for Strategic and International Studies (ISIS), Committee for Pacific Economic Cooperation (CPEC), Council of Europe–Asia Cooperation (CEAC), and so on	All key trade negotiations
Institute for Economic and Social Research (LPEM–Lembaga Penyeledikan Ekonomi dan Masyarakat)	General economic policies	ditto	Consultancies and international donors	Various economic-related government agencies and CSOs	Like-minded think-tanks in other countries	n/a
Advisory Group on Economics, Industry and Trade (ECONIT)	Economic, trade and industrial policies	ditto	ditto	ditto	n/a	n/a
Institute for Development Economics and Finance (INDEF)	Economics and finance policies	ditto	ditto	ditto	n/a	n/a

Table 5.4 (cont.)

NSAs	Policy interests	Constituencies served	Source of funding	Local affiliates	International affiliates	Negotiations active in
Centre for Information and Development Studies (CIDES)	Development and economic policies	ditto	ditto	ditto	n/a	n/a
CSOs						
Indonesian Farmers' Association (API)	Agricultural trade policy	28 farmers federations across Sumatra, Java, Bali, Sumbawa, Flores and Central Sulawesi	International donors (primarily from VECO of Belgium)	Ministry of Trade, Ministry of Agriculture	ASEAN Farmers' Association (AFA), Asia–Pacific Network for Food Sovereignty (APNFS)	Multilateral agricultural negotiations
Bina Desa (InDHRRA)	Sustainable agriculture and rural development	Peasant farmers, rural women and fisherfolks	International donors	Local civil society networks (e.g., Anti-Debt Coalition (KAU–Koalisi Anti Utang), Friends of the Earth Indonesia (Walhi–Wahana Lingkungan Hidup), and so on)	Asia–Pacific Women, Law and Development, APNFS, Asian Partnership for the Development of Human Resources in Rural Asia (Asiadhrra), Asian NGO Coalition for Agrarian Reform and Rural Development	Bilateral, regional and multilateral trade negotiations on agriculture

Organization	Focus	Constituency	Funding	Networks / allies	International partners	Trade focus
Business Watch Indonesia (BWI)	Social-economic policy, business democratization and corporate social responsibility (CSR)	Civil society groups, business, government and the academic community	International donors (primarily the Netherlands-based donor agencies)	Various civil society networks (e.g., CSR Consortium, Indonesian Tea Council, National Reference Group of Indonesia on Tea, Indonesian Cacao Alliance)	OECD Watch, Good Electronics, Corporate Europe Observatory (CEO)	Primarily multilateral negotiations
Federation of Indonesian Farmers' Union (FSPI)	Food sovereignty, farmers' rights, women farmers and migration	Members in 12 Indonesian provinces and farmers in general	Subscription and international donors (primarily from Switzerland and France)	Ministry of Agriculture, Ministry of Trade, Forum WTO Indonesia, People's Movements Against Neo-Colonialism and Imperialism	La Via Campesina	All key trade agreements
Hizbut Tahrir	Islamic	Muslims	Membership subscription	Nadhlatul Ulama (NU) and Muhammadiyah	n/a	Not specific, but generally critical of global capitalism
Institute for Essential Services Reform (IESR)	Energy policy and services trade	n/a	International donors (primarily from Europe)	Forum WTO Indonesia	Jubilee South, Solidarity for Asian People's Advocacy (SAPA)	Multilateral services trade negotiations

Table 5.4 (cont.)

NSAs	Policy interests	Constituencies served	Source of funding	Local affiliates	International affiliates	Negotiations active in
International NGO Forum on Indonesian Development (INFID)	Debt, poverty and civilian supremacy	Civil society groups	International donors	INFID is an international coalition	BAPPENAS, Ministry of Finance, and various Indonesian civil society groups (e.g., IGJ, Human Rights Working Group (HRWG), and so on)	Not specific, but generally critical of economic liberalization
Institute for Global Justice (IGJ)	International trade policy	Civil society groups and public	International donors (including the Ford Foundation (US) and 11.11.11 (Belgium))	Ministry of Trade, Ministry of Foreign Affairs, Indonesian WTO Forum	ASEAN, Our World Is Not For Sale (OWINFS), SAPA Working Group on ASEAN, APNFS, Asia–Pacific Research Network (APRN)	All key trade agreements
People's Coalition for Food Sovereignty (KRKP)	Food and agricultural policy	Civil society and farmers	International donors (primarily from VECO and HIVOS (Holland))	Various ad hoc civil society coalitions	APNFS, East Asia Rice Networking Group (EARNG), and G33 CSO Alliance	Agricultural trade negotiations at multilateral, regional and bilateral levels
Confederation of Prosperity Indonesian Labour's Union (KSBSI)	Labour policy on the mining, energy, garment, health, banking, metal, education and	Workforce from the aforementioned sectors	Subscription, entrepreneurship initiatives, and international donors	Labour federations from the sectors represented in the Confederation	International Trade Union Council (ITUC), World Confederation of Labour (WCL) and the International	WTO and ACFTA

					Confederation of Free Trade Unions (ICFTU)	
transportation sectors						
Migrant Care	Migrant labour policy	Migrant labourers	International donors (e.g., Cordait Foundation (Holland) and TIFA (Indonesia))	Justice Working Forum for Migrants, KAU, Women's Networks, and so on	ASEAN, Global Call Against Poverty (GCAP) and the NGO Platform on Migrant Workers Convention	Not specific, but generally involved actively on trade-related issues, such as movement of natural persons
Prakarsa	Globalization and governance	n/a	International donors	IGJ, INFID, and so on	New Rules on Global Finance, One World Trust, Oxfam	Not specific, but generally involved in dialogue about trade governance issues
Women's Solidarity (SP–Solidaritas Perempuan)	Food sovereignty and migration policies	Women, migrant labourers, etc.	International donors	Walhi, Consortium of Agrarian Reform (KPA–Konsorsium Pembaharuan Agraria), KAU, etc.	NGO Forum on ADB, APWLD, Migrant Forum in Asia (MFA), etc.	Not specific, but it has been active in disseminating information concerning the impacts of PTAs on women
Indonesian Consumer Organization (YLKI)	Public services	Consumers	International donors	INFID, Class Action Network, etc.	Health Action International, ASEAN Consumer Groups Association	Varies and depends on the issues discussed in specific trade negotiations

Table 5.5 *Indonesia's PTAs, October 2009*

PTAs	Type of agreement	Signing date	Entry into force
ASEAN Free Trade Area (AFTA)	PTA	1992	1992
ASEAN–China Free Trade Agreement (ACFTA)	PTA and Economic Integration Agreement (EIA)	PTA (2002) and EIA (2007)	Early Harvest Programme (EHP) (2004) and EIA (2007)
ASEAN–Japan Comprehensive Economic Partnership (AJCEP)	FTA and EIA	2003	2008
Indonesia–Japan Economic Partnership Agreement (IJEPA)	FTA and EIA	2007	2008
ASEAN–South Korea Free Trade Agreement (ASKFTA)	FTA	2005	2007
ASEAN–India Free Trade Agreement (AIFTA)	PTA	2009	2010
ASEAN–Australia & New Zealand Free Trade Agreement (AANZFTA)	FTA	2008	2010
ASEAN–EU Free Trade Agreement	FTA	To be negotiated	To be negotiated
Indonesia–US Free Trade Agreement	FTA	To be negotiated	To be negotiated

Note: Analyses in this chapter are based on these PTAs.

is expected that there will be more opportunities in the future for NSAs to influence the ASEAN agenda. Furthermore, collective action with NSAs from other ASEAN countries is also expected to make a significant difference to the nature and outcomes of ASEAN's approach to economic cooperation. Therefore, when it comes to choices in trade forum, regionalism scores relatively high in the preferences of Indonesian NSAs.

However, these preferences should be read against the emergence of strong economic nationalism and the strengthening of Islamic ideology in Indonesia. For example, an Islamic CSO, Hizbut Tahrir, prefers regionalism and bilateralism to multilateralism. Hizbut Tahrir is pessimistic about the prospects of the Doha Round negotiations achieving a win–win situation for both developed and developing countries, and it believes that Indonesia could have better leverage in advancing its interests in the context of southeast Asian regionalism and, to a certain extent, bilateralism, particularly with the countries in the East Asian region.[7]

Indonesian NSAs consider bilateral PTAs to be their least favoured forum for trade negotiations for several reasons. First, the acceleration of trade liberalization as a result of bilateral PTAs is a major concern. Second, Indonesia is seen to lack the financial and human resources and expertise necessary to deal effectively with bilateral negotiations. Third, the bilateral PTA option is perceived by even the most fervent supporters of aggressive liberalization as a way to divert Indonesia's attention from multilateralism.

Nonetheless, there is a view that it is only a matter of time before Indonesia is pulled into bilateral PTAs by its trade partners.[8] The Indonesian business sector shares this view. According to a representative from the Indonesian Entrepreneurs' Association (APINDO – Asosiasi Pengusaha Indonesia), since the government signalled its intention to pursue bilateral PTAs in 2006, the private sector is concerned about the potential for PTA agreements to open the doors to competition from abroad before business is adequately prepared to cope.[9]

Do NSA preferences affect government preferences and policies? As argued above, Indonesian bureaucracy is poorly equipped to develop a coherent and effective trade strategy, and this has contributed to the slow response by government to the PTA challenge.[10] Indeed, as articulated

---

[7] Interview with Hizbut Tahrir spokesman, Muhammad Ismail, 1 May 2009, Jakarta.
[8] Interview with Dr Hadi Soesastro, director of the Centre for Strategic and International Studies (CSIS), 20 April 2009, Jakarta.
[9] Interview with Sofjan Wanandi, chairman of the APINDO, 6 April 2009, Jakarta.
[10] Interview with Hadi Soesastro.

by the officials from Deplu and Depdag, although many trade partners are interested in pursuing bilateral PTAs with Indonesia, the government would prefer to focus on the implementation of existing agreements rather than initiating new ones. Technically speaking, therefore, the government has not changed its preference on its forum choice. Nonetheless, it is likely that the growing resistance of NSAs to bilateral PTAs has reinforced the traditional preference of the Indonesian government for multilateralism.

5.2   Non-state actor strategies to influence government

Indonesian NSAs deploy different methods of advocacy to influence the government's trade policy, and this depends in large part on the ideological leaning of the NSA, as well as attitudes towards the government in general. For example, given the traditional opposition to neoliberalism in Indonesia, many NSAs advocate protection of local industries and small farmers. However, given the inclination of the government to pursue a neoliberal economic policy, direct lobbying of policy-makers is often viewed as ineffective, and forces NSAs to adopt public campaigning activities in an effort to secure political support for their positions. By contrast, more pragmatic NSAs, especially those in the business sector who are willing to accept a gradual and managed approach to trade liberalization, are more confident than their protectionist counterparts in their ability to influence policy-makers through dialogue.

5.2.1   How to influence?

While conscious of the differences that distinguish the various trade fora, Indonesian NSAs do not necessarily adjust their advocacy strategies to specific trade agreements. Initiatives such as involvement in meetings or committees organized by the government, self-initiated interaction with the government and other lobbying activities, policy advocacy publications and public campaigns are used by different groups to influence trade policy. The following analysis further elaborates each of the commonly used advocacy methods in Indonesia (see Table 5.6).

Given its commitment to pursue transparency and openness, it is now common practice for government to invite the participation of NSAs in meetings to discuss and exchange views on the country's trade policy. However, only a minority of NSAs find this form of engagement very useful. Indeed, of eighteen respondents interviewed, only five thought that participation in the government-initiated meetings and committees would make some difference to Indonesian trade policy. The remaining thirteen NSAs gave modest importance to this advocacy method. This is

Table 5.6 *NSAs' methods of influencing trade negotiations*

NSAs	NSA's methods of influencing trade negotiations				
	Participating in meetings/ committees organized by government	Self-initiated interaction with government	Publication and broadcasting activities	Public campaigns	Others
Business associations					
APINDO	1	1	3	2	n/a
Academia					
CSIS	2	1	1	4	n/a
University of Indonesia, LPEM–UI	3	3	1	3	n/a
University of Indonesia, FISIP	3	3	1	3	n/a
CSOs					
API	1	1	1	1	Mass mobilization in international trade negotiations
Bina Desa	2	2	3	1	Capacity building to trade constituencies
BWI	1	1	1	1	n/a
FSPI	4	3	2	1	International networking
Hizbut Tahrir	5	2	1	1	n/a
IESR	2	2	1	5	International networking
IGJ	2	2	2	1	International networking
INFID	2	2	5	4	International networking
KRKP	1	1	3	4	Capacity building to trade constituencies
KASBI	2	2	5	5	International networking
Migrant Care	5	5	4	1	n/a
Prakarsa	3	3	3	3	n/a
YLKI	5	2	1	1	n/a

not surprising, and there appears to be a bias on the part of government to take advice from the business community and a handful of trade experts.[11] Instead of transforming inputs into policy, trade discussion forums, such as the Indonesian WTO Forum, have been used by the government only to *socialize* NSAs to the government's policy preferences and to serve as a form of public scrutiny of government policies.[12]

On the other hand, some members of the Indonesian business sector believe that the government has taken appropriate measures to involve them in trade policy-making. Since the implementation of any trade policy would generate significant impacts on the private sector, representatives of this sector believe that such an approach is logical.[13] Other non-business NSAs, however, do not share this view, and argue instead that given the extensive coverage of international trade today, it is an issue of concern for the Indonesian population as a whole, including for those working in sectors particularly exposed to the effects of liberalization, such as agriculture, health and education. Although liberalization makes available more options for consumers to purchase and consume the products and services they desire, it also comes with its share of burdens, particularly for poorer groups in the community, such as small farmers who are incapable of competing with the flood of foreign agricultural goods or general low-income consumers incapable of securing access to affordable and good quality health and education services.[14]

Overall, debates about international trade policy in Indonesia remain in the realm of the elites. Apart from a small number of individuals and organizations, there are very few CSOs that have a good grasp of trade policy issues.[15] This helps to explain the relatively low turnout of representatives from CSOs and grassroots community in government-initiated trade discussion fora.

Many Indonesian NSAs consider the use of self-initiated interaction directly with the government to be a crucial means of influencing the government's trade policy. Yet such a method has never been easy to implement, as this approach depends on the development of trusting

---

[11] Interview with Fabby Tumewa, executive director of the Institute for Essential Services Reform, 28 March 2009, Jakarta.

[12] Interview with Indah Sukmaningsih, executive director of the Institute for Global Justice, 8 March 2009, Jakarta.

[13] Interview with Sofyan Wanandi, chairman of the Association of Indonesian Entrepreneurs (APINDO–Asosiasi Pengusaha Indonesia), 6 April 2009, Jakarta.

[14] Interview with Indah Sukmaningsih of IGJ.

[15] Interview with David Ardhian of KRKP.

relationships with government officials as well as absorbs funds, time and energy.[16] Furthermore, the successful use of this method also depends largely on the knowledge of the NSAs about the network of the country's key trade policy-making actors. Apart from the private sector and a few research institutes and CSOs, such as the CSIS and IGJ, respectively, there are not many Indonesian NSAs that put considerable effort into identifying the trade policy network and policy-making process.

The publication of materials such as research studies, briefing papers, factual notes and public statements are normally used for two key purposes: (1) to raise awareness of the public, particularly those at the grassroots, or educate the members of NSAs' own networks;[17] and (2) to serve as policy inputs to the government. Although considered to be a popular advocacy tool, most NSAs, particularly CSOs, prefer their publications to be directed at the public, instead of specifically targeted at the officials. Nonetheless, educating and influencing the public on trade-related issues is not always easy. While some issues, such as the importation of rice, could easily be turned into populist advocacy, complex issues, such as intellectual property rights and financial sector liberalization, require greater awareness-raising among the public.

Some NSAs also carry out public campaigns for the purpose of creating public pressure on government in respect of trade policy.[18] In some instances, public campaigns have also been used to support the Indonesian government's position. For example, during the visit to Jakarta in February 2007 of WTO director general, Pascal Lamy, a group of Indonesian CSOs read out public statements at the Indonesian WTO Forum which were critical of Lamy's visit and supported the position of the Group of 33 in the WTO (Kinasih 2007).[19]

Another advocacy activity considered important by many NSAs, particularly the CSO community, is international networking. Many Indonesian NSAs have established contacts with like-minded foreign organizations, which not only provide key information and

---

[16] Interview with Huzna Zahir, executive director of the Indonesian Consumer Organization (Yayasan Lembaga Konsumen Indonesia), 3 June 2009, Jakarta.

[17] One example being the Indonesian Farmers' Association (API–Asosiasi Petani Indonesia). Interview with M. Nuruddin, secretary general of API, 27 March 2009, Jakarta.

[18] Interview with Achmad Yacub, the head of the Department of National Strategic Studies of the Federation of the Indonesian Farmers' Union (FSPI–Federasi Serikat Petani Indonesia), 3 April 2009, Jakarta.

[19] According to David Ardhian of KRKP, a number of Indonesian CSOs were also the initiators of the coalition group among G33 countries' CSOs. This coalition is composed primarily of Asian CSOs and generally supports the position of the G33 countries.

capacity-building assistance directly to local actors, but also provide, through their own advocacy work, leverage to local NSAs' position towards policy initiatives initiated by the government. The participation of international CSO activists in the advocacy work of Indonesian NSAs has helped to raise government and public awareness of trade-related issues of potential relevance to Indonesia. In this context, international CSO activists often complement the domestic policy dialogue by sharing knowledge and best practice on how to pursue an effective and accountable trade policy that reflects the socio-economic development needs of the country. Furthermore, it is not uncommon to find that some international CSOs help the formulation of the Indonesian government's trade policy. International CSOs, such as the Third World Network (TWN) and Oxfam, have developed a positive reputation among policy-makers in the country.

5.2.2   Whom to influence?

As Table 5.7 shows, different NSAs tend to have different target groups for their advocacy. NSAs that target policy-makers are often involved in exchanges and policy discussions with ministers, government officials and legislators. Other NSAs target their advocacy efforts entirely on the public.

Among those NSAs that target their advocacy efforts on key policy-makers, such as IGJ, the Institute for Essential Services Reform (IESR) and the Confederation of Indonesian Prosperity Trade Union (KSBSI– Konfederasi Serikat Buruh Sejahtera Indonesia),[20] having the economic-related ministers influenced by their policy input is important. In particular, they focus on influencing the Trade Minister, given his/her key role in shaping the country's trade policy as well as leading the international negotiation team. Other prime advocacy targets among the governmental network include the Coordinating Minister for Economy, the Minister of Finance and the Minister of Foreign Affairs. Advocacy efforts are also targeted at lower level officials within these ministries. For many NSAs, particularly CSOs, policy discussions with these officials are far more strategic than having the opportunity to carry out policy exchanges at ministerial level, in part because officials tend to have far better knowledge on the details and substances of the country's trade policy.[21] It is not

---

[20] Interview with Ediartho Sitinjak, a senior staff member at the KSBSI, 25 March 2009, Jakarta.
[21] Interview with David Ardhian of KRKP and Henry Herneardhi, the managing director of Business Watch Indonesia (BWI), 23 April 2009, Jakarta.

Table 5.7 *NSAs' targets of advocacies*

NSAs	NSA's targets of advocacies				
	Ministers/ vice ministers	Government officials	Legislators	Public opinion	Others
Business associations					
APINDO	1	1	4	3	n/a
Academia					
CSIS	1	1	4	2	n/a
University of Indonesia, LPEM	2	2	4	3	n/a
University of Indonesia, FISIP	2	2	4	3	n/a
CSOs					
API	3	1	5	1	n/a
Bina Desa	5	5	2	1	n/a
BWI	2	1	1	1	The academic community
FSPI	3	4	2	1	n/a
Hizbut Tahrir	1	2	4	1	n/a
IESR	1	2	5	4	n/a
IGJ	3	1	4	1	Mass media (journalists) and the academic community
INFID	1	2	3	4	n/a
KRKP	2	1	2	2	Mass media (journalists)
KSBI	1	5	5	5	n/a
Migrant Care	1	1	3	2	n/a
Prakarsa	3	3	4	3	n/a
YLKI	4	1	5	1	n/a

uncommon to find CSO activists develop both professional and personal relationships with officials from relevant ministries, which allows them more space and opportunities to relay their advocacy messages via these state actors.[22]

Indonesian NSAs generally make only modest efforts to influence the position of the DPR. In fact, among eighteen NSAs that participated in the research interviews, only three actually saw the DPR as 'very important' or 'important' as a key target of their advocacy efforts. There are several reasons for this. First, trade literacy remains a key problem for many members of DPR, and this applies to both members from Commission VI (trade) and other trade-related commissions. A member of parliament from Commission XI confirms this argument, and blamed the lack of financial and human resources as the source of legislators' incapacity to engage fully on trade policy discussion.[23] Consequently, the DPR lacks capacity to deal with international trade policy issues. And when the DPR does become active, it is often in reaction to strong public pressure.[24] However, given the public's lack of knowledge about international trade issues, it is rare that such pressures emerge in the first place. Furthermore, given its executive power to negotiate and implement trade agreements, the government can bypass the authority of the DPR,[25] and this has been the case with the implementation of the ASEAN–China FTA, which was never ratified by the DPR. Consequently, this lowers the importance of the DPR in the trade policy-making of the country.[26]

Most Indonesian NSAs consider the mobilization of public opinion on certain trade issues as critical in order to influence trade policy-making. Among eighteen NSA respondents, eleven ranked public opinion as 'very important' and/or 'important' to their advocacy work. For these NSAs, the rationale to secure public opinion is a given since the positions that they advocate are supposedly the concerns of the general public. One key challenge, though, is rendering trade policy issues that

---

[22] Interview with Huzna Zahir of YLKI.
[23] Interview with Dr Dradjat Wibowo, Member of Parliament, Commission XI, from the National Mandate Party (PAN–Partai Amanat Nasional), 21 April 2009, Jakarta.
[24] Interview with David Ardhian of KRKP.
[25] Interview with Fabby Tumewa of IESR.
[26] Articles 10 and 11 of the Law No. 24/2000 of the government of the Republic of Indonesia concerning international treaties also stipulate any international treaty that does not affect the existing law is not required to pass through the ratification process from the DPR.

are sometimes technical or complex accessible to the public. Some NSAs target journalists as a means of mobilising public opinion on trade-related matters.[27]

Non-state actors also seek to advance their interests by raising awareness among other NSAs. Civil society organizations often focus on measures to promote capacity-building among local community groups so as to enable them to engage further on trade policy discussions; but lack of support from donors has made this approach difficult in a country as big as Indonesia. Civil society organizations also target their counterparts in the academic community as a potential channel to reach out to the government. Indeed, many among the academic community are part of the so-called 'track two' process, an informal framework where academics have been able to develop good relationships with key economic policy-makers. In fact, many of these policy-makers have themselves worked to influence government policies through 'track two' processes, most notably the Indonesian Trade Minister, Dr Mari Elka Pangestu.[28] For many trade activists in the country, therefore, establishing a good relationship with the academic circle is nearly as important as developing relationships with key policy-makers.

6   Conclusion

This study has revealed some intriguing findings in relation to trade policy-making in Indonesia and the question of forum choice. First, in relation to trade policy-making, Indonesia is still faced with considerable challenges in its effort to make an effective trade policy that reflects both the concerns and aspirations of all its stakeholders. The current Indonesian administration, as was the case with its predecessors, has generally failed to acknowledge trade as an issue of concern for many sectors of society. Thus far, trade policy-making remains the business of government and the private sector. Although democratic governance has made it possible for CSOs to engage in the formal trade policy-making process, there is little evidence to suggest that their inputs are

---

[27] Interview with Indah Sukmaningsih of IGJ.
[28] Other prominent economists in the current cabinet include Dr Boediono, a former professor at the Gadjah Mada University, and Dr Sri Mulyani, a former professor at the University of Indonesia.

being taken into consideration by the government. Non-state actors that challenge or criticize trade liberalization, for example, are hardly considered as relevant actors to be consulted by the government due to their ideological views.

Second, while improvements to the existing trade policy-making structure are still needed, there is also a significant gap between the government's trade policy and the aspirations of the grassroots community. Apart from the failure of the government to communicate its policies effectively to the public, the gap is also due to the lack of understanding of trade issues on the side of the grassroots community. Outside the private sector and the academic community, NSAs have engaged government in debate on the merits of trade liberalization, but have failed to provide relevant technical inputs on trade policy. It is also important to note that few Indonesian CSOs have shown much enthusiasm for advocacy on trade issues; those that do are often doing this to comply with the interests of the donor community.

Third, in terms of the question of forum, there has been a major shift in the attitude of Indonesian NSAs from either hostility or indifference to favourable views towards the multilateral trading system. Although critical of WTO negotiations, which are perceived to favour the interests of developed countries, the proliferation of bilateral PTAs and their potential to accelerate liberalization are of concern to many NSAs.

References

Basri, C. and Patunru, A. A. 2009. '*Why Government Hurts the Poor? The Case of Indonesia's Rice Protection*', Paper prepared for the conference on 'Globalization, Growth and Development in Asia', organized by Leverhulme Centre for Globalization and Economic Policy, University of Nottingham, Kuala Lumpur, 13–15 January 2009, accessed 12 April 2009, available at: www.nottingham.ac.uk/shared/shared_levevents/conferences/Malaysia_ConferenceJan2009/Basri-Patunru-Notingham.pdf.

Bird, K., Hill, H. and Cuthbertson, S. 2007. '*Making Trade Policy in a New Democracy After a Deep Crisis: Indonesia*', Research School of Pacific and Asian Studies (RPAS) Working Paper No. 2007/01, RSPAS, Research School of Pacific and Asian Studies, the Australian National University, Canberra.

Chandra, A. C. 2007, 'Democratic Governance and Practices in the Future of US–Indonesia Free Trade Agreement', *Indonesian Quarterly*, **35**, 2: 53–77.

—— 2008, *Indonesia and the ASEAN Free Trade Agreement: Nationalists and Regional Integration Strategy*. Lanham, MD: Lexington Books.

Coleman, P., Cornish, S. and Drake, P. 2007. *Arndt's Story: The Life of an Australian Economist*. Canberra: Asia-Pacific Press.

Depdag (Departemen Perdagangan – Ministry of Trade) n.d. *Perkembangan Ekspor-Impor Indonesia (Indonesian Exports-Imports Update*, accessed 10 February 2009, available at: www.depdag.go.id/index.php?option=statistik&itemid=06.

Kinasih, H. N. 2007. 'Masyarakat Sipil Kritisi Kunjungan Pascal Lamy' ('Civil Society Criticizes Pascal Lamy's Visit'), *Kabar Indonesia*, 2 March, accessed 11 June 2009, available at: www.kabarindonesia.com/berita.php?pil= 8&jd=Masyarakat+Sipil+Kritisi+Kunjungan+Pascal+Lamy&dn= 20070302031742.

Pangestu, M. E. 2006. *Indonesia, International Trade Negotiations and Fair Trade*, Keynote Address at the 'Ke Arah Liberalisasi Perdagangan yang Lebih Luas: Strategi Indonesia dalam Menghadapi Tantangan Perundingan Perdagangan Multilateral, Regional, dan Bilateral' ('Towards Greater Trade Liberalization: Indonesia's Strategy in Facing the Challenges of Multilateral, Regional and Bilateral Trade Negotiations'), Ministry of Foreign Affairs, Jakarta, 2 February.

Pangestu, M. E., Aswicahyono, H., Anas, T. and Ardyanto, D. 2002. 'The Evolution of Competition Policy in Indonesia', *Review of Industrial Organization* **21**, 2: 205–24.

Soesastro, H. and Basri, M. C. 2005. *The Political Economy of Trade Policy in Indonesia*, CSIS Working Paper Series WPE 092, CSIS, Jakarta, accessed 10 October 2008, available at: www.csis.or.id/papers/wpf092.

Soesastro, H., and Soejachmoen, M. P. 2007. *Towards an Effective Trade Policy: Challenges for Indonesia*, the EU–Indonesia Trade Support Programme, Delegation of the European Commission to Indonesia, Brunei Darussalam and East Timor and the Ministry of Trade of the Republic of Indonesia, Jakarta.

Vanzetti, D., McGuire, G. and Prabowo 2005. *Trade Policy at the Crossroads – The Indonesian Story*, Policy Issues in International Trade and Commodities Study Series No. 28, United Nations Conference on Trade and Development, Geneva, accessed 23 June 2009, available at: www.unctad.org/en/docs/itcdtab29_en.pdf.

Weinstein, F. B. 2007. *Indonesian Foreign Policy and the Dilemma of Dependence: From Sukarno to Soeharto.* Jakarta: Equinox Publishing.

Zabriskie, P. 2008. 'After Suharto' *Prospect Magazine*, 143 (February), available at: www.prospect-magazine.co.uk/pdfarticle.php?id=10039, accessed 10 April 2009.

6

Thailand

THITINAN PONGSUDHIRAK

1 Introduction

The politicization of trade policy-making in Thailand is arguably more
pronounced than elsewhere in the world, including at the global level
where multilateral trade negotiations (MTNs) under the World Trade
Organization (WTO) are currently stalled. Indeed, the Thai case of trade
policy quagmire is quite dramatic for having adversely impinged on the
country's body politic to the extent that a popularly elected government
was ousted in a military coup, and an anti-free trade agreement (FTA)
bias worked its way into a new military-organized constitution, contributing to a prolonged and protracted political crisis. That Thai trade policy
has become increasingly politicized over the first decade of the twenty-
first century is attributable to a number of dynamics, some in parallel to
trade policy experiences in the rest of the world, others more specific to
domestic circumstances.

The end of the Cold War and the concomitant wave of democratization in the developing world opened up the arena of trade policy, which
had previously been insulated and considered the exclusive domain of
technocratic expertise and bureaucratic wherewithal at the policy level.
Inclusiveness and demands for public participation made logical headway as post-1988 politics in Thailand entered a period of inexorable political liberalization.[1] After a military coup in February 1991 threatened
to produce a disguised military dictatorship through elections and parliamentary rule, a 'people's power' movement took hold and expelled the
military from government in a Bangkok-based, middle class-led popular

---

[1] Following a long period of military–authoritarian rule during 1947–73, Thai politics
opened up to greater participation amid periodic turbulence and turmoil, and settled into
a relatively stable period of 'semi-democratic' rule during 1980–8, when electoral politics
and parliamentary rule came to the fore in earnest under an unelected prime minister,
General Prem Tinsulanond, who was supported by the military.

uprising in May 1992. The post-May 1992 political reform movement witnessed an unprecedented expansion of civil society organizations (CSOs), culminating in the reform-driven 1997 constitution.

This period of democratic exuberance in Thailand was accompanied by a dynamic international and regional trading environment. The final stretch of the Uruguay Round multilateral trade negotiations in the early 1990s coincided with the rise of regional preferential trade agreements (PTAs) in Southeast Asia. Thailand was instrumental in the formation of the ASEAN Free Trade Area in 1992, which arrived on the heels of the Asia–Pacific Economic Cooperation (APEC) forum in 1989, the latter promoted by Australia and the United States. The early and mid-1990s also saw the proliferation of sub-regional economic integration projects, such as the Indonesia–Malaysia–Thailand Growth Triangle and the Japan-supported Greater Mekong Sub-region economic cooperation and infrastructure development, comprising the mainland Southeast Asian economies and southern China. During this period of regional trade dynamism, Thai bureaucracy, particularly its foreign and commerce ministries, was in the lead in trade policy formulation, negotiations and implementation. Lacking the requisite expertise and technical know-how, elected politicians and the government of the day relied on technocrats and experts in the specialized bureaucratic agencies to formulate positions and carry out trade policy.

While the early to mid-1990s was filled with great promise of growth and dynamism for Thailand and its neighbouring economies, the regional economic environment soured after the 1997–8 economic crisis set in, which began in Thailand in July 1997 and infected other economies in Asia soon thereafter. The International Monetary Fund (IMF) was called in to set up bail-out programmes for three major Asian economies: namely, Indonesia, South Korea and Thailand. The severe sociopolitical repercussions of Asia's sharp economic downturn brought down the incumbent governments in Thailand and Indonesia. During the crisis and recovery phases, finance and banking dominated economic policy discussions. The headlines were about bail-out conditionalities, hedge funds, exchange rate gyrations and corruption and cronyism, on the one hand, and the perils of speculative capital, on the other hand. The post-Uruguay Round trade arena was subsumed by these financial sector and exchange rate crises. GATT itself, moreover, was being retooled and institutionalized into the WTO.

But trade regained importance by the start of the twenty-first century. As a new round of MTNs was broached, and as the effects of the 1997–8

Asian crisis dissipated, international economic cooperation turned once again to the global trade arena. For Thailand, the Asian crisis and its wrenching and latent impact was critical to trade policy in the new Doha Round multilateral negotiations, because it gave rise to economic nationalism, which was exploited by Thaksin Shinawatra and his Thai Rak Thai (TRT) party to spectacular success. The TRT won the election in January 2001 and in February 2005 won a landslide election victory, becoming the first to be re-elected and command a one-party government. Thaksin, a telecommunications tycoon, parlayed his formidable parliamentary majority into an authoritarian style of government. Trade policy was a key plank of his policy-making apparatus. His authoritarian tendencies personalized and centralized trade policy-making, turning the emphasis away from multilateral negotiations towards PTAs, particularly bilateral FTAs. Thaksin's bilateral FTA focus, in turn, generated opposition from a wide range of vested-interest groups, particularly non-state actors (NSAs) comprising a broad array of CSOs and non-government organizations.

During the period when mounting opposition to his conflicts of interest and abuses of power gathered force from late 2005 to the military coup that ousted his administration in September 2006, Thaksin's FTA preferences were cited by his opponents among the NSAs as a justification for his overthrow. As enumerated below, these NSAs had already been biased against free trade orthodoxy in general, and the MTNs in particular, in the belief that the WTO was the lopsided den where powerful and developed economies exploited unfair advantages over less developed countries. Thaksin's top–down, authoritarian trade policy preferences galvanized these NSAs to turn against bilateral FTAs. The post-Thaksin political environment is unsurprisingly hostile to bilateral FTAs, with the glaring exception of the Japan–Thailand Economic Partnership Agreement (JTEPA). Overall, Thailand after Thaksin's downfall has yet to recover its trade policy footing. Thailand's trade policy-making is stuck in the quicksand of the country's political crisis. The concentric circles of FTA negotiations and agreements started by Thaksin have yet to be recalibrated and reset. Thailand's trade policy is thus in a holding pattern, a hostage to its domestic political turmoil (see Pasuk and Baker 2004; Thitinan 2008).

Accordingly, this chapter examines trade policy-making in Thailand's domestic setting, teasing out the political context and contours of trade policy and the inner workings and underpinnings behind them, with particular reference to the role of NSAs. The underlying assumption is that NSAs exert palpable pressure on trade policy-making, a pivotal role hitherto neglected. In the Thai case, as substantiated by semi-structured interviews and relevant secondary sources, the NSAs coalesced and generated decisive momentum as part of the build-up to the crisis and coup that expelled Thaksin from office. These NSAs, which cohered under the banner of 'FTA Watch', seized the post-coup landscape to inject provisions into a new constitution to widen participation and government accountability, but in the process has rendered Thai trade policy sticky, unworkable and unable to move in any meaningful direction, generally opposed to further liberalization measures such as privatization and the relaxation of legal restrictions on foreign investment. The upshot is that both trade policy-making at home and MTNs abroad must find ways to reconcile with and accommodate NSA preferences in order to achieve freer trade at a time when the future of the world trading system hangs in the balance.

2   Thailand's trade patterns

While the value of Thailand's international trade as compared with its gross domestic product (GDP) has represented more than 120% for the past two decades, with exports accounting for more than 60%, its origins and destinations have shifted significantly over the years since the country joined GATT in November 1982; a membership that carried over into the WTO from 1995. In the 1980s and 1990s, the proportion of Thai–US and Thai–EU two-way trade declined from more than 25% to less than 20%, respectively, whereas trade with Japan increased from 15% to 20%. Thailand's intra-regional trade in the ASEAN framework similarly rose from single to double digits after the creation of the ASEAN Free Trade Area (AFTA) in 1992 based on the Common Effective Preferential Tariffs (see Naya *et al.* 1992). The most significant change was the trade expansion with China, which has become Thailand's third largest trading partner after ASEAN and Japan, owing to Chinese membership of the WTO in the mid-1990s. Another important trade partner is Australia, which signed an FTA with Thailand in July 2004.

Table 6.1 reflects these trends. The value of Thailand's international trade has increased in absolute terms over the past two decades, thanks largely to trade liberalization efforts in GATT/WTO negotiations, but also to structural reforms that have diversified Thai exports (see Chaipat 1992). In percentage terms, intra-regional trade with post-AFTA ASEAN is Thailand's trade linchpin. The genesis of AFTA was as much political as economic. The end of the Cold War in the late 1980s and ensuing trade integration in North America (i.e., the North American Free Trade

Table 6.1 *Thailand's major trade partners, major destinations and major suppliers*

Country	Value (US$ million)				Share (%)			
	2005	2006	2007	2008	2005	2006	2007	2008
Major destinations								
World	110,937.66	129,720.43	153,864.96	177,775.20	100.00	100.00	100.00	100.00
ASEAN (9)	24,390.42	27,021.71	32,791.08	40,151.28	21.99	20.83	21.31	22.59
Japan	15,089.85	16,385.90	18,119.05	20,093.64	13.60	12.63	11.78	11.30
USA	16,996.64	19,449.60	19,415.61	20,274.76	15.32	14.99	12.62	11.40
EU (27)	15,100.07	18,006.24	21,688.17	23,392.07	13.61	13.88	14.10	13.16
Major suppliers								
World	118,175.23	128,772.33	139,958.90	179,223.26	100.00	100.00	100.00	100.00
ASEAN (9)	21,623.66	23,598.77	25,066.88	30,139.92	18.30	18.33	17.91	16.82
Japan	26,032.78	25,667.61	28,381.53	33,534.25	22.03	19.93	20.28	18.71
USA	8,683.15	9,587.90	9,494.37	11,423.25	7.35	7.45	6.78	6.37
EU (27)	10,802.79	11,242.57	11,952.19	14,332.58	9.14	8.73	8.54	8.00

Source: Ministry of Commerce.

Agreement) and Europe (i.e., the EU Single Market) prompted ASEAN to get its act together and bolster its economic cooperation (see Stubbs 2000). Since then, AFTA's intra-regional trade has steadily expanded. For Thailand, by 2008 AFTA accounted for more than US$70 billion in trade, whereas trade with Japan came in at more than US$53 billion. The composition of trade with AFTA is dominated by Malaysia, Singapore and Indonesia. In 2008, Thailand's trade with these three ASEAN members was more than twice that of the other six members combined.

Trade with China, on the other hand, more than doubled in a decade to US$36 billion in 2008. Trade with Australia, Thailand's seventh largest partner, totalled more than US$13 billion in the same year. Corresponding figures indicate a gradual rise in trade value with the United States, but at a slower pace compared with others such as ASEAN and China. From the status of Thailand's largest and most strategically important trade partner in the 1980s, the United States now ranks fourth, behind ASEAN, Japan and China. The expanded European Union naturally accounted for a substantial amount, but this is spread out among its twenty-seven members, led by Germany, the United Kingdom and the Netherlands, Thailand's thirteenth, eighteenth and nineteenth largest partners, respectively. The overall pattern of trade expansion suggests that Thailand's international commerce with the rest of the world, apart from traditional partners such as ASEAN, Japan, the United States and the European Union, has expanded markedly, led by new and burgeoning players such as China and Australia.[2]

In terms of major export and import items, Thailand remains an important commodity producer of rice and rubber (see Table 6.2). More important, it has become a regional assembler of automobiles and electronics. The auto industry has spawned related auto parts and accessories competencies. Thailand's auto story has been so successful that it has earned widespread acclaim as being the 'Detroit of Asia'. This story harks back to the post-Plaza Accord conditions in the late 1980s that enabled Thailand to become a hub for the relocation of Japanese auto companies due to the appreciation of the yen and local export promotion policies. The electronics and electrical products followed a similar route due to conducive government policies and tax incentives from the Thai Board of Investment. The petrochemicals export industry is a relative newcomer to the scene, but it has shown immense potential. In addition, the export

---

[2] For figures in this section, see also trade statistics on the Ministry of Commerce's website: available at: www.dtn.go.th/dtn/tradeinfo.

Table 6.2 *Thailand's major exports and imports*

Main exports from Thailand (2005–8)

No.	Products	Value (US$ million)				Share (%)			
		2005	2006	2007	2008	2005	2006	2007	2008
1	Automatic data pro-cessing machines and parts thereof	11,848.66	14,869.39	17,331.58	18,384.16	10.68	11.46	11.26	10.34
2	Automobiles, auto parts and accessories	7,745.44	9,524.19	12,978.12	15,585.53	6.98	7.34	8.43	8.77
3	Precious stones and jewellery	3,232.66	3,668.29	5,381.75	8,270.07	2.91	2.83	3.50	4.65
4	Refined fuels	2,352.11	3,648.86	4,097.09	7,913.19	2.12	2.81	2.66	4.45
5	Electronic integrated circuits	5,950.64	7,029.98	8,418.14	7,241.30	5.36	5.42	5.47	4.07
6	Rubber	3,709.99	5,396.59	5,639.98	6,791.73	3.34	4.16	3.67	3.82
7	Rice	2,328.96	2,583.04	3,467.43	6,204.08	2.10	1.99	2.25	3.49
8	Polymers of ethylene, propylene, etc. in primary forms	4,198.45	4,498.43	5,212.30	5,520.00	3.78	3.47	3.39	3.11
9	Iron and steel and their products	2,895.63	3,528.61	4,570.55	5,361.49	2.61	2.72	2.97	3.02
10	Rubber products	2,351.20	3,082.00	3,653.74	4,549.81	2.12	2.38	2.37	2.56
Total 10 records		46,613.73	57,829.37	70,750.69	85,821.36	42.02	44.58	45.98	48.28
Other		64,323.93	71,891.05	83,114.27	91,953.84	57.98	55.42	54.02	51.72
Total		110,937.66	129,720.43	153,864.96	177,775.20	100.00	100.00	100.00	100.00

Table 6.2 (*cont.*)

Main imports to Thailand (2005–8)

No.	Products	Value (US$ million)				Share (%)			
		2005	2006	2007	2008	2005	2006	2007	2008
1	Crude oil	16,998.74	20,111.60	20,405.79	30,159.78	14.38	15.62	14.58	16.83
2	Machinery and parts	10,970.27	11,315.36	12,172.07	14,880.86	9.28	8.79	8.70	8.30
3	Iron, steel and products	8,696.24	7,412.42	8,575.37	13,759.10	7.36	5.76	6.13	7.68
4	Chemicals	8,168.52	8,828.11	10,020.87	12,644.50	6.91	6.86	7.16	7.06
5	Electrical machinery and parts	9,209.78	9,393.29	9,503.13	10,742.87	7.79	7.29	6.79	5.99
6	Electrical circuit panels	7,985.72	8,628.65	9,822.57	9,197.13	6.76	6.70	7.02	5.13
7	Jewellery including silver bars and gold	3,924.59	3,890.83	4,117.30	8,856.15	3.32	3.02	2.94	4.94
8	Other metal ores, metal waste scrap	4,339.72	6,081.34	7,129.55	8,004.60	3.67	4.72	5.09	4.47
9	Computers, accessories and parts	6,803.47	7,597.40	7,520.38	7,815.32	5.76	5.90	5.37	4.36
10	Vegetables and vegetable products	2,241.58	2,298.78	2,847.56	4,367.46	1.90	1.79	2.03	2.44
Total 10 records		79,338.62	85,557.77	92,114.59	120,427.77	67.14	66.44	65.82	67.19
Other		38,836.62	43,214.56	47,844.31	58,795.49	32.86	33.56	34.18	32.81
Total		118,175.23	128,772.33	139,958.90	179,223.26	100.00	100.00	100.00	100.00

Source: Ministry of Commerce, Thailand.

of services by way of tourism has accounted for more than 6% of GDP, giving rise to spill-over development of hotels, restaurants and other services. In turn, these have turned into meetings, incentives, conventions, and exhibitions (MICE) activities.

Traditionally, the largest imported product is crude oil, which has taken up around 10% of the overall import bill. Despite considerable deposits of natural gas at home and purchase from nearby resource-rich neighbours such as Myanmar and Laos for gas and hydropower, respectively, imported petroleum remains Thailand's energy lifeline. But local refinery capacity has expanded into petrochemicals and chemicals, enabling Thailand to develop heavier industries in the process. The story of imported inputs is the same for electronics and electrical products. Tax incentives, industrial estates and export processing zones have transformed Thailand into a hub for exports of integrated circuits, computers and computer parts and electrical products, driven by imported inputs. The Thai economy remains sandwiched between the economies with higher value-added labour productivity, such as South Korea, Taiwan and Malaysia, and those with cheaper labour, particularly China and India. During the Thaksin years, industrial upgrading efforts and cluster development projects were mooted with the lofty aim of becoming a member of the Organization for Economic Cooperation and Development. But the military coup and its aftermath have landed the Thai economy back in the structural sandwich between competitors with higher skills and a cheaper labour pool. The broad sectoral outlook views services output as representing just over 50% of GDP, with industry around 40% and agriculture around 9%.

3   State and non-state actors

While Thailand's trade policy framework revolves around cabinet decisions, its formulation in all facets (i.e., bilateral, sub-regional, regional and multilateral) is more complex. It is conventionally governed by the International Economic Policy Coordination Committee (IEPCC), comprising the ministers of the finance, foreign affairs, agriculture and cooperatives, and industry ministries, along with the permanent secretaries of foreign affairs and commerce. The prime minister or a designated deputy prime minister chairs the committee, and the commerce minister is *ex officio* vice chair, with the director general of the International Economic Affairs of the Ministry of Foreign Affairs (MFA) acting as committee secretary. Although the IEPCC has long been the dominant body in setting out trade policy directions, the Thaksin government appointed a clutch of negotiating teams, each with an overall team leader, to supervise Thailand's PTAs (see below) in November 2004. In addition, an FTA Strategy and Negotiations Committee was established around the same time.

At the height of Thaksin's rule and its FTA momentum, the various FTA teams and the Strategy and Negotiations Committee effectively eclipsed the IEPCC, which became temporarily dormant. This line of trade policy command was part and parcel of Thaksin's top–down CEO economic policy-making approach (Bidhya 2004). It circumvented the bloated bureaucracy[3] and sidestepped senior bureaucrats by streamlining and centralising decision-making at Government House. Prior to Thaksin's rule, the ministries of commerce and foreign affairs would normally have been the lead agencies in trade policy formulation and consideration through the IEPCC. But under the Thaksin regime, they were bypassed in favour of cabinet members and political appointees, who reported directly to the Strategy and Negotiations Committee and to Thaksin himself at Government House. On the other hand, parliamentary oversight was marginalized by Thaksin and his ruling TRT party's firm control over the lower house. Business associations appeared subservient to the Thaksin government's FTA preferences. Non-state actor stakeholders, however, took Thaksin to task. In October 2003, a hitherto motley mix of seventeen NGOs formed an effective and ultimately powerful 'FTA Watch' group that opposed trade policy-making under Thaksin. The FTA Watch activists and proponents and their extensive networks ultimately became a potent and decisive political force to reckon with on trade policy, as outlined below.

As Thaksin's CEO-style of management over Thai FTAs became a source of street protests against his rule, the post-Thaksin era engendered strong NSA reactions. The NSA backlash was so severe that anti-FTA provisions were incorporated into Article 190 of the post-coup 2007 constitution.[4] This charter provision stipulated that international agreements with binding treaty characteristics were required to be approved by parliament before negotiations took place and after they had been signed. Article 190 later became an albatross to foreign (political and economic)

---

[3] The bureaucracy most attuned to Thai trade policy was the Department of Trade Negotiations (DTN) under the Ministry of Commerce. It became the policy hands that provided input and technical advice to both the IEPCC and the FTA teams.
[4] Constitution of the Kingdom of Thailand, BE 2550, Bangkok: The Constitution Court.

policy-making, deterring ministers and officials from engaging in international negotiations and commitments. Indeed, the pendulum swung back against the executive branch. Parliament, which under the 2007 charter comprised a half-appointed senate, was given much more latitude over international obligations. Unsurprisingly, PTA negotiations were mired in acrimony and inactivity as a result of the stipulations laid out in Article 190 due to the critical role of NSAs. In view of the powerful role of the anti-FTA coalition, it is instructive to delve deeper into its background, composition and policy preferences.

3.1   FTA Watch[5]

To be sure, NSAs in Thailand long preceded the controversy surrounding FTAs. Although varied and disparate, Thai NSAs have long been a force in determining political outcomes. Their rise as political actors tracked Thai economic development and political liberalization. The high water mark for Thai NSAs was the popular uprising that overthrew a *de facto* military dictatorship in May 1992, following in the footsteps of a similar anti-military protest led by university students in October 1973. Among the NSAs, the media, environmental protection groups and the medical profession demonstrated early effectiveness (see Bamber 1997; Prudhisan and Maneerat 1997; Thitinan (1997). Private sector NSAs have featured the three main business chambers: namely, the Federation of Thai Industries, the Thai Bankers' Association and the Thai Chamber of Commerce. These three business associations also participated in the ejection of the military from political power in the May 1992 uprising, but they were less vociferous than civil society NSAs in their opposition to Thaksin's rule. Towards the late 1990s, NSAs became more diversified, albeit still focused on similar single issues such as the environment and healthcare. Yet relatively new NSAs came to the fore during the 1997–8 economic crisis to oppose the IMF, financial globalization and 'neoliberal' reforms and development mandated by the 'Washington Consensus'. The opposition to economic neoliberalism was the basis of the local movement against freer trade under the WTO framework. In fact, a host of NSAs had been working against the WTO provisions and negotiations until the convergence of timing and circumstance propelled them onto the national stage as anti-FTA and anti-Thaksin activists.

---

[5] This section is based on author's interviews with FTA Watch activist (Nos. 1–6), June 2009.

The campaign by civil society NSAs against Thaksin's bilateral FTAs began in earnest when the then Thai premier together with then US President George W. Bush declared during the APEC leaders' summit in October 2003 that negotiations between Thailand and the United States would commence. It was part of a package deal that stemmed from Thaksin's visit to the White House in June 2003, where Thailand fully signed on to the US-led war on terrorism, including the Container Security Initiative and the arrest of key members of Jemaah Islamiyah, the regional outpost of Al Qaeda, and America's designation of Thailand as a major non-NATO ally. Consequently, the Thai–US FTA negotiations became FTA Watch's primary target, although it had protested earlier against the early harvest scheme with China and the Thai–Australia FTA. It was during this period of Thaksin's rule that the civil society NSAs began to campaign on FTA issues for popular support, initially under adverse conditions as Thaksin's popularity was reaching a crescendo.

After extended discussions and debates in October 2003, the anti-FTA FTA Watch coalition was established, comprising CSOs and academics generally sceptical of, or opposed to, neoliberal economic development, as well as officers and members of independent regulatory organizations, such as the National Human Rights Commission (NHRC) and the National Economic and Social Advisory Council (NESAC) (see also Pavida and Veerayuth 2004). Leading the FTA Watch consortium were notable CSOs such as AidsAccess, Biothai, Focus on the Global South and Alternative Agriculture Network. Each came with a wide array of constituents, supporters, networks of contacts and like-minded institutes and organizations with regional and international counterparts. However, the agenda was set up locally. Regional and international solidarity was informal and manifested on a case-by-case basis.

FTA Watch focused on a range of trade-related issues, including biological resources, intellectual property (especially pharmaceutical patents), public health and consumer protection, the WTO and globalization, farmers' networks for sustainable agriculture and networks of people living with HIV/AIDS. It launched a plethora of literature, including seminar books (Kannikar *et al.* 2004; Sornchai *et al.* 2004; Chanida *et al.* 2005) and other paraphernalia such as t-shirts. It aimed to coordinate analysis and advocacy on trade issues among CSOs and their various alliances. It had no permanent office, but worked horizontally in collaboration and coordination with thirty to forty core members from about twenty organizations. Email and electronic communication was its main platform for discussions and decisions, whereas more sensitive issues and important decisions were sorted out in regular meetings hosted alternately among various member organizations. FTA Watch came up with a savvy website[6] to act as an official online advocacy tool and to disseminate information. Reports, analyses and pertinent debates on FTA issues from various media outlets involving the Thaksin government, its FTA negotiation teams and CSOs were compiled and kept. More than 20,000 news items eventually found their way onto the FTA Watch website, which has been accessed by several million viewers. Live Internet broadcasts for large public forums also came into use. Small focus groups of thirty to forty people were held, some expanded into nationwide seminars with several hundred participants held in different provinces. Topics discussed included farmers and health patients, intellectual property provisions, investment clauses and an overall analysis of FTA issues, such as the lack of transparency in the negotiation process, conflicts of interest and the roles played by multinational companies.

Once it gained sufficient public exposure, FTA Watch developed into a coordinating centre among activists campaigning on relevant issues. It started with a demonstration against the signing of the Thailand–Australia FTA in 2003 in front of Government House with around 1,000 demonstrators, then a demonstration against the third round of Thai–US FTA negotiations in Pattaya in April 2005, followed by a massive protest in Chiang Mai in January 2006. Attacking Thaksin for authoritarianism and cronyism as leading cabinet members hailed from the country's largest agro-industry conglomerate and a major auto-parts business group, FTA Watch joined forces with the anti-Thaksin protesters under the People's Alliance for Democracy (PAD) to oppose the privatization of state-owned enterprises. This helped PAD to attain the critical mass it needed to topple the government at a time when Thaksin was embattled following the controversial multi-billion dollar sale of his Shin Corp telecommunications conglomerate to Temasek Holdings. FTA Watch's Chiang Mai demonstration against the Thai–US FTA negotiations in January 2006 was crucial in other ways. It brought out more than 10,000 protesters who blockaded the hotel venue, a protest that grabbed the headlines and hastened the downward spiral of Thaksin's rule. The bilateral meeting was adjourned abruptly, and the lead Thai negotiator resigned a week later.

As Thaksin's power waned, FTA Watch activists became adept at lobbying and mass mobilization. Some of them and their allies had been members of various committees straddling the lower house and the senate,

---

[6] See www.ftawatch.org.

such as the Standing Committee on Foreign Affairs and the Standing Committee on Social Development and Human Security. Other FTA Watch members took part in sub-committees appointed by independent regulatory organizations such as NHRC and NESAC. They held dialogues with MPs and met officially with Thaksin and his deputies, and leaders of parties from the opposition. They generated briefs and brochures, and disseminated them widely to the legislative members. After the coup in September 2006, FTA Watch activists stepped up their lobbying activities by drafting and presenting proposals directly to the coup-appointed National Legislative Assembly (NLA) and pushed for clauses in the new 2007 constitution that guaranteed transparency and participation in the trade policy-making process on trade agreements. The pinnacle of the FTA Watch campaign was the initiative and incorporation of Article 190 of the charter, which they 'practically wrote themselves'.[7]

4 Thai PTAs in play

Notwithstanding Thailand's topsy-turvy and contested political directions since late 2005, Thai PTAs were implemented against the backdrop of uncertainty behind the Doha Round, following in the footsteps of Singapore, the first ASEAN country to embark on the bilateral FTA road. During Thaksin's tenure, a handful of bilateral FTAs were finalized, and while his emphasis on bilateral preferences was halted when his government was ousted in the September 2006 military coup, the coup-appointed government of General Surayud Chulanont still managed to seal the FTA with Japan (the Japan–Thailand Economic Partnership Agreement or JTEPA). As of mid-2009, Thailand's stalled PTAs focused on a clutch of bilateral FTAs, complemented by at least two regional PTAs (see Table 6.3). What follows is a cursory look at their dynamics and outcomes.

The Framework Agreement on Thailand–Bahrain Economic Partnership was signed on 29 December 2002. Thai–Bahraini bilateral trade was relatively small, but its potential for expansion was cited as justification. As Bahrain is a member of the Gulf Cooperation Council and in the strategic Persian Gulf area, this partnership was considered to hold geo-strategic significance. The necessary follow-up implementation on this framework agreement has been dormant.

---

[7] Author's interviews with FTA Watch activists (Nos. 2 and 3), June 2009.

Table 6.3 *Thailand and ASEAN FTAs*

FTA	Date of Implementation	Objective			Rules of origin	Year to complete FTA framework agreement
		Goods	Services	Investment		
Thailand–Australia	1 January 2005	x	x	x	x	
Thailand–New Zealand	1 July 2005	x	x	x	x	
Thailand–Japan	1 November 2007	x	x	x	x	
Thailand–India		xx	xx	xx	x	
Thailand–Peru		xx	xx	xx	xx	2015
Thailand–US	Suspended	xx	xx	xx	xx	
Thailand–EFTA		xx	xx	xx	xx	
Thailand–BIMSTEC	1 January 2010	x	xx	xx	x	
ASEAN–China	1 October 2003*	x	x	x	x	
ASEAN–Korea	1 June 2009 (services) October 2009 (goods)	x	x	xx	x	
ASEAN–India	1 January 2010**	xx	xx	xx	xx	
ASEAN–Japan	June 2009	x	xx	xx	x	
ASEAN–EU	Temporary suspension	xx	xx	xx	xx	
ASEAN–Australia–New Zealand	Prospectively late 2009 or early 2010	x	x	x	x	

Note: x = negotiations concluded.

xx = covered under negotiations but inconclusive/not yet started.

* Thailand's and China's leaders agreed to eliminate tariffs on bilateral trade in fruits and vegetables from 1 October 2003 before the ASEAN–China FTA took full effect on 1 January 2004.

** Draft agreement begins tariff reduction in goods on 1 January 2010, but has not been signed as of July 2009.

The ASEAN–China FTA was China's strategic move to build on its relations with the ASEAN countries. Until the mid-1990s, ASEAN–China relations were characterized by enmity and friction, largely due to overlapping territorial claims in the South China Sea and the legacy of communist expansionism in Southeast Asia. But China followed a different tack after the 1997–8 economic crisis, and began its so-called 'charm' offensive of 'soft power' projection in Southeast Asia. The ASEAN–China FTA has been the economic linchpin of China's soft, non-military power. In this context, Thailand and China spearheaded the broader regional PTA with tariff reductions under the Thailand–China Early Harvest Scheme from 1 October 2003, only to be suspended in the following year due to an import surge and adverse effects on Thai agricultural producers. Progress on the wider ASEAN–China FTA has also made limited headway in the interim.

The Framework Agreement on Thailand–India Free Trade Area was signed on 9 October 2003. The necessary follow-up on the Thai–Indian framework agreement remained inactive over 2006–8. The Thailand–Australia Free Trade Agreement was signed on 5 July 2004 and it came into force on 1 January 2005. Apart from the FTA with Japan, the Thai–Australian FTA is the most comprehensive and substantial. Its implementation continues apace despite the Thai political crisis.

The Thailand–New Zealand Closer Economic Partnership Agreement was signed on 19 April 2005 and took effect on 1 July in the same year. Amounting to around US$500 million in bilateral trade, the Thai–New Zealand FTA is relatively small, but holds symbolic significance in Thailand's FTA map because New Zealand is a developed country with close relations with Australia and substantial credibility in the international arena.

The JTEPA was signed and was implemented from 3 April 2007. This FTA is crucial as Japan is Thailand's largest foreign investor. It was passed during the coup period under interim Prime Minister Surayud, and remarkably overcame civil society opposition that was staunchly opposed to Thaksin's FTA schemes. Having been appointed by the military coup-makers, the Surayud government felt that JTEPA provided much needed international credibility.[8] The civil society NSAs under FTA Watch, on the other hand, were aware of the drawbacks of JTEPA, but were not able to mobilize in time to oppose it.[9] However, some FTA Watch activists

---

[8] Author's interview with a former member of National Legislative Assembly, June 2009.
[9] Author's interview with FTA Watch activist (No. 1), June 2009.

were able to raise sufficient reservations to eke out two side agreements on bio-hazardous waste and the use of organic fertilizer.[10] Because of their virulent protests against Thaksin, the civil society NSAs were effectively co-opted by the anti-Thaksin forces who took power after the September 2006 putsch, and hence their relative lack of vehement opposition to JTEPA.

The Bangladesh–India–Myanmar–Sri Lanka–Thailand Economic Cooperation (BIMSTEC) was signed in 2004, representing a trade cooperation scheme comprising the South Asian countries. With the subsequent additions of Bhutan and Nepal, this regional PTA has geo-strategic and political significance due to its involvement of giant India and reclusive Myanmar. Its follow-up agreements and implementation, however, have since made little progress. The Thailand–Peru Free Trade Agreement remains under negotiation despite early signs of a breakthrough during Thaksin's rule.

The Thailand–US Free Trade Agreement was first negotiated in 2003, but became bogged down and problematic as mentioned above. It would be Thailand's most significant and comprehensive FTA as the United States remains Thailand's most important strategic partner, but it has made no headway following the disrupted meeting in Chiang Mai in January 2006. Indeed, the Thai–US FTA negotiations have been put on a backburner indefinitely. When President Barack Obama and the coalition government of Prime Minister Abhisit Vejjajiva took office in January 2009, this FTA re-entered discussions, but remains a distant realization due to economic adversity in both countries and Thailand's protracted political polarization and persistent turmoil.

On the regional front, Thailand is engaged in the planned economic integration under the ASEAN Charter by 2015. While the charter stipulates an integrated economic community, the ASEAN members have faced a host of obstacles. Compliance and dispute mechanisms are inadequate, and the development gaps between the older members (Indonesia, Malaysia, the Philippines, Singapore and Thailand) and the newer ones (Cambodia, Laos, Myanmar and Vietnam) remain large. The older members are likely to see greater trade integration among themselves much more than between them and the newer members. Beyond ASEAN, the ASEAN Plus Three (APT) framework comprising ASEAN, China, Japan and South Korea has also broached the idea of an East Asia Free Trade Area, but it has not taken off due to a lack of agreement and resolve.

---

[10] Author's interview with FTA Watch activist (No. 3), June 2009

Similarly, the East Asia Summit members, essentially ASEAN plus six, or APT with India, Australia and New Zealand, has also expressed interest in a region-wide free trade area without concrete ways of achieving this having been put forward thus far. The older and more established regional trade vehicles, particularly APEC, have lost momentum and are in need of reinvention. Meanwhile, other economic cooperation schemes have been floated, including Australia's Asia–Pacific community, which might be a revamped version of APEC with fewer members and a broader mandate. These schemes are as much political and strategic as economic with a trade integration focus.

Moreover, Thailand's trade policy strategy and capacity in undertaking these FTAs both at the bilateral and regional levels remains a matter of contention. Rangsan (2005) has suggested that the immense cost of non-participation is prohibitive, whereas Thitinan and Sally (2008) have pointed to the incoherence and inefficiency in Thai FTA initiatives. Senior negotiators were few and spread out across different agencies, led by the Ministry of Commerce's Department of International Trade Negotiations and the Foreign Ministry's Department of International Economic Affairs, resulting in inter-agency turf conflicts and lack of coordination. Because senior negotiators who are well-versed on negotiating skills and technical expertise are few, they have had to look after a number of FTAs and sectoral issues at the same time.[11] Clearly, Thaksin appeared intent on not missing the boat, especially since the Doha Round of MTNs ran into a dead end and nearby countries such as Singapore hopped on the bilateral FTA bandwagon. At the same time, FTAs under Thaksin harboured strategic and foreign policy implications as a pillar from which to manage relations with the major powers in the context of the Asia Cooperation Dialogue and the Ayeyawady–Chao Phraya–Mekong Economic Cooperation Strategy for greater cooperation on the Asian landmass, with a Thailand-driven mainland Southeast Asia as the centre of gravity (Thitinan 2007).

For FTA Watch, the broad push for FTAs was seen as being driven by vested interests among the major economic powers, particularly the United States, and the Thaksin government and its cronies who stood to gain from trade liberalization. To the civil society NSAs, the Thaksin government realized that the efforts towards trade and investment liberalization through WTO were fraught with difficulties, particularly after several major developing countries, including Brazil, India and

---

[11] Author's interview with a senior Ministry of Commerce official, April 2009.

China united with other smaller developing countries. Meanwhile, FTA Watch was part of the broader international movement against globalization. This is how they viewed the US government's intentions under the Thai–US FTA. Because the United States could not achieve its targets at the MTNs, it has turned to bilateral FTAs to exploit its overwhelming advantages. In Southeast Asia, this bilateral FTA started with Singapore, then moved on to Thailand, Malaysia, the Philippines and Indonesia, in that order. In Thailand, the major drive for the FTA came from Thaksin, the Charoen Pokphand (CP) group, the largest agro-industry conglomerate in Thailand and one of the largest in the region, and the family-owned Thai Summit auto parts manufacturer, whose scion was a Thaksin cabinet member and key financier to the ruling TRT party.

Civil society NSAs saw the Thai–China FTA as an unmitigated disaster for Thai farmers who grew temperate climate fruits and vegetables in northern Thailand. Chinese fruits and vegetables, such as garlic, broccoli, kale, apples and peaches, flooded into the Thai market at half or even a quarter of prices of home-grown equivalents, adversely affecting the livelihoods of untold thousands of farming families.

On the Thailand–Australia FTA, signed in July 2004, civil society NSAs took to the defence of local dairy farmers. They argued that cheaper dairy products, especially milk powder, crowded the Thai market and tens of thousands of small-scale local dairy-producing families could not cope with their Australian competitors, as production costs in Australia were just half of those in Thailand. It was estimated that one-third of Thai dairy farms went bankrupt within a year of implementation of the bilateral agreement.

Moreover, local vested interest groups were positioned to gain from these FTAs, including key business groups who financed the ruling party, and including Thaksin himself whose family owned a telecommunications conglomerate at the time. These businesses benefited from the FTAs with China, Australia and New Zealand. Shrimp and seafood exporters, such as the CP Group, enjoyed a 50% increase in exports in the first year of the FTA with Australia. The auto parts firms, one owned by then Transport Minister, Suriya Jeungrungruengkit, benefited from a 75% increase in exports of auto parts to Australia. Apart from these conflicts of interest and apparent cronyism, the FTA negotiations processes were shrouded in secrecy with no transparency and participation. Negotiating objectives were subject to the exclusive manipulation and exploitation of big business and government officials. Issues under negotiation and the related documents were kept from public access, only to be revealed as a fait accompli after the agreement had been signed. The full details of Thai FTAs with Australia and Japan, for example, were publicized only after the respective signing ceremonies.

The governments of both Thaksin and Surayud refused to table FTA texts for deliberation and approval by the lower house despite their palpable impact on the general public. For the FTA with the United States, which would have been wider and deeper in its impact compared with those with China and Australia because the framework for negotiation was more comprehensive, including intellectual property and investment liberalization, details were even more scant and the negotiations process more furtive. The mass mobilization in Chiang Mai in January 2006 against the Thai–US FTA made a substantial public impact and unnerved government officials. By the time of the coup, many Thais had turned against Thaksin for reasons of disgust and distrust in the face of his corruption allegations, abuses of power and authoritarian governance. A central source of the public discontent was undeniably Thaksin's bilateral FTAs. Coming at a time when Thaksin's regime was unravelling, the Thai–US negotiations were the last straw for civil society NSAs who mistrusted bilateral free trade. They were adamant that the inclusion of gene patenting clauses and liberalization of genetically-modified (GM) products would pave the way for the domination and exploitation of biological resources and monopoly control of local plant varieties. Similarly, they believed that drug patenting in accordance with US standards would have forced Thai patients and consumers to buy drugs at prices between thirty and several hundred per cent higher than current costs. The impact of higher prices would be felt most severely by those who depended on life-sustaining medication (e.g., those afflicted by HIV/AIDS).

Overall, the FTA Watch activists and advocates harboured distrust on several levels in their opposition to Thai FTAs. First, they suspected crony interests within the Thaksin government, not least Thaksin himself for his far-flung telecommunications-related businesses. For his part, Thaksin was never able to dispel doubts about his conflicts of interests and abuses of power, but instead compounded the distrust of CSOs by issuing a number of legislative measures that benefited his family-owned firms (Pasuk and Baker 2004). This is why the FTA Watch's motto and book titles were coined as 'sovereignty not for sale'. Related to Thaksin's vested interests were those of his cabinet colleagues and associates, particularly Thai Summit and CP representatives in cabinet. Because these large business groups held power over trade policy-making, the civil society NSAs had an easy target when they opposed Thaksin's FTA plans.

On the other hand, FTA Watch did not oppose the JTEPA as fiercely, partly because its activists were aligned with the Surayud government and its backers when they all protested against and ousted Thaksin in 2005–6. Second, and more broadly, civil society NSAs were similarly distrustful of the MTNs at the WTO level. It was a distrust that grew out of a broader scepticism and opposition to the principles of freer trade. With their counterparts elsewhere, they considered Cancun in 2003 to be a success for turning back the tide of free trade. They viewed the WTO as exploitative, as an arena where the larger and more powerful had their way with the small and powerless.

Third, as preferences of powerful players like the United States were unmet in multilateral settings, the shift to bilateral FTAs was seen as transferring MTN preferences by large economies to exploit advantages under bilateral FTAs with smaller economies. But in the Thai case, such opposition involved timing and circumstance. The civil society NSAs opposed the Australian deal, and to a lesser extent the smaller New Zealand pact, but could not galvanize enough public support to make a difference. This opposition spilled over into the early harvest in the Thai–China FTA, but they were unable to muster the wherewithal to derail Thaksin's FTA train. The turning point came with the US deal. It became a punch-bag for the CSOs. There is an inherent bias against US interests among all NSAs and even among state agencies, except the security and foreign policy establishment. But as one round of negotiations led to the next, the tipping point came with the anti-Thaksin movement by the PAD. FTA Watch, its networks and allies naturally joined the anti-Thaksin coalition. They ended up laying the conditions for the September 2006 coup that deposed Thaksin, and consequently have put Thailand's political and economic prospects into a tailspin since.

5   Concluding summary and analysis

The formidable role of civil society has been unmistakably critical to Thai trade policy-making. It was a function of domestic politics and regional and international dynamics. Almost three decades of democratization on the back of sustained economic development had given rise to a vibrant NSAs sector, which was able to organize and cohere around preferences that were critical of globalization dynamics (e.g., freer trade). At the outset of the Doha Round in late 2001, trade policy-making authority was relatively diffused among various stakeholders, from macro-economy-related cabinet members and trade policy bureaucrats to business associations and civil society NSAs. But as Thaksin consolidated his power from mid-2001 to his landslide and unprecedented re-election in February 2005, the role of NSAs became more pronounced. They ultimately provided a protest platform and network that challenged his authority and eroded his legitimacy enabling his overthrow.

CSOs, as distinct from other stakeholders concerned, such as media or business associations, were instrumental in Thai trade policy directions. Their opposition to the various bilateral and regional PTAs as well as the Doha Round raised the bar for Thai policy-makers. Ultimately, the symbiotic networks of CSOs substantially shaped the trade policy-making framework, constraining negotiations and agreements at all levels. Yet several bilateral FTAs were rammed through, especially the JTEPA under the coup-appointed Surayud government, which enjoyed acquiescence from the CSOs who had played a part in toppling Thaksin's regime. How CSOs treat the Democrat Party-led government, which took power in December 2008, should merit close observation. Having worked hand-in-glove with a wide array of NSAs in the anti-Thaksin protests, the Democrat Party is likely to be put on the spot because it has revived negotiations for bilateral and regional FTAs.

As the protracted political crisis during 2005–9 virtually ground Thai trade policy-making to a standstill (except the JTEPA), the logic and strategy behind the disparate geographic range of Thai FTAs deserves to be addressed. At the government level, inter-agency conflicts and lack of coordination, especially between the Ministry of Commerce's Department of International Trade Negotiations and the Foreign Ministry's Department of International Economic Affairs, have hindered Thai trade policy-making.

Equally important has been the role of the private sector at the company and industry levels, as well as local trade associations and chambers of commerce, although they have not played such a large part as the CSOs. The FTA Watch consortium has been the central agent of NSAs. It succeeded beyond its own expectations due its own hard-won efforts, but also to timing and circumstance. Its opposition to MTNs, and later the PTAs in Thaksin's bilateral FTAs, was fortuitously boosted by the PAD's anti-Thaksin movement. But partaking in the PAD's coalition also compromised FTA Watch in the case of JTEPA under the Surayud government, where it did not apply the same stringent and critical criteria, except to effect two side agreements. This outcome was partly attributable to the networks and contacts of FTA Watch who were in the coup-appointed NLA and in the Surayud government. The dialogue and participation allowed under Surayud partly explains the passage of JTEPA.

Moreover, FTA Watch's lobbying after the coup enabled its preferences to be codified into Article 190 of the 2007 constitution. Its ability to push for Article 190, which placed strict endorsement criteria on binding international agreements such as FTAs was a remarkable outcome and testified to Thai civil society NSAs' effectiveness. It was designed to deter and constrain the executive branch of government from forcing through FTAs as experienced under the Thaksin administration.

That civil society NSAs were more opposed to MTNs and bilateral FTAs than regional trade liberalization also warrants attention. Respondents in interviews and the corresponding literature were less critical of ASEAN economic integration and wider intra-Asian cooperation than MTNs and bilateral FTAs. One respondent preferred a South–South trade and investment integration.[12] PTAs on a regional level benefit from a sense of solidarity that stems from longstanding East Asian regionalism, such as ASEAN and APT, the latter having produced currency swap agreements under the Chiang Mai Initiative in response to the 1997–8 crisis.

But by and large, FTA Watch activists were not as opposed to the FTAs as they were to the ways and means by which they were formulated, negotiated and decided. They merely rejected the lack of participation and Thaksin's roughshod and top–down methods, which must also be juxtaposed to what they saw as Thaksin's abuse of power, conflicts of interest and corruption. Because it allowed more NSA participation and deliberations, the JTEPA is a case in point where inclusiveness led to signed agreement. JTEPA also signified trade-offs and co-option that besotted Thai NSAs. After they aided the overthrow of Thaksin, Thai NSAs became a player in constitution draft-making and policy-making processes that dampened their otherwise opposition to bilateral free trade deals.

The Thai case of NSAs' impact on trade policy-making appears salient. It bears lessons for the WTO to take a more nuanced, relatively more bottom–up approach, which can still be workable and effective. Midway–up approaches by way of regional PTAs should also be considered as more preferable than bilateral outcomes. Freer trade at the regional level could then be promoted and expanded into inter-regional schemes, such as an ASEAN–EU FTA for example. Lessons from Thai trade policy-making and its NSA impact should behove the WTO to take a more inclusive and accommodating stance as the future of the Doha Round remains murky.

---

[12] Author's interview with FTA Watch activist (No. 1), June 2009.

The WTO may have to bite the bullet and accept bilateral FTA realities, but it could also focus on regional roads that subsequently lead to multi-lateral outcomes. The era has come for a more nuanced and sophisticated multilateralism.

More specific to the Thai case would be the role that the politics of trade policy-making – under the Thaksin regime in this case – has impacted on national politics. The bilateral FTAs in Thailand were a crucial compo-nent of the domestic discourse and a key rationale for the protest move-ment that deposed Thaksin. Accordingly, the Thai case is instructive not only because of how trade policy-making has become politicized, but also because that politicization of trade policy-making has adversely affected the course of domestic politics and progress towards greater democra-tization. While Thailand's political crisis has put its bilateral FTAs in tat-ters, the absence of progress at the multilateral level has placed Thai trade policy in limbo in view of the little headway that has been made in the regional setting.

References

Bamber, S. 1997. 'The Thai Medical Profession and Political Activism', in K. Hewison (ed.), *Political Change in Thailand: Democracy and Participation*. London: Routledge.

Bidhya, B. 2004. 'Thaksin's Model of Government Reform: Prime Ministerialization Through "a Country is My Company" Approach', *Asian Journal of Political Science* **12**, 1.

Chaipat, S. 1992. *Lessons from the World Bank's Experience of Structural Adjustment Loans (SALs): A Case Study of Thailand*. Bangkok: Thailand Development Research Institute.

Chanida, C. B. *et al.* 2005. *Free Trade Agreements And Their Impact on Developing Countries: The Thai Experience*. Bangkok: FTA Watch.

Kannikar, K. *et al.* 2004. *Sovereignty Not For Sale: Free Trade Agreements and Their Impact on Thailand*, Vol. II (in Thai). Bangkok: FTA Watch.

Naya, S. *et al.* 1992. *ASEAN Free Trade Area: The Way Ahead*. Singapore: Institute of Southeast Asian Studies.

Pasuk, P. and Baker, C. 2004. *Thaksin: The Business of Politics in Thailand*. Chiang Mai, Thailand: Silkworm Books.

Pavida P. and Veerayuth K. 2004. '*FTAs From the Perspectives of Academics and NGOs*', unpublished report submitted to Ministry of Commerce.

Prudhisan, J. and Maneerat, M. 2007. 'Non-governmental Development Organisations: Empowerment and Environment', in K. Hewison (ed.), *Political Change in Thailand: Democracy and Participation*. London: Routledge, ch. 12, pp. 195–216.

Rangsan T. 2005. *Thaksinomics III* (in Thai). Bangkok: Open Books.

Somkiat T. *et al.* 2009. 'Reaping Benefits for Thai Businesses From JTEPA', *Thailand Development Research Institute Report No. 69*, TDRI, Bangkok, April.

Sornchai J. *et al.* 2004. *Sovereignty Not For Sale: The Thai–United States Free Trade Agreement and Its Impact on Thailand*. Bangkok: FTA Watch.

Stubbs, R. 2000. 'Signing on to Liberalization: AFTA and the Politics of Regional Economic Cooperation', *The Pacific Review* **13**, 2.

Thitinan P. 1997. 'Thailand's Media: Whose Watchdog?', in K. Hewison (ed.), *Political Change in Thailand: Democracy and Participation*. London: Routledge.

— 2007. 'Mainland Southeast Asia, ASEAN and the Major Powers in East Asian Regional Order', in J. Tsunekawa (ed.), *Regional Order in East Asia: ASEAN and Japan Perspectives*. Tokyo: National Institute for Defence Studies.

— 2008. 'Thailand Since the Coup', *Journal of Democracy*, October–December.

Thitinan P. and Sally, R. 2008. *Thailand's Trade Policy Strategy and Capacity* (in Thai). Bangkok: Department of International Relations, Chulalongkorn University.

7

Jordan

RIAD AL KHOURI

This chapter explores how non-state actors (NSAs) seek to influence government policy in relation to the World Trade Organization (WTO) and preferential trade agreements (PTAs) as alternative venues for international trade cooperation. Little research has been done on NSA–government interaction on trade policy development in Jordan, and almost no analysis exists that captures and contrasts this interaction in relation to multilateral as opposed to bilateral or plurilateral negotiations. This chapter, based on interviews with representatives of government and NSAs, focuses on recent developments in Jordan's trade policy-making. It has found that NSA activity in Jordan is relatively weakly developed compared with the other cases in this study, but that it is growing, in large part as a result of the influence of international actors, including US foreign aid donors and some other international business and civil society organizations (CSOs).

Section 1 surveys the evolution of trade policy and Jordan's trade patterns. Section 2 outlines the key state and non-state actors involved in trade policy-making and the mechanisms for government consultation. Section 3 outlines Jordan's key multilateral and preferential trade agreements. Section 4 explores the interactions between state and non-state actors in relation to trade negotiations, and considers the question of forum choice. Section 5 concludes.

1   The evolution of trade policy in Jordan

Jordan is a lower-middle income country that is poor in energy and water resources. As such, the kingdom has depended for survival on a strategic relationship with the West, mainly with the United States, which supports Jordan with aid and preferential trade agreements.

Encouraged by the United States, over the past two decades Jordan has undertaken limited political liberalization in an effort to promote social stability. However, despite steady reform, Jordan still needs to do much in terms of the 'voice and accountability' component of governance; on the other hand, regarding the rule of law, the country has done better in recent years, though it is still far behind developed states. Compared with other countries in the region, Jordan ranks well in terms of the rule of law, but it is still behind in terms of other aspects of democratic govern-ance, especially in relation to participation. This reluctance by the state to allow others a voice in public policy and to accept the principle of govern-ment accountability to the people helps to explain the weak development of NSAs in the kingdom.

Jordanian economic policies prior to the mid-1990s were based on strong state control, including control of major producers of raw materials such as potash and phosphates, the country's leading exports of goods at that time. Trade policy then was heavily protectionist in an effort to pro-mote local manufacturing and move the country away from its reliance on traditional agricultural and mining production. By the mid-1980s, this strategy had succeeded in helping to establish a light manufactur-ing sector producing goods such as processed food, furniture and house-hold appliances, which were mainly exported to Iraq and other regional markets. However, as the economies of Jordan's oil-producing neighbours contracted in the late 1980s, these exports collapsed and manufacturing contracted when it failed to find alternative markets. This contributed to a balance of payments crisis in 1989 that triggered political liberalization, on the one hand, and economic reform, on the other hand.

Having undergone major economic reforms since the 1990s, including trade liberalization, customs and tax reforms, as well as the strengthen-ing of intellectual property rights (patents, copyright and trademarks), Jordan is an open economy. These domestic reforms have been supported by trade liberalization undertaken as a result of its accession to the WTO in 2000, and through a range of PTAs with a broad range of Arab and non-Arab countries.

Jordan has PTAs with the United States (2001), Singapore (2005), Canada (2009), and its relations with the European Union are governed by a Euro-Med Association Agreement signed in 1997 and implemented in 2002. Jordan also has a range of PTAs with countries in Africa and the Middle East, including Israel (1995), and it is a member of the Agadir Agreement with Egypt, Morocco and Tunisia, who are also part of the Arab Free Trade Agreement (AFTA) that Jordan joined in 1997.[1]

---

[1] AFTA includes all League of Arab States members except for Algeria, the Comoros, Djibouti, Mauritania and Somalia.

Table 7.1 *Composition of merchandise exports and imports, 2008*

	US$ (million)
Total exports:	6,181
Of which greatest by value:	
Garments	1,011
Potash	768
Fertilizers	587
Phosphates	520
Medical and pharmaceutical products	498
Total imports:	16,883
Of which greatest by value:	
Crude oil	2,711
Transport equipment and parts	1,290
Iron and steel	854
Telecoms equipment	804
Textile yarn, fabric, manufactured articles and related goods	650

Source: Central Bank of Jordan 2009.

Following major liberalization in the context of accession to the WTO in 2000, Jordan now has relatively low tariffs, with an average most favoured nation (MFN) applied rate of 11.2%. There are still high tariffs in some sectors, notably beverages and tobacco (69.5%), clothing (23.3%) and textiles (5.5%). Tariff policy generally favours imports of primary and intermediate inputs over finished goods.

1.1   Patterns of trade

Jordan's bilateral and regional trade liberalization has contributed significantly to export growth and has transformed the structure of its exports and imports. A summary of trade patterns by product composition (see Table 7.1) and by trade partners (Table 7.2) shows that Jordan is experiencing imbalances in some bilateral trade relations, especially with exporters of oil. This is unavoidable and may matter little provided the overall balance of payments is sound; even a persistent overall trade deficit over several years as experienced by Jordan is not an issue of concern for a country that is undergoing economic growth and modernization, as long as such an imbalance is offset by sustainable service exports, remittances and private capital inflows.

Table 7.2 *Major trade partners by merchandise exports and imports, and aggregates for trade with the EU-29, 2008*

	US$ (million)
Exports:	
India	1,280
US	1,038
Iraq	808
Saudi Arabia	475
United Arab Emirates	219
EU-29	257
Imports:	
Saudi Arabia	3,643
China	1,751
Germany	1011
US	774
Egypt	719
EU-29	3,531

Source: Central Bank of Jordan 2009.

Nevertheless, the current high level of the Jordanian trade deficit may become difficult to sustain in the longer run. This warrants the attention of policy-makers in order to broaden and expand the country's export potential. With a view to this objective, the current regional and com-modity structure of Jordan's exports raises the question of whether the misallocation of productive factors that has taken place in Jordan's export industry should be adjusted over time by measures to encourage a greater diversity of manufactured exports and, thus, more scope for export expansion.

Chemicals and pharmaceuticals, arguably Jordan's most promising export sectors, have underperformed in the last ten years, having not been able to expand their share of Jordan's exports. At the same time, since 2001 a huge sectoral trade diversion has taken place as result of pref-erential agreements between Jordan and the United States. The bias in the structure of Jordan's exports to the United States is not replicated in exports to other regions. The composition of Jordanian exports to Europe is less lopsided with regard to garments, but it is also rather unsteady. By contrast, Jordan's exports to Arab countries are quite diversified.

The structural aspects of Jordan's exports should be seen against the background of its overall trade expansion. In recent years, the kingdom's total exports have grown faster than global trade. Much of this growth is accounted for by exports to the United States, whereas exports to the European Union remained mostly stagnant. Since 2004, however, the growth in exports resulted mainly from exports to Arab countries and to other non-Western markets

Exports as well as imports have risen much faster than gross domestic product (GDP); the merchandise trade to GDP ratio reached 120% in 2008, up from 82% in 1997. The trend of the past few years has been for imports to rise faster than exports. The export:GDP ratio increased from 25% in 1997 to 35% in 2009, while the comparable import ratio rose from 57% to 85% over the same period.

In trade as with other areas, Jordan's official National Agenda for 2006–15 has spelled out ambitious goals, including a determination to reduce the net trade imbalance to US$1.7 billion by 2012 and US$0.9 billion by 2017. Nonetheless, the economy remains characterized by a persistent and growing deficit, which in 2008 was a staggering US$9.1 billion or 49% of GDP. This shortfall is partly financed by remittances into the kingdom, estimated at US$2.4 billion for 2008. Also important in this respect are inflows of private capital, aid and some services income, particularly from tourism.

Such structurally weak characteristics of Jordan's exports thus warrant attention. In 1999–2008, Jordan's total exports grew around threefold. Much of this growth is accounted for by exports to the United States. The share of total Jordanian exports destined for the United States increased from less than 1% in 1997 to more than 25% in 2008. However, Jordan's exports to the United States, heavily dominated by apparel, may decrease as Jordan's preferential access to the US market is eroded. Jordan will thus need to diversify its exports to the United States in order to compensate for flat or falling apparel exports.

In 2008, Jordan's main source of imports was the AFTA, which exported US$5.64 billion of merchandise to Jordan, a 30% increase from 2007. The European Union was the second largest source of imports (US$3.54 billion – a 6% increase from 2007), third was China (US$1.75 billion – up 34% from 2007) and, finally, the United States (US$0.78 billion – an increase of 22% from 2007). The latter is especially noteworthy, having risen steadily and strongly over the last five years, though during the last two years this increase was not matched by an expansion of US imports from Jordan.

During the first decade of the twenty-first century, the impact of the Israel–Jordan–United States Qualifying Industrial Zone (QIZ) and the Jordan–US FTA on Jordan's exports has been considerable, with both regimes allowing higher exports to the United States. US imports under the Jordan–US FTA increased more than twentyfold between 2002 and 2008. Jordanian exports to the United States under the QIZ rose from US$0.2 million in 1999 to over US$750 million in 2008. Despite this generally stellar performance, bilateral trade between Jordan and the United States decreased by 5% between 2007 and 2008. In the latter year, Jordanian exports to the United States fell 15% from 2007; and in 2008, apparel exports totalled around US$1 billion, a 15% decrease from the previous year, but still 85% of total Jordanian exports to the United States. At the same time, Jordanian imports from the United States in 2008 rose 10% from 2007.

2 State and non-state actors in Jordan's trade policy-making

2.1 State actors

2.1.1 The executive

The Council of Ministers is collectively responsible for trade policy formulation, though in some cabinets there has been an 'economic team' headed by a vice premier that focused on these and related matters. Cabinet also decides customs duties.

2.1.2 The legislature

The role of legislative processes in trade policy formulation in Jordan is meagre. It would be an exaggeration to describe Jordan's bicameral parliament as a rubber stamp; nevertheless, in considering issues relating to trade agreements, the legislature has not substantially stood in the way of the accords put forward by the executive branch of government for ratification. In this respect, the Islamist bloc in parliament has been the most outspoken, but its remarks on these agreements tend towards general political positions as opposed to dealing with specific economic issues. The appointed Senate, the upper house of parliament, has traditionally taken a more serious interest in economic matters, but there too little serious discussion of trade agreements has taken place. Generally, Parliament is weakened by some members' ignorance and their inappropriate understanding of their public roles as parliamentarians, as opposed to their private business or family interests.

2.1.3   Government departments

Trade policy is implemented by the Ministry of Finance (MoF), which coordinates implementation by other ministries and agencies where necessary, including the Ministry of Industry and Trade (MoIT), the main body involved in the drafting and negotiating of trade agreements. Within MoIT, the Foreign Trade Policy Department (FTPD) deals with WTO agreements, PTAs and other bilateral agreements, and it is responsible for negotiation, supervision of implementation and research and evaluation of trade agreements.

The FTPD is the focal point for the WTO in Jordan, and functions as a Jordanian notification point for the various agreements of the WTO (with the exception of notifications relating to sanitary and phytosanitary measures) and as the Jordanian inquiry point for trade of services. The department also ensures that Jordan complies with its commitments towards the WTO, as well as regional and bilateral agreements. It fulfils its duties through cooperation and coordination with other governmental, as well as Jordanian private sector, institutions. The department is Jordan's focal point for the Social and Economic Council of the Arab League. The department deals closely with Jordan's economic counsellors' offices worldwide in order to follow up on international and bilateral relations with its trading partners. The MoIT has economic counsellors within Jordanian permanent missions/embassies in Switzerland (Geneva), Egypt (Cairo), and the United States (Washington, DC) among others places.

2.2   Trade policy consultation mechanisms and the role of foreign donors

Much of Jordan's trade reform has been undertaken at the instigation of foreign donors rather than the government. Indeed, the constellation of stakeholders that drove reform in Jordan's external sector was largely made up of foreign bilateral and multilateral aid and lending agencies, including the World Bank and the German Agency for Technical Assistance. But most influential of these foreign donors was the US Agency for International Development (USAID). As part of its efforts to secure change in Jordan's trade policies, USAID sought to engage Jordanian stakeholders in consultative processes in a way that had not occurred in the past.

For example, in the mid-1990s, USAID conducted a programme designed to drive changes in Jordan's custom regime and tariff structures.

The work conformed to the USAID trade development policy, which was designed to encourage countries like Jordan 'to use international trade as a key instrument in the process of achieving broad based, sustainable economic growth, and place a greater reliance on complementary domestic competitive markets that support more open trade policies' (see al Khouri 2004). As part of this it adopted a consultative approach, which brought together representatives of Jordanian stakeholders concerned with trade issues in general and customs in particular. Participants from Jordan's business sector included the Federation of Chambers of Commerce and the Amman Chamber of Industry, as well as representatives of the public sector. In its work on Jordanian customs reform USAID also used focus groups, creating a precedent for future reform.

These developments provide two important insights: first, the influence of USAID in Jordan and; second, the relative lack of normal interface between government and NSAs in Jordan. It is notable that these programmes were well received by the private sector and gradually gained the acceptance and endorsement of government officials.

As a result of its trade reforms, Jordan has developed a more coherent approach to trade policy development, with a clear separation of responsibilities among the Cabinet (deciding collectively on strategy), MoIT (negotiating and following up) and the MoF (overseeing implementation of regulations). Moreover, in respect of stakeholder consultation, the FTPD in the MoIT now oversees a process of stakeholder consultation, which the MoIT is hoping to develop further.

However, this division of labour still suffers from the intrusion of personal or tribal interests, as well as from the lack of technical capacity needed at some levels. When such situations arise, it sometimes happens that an outside state actor, or even an NSA, becomes involved in the trade policy process. Yet on the whole this state system of development and conduct of trade policy is working much better now than it did a decade or so ago.

2.3   Non-state actors

The role of NSAs in trade policy in Jordan has been limited, but is growing somewhat. The past decade has witnessed a rapid emergence of NSAs in Jordan, although many of these organizations have strong associations with the state. Furthermore, multilateral organizations and bilateral donors for the most part still engage primarily with government in Jordan, with NSAs largely given a back seat in relation to trade issues.

Jordanian NSAs generally face problems vis-à-vis the authorities, which seek to impose control directly or indirectly on these organizations by containment and repression. The state interferes with the establishment, financing and focus of NSAs and resorts to establishing semi-official organizations to undertake functions that are in line with and defend the state's positions. Government also constrains the work of NSAs. Consequently, the impact of Jordanian NSAs remains limited, including their effect on the process of negotiating trade accords. Yet the appearance of new NSAs and a certain amount of activity in this sphere in the past few years is noticeable. At the same time, the acquiescence and relative silence of society on trade issues is because the authoritarian nature of the Jordanian state has not changed.

Non-state actors include business, professional and labour groups, as well as private voluntary organizations (see Table 7.3). Because of the weakness of political parties, political activity spills over into professional associations, while various types of charities are politically involved, as are labour organizations. These may all be labelled 'old' NSAs, in contrast to the newer ones set up or introduced in the 1990s. In terms of strength and weakness and overall presence on the landscape of trade reform, the newcomers are more active with a higher profile, but the older and more well-established NSAs retain behind-the-scenes power.

As a result of democratization, the 1990s saw an increase in NSA activities in Jordan. However, generally NSAs do not wield any serious pressure on government in relation to trade policy-making. Apart from their problems with funding and human resources, such organizations have developed in an unfavourable political, legal and socio-cultural environment. This is partly because of the nature of the Jordanian system, which is a tribal monarchy, with public policy decision-making generally flowing from the top rather than being generated as a result of pressures from societal interests. The king can appoint and dismiss the prime minister and the government, and is the commander-in-chief of the defence and security establishment. While security apparatus and other state interventions in NSAs are common, they are also often linked to the royal family or tribal and religious leaders. There is strong competition for foreign funding, and often those NSAs backed by members of the royal family and by others in the country's establishment crowd out smaller organizations.

The interests of NSAs in Jordan remain generally outside the economic sphere. Though there has been an increase in the number of NSAs in the country, few focus on overtly trade-based issues. Jordanian democratization and liberalization have not led to business or consumer grassroots

Table 7.3 NSAs involved in trade policy-making in Jordan

Non-state actor	Policy interest	Constituencies served	Local affiliates	International affiliates	Negotiations active in
Federation of Jordanian Chambers of Commerce	General economic policies	Business community	MoIT, MoF	International Chamber of Commerce	WTO
Federation of Jordanian Labour Unions	General economic policies	Workers	Ministry of Labour	ITUC, ILO, Ebert Foundation	WTO, Jordan–US FTA
Jordan Garment Accessories and Textile Exporters (JGATE)	Measures with an impact on textile and garment production	Textile and garment producers	MoIT	USAID	PTAs especially more recent ones (e.g., with Canada)
Association of Jordanian Banks	Banking and financial policy	Banks	MoF, Central Bank of Jordan	Union of Arab Banks	WTO
Jordan Intellectual Property Association (JIPA)	Intellectual property issues	Producers of and dealers in intellectual property products	National Library	WIPO	WTO, Jordan–US FTA
Jordan Chamber of Industry	Market access policies	Manufactures	MoIT, MoF	None	PTAs especially more recent ones (e.g., with Canada)

Source: Compiled by author from individual NSAs.

movements having any great influence, partly because of the prevalence of security-oriented decision-making in politics and economics by relatively self-contained tribal–security–commercial elites linked to the monarchy. This has left little scope for NSAs to develop significant credibility at the grassroots or power within the establishment. Nonetheless, the pace and scope of trade reforms since the mid-1990s have started to transform aspects of economic life, slowly asserting the dominance of formal transparent rules based on law over tribal and personal connections, and giving NSAs a small window within which to move into lobbying and influencing law-making. Meanwhile, the Jordanian state's influence on NSAs is as important (if not more so) than their influence on the state, including the process of trade negotiation.

The legal framework of Jordanian civil associations imposes rules that constrain activities and restrict forming or joining. The law usually imposes restrictions that can prevent these associations from achieving their goals, allowing the executive authorities to interfere in activities and affect NSAs' performance. Adding to this the circumstances surrounding associations' activities along with the political situation in Jordan and the absence of democracy may lead to the assumption that NSAs are ineffective, but this is not entirely the case.

The Jordanian constitution explicitly states that Jordanians have the right to assemble under the law, and to establish associations provided that they have goals and rules that do not violate the law. Thus, the constitution guarantees the right to form associations but also mentions 'monitoring their resources', that is, scrutinizing their sources of finance. This point is elaborated further in legislation which classifies associations into local and foreign. The latter are defined as those with headquarters located outside Jordan or having more than half of their board as non-Jordanians, which draws attention to the importance of international NSAs in Jordan's political life.

The sources of NSA influence in Jordan are often tribal, and in some cases paradoxically related to the state. At the other extreme are NSAs that rely more on foreign support and funding, though these can come also under state pressure and find their activities restricted. Few NSA members sit in parliament or are otherwise involved in political life through a party, while the political parties of Jordan are often built around family and clan affiliations. The extent to which NSAs influence the process of policy- and law-making is thus limited by weak organizational structures and a near absence of NSA lobbying in parliament on economic issues.

Some in Jordan feel that for NSAs to bolster policies and bypass the state level by communicating directly with the public is a threat to the security of the state and society. Indeed, allegations are periodically made regarding the sources of 'foreign funding' for NSAs, with questions being raised about their regional and international networks. It is only in recent years, with increasing emphasis on trade liberalization, that the state has begun to withdraw from some areas of public life. However, the regime continues to co-opt NSAs. Jordan thus allows the development of relatively abundant NSAs, but has also helped to create captive organizations that actually aid the regime in controlling opposition.

Thus, the preference of many NSAs in Jordan today is to proceed cautiously with lobbying in the trade and other spheres. In fact, such is the strength of the executive branch of government that NSAs must not exhibit critical opposition leadership. This narrows the range of activities of an NSA to a specific sub-set within the broader field of interest; the state is armed with legal instruments to dissolve organizational non-compliance; it controls emergence of an organized opposition; and prevents the emerging leaders in NSAs who could constitute viable threats to the regime's power (Wiktorowicz 2002).

At the same time, the state purports to recognize NSAs and ask for their support in policy-making. Confirmation of this situation came in June 2004 when the then Prime Minister, Faisal Fayez, said, 'The sad fact is that we have no Jordanian public opinion because the silent majority constitutes 90% of the population and the only voices heard are those of the professional associations, the Islamic Action Front and the leftist parties.' He complained that the government has received no official reactions to various key pieces of draft legislation (ar-Ra'i 2004).

Jordan's trade reform has led to, among other things, important liberalization. However, despite progress in the implementation of trade reform, the role of the state in Jordan is still strong. As long as many of the relatively new NSAs have strong links with the state, change will remain shaped by the interests of competing elite groups and individuals. The continuing dependency of the people on the state also mirrors Jordan's increasing reliance on international institutions and Western governments; achieved through the transfer of growing amounts of development aid.

Donors and others see Jordan as needing to move towards a more outward-oriented trade strategy in order to rectify the current imbalance in its foreign exchange position. After a precarious debt position forced Jordan to seek outside assistance, since the 1990s the country has been engaged in trade reform in collaboration with various international organizations and foreign governments. Thus, the country's main drivers of trade reform in general were foreign governments and lending agencies, though the demand for change came partly from the local private sector. However, this was not necessarily expressed in the activities of business chambers, but came mostly from owners of large businesses dealing directly with top officials on an individual basis.

In conclusion, it remains the case that the specific trade policy aims of many Jordanian NSAs are imprecise, except possibly where an international NSA has become involved to offer support and shape agendas and policy objectives. However, as discussed above, the involvement of international NSAs has proven to be a sensitive topic, and the state still tries to restrict foreign participation in the country's public life that is not directly channelled through government aid programmes. Yet the latter have openly taken a role in the beginning of change in the Jordanian trade regime and continue to participate in influencing trade policy, though with greater participation by Jordanian NSAs.

3   Jordan's trade agreements

In this case study, particular agreements and on-going negotiations selected as the main basis for analysis are, at the multilateral level, WTO accession and the Doha Round, and, in the case of PTAs, the Jordan–US FTA and the Israel–Jordan–United States QIZ accord.

3.1   Multilateral trade agreements

3.1.1   WTO accession negotiations

In the 1990s, the Jordanian leadership's preoccupation with regional politics meant that the decision to join the WTO and the economic rationale of what the country hoped to achieve by becoming a member were overshadowed by strategic considerations. However, with the ascension in 1999 of King Abdullah II, Jordan's decision to join the WTO became a central element of the country's development strategy. Once full membership in the WTO was successfully reached in April 2000, Jordan agreed to assume all its market access commitments on goods. Under the terms of Jordan's membership of the WTO, custom tariffs must be reduced to 20% by 2010. Jordan also made commitments in its services schedules, primarily in business services, transport, financial services and tourism, which are strategic to supporting the diversification of its economic structure. As a member of the WTO, Jordan has fully implemented wide-ranging commitments under the General Agreement on Tariffs and Trade (GATT), the General Agreement on Trade in Services (GATS) and the agreement on Trade-Related Aspects of Intellectual Property (TRIPS), signed the Information Technology Agreement, and is currently in an advanced stage of negotiations for its accession to the Government Procurement Agreement.

3.1.2 The Doha Round negotiations

In the Doha Round, Jordan is classified as a small and vulnerable economy (SVE), and, as a net food importer developing country, it has called for additional flexibilities in this round of agricultural negotiations. Jordan upholds Doha and Hong Kong mandates for the phasing out of export subsidies, more stringent rules on domestic support, and it supports demands for developing countries to designate special and sensitive products in addition to creating a new special safeguard mechanism. In terms of non-agricultural market access, Jordan is actively participating in the 'recently-acceded members' grouping. It has submitted a proposal with other SVEs calling for additional flexibilities and a balanced tariff reduction formula, which will allow these groups of countries to achieve industrial policies and diversification objectives, as well as securing effective market access for their exports. Jordan also strongly supports eliminating all market access barriers on products of export interest for developing countries. Jordan officially considers the success of Doha negotiations as 'paramount for its own prosperity and for the region's and the global economy's prospects'. The failure to revive Doha would mean 'a triumph for protectionism, which would be detrimental to the multilateral trading system and interests of all countries, particularly the smaller and developing members. Jordan will spare no effort in working with all WTO members in any attempts to revive the Talks.' (Government of Jordan 2008)

3.2 Preferential trade agreements

3.2.1 Israel–Jordan–United States Qualifying Industrial Zone

The QIZ is a trade agreement instigated by the United States between itself, Jordan and Israel, established in 1996 and aimed at enhancing regional economic cooperation and integration (Ruebner 2000). The legal basis for the agreement is the existence of an Israel–US FTA, on the one hand, and a Jordan–Israel free trade accord (signed in 1995), on the other hand. Merchandise produced in a QIZ enclave may enter the US market without payment of duty or excise taxes. A product is granted duty-free and quota-free access to the United States provided that the sum of the cost or value of materials produced in the West Bank, Gaza Strip, a QIZ or Israel, plus the direct costs of processing operations performed in the West Bank, Gaza Strip, a QIZ or Israel, is no less than 35% of the appraised value of such articles when imported into the United States. More specifically, the local content requirement states that to qualify for duty-free access to the US market, a good must have 11.7% of Jordanian QIZ content, and 7% or 8% of Israeli content (7% for high-tech products, 8% for others). The remaining 15.3% (16.3% for high-tech) to reach the 35% value-added requirement, may be provided by Jordan, the United States, the West Bank, Gaza or Israel.[2] Qualifying industrial zones were successful in expanding Jordan's exports: the kingdom became a processing base for exports of garments to the United States, and the industry became Jordan's largest export sector. QIZ has helped the garment industry to develop into Jordan's second most important manufacturing sector.

3.2.2   Jordan–US FTA

This agreement, in force since 2001, eliminates tariffs on virtually all industrial and agricultural products over ten years, and opens Jordan's services market to US companies in key sectors, including energy distribution, printing and publishing, health, audiovisual, tourism and transport services. The agreement also promotes more effective protection of intellectual property rights (IPR). The rules of origin (RoO) provide that at least 35% of the customs value of imported products must originate in the United States. Finally, the FTA has a special set of 'substantial transformation' rules for textile and apparel products. The US–Jordan FTA provides for a tariff system made up of 14,000 tariff lines over thirteen categories. The average tariff rate for Jordan is 6%, half of the weighted average tariff rate in 2003. The agreement for five categories of products, defined according to the tariff phase-out rules, is asymmetrical and provides for the elimination of all duties in ten years, while for the remaining eight categories special provisions will be applied unilaterally. The FTA also defines special staging categories covering, among others, certain alcohol, textile and agricultural products, as well as cars. To receive

---

[2] A different RoO regime in each FTA is a burden for Jordanian exporters, especially small firms. Large firms with stronger administrative capacities are thus the main beneficiaries of PTAs.

duty-free treatment an article must 'originate' in Jordan, or if any third-country materials are used, those materials must be substantially transformed into a Jordanian 'origin' product through a manufacturing or processing operation, and be imported directly into the United States.

4   State–non-state actor interactions and forum choice

Interviews for this research revealed that state agency views on alternative negotiating forums (multilateral or regional) differed, with various officials finding one or the other easier to deal with. Yet there was consensus that the forum in which to negotiate and manage trade relations was exogenously determined and not the result of government deliberation. There are no processes for consultation with NSAs as part of government deliberations to determine whether particular issues should be dealt with in a multilateral or regional context.

Within government, key trade negotiation and policy decisions are usually taken at the highest level, that of the prime minister (or sometimes vice premier). Some inter-agency processes are in place for trade policy deliberation, policy formulation and negotiation, but these processes do not differ according to whether the negotiation is multilateral or regional.

Interaction with NSAs has developed since the 1990s when WTO and other negotiations were launched. Steps taken by the government to organize and prepare for its participation in WTO accession negotiations were uncertain at the outset, having started with the designation of the office of the secretary general of the Ministry of Planning as a focal point of the process. However, this soon shifted to the MoIT, where a small WTO secretariat was formed in 1995. After that, gradual but accelerating involvement of NSAs – including business chambers, as well as a few individual companies and some consultants – in the WTO accession process helped the government to take the issue more seriously and commit resources to a strengthened technical team in the MoIT, as well as devote more time at cabinet level to accession issues.

Some processes now exist for NSA consultation, but whether this consists of genuine participation in decision-making is unclear. On the whole, such processes work best when personal relationships exist among interlocutors (i.e., ministers, on the one hand, and chamber heads, on the other hand). Processes are different depending on the NSAs involved, with, for example, chambers, and more recently labour unions, becoming more proactive. Processes can differ as between multilateral

Table 7.4 *State actors' reasons for consultation*

	%
Seeking technical advice and commercial intelligence	28
Promoting transparency	20
Gauging potential public views in relation to potential points of opposition to negotiating positions	20
Creating coalitions to support negotiating positions and outcomes	16
Satisfying public policy (including statutory) requirements	16

Source: Author's calculations from survey data.

and regional negotiations, with the latter tending to be more dynamic thanks to the overt involvement of the foreign stakeholder, especially in the case of significant involvement of USAID and of mixed chambers/business groups in the process leading up to and following signature of the Jordan–US FTA.

Research for this study has found that state actors engage with non-state actors in trade policy-making for the following reasons (in order of importance): for 'seeking technical advice and commercial intelligence'; for 'promoting transparency' and 'gauging potential public views in relation to potential points of opposition to negotiating positions' (equal second preference); and 'creating coalitions to support negotiating positions and outcomes' and 'satisfying public policy (including statutory) requirements' (equal third preference). Government views as to how far NSAs have influenced negotiating positions tended to be mixed, but it was not thought that NSAs exerted any influence over forum choice for trade negotiations, or that NSA attitudes towards alternative forums differed.[3] Table 7.4 summarizes state actors' reasons for consultation.

With a few exceptions, which will be discussed below, it was generally found that in the case of Jordan, NSA preferences had a minor influence on trade policy decision-making in relation to specific negotiations. Part of the problem is that for most Jordanian NSAs surveyed, areas of policy interest were not clearly defined except in broad general terms. The various constituencies served by most NSAs were also defined in terms of the narrow membership of, for example, a business chamber without making

---

[3] The Annex lists state, NSA and INSA representatives interviewed.

an effort in most cases to define a broader constituency, which could if identified be engaged in support of their aims. For example, the two NSAs interviewed that focused on garment manufacturing (involved in issues related to the QIZ agreement) simply defined their constituents as 'garment manufacturers' without mentioning, for example, designers, raw material producers, workers, consumers or other stakeholders. Put in other terms, there was little recognition of industrial clusters, on the one hand, or of political networking, on the other hand. This pointed up a general weakness in Jordan's public affairs culture, where the state had previously been all powerful and NSAs very weak or non-existent. Naturally, the objective reality underpinning such a situation has changed with the advent of trade liberalization and globalization, but the mentality needed to cope with the new economic situation has developed more slowly.

Turning to the NSAs themselves, their sources of funding in most cases were declared to be internal, with members providing the bulk of finance for organizations. As mentioned above, there is great sensitivity in Jordan regarding this issue, as there is concerning the question of international affiliates, who were in most cases limited. On the other hand, the lack of a political culture also meant that national affiliates of most NSAs were few; once again, the state's previous attitude of controlling public life and repressing civil society organizations and labour groups contributed to this reluctance by NSAs to networking and forming alliances with other stakeholders.

Affiliations, again, were not well developed: explicit or constitutional international affiliates existed for several of the NSAs examined, in two cases international NSAs were relevant, namely, the International Trade Union Confederation (ITUC), and to a lesser extent the Ebert Foundation, which will be elaborated on below. Yet apart from these instances, in general the contribution to local NSA activities in Jordan of explicitly affiliated international associations was limited. The suspicion here is that this process of interaction, with even those legal and explicitly permitted organizations, was meagre due to the reluctance of Jordanian NSAs who were wary of the state frowning on their outside connections. By the same token, coordination with international NSAs by NSAs with no international affiliates was practically non-existent. Regarding coordination work in the domestic process, the existence of national affiliates or coalitions was also limited in most cases.

Trade interests and activism focused in most cases on a mix of very narrow concerns of specific NSAs (e.g., garment exports) or a too wide preoccupation with grand national issues, which were nevertheless not

Table 7.5 *Ways in which NSAs try to influence trade policy*

	%
Participating in meetings or committees organized by government	32
Self-initiated interaction with government or other lobbying activity	32
Publishing or broadcasting material	19
Conducting public campaigns	17

Source: Compiled by author from individual NSAs.

properly digested or considered (e.g., opposition to Israel). The particular areas of interest as they relate to trade policy tended not to be sharply focused or expressed in the context of WTO issues or matters connected to a PTA. In the case of Jordanian NSAs today, it is in bilateral PTA trade negotiations where they have been most active. Yet this does not necessarily indicate a clear preference for bilateralism or PTAs; rather, this is a reflection, on the one hand, of the high level of activity in bilateral negotiations being negotiated by Jordan currently, as well as on the relatively moribund situation of the Doha Round, on the other hand. It should also be remembered that NSAs on the whole were less active in Jordan in the late 1990s when accession to the WTO was being negotiated.

As for the issue of forum choice, most NSAs stated in interviews that they did not act differently in multilateral and regional settings, feeling that government gave the same space to participate in decision-making regardless of whether negotiation was multilateral or regional; with similar government attitudes towards multilateral and PTA forums.

Regarding efforts at seeking to exercise influence (see Table 7.5), the ways in which NSAs tried to have an impact on particular trade negotiations were in order of importance: 'participating in meetings or committees organized by government' and 'self-initiated interaction with government or other lobbying activity' (equal first); 'publishing or broadcasting material'; and 'conducting public campaigns' (a distant second and third preference, respectively).

Table 7.6 shows that those whom NSAs sought most to influence were 'ministers/vice ministers' (a clear favourite) followed by 'government officials' and, finally, 'legislators' and 'public opinion', the latter two noticeably not of interest to NSAs. There were no significant differences in approach to influencing policy outcomes according to whether the context is multilateral or preferential. These responses suggest that NSAs are

Table 7.6 *Policy-makers that NSAs seek to influence*

	%
Ministers/vice ministers	40
Government officials	29
Legislators	18
Public opinion	13

not particularly focused on grassroots activity, choosing instead to deal with government directly, preferably at cabinet or other high level.

Jordan's NSA experience has shown that their government interlocutors were more interested in form as opposed to genuinely listening. On the other hand, some NSAs felt that they had exercised a certain amount of influence, with the MoIT most often cited as the main agency involved. With regard to their degree of influence in relation to different fora, there was no significant difference due to government attitudes, consultation opportunities offered or public responsiveness. As for possible improvement in the manner in which NSAs are permitted or invited to participate in decision-making, the answer was generally that the state should take NSAs more seriously. However, this was not nuanced by whether negotiating contexts were multilateral or regional. In any case, such simplistic responses are partly a testament to the relative immaturity of Jordanian NSAs. At the same time, the number and type of trade accords has been rising, as seen in Table 7.7. This proliferation complicates the task of advocacy groups and other NSAs in taking positions, on the one hand, but offers a richer area of work for an NSA willing and technically able to rise to the occasion, on the other hand.

In summing up these findings, it is possible to say that although NSA influences on negotiating agendas and outcomes are not extensive, some cases nevertheless exist. For example, a challenge Jordan faced when negotiating WTO accession related to TRIPs. This provides an interesting example of the work of NSAs in trade policy-making in the country. The Jordan Intellectual Property Association (JIPA) is an NSA that is aware of the major impacts of WTO membership on the Jordanian economy through TRIPS. Unlike many other NSAs in Jordan, JIPA has been active in emphasizing the role of WTO compliance in attracting foreign investment to Jordan. That JIPA is perhaps the exception that proves the rule regarding relative NSA inactivity in the trade sphere is

Table 7.7 *PTAs negotiated by Jordan*

Country/group	Type of agreement	Year signed	Year entered into force
Israel	Partial scope agreement (PSA)	1995	1996
QIZ (Israel–US)*	PSA based on RoO cumulation	1995	1996
AFTA	FTA with 16 other Arab countries, all of which had PSAs with Jordan	1997	1998
EU	FTA and association agreement	1997	2002
US*	FTA	2000	2001
European Free Trade Area	FTA	2001	2002
Agadir (Egypt–Morocco–Tunisia)	Provides for RoO cumulation with three Arab states that are also members of AFTA	2004	2006
Singapore	FTA	2004	2005
Canada	FTA	2009	Ratification process underway

Source: MoIT website at: www.moit.gov.jo, accessed July 2009.
* Analysed in this case study.

due to various factors. One of them is that JIPA is largely made up of lawyers, who also tend to be from the higher socio-economic class of Jordanians. Their skill and connections allow them to talk to parliamentarians more freely, but they have also succeeded in soliciting the help of international organizations such as the World Intellectual Property Organization (WIPO). At the same time, JIPA's aims are roughly those of the Jordanian government, which made for a harmonious partnership of local and international officialdom with JIPA. Another factor explaining JIPA's role is the involvement of the international NSA, the Business Software Alliance, an international organization committed to advancing world trade for legitimate business software by advocating strong copyright protection. (However, the situation in other cultural industries did not develop as positively, with book, music and audio-visual piracy levels still quite high. Protection of IPR still requires major efforts in educating the Jordanian public and private sectors, a task in which JIPA continues to play a role.)

JIPA provides a good contrast to many otherwise lame Jordanian NSAs. In this case, lobbying the government was done by well-connected experts who actually helped the state accomplish what it was being asked to do under WTO rules. Thus, in a country where the government is more or less authoritarian, state support of the cause of JIPA should not be seen as a 'victory' for an NSA 'fighting' the powers that be. Rather, this is an example of cooperation between the public and civil sectors on an economic issue.

Apart from the TRIPS issue, social standards debates have most notably been raised recently in the context of Jordan's trade agreements. In particular, this occurred with the lobbying by the ITUC office in Amman for the Jordan–US FTA's clause on labour rights, which was the first such element in a US trade accord internationally to base these rights on International Labour Organization conventions as opposed to national laws. In this respect, it is interesting to note that labour rights issues in Jordan have started to acquire a higher profile, especially since 2006 when work conditions in the country's garments sector began to be widely debated. Also active in this respect has been the Ebert Foundation, an international NSA working through its Amman office.

In particular, with the impetus provided by the Jordan–US FTA's labour clause, in 2006 the US National Labor Committee published a report, titled 'US–Jordan Free Trade Agreement Descends into Human Trafficking and Involuntary Servitude', that effectively threatened the success of Jordan's QIZs. The report gave a detailed account of violations of labour rights, highlighting poor working conditions in the industry. This caused concern among US apparel companies that source their garments in Jordan; it also created awareness regarding the status of Jordan's foreign workers.

Working conditions in some QIZ factories were found by the report to be poor in many respects. QIZ labour turnover is high, productivity is low and absenteeism is common. To help combat these problems, in January 2009, Jordan's Labour Ministry, the General Trade Union of Workers in Textile Industries and one of the newer more specialized NSAs, the Jordan Garment Accessories and Textiles Exporters (JGATE), signed a memorandum of understanding under which garment employers agreed to improve the conditions of Jordanians working in QIZ factories.

It is too early to say that this issue has been resolved in a satisfactory manner, nevertheless this is a clear example of the direct involvement of an international NSA (the ITUC), working with Jordanian NSAs, lobbying in negotiations for a bilateral trade agreement (the Jordan–US FTA) that resulted in an important change being made that eventually had a practical result. Unfortunately, this is perhaps a rare exception that proves that rule regarding the quiescence of Jordanian NSAs in trade matters. Yet it is interesting that this should have taken place in the context of a bilateral agreement, perhaps an easier forum in which NSAs can be active.

Finally, regarding the paralysis of the Doha Round talks, the government of Jordan is officially 'dismayed' according to its WTO Trade Policy Review 2008, though it is unclear whether many NSAs share this concern or are even seriously involved in the Doha work programme. While Jordan is concerned with various aspects of the Doha agenda, the country's limited negotiation resources and technical expertise are drawbacks. One way out of such a situation is for a much larger role to be taken by NSAs in support of the government, but this has yet to happen in the current public culture of the kingdom. However, it should be remembered that such an unsatisfactory situation is the fault of both the state and NSAs, as it is no longer possible to speak of open repression of civil society by the government in Jordan. Nevertheless, the practical implications of the Doha Round are still far from the agendas of NSAs in Jordan.

5   Conclusion

In the mid-1990s when Jordan began negotiating a QIZ trade accord with Israel and the United States, a free trade agreement with the United States and entry into the WTO the impression in the country was that trade policy decisions were settled by a handful of government bodies and conveyed to parliament and society at large. Since then, the manner in which Jordanian national trade policy is formulated has changed, with an increasing, though still relatively small, involvement by NSAs in these processes.

The visible impact of PTAs seems to have been higher in Jordan, though this is partly thanks to effective publicity by the foreign power involved, in this case the United States. However, it is a fact that reforms were implemented by the Jordanian government as companion measures to the Jordan–US FTA to boost the payoff from free trade with America both at and behind the border. Those included improvements in gender mainstreaming, labour rights and intellectual property protection.

One of the main benefits of the Jordan–US FTA came from addressing labour issues that are related to trade, especially by invoking the Jordan–US FTA labour clauses. The previously mentioned report on labour and human rights published in 2006 caused concern among US apparel companies that source their garments in Jordan and created confusion regarding the status of the country's foreign workers. The Jordanian government's swift and effective response in this situation has helped to enhance Jordan's reputation globally, and to improve the condition of workers inside the country.

Another benefit concerned intellectual property protection which was improved through the FTA. Jordan's intellectual property legislation contains TRIPS-plus provisions, which were adopted to further enhance intellectual property protection and respect Jordan's international commitments. The Jordanian pharmaceutical industry in particular has benefited from strengthened TRIPS-plus IPR legislation inspired by the Jordan–US FTA. As a result, Jordanian companies have entered into licensing relationships with firms from the United States and elsewhere.

QIZs helped to address the problem of gender inequality in the labour market, and the low productivity of women through increasing employment and training. Recently, five QIZ 'satellites' have opened operations in areas of high female unemployment.

By interacting with some NSAs, the Jordan–US FTA raised the understanding of the impact and role of trade policy on the environment. This has happened especially through activities such as the US-sponsored environmental forum held in Jordan in March 2009 to examine the impact of the Jordan–US FTA environmental clause on Jordan. Along with the impact of the accord's labour clause mentioned above this is noteworthy.

By streamlining its system and making better use of international trade agreements such as the Jordan–US FTA, Jordan will hopefully cope better with the current global financial crisis. Apart from directly helping to lift exports, the Jordan–US FTA has also helped Jordan to improve its economy and its regulations, which will allow it to compete more effectively in global markets. QIZ, on the other hand, now appears to be unravelling. The Jordan QIZ's shortcomings are a result of fecklessness on the part of Amman, and not an inherent weakness in the model itself. Bad management and unsound business models are likely to have been behind the retreat in garment exports rather than the financial crisis, as well as fierce competition from Egyptian QIZs in exporting garments to the United

States. An indigenously-rooted QIZ model (not just a footloose collection of offshore manufacturers) could have been a powerful tool for export promotion and development.

Preference duplication and erosion happened to the Jordan QIZs after Egypt obtained the same privileges. Had the approach to QIZs been better planned from the beginning, it is possible that stronger backward linkages and technology transfers could have taken place. At present, there is an attempt to fill this gap by JGATE, which asked the government for an incentive package to minimize the impact of the current crisis and of the downturn in US imports, so far with no resolution.

Unlike the case of QIZ, reforms directly or indirectly spurred by the PTA with the United States – in human rights and intellectual property protection – have helped to deal with the important role of the state in the economy, shifting the government from being an interfering, punitive and generally counter-productive economic actor to having a more constructive role as regulator, facilitator and defender of rights.

At the same time, international NSAs have involved themselves in Jordan. For example, the ITUC has an increasingly active office in Amman and supports local trade unions, becoming directly involved in lobbying. A strong attempt by the ITUC to lobby for changes in the law produced a positive reaction. The impact that such support has left on the capability of the local unions to participate more fully in public life is generally positive.

Interest of NSAs in economic policy and law-making in Jordan was limited, and pressure to change laws and reform came from other directions. Such pressure included Jordan's application and eventual membership of the WTO, which led to, and continues to result in, measures assuring a more liberal and open foreign trade regime, including significant changes in economic laws. Though the general perceptions in Jordan about the WTO are largely impressionistic with mixed views about the ramifications of joining, there is no doubt that WTO accession was the prime mover in the reform of Jordanian laws in the late 1990s. NSAs were not seriously involved in this change, and the WTO process and its heavy technical workload raise the issue of the limited ability of a Jordanian NSA to participate in it.

Jordan has attempted to conform to WTO requirements from 1995, and the country's membership was even delayed due to the slow pace of legal and policy reforms. Before and after accession, Jordanian trade unions have been quiescent regarding the WTO, but business chambers are becoming more vocal. Seminars were held for NSAs and government to exchange views before and after joining; at the same time, the technical and human resources of NSAs in Jordan are limited, and therefore their ability to engage in legislative lobbying is circumscribed.

On the other hand, various foreign stakeholders with an interest in Jordan's stability wanted trade reform, and the support at high levels in Jordan that they were able to marshal was considerable. There was thus no serious effort to build consensus through NSAs or a need to compromise with them to be able to implement reform, which nevertheless was done very gradually in order to placate elements of the bureaucracy. In sum, the legitimacy of trade reform and the power of the reformers to push it through were not questioned, and the political and institutional processes by which affected groups influenced decisions about reform were not significant or problematic.

The interplay of powerful outside forces allied to the upper echelons of the regime pushing reforms, with some bureaucrats and grassroots opposition against change, has affected the design of trade reform, tending to make it Western-oriented in spirit and presentation. In any case, reform was top-down, initiated by government, and only secondarily reacting to pressures from NSAs. Parliament and the media were, and often remain, timid and unprofessional, and it remains crucial to familiarize parliamentarians and journalists with WTO issues.

In the mid-1990s Jordan started its WTO negotiations unprepared: otherwise, why was the technical side of WTO entry left for thirty months to a staff of two people? Now, after serious expansion and strengthening on the technical side, Jordan has even managed to export its WTO accession expertise to other Arab states, to the mutual benefit of provider and recipient.

Close to a decade after accession, the benefits of WTO membership for Jordan are still misunderstood at a popular level. Greater participation of NSAs from the beginning would have helped, but the state's paternalism is not entirely to blame, as the anti-WTO arguments that NSAs sometimes advanced were in some cases spurious and propagandistic. To remedy this, technical assistance could have been extended to NSAs. However, this is not easy as such organizations are often unequipped to handle serious assistance. The process is also expensive. In such a situation, possible entry points for aid policy could be the granting of support to the research and documentation departments of business associations. Other suggestions for entry points to support NSAs would be more practical training for journalists in economic reporting, and for civil society activists in lobbying.

In conclusion, the question of which kind of trade agreement is preferred by NSAs in Jordan remains unanswered, and possibly not of
major relevance. The role of Jordan's NSAs in development of national
approaches to WTO and PTA policy formulation is still limited, and the
implications of the interactions between these NSAs and the Jordanian
government in terms of preferred instruments for trade cooperation are
not very important. The 'optimum' mode for cooperation between the
state and NSAs seems to be the current mixture of WTO and PTA negotiations, always provided that the government is sincere in its engagement of NSAs, and the latter are professional and mature enough to
work effectively alongside the state. Issues of forum choice are still not
publicly articulated grassroots issues among domestic Jordanian political and economic interests, so there are no major lessons to be drawn
about government choices vis-à-vis multilateralism and preferentialism,
beyond noting that these are influenced by the country's highest political
authority (the king) and by outside powers. Broader lessons about the
multilateralism/regionalism debate more generally will thus have to be
sought outside Jordan.

References

Central Bank of Jordan 2009. *Monthly Statistical Bulletin*, June.

al Khouri, R. 2008. '*WTO Trade Policy Review*', WT/TPR/G/206, Government of
Jordan.

ar-Ra'i 2004. '*Prime Minister Faisal Fayez Interviewed*', ar-Ra'i Arabic daily newspaper, Amman, 15 June.

Ruebner, J. 2000. '*US–Israel Free Trade Area: Jordanian–Israeli Qualifying
Industrial Zones*', CRS Report for Congress, Congressional Research
Service, the Library of Congress, Washington, DC, 30 March.

US Government Printing Office Washington 2001. '*Jordan Free Trade Agreement*',
hearing before the Committee on Finance, US Senate, 107th Congress, first
session, Washington, DC, 20 March.

US National Labor Committee 2006. '*US–Jordan Free Trade Agreement Descends
into Human Trafficking and Involuntary Servitude*', New York.

Wiktorowicz, Q. 2002. 'Embedded Authoritarianism: Bureaucratic Power and
the Limits to Non-Governmental Organizations in Jordan', in G. Joffe (ed.),
Jordan in Transition: 1990–2000. London: Hurst.

ANNEX

Interviewees

State entities

Maha al-Ali, director, MoIT FTPD.

Maen Nsour, executive director, Jordan Investment Board.

Fakhry Hazaimeh, economic counsellor, Government of Jordan Delegation, Geneva.

Jawad Anani, former deputy prime minister/head of cabinet economic team, former Minister of Industry and Trade, Council of Ministers.

Tamam al-Ghul, former head of WTO Technical Unit, MoIT.

NSAs

Dana Bayyat, executive director, JGATE.

Samir Maqdah, head of Garment and Textile Chapter, Jordan Chamber of Industry.

Achim Vogt, resident representative, Ebert Foundation, Amman.

Adly Qandah, executive director, Association of Jordanian Banks.

Bassam Hajjawi, president, JIPA.

Nezam Qahoush, coordinator, ITUC, Amman office.

Zaki Ayoubi, secretary general, Jordan Chamber of Industry.

The following were also consulted in unstructured informal discussions: Haider Rashid, president, General Trade Union of Banks, Insurance and Audit Employees in Jordan; Muntaser Oklah, secretary general, MoIT; Ziad Abdessamad, director, Arab NGO Network for Development, Beirut; Hassan Nsour, director, QIZ Unit MoIT; Esther Busser, deputy director, ITUC, Geneva office; and Stefan Gremmling, Ebert Foundation, Geneva office. I would like to thank them all, and absolve them of any of this study's errors or omissions, which are entirely my responsibility.

8

Kenya

NJUGUNA NG'ETHE AND JACOB OMOLO

1 Introduction

It is almost axiomatic that trade policies of a country affect in one way or another many sectors of that country and those of its trading partners. In other words, the impact of trade policy quite often goes beyond the participating countries or the direct beneficiaries, be they producers or consumers. One would have thought, therefore, that in line with the principle that the governed must have a voice on matters that affect them, there would be no decision, agreement, treaty, convention or protocol on trade signed without the input of the governed. This, however, is often not the case. Thus, despite the increasing and widening of democratic space in most African countries, trade policy-making in many of these countries is still shrouded in mystery, secrecy and mainly the preserve of the executive branch of government. This situation persists even though most African governments have over the last fifteen years or so tended to embrace participatory planning, which should enlist non-state actors (NSAs) policy-making. Thus, in trade policy-making, NSAs often remain at the periphery of decision-making. One reason for this situation could be that consultation forums, where these exist, are perhaps deliberately limited in numbers and scope of action and, therefore, do not carry much weight.

This chapter examines the trade policy-making regime in Kenya and the role of stakeholders in preferential and multilateral trade negotiations. It analyses the role of state and non-state actors in the trade policy-making process and how the actors can increase their role in influencing the policy outcomes. The chapter is structured in five parts. Section 1 opens. Section 2 provides the background and context of the study, the overview and context of trade policy in Kenya, and its trade patterns over time in terms of the composition of trade and trade partners. Section 3 discusses the role of state and non-state actors in trade policy-making. It highlights the interests of the actors, their specific trade policy aims, sources of their influences and how they seek to exert it. Section 4 contains a discussion and analysis of Kenya's trade agreements, the influence of NSAs on their negotiation and outcomes, and issues of forum choice. Section 5 concludes.

2 Historical overview of trade policy in Kenya

Kenya's trade policy objectives are articulated in various policy documents developed since independence from Britain in 1963. Concrete elaboration of trade policy in Kenya was made in the Sessional Paper No. 1 of 1986 on Economic Management for Renewed Growth. Since then, Kenya's trade policies have evolved over time as articulated in the Economic Recovery Strategy for Wealth and Employment Creation (2003–7), the Kenya Medium Term Plan (2008–12) and Vision 2030 (2007).

After independence, Kenya relied on an import-substitution trade strategy. As elsewhere in Africa and the rest of the world, this policy was biased towards protection of domestic industries at the expense of their competitiveness since it enabled entrepreneurs, especially manufacturers, to make profits even in cases of under-utilized capacities. Kenyan manufacturers thus became inward-oriented and failed to venture into international markets.

By the beginning of the 1990s, the importance of the inward-looking development strategy had begun to wane. A review of the strategy showed that this strategy discouraged export promotion and resulted in the consistent shortage of foreign exchange. In addition, many other countries had begun to liberalize their trade regimes unilaterally. Furthermore, Kenya was forced to embark on economic reforms as a pre-condition for receiving aid.

Arising from these developments, the government embarked on a reform programme to promote trade, among other national growth and development areas. Thus, the primary objective of the current trade regime is the promotion of exports of consumer and intermediate goods, while at the same time laying the base for eventual production of capital goods for both domestic and export markets. Some of the incentives provided by the government to promote this are manufacturing under bond scheme, removal of export licensing, establishment of export processing zones, removal of exchange and price controls, pursuance of flexible exchange rate systems, trade licensing reforms and rationalization and removal of duties.

2.1   Patterns of trade

The volume of Kenya's exports has increased over time, albeit at a less proportionate rate compared with the increase in imports (Republic of Kenya, 2008). Kenya's international trade data for the period 1997–2007 show that the volume of the country's exports increased by an annual average of 13% between 1997 and 2008, compared with a 22% annual increase in imports over the same period (Republic of Kenya, 1998; 2009).

Kenya's export earnings continue to be generated mainly from exports of primary agricultural products, including coffee, tea and horticulture. The contribution of food and beverages to the total exports remained relatively high, though exhibiting a declining trend over the period, from 53.7% of total exports in 1997 to 40.4% in 2008. Second in importance to agricultural products, industrial supplies accounted for about 29% of the total exports in 2008 (Republic of Kenya, 2009). Trade data also show that Kenya's import demands increased considerably especially after 1999. This was due mainly to the trade liberalization policies adopted by the government. Specific areas of liberalization that may have contributed to the phenomenal growth in imports include the removal of import licensing, quantitative import restrictions and foreign exchange controls. The country's imports increased from US$3.04 billion in 1997 to US$3.18 billion in 2000. By 2008, the imports had more than tripled to stand at US$10.41 billion.[1] Industrial supplies and fuel and lubricants were the largest contributors to the country's import bill, constituting 31% and 26.8%, respectively, in 2008.

The export cover ratio, measured as total exports divided by total imports, also gradually declined over the period, from 63% in 1997 to 44.8% in 2008 (see Figure 8.1). The implication is that while the country's export earnings could finance about 63% of the imports in 1997, by 2008 the country's total exports could only cover close to 45% of the imports.

Owing to the considerable increase in imports vis-à-vis the marginal growth in exports, Kenya's trade deficit has worsened over time. The trade deficit increased by more than fivefold from US$1.1 billion in 1997 to US$5.8 billion in 2008.

Figure 8.2 gives a summary of Kenya's total exports by destination. It shows that Africa continues to be the major destination of Kenya's exports followed by Europe. In 2003, for example, the market share of Kenya's

---

[1] Converted at the mean exchange rate of US$1 to K.Shs.62.7, 78 and 74 in 1997, 2000 and 2008, respectively.

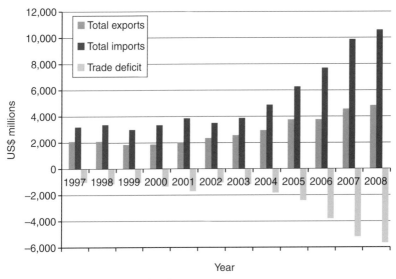

Figure 8.1 Kenya's balance of trade, 1997–2008

total exports to African countries and the European Union stood at 46.2% and 30.6%, respectively. The share of total exports to the European Union was 28.5% of the total exports, while exports to Asia accounted for 15.2%. By 2008, Kenya's share of exports to African countries stood at 47.6% of total exports, while that of Europe was 28.9%. The marginal decline in the market share of exports to African and European countries between 2003 and 2008 may be attributed to the increase in the exports to the United States, whose share of imports from Kenya more than quadrupled from 2% in 2003 to 9% in 2006 before easing to 6% in 2008.

Kenya's key commodity exports to Europe are coffee, tea, pyrethrum extract and tinned pineapples, with beans, peas and lentils of lesser importance. The principal commodities exported to the United States were tea, pyrethrum extract and tinned pineapples. Others included oil seeds, nuts, kernels, beans, peas and lentils.

Figure 8.3 gives a representation of the trend of Kenya's imports by region of origin. It reveals that the country's imports are mainly drawn from Asia, Europe and Africa. In 2008 the contribution of Asia, Europe and Africa to Kenya's total imports stood at 61.1%, 21.7% and 11.2%, respectively. The trade data also reveals that while the share of Kenya's imports from Africa and Europe declined over time, the proportion of the country's imports obtained from Asia increased over time. Imports

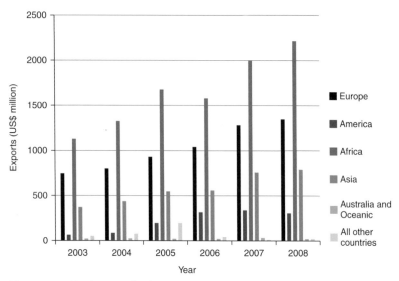

Figure 8.2   Total exports by destination, 2003–8

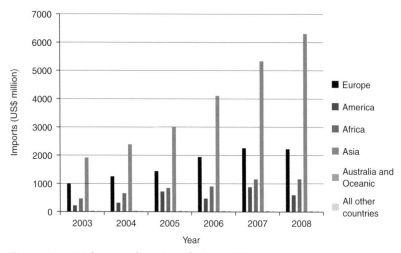

Figure 8.3   Total imports by region of origin, 2003–8

are mainly drawn from the United Arab Emirates, China, Japan, Saudi Arabia and Singapore.

The bulk of Kenya's exports are consumed within the East African Community (EAC), followed by other countries within the Common Market for Eastern and Southern Africa (COMESA). In 2008, for instance,

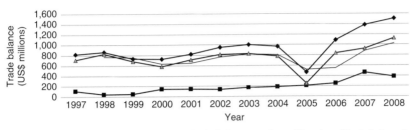

Figure 8.4   Kenya's pattern of trade in COMESA region, 1997–2008

51.6% of Kenyan exports were destined for the EAC, while 34.8% were sold in the COMESA countries other than Uganda, Burundi and Rwanda, who are also members of the EAC (Republic of Kenya, 2009). Tanzania and Uganda are the single largest consumers of Kenya's export products under the EAC trade area, while Sudan, Democratic Republic of Congo and Egypt are the largest export markets for Kenyan products outside the EAC. Kenya's imports from Africa mainly originate from within the COMESA region, but outside the EAC member countries. In 2008, for example, South Africa supplied 54.3% of Kenya's imports, Egypt 12.6% and Swaziland 5.8%. The imports from South Africa are mainly maize, sugar, petroleum products, paper and paperboard, motor vehicles, fertilizers and medicinal products.

Figure 8.4 shows the pattern of Kenya's trade within the COMESA region. It shows that Kenya's trading position within the COMESA region has been positive with the exports far outweighing the imports. Consequently, Kenya has over time experienced a positive trade balance.

The trade patterns summarized above give an indication of the growing importance of regional preferential trade agreements (PTAs) to the Kenyan economy compared with WTO agreements. The trade data analysed in the following discussions, for example, shows that African countries absorb up to 48% of Kenya's exports compared with the European Union's 29%, and that the share of Kenya's trade within the region has been growing at a relatively faster rate than the rate of increase in the proportion of its trade with other regions under the WTO framework.

3   State and non-state actors in trade policy-making

The development of trade policies in Kenya, particularly since the ushering in of democracy in 2003 for the first time since independence, has attempted to embrace consultation among and between both state and non-state actors. Negotiation of trade pacts have also started, albeit at a slow pace, to be participatory, enlisting the involvement of both governmental and non-governmental institutions and actors.

3.1   State actors

Trade policy-making in Kenya, like the formulation of other development policies, is mainly guided by the government. The presence of a strong executive in Kenya's governance system also points to the key role that the Office of the President plays in trade policy-making, especially in terms of approval and subsequent legislation. However, the focal point for trade policy-making in Kenya is the Ministry of Trade (MoT). The MoT is responsible for the promotion of trade and investment and is mandated to formulate trade and investment policies. The main functions of the Ministry are: (i) formulating, implementing, coordinating, reviewing and monitoring policies in trade and investments; (ii) facilitating the orderly development, promotion and growth of domestic and international trade; and (iii) facilitating the development and promotion of domestic and foreign direct investment. The MoT is also responsible for leading all industrial and trade policy negotiations at the EAC, COMESA and bilateral agreements. Specific mandates include monitoring the implementation of EAC specific trade agreements, common market negotiations and integrating trade and industrial policies in the regional policies.

A number of other government ministries and departments contribute to trade policy-making in Kenya. Key among these is the Ministry of East African Community (MEAC), which coordinates all activities related to the EAC. The MEAC coordinates, monitors and evaluates the implementation of EAC policies, projects and programmes, and liaises with public and private sector stakeholders on EAC matters. It also maintains linkages between the East African Legislative Assembly and the Kenya National Assembly, as well as linkages between EAC institutions, line ministries and other related institutions. The MEAC also facilitates the review of treaties, protocols and agreements under the EAC, including those related to regional integration.

Other ministries play some role in trade matters, albeit indirectly. The Ministry of Industrialization develops and implements the national industrial policy; the Ministry of State for Planning, National Development and Vision 2030 is responsible for national development planning; the Ministry of Finance sets and administers the national budget including revenues and expenditures; the Ministry of Foreign Affairs has overall responsibility for dealing with international relations; the Ministry of Agriculture formulates agricultural policies, including plans to ensure sufficient domestic capacity to produce and supply the staple food commodities; and the Central Bank of Kenya sets the monetary and exchange rate policies, as well as ensuring macro-economic stability.

Other government agencies and parastatals responsible for dealing with matters that are related to selected trade policy measures and/ or implementation of commitments under multilateral and other trade agreements include: the National Economic and Social Council, which is Kenya's apex economic and social policy body, whose role is to advise the government on appropriate social and economic policies that the country needs to pursue for sustained economic growth and development; the Kenya Bureau of Standards which deals with the development and enforcement of domestic standards and acts as the focal point for issues related to standardization and quality control; the Kenya Revenue Authority which collects governmental revenues, including customs duties; and the Kenya Industrial Property office which administers laws related to intellectual property. The Kenya Export Promotion Council and the Kenya Exports Processing Zones Authority perform the main function of export promotion, while the Horticultural Crops Development Authority is tasked with the development of the horticultural sector, which has emerged as the key export sector in recent years. The Kenya Investment Authority works to promote investment. The Privatization Steering Committee deals with disinvestments of state enterprises and the Development Bank of Kenya is mandated to provide development financing for projects. The Kenya Plant Health Inspectorate Service enforces plant protection standards and laws, while the Kenya Institute for Public Policy and Research Analysis provides research and analysis to government.

The state actors are involved in trade policy in different ways. Table 8.1 summarizes the results of the field interviews conducted with a selected number of key state actors in terms of their respective areas of policy interest, constituencies served, local and international affiliates and the specific trade negotiations in which they have been involved.

In Kenya, the MoT and EAC are the only government ministries with a mandate of developing trade policies and undertaking trade negotiations at the bilateral, regional (EAC and COMESA) and multilateral level. The other ministries and government departments facilitate the trade policy-making and negotiation processes by providing support services, such as guidance on the focus of the national development agenda, revenue, investment and export implications of specific trade pacts and research

Table 8.1 *Key state actors and areas of policy interest*

Agency name	Policy interest	Constituency served	Source of funding	National affiliate(s)	International affiliate	Trade negotiations involved in
Ministry of Trade	Trade policies: regional and multilateral	Government, public	State and donor funds channelled through Treasury	Ministry of Planning, Ministry of Finance and KRA	WTO	COMESA, EAC, EPA, WTO and virtually all trade agreements
Ministry of Finance	Prudent financial management	Government, public	State and donor funds channelled through Treasury	Ministry of Trade, Ministry of Planning, KRA, CBK		EAC, EPA, COMESA, WTO
Ministry of Planning	Development policies on trade and other developmental issues	Government, public	State	All ministries in the government		EAC, EPA
Ministry of EAC	Facilitation of trade by creating conducive environment for trade within the EAC	Government, public	State	Ministry of Trade, Ministry of Finance and Ministry of Planning	Ministries of EAC in member states	EAC

Kenya Revenue Authority	Revenue protection policies	Government, public	Taxation	Ministry of Trade, Ministry of Planning and Ministry of Finance		EAC, COMESA
Kenya Investment Authority	Investment-oriented trade negotiation policies	Investors, public	State	KRA, Ministry of Trade, Ministry of Finance, Ministry of Planning and Ministry of EAC		EAC, COMESA, EPA
KIPPRA	Research and policy analysis	Government of Kenya, CSOs, public	State, donors	KEPLOTRADE	None	EPA, WTO, COMESA, EAC
KEPLOTRADE	Capacity building in trade negotiations	Government, private sector, CSOs, public	State, donors	MoT, Ministry of Finance		EPA, WTO, COMESA, EAC

Source: Survey results (2009).

and policy analysis. Table 8.1 also shows that the trade policies and negotiations have mainly concentrated on EAC, COMESA and economic
partnership agreements (EPAs). This reflects the relative importance of
regional blocs in the trading pattern of Kenya.

3.2   The role of parliament

The National Assembly is an important institution in the growth, democratization and general development of any country. Parliaments worldwide legislate and put in place appropriate legal instruments necessary
for effective enforcement and implementation of national, regional and
international laws and treaties. For example, parliaments of EAC countries are required to enact laws to domesticate regional and international
agreements. The International Labour Organization (ILO) also encour-
ages member states that have ratified its conventions to domesticate them
by enacting new laws or incorporating the key provisions of the conventions in the existing domestic laws.

Analysis of the extent of participation of parliament in trade policy-
making in Kenya shows fairly low levels of participation of the legislature
in trade policy-making processes. Ordinarily, Members of Parliament
(MPs) participate in the process only when the draft policy is submitted to
parliament for consideration and approval. This is done both at the level of
the departmental committee responsible for trade matters, and when the
draft policy is brought to the floor of the house for debate. Occasionally, a
few parliamentarians may get the opportunity to give their views on the
policy during the stakeholder consultation stages, but this involvement is
limited to the extent of their invitation by the host ministry.

In regard to participation of the National Assembly in trade negotiations, there are no formal systems, procedures or structures that provide
for parliament's participation in trade negotiations and approval. On a
few occasions, such as the Cancun and Hong Kong WTO Ministerial
Meetings, some MPs participated in the Kenyan delegation, but their
involvement is at the discretion of the executive rather than as a consequence of an established legal and institutional framework.

At the level of the EAC, initiatives have been made to involve and
ensure parliamentary participation in trade negotiations. This was given
effect through the formation of the East African Parliamentary Liaison
Committee (EAPLC) on Trade in 2003. The objective of the EAPLC is
to ensure that MPs participate in trade negotiation processes, as well as
lobby and influence national governments to adopt a common position

during negotiations. The EAPLC is composed of the members of the trade committees of the national parliaments of the EAC member states. In addition, the members of the Communication, Trade and Investment Committee of the East African Legislative Assembly (EALA) are also members of the EAPLC.

The EAPLC initiative seeks to ensure coordinated trade policy within the EAC. However, the EAPLC itself suffers from ineffective coordination at the national and regional levels. The MPs serve their constituents, to whom they give priority and, thus, may not have sufficient time to devote to trade issues both at the national and regional levels. For the EAPLC to discharge its role effectively, there is a need for infrastructural and research support for MPs to ensure that they are fully appraised of the developments in the trade fields and the social, economic and political circumstances in the countries and the region.

3.3   Non-state actors

In Sub-Saharan Africa, Kenya is known for its vibrant civil society in all sectors of the economy. Not surprisingly, NSAs from both the business and civil society sectors are involved in trade-related policy issues. The business sector is organized into umbrella and sector-specific organizations to facilitate provision of, and access to, a range of advisory services, and to provide a platform for policy advocacy.

There are three key broad-based business umbrella organizations that aim to coordinate and represent the collective interests of the private sector and businesses in Kenya. The Kenya National Chamber of Commerce and Industry (KNCCI) represents small-, medium- and large-scale traders. The Federation of Kenya Employers (FKE) represents the collective interests of small, medium and large employers in matters relating to industrial relations, trade and taxation policies, public policy and the general promotion of a favourable investment climate. The Kenya Private Sector Alliance (KEPSA) is the umbrella organization of private business associations. KEPSA's policy advocacy centres on improving the enabling environment for business, particularly the formulation of investor-friendly public policy and a harmonized approach to cross-cutting issues that affect growth and development of the private sector. KEPSA mobilizes and coordinates the engagement of private sector associations in policy debate through sector working groups, ministerial stakeholder forums and roundtable discussions. Since 2008, KEPSA has been instrumental in engaging the government on key issues of concern to the private sector, such as trade and taxation policies, security, infrastructure development and the generally unfavourable business environment among others. This is done through monthly roundtable meetings with various government ministries and departments under the stewardship of the Prime Minister of the Republic of Kenya.

The sector-specific associations cater for the unique interests of their members. The best known of these associations is the Kenya Association of Manufacturers (KAM), which brings together the enterprises engaged in manufacturing only. KAM is regarded as the voice of industry and premier representative organization for value-adding industries and other related sectors in Kenya. According to KAM, the association provides an essential link for cooperation, dialogue and understanding with the government by participating in formulation and implementation of trade policies, promoting trade and investment, upholding standards and representing members' views and concerns to the relevant authorities.

Other sector-specific business associations whose interests are in trade policy-making are the Kenya Flower Council which represents flower producers, the Fresh Produce Exporters Association of Kenya (FPEAK), and the Kenya Small Scale Farmers Association (KSSFA). FPEAK is a premier private association in the horticultural industry. It draws membership from fruit and vegetable exporters, flower exporters, Kenyan embassies, international partners and other agricultural support institutions such as banks, suppliers of agricultural inputs and development partners that support the sub-sector. FPEAK provides a forum for raising the voice of horticultural farmers and exporters, and promoting policy dialogue between the farmers/exporters, government and other stakeholders. KSSFA represents the interests of small-scale farmers in almost all spheres of public policy-making, with a particular bias in trade policy-making in order to moderate the negative impacts of regional and multilateral trades on small-scale farmers and rural livelihoods.

According to both the state and non-state actors interviewed for this study, the private sector has been quite influential in trade policy-making in Kenya. This has been through participation in established trade consultative mechanisms, standing committees, taskforces and other key decision-making organs where government solicits the views of the private sector; lobbying either as individual firms or as associations; holding consultations with policy-makers in the form of roundtables, meetings, workshops and seminars; and through petitions and threats to the relevant authorities on specific trade policy issues/concerns.

The civil society organizations (CSOs) involved in trade policy issues are active in a variety of areas, such as research, policy analysis, dissemination, capacity-building, advocacy and policy influencing. In respect to trade policy-making and trade negotiations, the key CSOs are Action Aid, CUTS International, the Kenya Human Rights Commission and EcoNews Africa. Others are Friedrich Ebert Stiftung (FES), Oxfam, Southern and Eastern African Trade Information and Negotiations Institute, and the Central Organization of Trade Unions (COTU-K).

The number and diversity of interests of Kenyan CSOs make it even more important to have some mechanism for information and knowledge sharing and facilitating joint activities. Consequently, the Kenya Civil Society Alliance was established in 2002 to respond to this need. Other CSOs involved in trade policy are universities and policy analysis and research institutions, whose work is used by government as well as by other CSOs to support their lobbying and advocacy activities. The Institute of Policy Analysis and Research, Institute of Economic Affairs, Institute for Development Studies and the African Economic Research Consortium are some of the research and policy analysis institutions that have produced relevant research and analysis papers on trade issues.

3.4 Key consultative mechanisms

A number of mechanisms have been established to facilitate consultations among the various stakeholders and participation of the groups in trade policy issues. The existing consultative mechanisms include the Cabinet's Sub-Committee on Trade and Inter-Ministerial Committee, the Joint Industrial and Commercial Consultative Committee (JICCC), the National Committee on WTO (NCWTO), the Kenya–European Union Post-Lomé Trade Negotiations (KELPOTRADE)[2] and the Support Programme/National Development and Trade Policy Forum (NDTPF).

As previously discussed, the government plays a crucial role in the formulation and implementation of trade policies in Kenya. Kenya has a standing Cabinet Sub-Committee on Trade, where ministerial-level consultations and coordination take place on trade-related issues. This sub-committee performs an important role in resolving issues among government ministries and ensuring a coherent and coordinated approach to trade policy. Coordination among various government ministries and agencies also takes place through inter-ministerial committee

---

[2] Kenya–European Post-Lomé Trade Programme, available at: www.keplotrade.org/subsection.asp?ID=10, 23/05/09.

meetings, which are initiated and coordinated by relevant ministries. Bringing together all governmental stakeholders, these meetings facilitate the provision of technical inputs, the input of substantive comments and the harmonization of various policies being pursued by different government ministries.

The JICCC is another trade-related consultative mechanism that works within the framework of the inter-ministerial committee process. The MoT convenes and chairs the meetings of the JICCC and provides the secretariat for its functioning. The JICCC consists mainly of public and private sector representatives and meets only to deliberate on specific issues related to industrial and commercial matters. However, the functioning of the JICCC has not been very visible, hence, there is little information available in the public domain on the frequency, agenda and outcome of its meetings.

The NCWTO is a forum mandated to develop national positions on the WTO. This is the main trade consultative forum for bringing together all stakeholders from the public sector, private sector and civil society to discuss trade policy issues related to the WTO. The NCWTO was established by government in response to demands for policy involvement and participation from CSOs and development partners. The NCWTO is mandated to meet once a year and more often if needed. All stakeholders have the opportunity to raise issues and present positions of their constituents and relevant stances on WTO trade agreements. NCWTO also provides resources, workshops, consultative meetings, research and analysis to inform national positions and build capacity of stakeholders. The NCWTO is often consulted regarding representation in the WTO ministerial conferences. Consequently, representatives of NSAs are now included in the official delegation to the WTO ministerial conferences. Our interviews have found that business and CSOs feel that they have been able to engage with the government through the NCWTO on WTO issues.

Preparations for the EPA negotiations are being facilitated through KEPLOTRADE Negotiations Support Programme, which has an inbuilt National Development and Trade Policy Forum. KEPLOTRADE was established by the MoT in 2001 as a national EPA negotiation structure to facilitate the country's negotiations of EPA with the European Union. Its purpose is to facilitate and promote stakeholder consultations as a key means to defining broad-based national positions on EPA issues, as well as disseminating EPA-related information. KEPLOTRADE's mandate is to (i) undertake required analytical studies, (ii) coordinate the participation of stakeholders in EPA negotiations and (iii) build the capacity of government and NSAs to effectively engage and participate in the actual negotiation process.

KEPLOTRADE is housed within the MoT, where its operations are overseen by a national steering committee, assisted by a technical team. KEPLOTRADE benefits from financial and technical support provided by the European Union. Its membership is broad-based, with representation from the public and private sectors, CSOs and research institutions that are engaged in trade and development work. The forum works through seven clusters/groups, namely, market access, agriculture, services, trade-related issues, fisheries, development dimensions and legal and institutional. The clusters/groups are responsible for undertaking analytical studies and consultations to help formulate the national position on the issues under the cluster. Figure 8.5 shows the structure of Kenya's negotiating team for EPAs.

The structure of Kenya's team for EPAs shows heavy representation of government augmented with a fair representation from NSAs. The negotiating team is headed by the minister in charge of trade as the chief negotiator. The other members of the team are the permanent secretary in the MoT, leaders of the seven clusters, key trade experts drawn from both the private and public sectors of the economy and civil society and government officials representing key ministries. Non-state actors are either directly invited by the government or nominated by their respective organizations. The NSAs interviewed for this study also argued that the National Committee on Trade Negotiations makes final trade negotiation decisions. They observed, however, that even though government representation is heavy in the team, decisions are made through consensus, unless there are cases of conflicting interest when the issue is put to a vote.

The foregoing discussions reveal two distinct processes for consultations on WTO and PTA negotiations. It also reveals very rare meetings of the WTO group as compared with the PTA group. This state of affairs reflects the Kenyan state view and at the same time is a reflection of the relative importance attached by both state actors and non-state actors to the PTAs as opposed to the WTO. The PTAs, especially the EPAs, EAC and COMESA have generated a lot of interest and public debate in Kenya, hence, the significance attached to the trade agreements. The same is reflected in the importance of regional trade to Kenya, where the African region remains the major destination of Kenya's exports. In addition, both the state and non-state actors interviewed concurred that the relevance

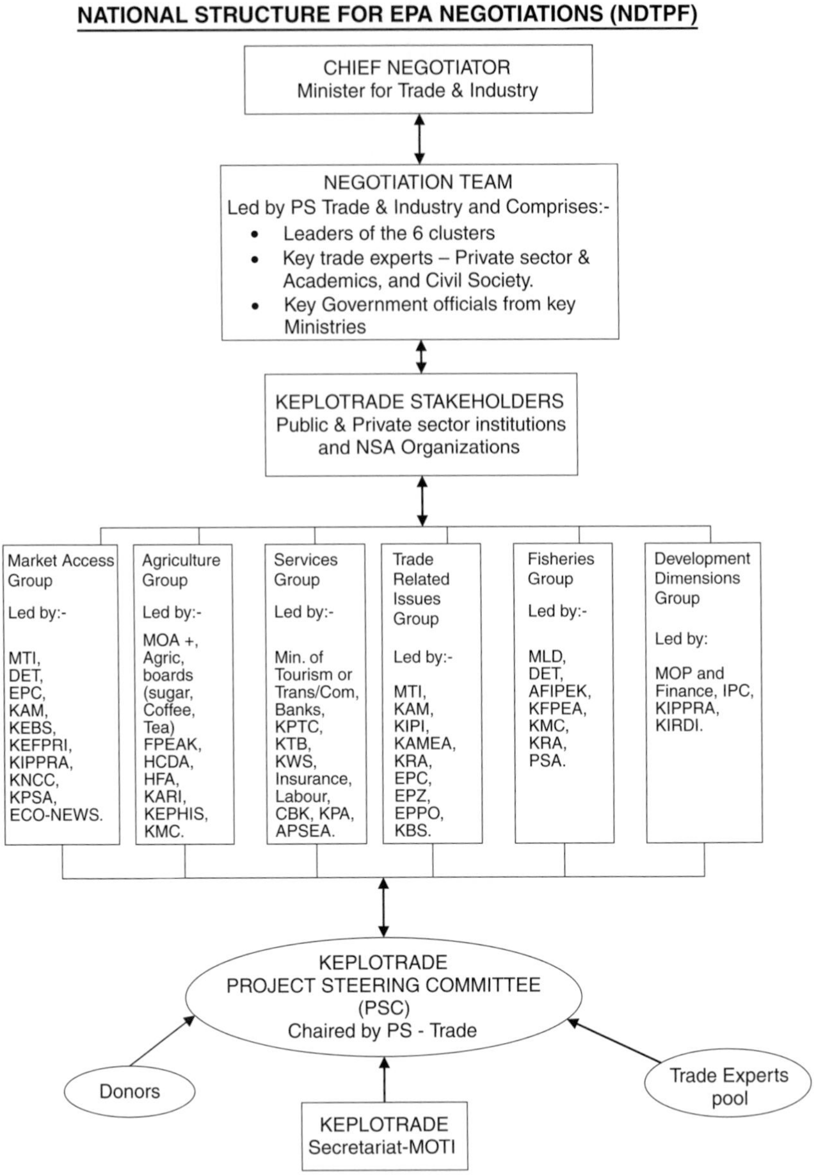

NATIONAL STRUCTURE FOR EPA NEGOTIATIONS (NDTPF)

Figure 8.5   Structure of Kenya's negotiating team for EPAs

and visibility of the NCWTO as a framework for developing country positions in the WTO and by extension the WTO-related consultation mechanisms have declined in recent years mainly due to the lack of progress in the Doha Round of negotiations. Interviewees also contended that the NCWTO lacks a legal mandate to play a more influential role, given that its functions are limited to information sharing, deliberations and consultations and advising the government on the Kenyan position regarding WTO issues/negotiations. The functioning of the NCWTO is also constrained by inadequate funding, unlike KEPLOTRADE, which facilitates preparations for EPAs, and other mechanisms for developing regional trade agreements such as the EAC and COMESA.

3.5   How non-state actors seek to influence trade policy

In Kenya, the influence of NSAs in trade policy is exerted in several ways. These include targeted lobbying and advocacy programmes involving individual NSAs and/or alliances of NSAs. Such influence is also exerted through coordination with donors, the WTO secretariat, legislators, ministers, government officials, the general public and the media. Table 8.2 summarises the methods used by NSAs to influence particular trade negotiations, whom they seek to influence and the relative importance (rank) attached to each alternative by the NSAs.

Table 8.2 shows that the majority (eight of eleven) of the NSAs prioritized participation in meetings or committees organized by the government as their key means to influence particular trade negotiations. Others (two of eleven) and (one of eleven) identified publishing or broadcasting material and self-initiated interaction with government or other lobbying activity as the second and third best means of seeking to influence trade negotiations, respectively. The conducting of public campaigns is the least preferred means of influencing particular trade negotiations. This revelation is inconsistent with the popular view held by most advocacy and lobby groups that public campaigns are an important strategy for influencing public opinion. In the Kenyan context though, the limited use of public campaigns may be attributable to the intolerance of government, and the police in particular, to any form of public campaigns and demonstrations held by CSOs. It is also a reflection of the cumbersome procedures that need to be followed to acquire government approval to hold such campaigns.

From Table 8.2, it appears that lobbying and advocacy interventions by NSAs seek mostly to influence government officials. Only a few NSAs aim to influence public opinion with KHRC and COTU-K giving it the highest ranking. According to the NSAs interviewed, there are no significant differences in approach to influencing policy outcome, whether the context is the WTO or a PTA.

Table 8.2 *Ways to influence and whom to influence (ranks)*

NSA/rank	Ways to influence particular trade negotiations					Whom the NSAs seek to influence				
	1	2	3	4	5	1	2	3	4	5
Institute of Economic Affairs	2	1	3	0	4	0	1	0	0	2 (media)
Central Organization of Trade Unions	1	2	3	0	4 (labour day)	0	2	0	1	0
EcoNews Africa	1	0	2	0	3	4	3	2	0	1
KHRC	3	4	2	0	1	0	0	3	1	2
CUTS	1	2	3	0	0	0	1	0	0	2 (lobbying groups)
KNCCI	1	2	0	0	0	2	1	3	4	0
KAM	1	2	3	0	4 (consultation)	2	1	3	4 (members)	0
Action Aid	1	2	0	3	4 (WTO secretariat)	3	1	2	4	0
KEPSA	1	2	0	0	0	3	1	2	0	0
FKE	1	2	0	0	0	1	2	0	0	0
IPAR	3	2	1	0	0	1	3	2	3	0

Source: Survey results (2009).

Key ways: (1) participating in meetings or committees organized by government; (2) self-initiated interaction with government or other lobbying activity; (3) publishing or broadcasting material; (4) conducting public campaigns; (5) other ways.

Ranks: these have been assigned numbers 1–5, with rank 1 being the most important and rank 5 the least important. The number zero is given to an alternative that is not used at all by the NSAs.

The level of influence exerted by NSAs on specific trade agreements is indeterminate given that there is nothing, in terms of a legal framework or accountability mechanism, which compels the state actors to adopt the positions or recommendations advanced by the NSAs. Nevertheless, according to those interviewed for the study, some NSAs have managed to push their proposals through, but only after a thorough discussion with the government. For example, the High Tariff Binding (HTB) adopted by the Kenya government was a proposal from one of the NSAs (IEA). KAM has also been contracted by the government occasionally to develop trade policies which the government has finally adopted for trade negotiations. It was also revealed that some NSAs, especially the business organizations, are at times invited and incorporated in the government delegations for bilateral, multilateral and regional trade negotiations. Since participation of NSAs in the specific trade negotiations is at the behest of the government, these NSAs cannot advance positions which are at variance with that of the government. In most cases, the views and/or positions of NSAs on respective trade agreements, where sought, are synchronized with those of the government and advanced as the government position.

The major influence of Kenyan NSAs has been in the EPA negotiations, where NSAs have succeeded in forcing the government not to sign the agreement with the European Union until such time as all the pending issues are ironed out. This explains the continued postponement of signing of the EPA as a tactic aimed at allowing for more consultation between state and non-state actors. The level of influence also varies with the trade agreement. For example, KAM is believed to have more influence on COMESA negotiations; Action Aid with its global perspective, has more influence on WTO negotiations, while Econews Africa and IEA believe they have more influence on EPA negotiations. The perception by NSAs of relative influence on specific trade agreements is based on the existence/non-existence of scheduled programmes and links/rapport with the secretariats of the respective trade agreements. Non-state actors with structured links to a specific trade secretariat naturally believe that they have more influence in that particular secretariat.

3.6   Why governments engage non-state actors in trade policy

The key finding of this study is that involvement and participation of NSAs in the formulation and implementation of trade policies is gaining acceptance in Kenya. There are three main reasons for this. First, policy-makers, development partners and CSOs have come to acknowledge that past structural adjustment policies failed mainly because of a lack of local commitment, or 'ownership'. Participation by local CSOs is, therefore, expected to broaden trade policy ownership beyond the government arena. Second, pro-poor outcomes of trade policies are likely to increase with greater CSO participation, on the strength of their proximity to the poor, their capacity to grasp the nature of poverty in Kenya and, therefore, correctly assess the impact of trade policies on the poor. Third, since governments worldwide are better at making promises than in delivering on the promises, development partners are keen for CSOs to 'follow the money' and monitor policy implementation in trade policies. Our findings on why the government is seeking NSA's participation in trade matters are generally consistent with the above public policy context, but mainly reflect government interests.

Table 8.3 summaries the reasons why state actors in Kenya now seek to engage NSAs in trade matters and the relative importance attached to each reason by the respective state actor. It shows that for state actors, seeking technical advice and commercial intelligence is the most important reason for engaging with NSAs in trade policy-making. This may imply that the government has recognized its capacity gap, especially in terms of understanding the needs of particularly the weak and the vulnerable on whose behalf NSAs mainly speak. The prioritization of technical advice and commercial intelligence from the NSAs is also consistent with the fact that NSAs have wide outreaches in the rural areas, where the majority of the population and the poor live. The NSAs also have local, regional and international networks and may have a better view of the market, including best trade practices. Thus, by involving NSAs in policy-making, the government would be bridging the information and the market intelligence gap.

The government ministries and agencies identified satisfaction of public policy requirements and promotion of transparency as the second and the third most important reasons for engaging with NSAs in trade policy-making, respectively. Surprisingly, engagement of state and non-state actors as a means of creating coalitions to support negotiating positions and outcomes was ranked as the least important reason, suggesting that the government does not feel that it needs much support in the actual negotiations or in selling the negotiation outcomes to the public. This is also true with partnering with NSAs to facilitate gauging of public opinion in relation to potential points of opposition to negotiating positions. This reason is not given by any of the state actors, save for the Kenya Revenue Authority and even then it is ranked last.

Table 8.3 *Reasons for seeking state–non-state actor engagements in trade policy-making*

State actor/rank	Reasons for engagement with NSAs					
	1	2	3	4	5	6
Ministry of Trade	3	2	1	0	4	0
Kenya Investment Authority	2	3	1	0	4	5
Ministry of EAC	4	3	1	0	2	0
Ministry of Planning	4	3	1	0	2	0
Ministry of Finance	3	1	2	0	0	4
Kenya Revenue Authority	2	4	1	5	3	0
KEPLOTRADE	2	4	1	0	3	0
KIPPRA	2	3	1	0	4	0

Source: Survey Results (2009).
Key reasons why state actors engage with NSAs in trade policy-making: (1) satisfying public policy, including statutory requirements; (2) promoting transparency; (3) seeking technical advice and commercial intelligence; (4) gauging potential public opinion in relation to potential points of opposition to negotiation positions; (5) creating coalitions to support negotiating positions and outcomes; (6) others. Ranks: these have been assigned numbers 1–5, with rank 1 being the most important and rank 5 the least important. The number zero is given to an alternative that is not used at all by the state actor.

Prioritization of 'satisfying public policy (including statutory) requirements' as one of the important reasons for engagement of NSAs in trade policy-making confirms the fears NSAs have held over time about their engagement with government in trade policy-making. Non-state actors have a strong feeling that they are yet to be fully accepted and appreciated by the government as partners in trade policy-making. The NSAs argue that this explains why their engagement in this important process is *ad hoc*, with no legal and institutional framework for effective enforcement and representation. One of the state actor interviewees quipped 'there is a general feeling within the state agencies that NSAs are not genuine in their undertakings and are commonly used by critics of the government. In addition, their source of funding is, to the government, questionable which is always suspicious of their activities in the country'.

According to NSAs, some of them are less engaged by the government or are left out of trade policy-making and trade negotiations altogether because of their controversial approach to development issues. In the opinion of some NSAs, the government works with them only because it is forced to by international organizations such as the International Labour Organization, and development partners such as the European Union. Non-state actors further suspect that the government is not serious on trade policy-making, negotiations and agreements, which has often led to a working environment rife with suspicion, confrontations and generally poor working relationships with NSAs. In addition, NSAs also attributed the perceived limited engagement between themselves and state actors to the absence of a legal and accountability framework to ensure their involvement and participation in trade policy-making, and to guarantee that their views are taken on board.

The NSAs identified the following as some of the state-centred constraints to their effective participation in trade-related matters: the lead role, as opposed to facilitative role, played by the government in trade policy-making and trade negotiations; poor coordination; lack of transparency; information asymmetry; and the bureaucratic and confidential nature of government operations. Non-state actors observed that these state-centred constraints have occasionally forced them to lobby and seek support for inclusion in trade policy-making from the would-be markets and partners such as the European Union, WTO and ILO among others. Non-state actors, however, acknowledge their own limitations, including inadequate human and financial resources, ineffective coordination of NSA issues and positions, irregular participation of NSAs in trade policy issues and weak feedback mechanisms to the NSA-nominating bodies.

4   Kenya's trade agreements

Kenya is a signatory to a number of agreements aimed at enhancing trade among member states. While country-specific bilateral agreements are important to Kenya in terms of promoting trade, Kenya's export trade patterns indicate that the regional agreements with EAC and COMESA are critical to the country. Similarly, the importance of the European Union as one of Kenya's main export destinations and origin of the bulk of its imports should not be underestimated.

4.1   WTO agreements

Kenya became a contracting party to the GATT on 5 February 1964, and has been a member of the WTO since its inception in January 1995.

4.2   Preferential trade agreements

4.2.1   Regional agreements

4.2.1.1   COMESA.   Kenya is a member of COMESA, which was formed in December 1994. COMESA seeks to promote regional and economic integration through trade and investment in eastern and southern Africa. COMESA has a total membership of nineteen states and a population of 416 million as of 2007. With an annual import bill of around US$95 billion and an export bill of US$107 billion, COMESA forms a major marketplace for both internal and external trading.

The aims and objectives of COMESA have been designed so as to remove the structural and institutional weaknesses in the member states by pooling their resources in order to sustain their development efforts either individually or collectively. The COMESA agenda is to deepen and broaden the integration process among member states through the adoption of more comprehensive trade liberation measures such as the complete elimination of tariff and non-tariff barriers to trade and elimination of customs duties. Some member states have already signed a free trade area protocol, and the rest are working towards this goal. Efforts are at an advanced stage to establish a common external tariff (CET). COMESA is one of Kenya's dominant export destinations (Republic of Kenya, 2009).

4.2.1.2   EAC.   EAC is the regional intergovernmental organization of the republics of Kenya, Uganda, Tanzania, Rwanda and Burundi, with headquarters located in Arusha, Tanzania. The EAC was formerly established on 30 November 1999 through signatures of heads of state and governments of Kenya, Uganda and Tanzania. The East African countries have a population of slightly above 100 million people. Three of the countries in the region, namely, Kenya, Uganda and Tanzania share a common history, language, culture and infrastructure, while Rwanda and Burundi are the closest neighbours. These advantages provide the partner states with a unique framework for regional cooperation and integration. The EAC is an important trading bloc for Kenya. In 2008, the share of Kenyan exports to the African continent was 47.6%, out of which 51.6% was consumed by the EAC member states (Republic of Kenya, 2009).

4.3   Economic partnership agreements

Economic partnership agreements are a scheme to create a free trade area (FTA) between the European Union and the group of African, Caribbean and Pacific (ACP) countries. The EPAs are a response to continuing criticism that the non-reciprocal and discriminating PTAs offered by the European Union are incompatible with the WTO rules. The EPAs are an important element of the Cotonou Agreement, whose key principles are reciprocity, regionalism and special treatment. The EPAs are still under negotiation, with negotiations being conducted in accordance with the procedures agreed upon by the ACP Group. The countries are conducting the negotiations in two phases: the first phase is the All-ACP level, which began in September 2002 with the launch of negotiations on the objectives and the principles of the EPAs, as well as issues of common interest to all ACP states. The second phase, which began in 2003, is at the regional level. This phase deals mainly with tariff negotiations and other negotiations and commitments at national or regional levels. It also deals with issues specific to ACP countries or regions.

The ACP region has configured itself into six distinct regional groups under which negotiations with the European Union are taking place. These regional groups are: east and southern Africa (ESA); Southern Africa Development Cooperation (SADC); Economic Commission of West African States (ECOWAS); Central Africa Monetary Union (CEMAC); and the Caribbean and Pacific.

Since the launch of the EPA negotiations, Kenya along with the other three EAC countries (Burundi, Rwanda and Uganda) has been negotiating EPAs under the ESA configuration. The ESA has sixteen member countries: Burundi, Comoros, DR Congo, Djibouti, Eritrea, Ethiopia, Kenya, Madagascar, Malawi, Mauritius, Rwanda, Seychelles, Sudan, Uganda, Zambia and Zimbabwe. Tanzania, a member of the EAC Customs Union, has, on the other hand pursued EPAs under the SADC configuration.

Negotiation of EPAs by the EAC countries under different configurations has posed a great challenge to the EAC countries. By virtue of being members of the EAC Customs Union, EAC countries are bound by the EAC Customs Union Protocol. They are also bound by the EAC Customs Union Management Act to sign EPAs as a customs territory. The EAC negotiating structure comprises the EAC Ministers of Trade, EAC senior officials (permanent secretaries in trade ministries) and the National Development and Trade Policy Forum (NDTPF). The NDTPF is multi-sectoral (agriculture, trade, investment, services, etc.) and representative of the public and private sectors and NSAs involved in trade and development work. The function of the NDTPF is to determine what the optimal development and trade negotiating position for the country should be and to prepare briefs outlining these positions. These are then used by the representatives of the country in the EAC/ EPA Experts Committee meetings in preparation of the EAC position for the negotiations with the European Union.

4.4 Bilateral trade agreements

Kenya has signed bilateral trade agreements with several countries around the world including Argentina, Bangladesh, Bulgaria, China, the former Czech and Slovak Republic, Djibouti, Egypt, Ethiopia, India, Iran, Lesotho, Nigeria, Pakistan, Poland, Romania, Rwanda, Republic of Korea, Sudan, Tanzania, Thailand, the former USSR, the former Yugoslavia, Zambia and Zimbabwe. Some of the countries are already members of existing schemes offering market access/duty reduction preferences as above. Under these agreements, trading partners accord each other preferential treatment in matters with respect to their mutual trade relations. These are not free trade agreements and they have been used primarily as instruments for promoting trade and improving economic relations between Kenya and the respective countries.

4.5 Non-state actors, trade policy-making and forum choice

As indicated earlier, trade policy-making in the country is spearheaded by government with some level of participation by NSAs. This section presents our research findings on the role of stakeholders in trade policy-making and trade agreements, with specific reference to the trade agreements outlined in the preceding section. We start with the role of NSAs.

4.6 Nature of non-state actor engagement

Table 8.4 summarises the key NSAs involved in trade policy-making in Kenya, their areas of policy interest, constituencies served and the trade negotiations in which they have been active.

Table 8.4 *NSAs involved in trade policy-making in Kenya*

NSA	Policy interest	Constituencies served	Source of funding	Local affiliates	International affiliates	Negotiations active in
Kenya National Chamber of Commerce & Industry	Trade advisory policies	Business community	Subscription, donors, consultancies	MoT, Ministry of Finance, KRA, Ministry of EAC	None	COMESA, EAC, EPA, WTO
Federation of Kenya Employers	General, economic policies	Traders and employers	Subscription, donors, consultancies	Ministry of Trade, Ministry of Finance		WTO, EAC, EPA, COMESA
Kenya Private Sector Alliance	All policy-related issues	Private sector business community	Members' subscriptions	Ministry of Trade, Ministry of Finance, KRA		None
Kenya Association of Manufacturers	Market access policies	Manufactures and business community	Subscriptions and donors	Ministry of Trade, Ministry of Finance, KEPLOTRADE and KRA		WTO, EAC, EPA, COMESA
Kenya Small Scale Farmers Association	Trade policies that impact on small-scale farmers and rural communities	Small-scale farmers	Membership subscriptions	CUTS, EcoNews Africa, Action Aid		EAC, COMESA, EPA
Action Aid CUTS International	Poverty reduction policies, consumer protection	Public and the poor, consumers and general public	Sponsors, donors, 100% donor	KHRC, KEPLOTRADE, MoT Action Aid, Oxfam	OWINS, GCAP CUTS India	WTO, COMESA, EPA, EAC EAC, EPA, COMESA, WTO

Kenya Human Rights Commission	All issues related to human rights	Public	100% donor	Action Aid	International human rights commission	EPA
EcoNews Africa	Policy and advocacy	CBOs and SMEs	100% donor	KEPLOTRADE Action Aid	No	EPA, multilateral and bilateral trade
Friedrich Ebert Stiftung	Not specific	NSAs	100% donor	CUTS, Oxfam, Action Aid	FES Bonn Germany	Supports the NSAs
Central Organization of Trade Unions	Labour market policies	Employers and employees	Subscription from members and donors	Each sector of production forms an affiliate	ILO, ITUC, LO/FTS	EAC at some stages
Institute of Economic Affairs	Trade policies and their impacts	Government and the general public	100% donor	CUTS, EcoNews Africa	CUTS International	COMESA, EAC, EPA, WTO
Institute of Policy Analysis and Research	Trade, agriculture and labour policies	Government, private sector, civil society and general public	Donors and consultancies	FKE, COTU, Action Aid, KEPSA, KHRC, KAM, others	Brookings Institute, FASID, ILO	Provides research and policy analysis inputs

Source: Survey results (2009).

Not directly evident from Table 8.4 is the fact that the NSAs' activities on trade policy issues in Kenya started in late 1990s and initially focused on the WTO. More recently, their focus of attention has been the EPA negotiations with the European Union, COMESA and the regional integration and trade arrangements under the EAC. Non-state actors have tried to work with the government including, for example, through commissioning research. Thus, the research that informed national positions on the two immediate past WTO ministerial conferences were commissioned and undertaken by a consortium of NSAs consisting of EcoNews Africa, Oxfam, Traidcraft and KHRC. This research focused on trade in the cotton, textile, footwear and dairy sub-sectors.

Field interviews revealed that NSAs engage in trade policy negotiations in several ways. First, they conduct research on various aspects of trade and avail the information to both government and other actors through a number of forums, such as formal meetings and the media. Second, NSAs organize debates with the aim of sensitizing the public and the government to issues that are of interest to the NSA and that, if included in such agreements, would benefit the country. Third, NSAs mobilize specific stakeholders, such as farmers, industrialists, trade unions, employers and other private sector entrepreneurs to inform them of the possible implications of trade policies and encourage them to air their concerns and views to the government during the trade policy-making process. Fourth, some of the NSAs, specifically those with some clout and the requisite capacity such as the IEA and KAM, are directly involved in the WTO, EAC, COMESA and EPA negotiations. Fifth, some of the NSAs listed in Table 8.4 have affiliations or collaborate with the international NGOs based in Geneva (e.g., FES, KNCCI, FKE, KAM, Action Aid, CUTS International and COTU). Both FES and CUTS International have offices in Geneva; KNCCI and KAM have working collaboration and affiliation with the International Chamber of Commerce Representation Office; FKE is affiliated to the International Organization of Employers and the ILO; COTU is affiliated to both the ILO and the International Trade Union Confederation (ITUC); while Action Aid collaborates with Oxfam International and World Vision in promoting their trade policy formulation and negotiation agenda.

4.6.1   Trade agreements preferred by non-state actors

Non-state actor preferences for different trade agreements and negotiating forums depend on their constituencies and the potential welfare improvement of the trade agreement in question. This study reveals

Table 8.5 *Trade agreements preferred by NSAs*

NSAs	Trade agreements			
	EAC	COMESA	EPA	WTO
Action Aid	1	1	?	1
CUTS International	1	1	1	0
KHRC	1	1	?	0
EcoNews Africa	1	1	1	1
COTU-K	1	0	?	0
IPAR	1	1	?	1
IEA	1	1	?	1
KNCCI	1	1	?	0
KEPSA	1	1	1	1
FKE	1	0	?	0
KAM	1	1	?	0

Source: Survey data (2009).
Key: 1= preferred; 0 = not preferred; ? = issues still pending.

unmatched preference of NSAs to trade agreements under EAC, COMESA and WTO. However, a number of the NSAs still have queries about the EPA (Table 8.5).

From Table 8.5, it is evident that all NSAs prefer trade agreements under the EAC. All NSAs except the labour-based NSAs – COTU-K and FKE – do not prefer COMESA. The non-preference of COMESA by the two social partners could be attributed to the fact that COMESA trade agreements provide for certain trade conditions which have been blamed for exposing local industries to unfair competition resulting in considerable job losses. By contrast, the EAC trade agreements seek to widen the market frontiers for all the factors of production with provision of free movement of labour. This provision has received considerable support from the labour market players in Kenya since it is considered as a means to ease unemployment, increase union membership and enhance labour market flexibility, especially wage flexibility and labour mobility. In addition, the EAC duly recognizes the participation of workers' and employers' bodies in the trade negotiations. For example, the East African Trade Union Confederation (EATUC), a confederation of workers' umbrella bodies from Kenya, Uganda, Tanzania, Rwanda and Burundi, is legally recognized under the EAC rules to represent workers' interest in the EAC trade negotiations. EATUC is, thus, instrumental in ensuring that the EAC involves workers in all issues concerning regional integration and promotion of tripartism as an important mechanism of consultation and dialogue. The regional workers' body also promotes the ratification of international labour standards by partner states besides enhancing integration of youth and women in all spheres of socio-economic development. It also promotes decent work agenda and advocates for free movement of factors of production in the region.

The general support for EAC and COMESA can be explained by the magnitude of Kenya's trade with African countries and the immediate relevance of the agreements to the country. By contrast, the summaries in Table 8.5 show limited preference for the EPA. This is attributed to a number of issues with the EPA which remain unresolved. One prominent issue is the continued subsidization of agriculture production in the European Union, and the concern on the part of Kenyan NSAs that this will be to the detriment of domestic producers. While the Kenyan government contends that the trade pact will be beneficial to Kenyans, local lobby groups have voiced concern against the trade agreement, arguing that it will worsen the country's trade position and the general welfare of citizens.

Table 8.5 also shows that Kenyan NSAs do not prefer the multilateral trade agreements negotiated under the WTO. Interestingly, of the NSAs that prefer multilateral trade agreements, most have a mandate to seek to influence any trade policy that affects human welfare, regardless of negotiating forum. These include Action Aid and EcoNews Africa, whose mandate is to alleviate human suffering including consumer awareness and protection; IPAR and IEA, national think-tanks whose goal is to undertake objective and data-based policy research and analysis for socio-economic development; and KEPSA whose advocacy programmes centre on improvement in the enabling environment and expansion of business opportunities for Kenyan private sector entrepreneurs.

More generally, the preference among Kenyan NSAs for regional rather than multilateral trade agreements can be explained by trade patterns, the nature of the government consultative mechanisms and the financial and institutional support mechanisms that exist for furthering the negotiation of regional PTAs and EPAs. Indeed, Kenya's trade is heavily regionalized: half of its exports are consumed within the African region, and if the European Union's share is added (28.9%), then upwards of three-quarters of the country's exports are accounted for by two regions, while the majority of Kenya's imports come from East Asia (61.1%). Such heavily regionalized trade patterns may explain the high priority attached by most players to PTAs.

That being said, while most NSAs prefer regional trade forums our research has found that they do not participate in discussions regarding forum selection. This, they argue, is normally taken to be the prerogative of the government, primarily the MoT. In addition, some trade agreements, such as EAC and COMESA, are negotiated in specific venues where their secretariats are based. Non-state actors, however, underscore the importance of forum choice because of the way that it affects the bargaining power of the actors, including the extent to which NSAs can mobilize their constituents and key alliances to participate in the negotiations and/or advocacy programmes outside the negotiation room. The NSAs involved in manufacturing and the business community, such as KAM, KNCCI, FKE and KEPSA, hold the opinion that it is normally very difficult to influence trade policy outcomes in forums outside Geneva. This view is also held by those NSAs with international affiliates such as Action Aid, CUTS International, COTU and the Kenya Human Rights Commission who are also comfortable with Geneva for the same reasons. In all, therefore, most actors, according to the interviews, are comfortable with Geneva forums. State actors concur with NSAs on the importance of Geneva forums in terms of their ability to exercise influence, but are of the opinion that NSAs support alternative forums only if their interest is well taken care of; an observation that is hardly surprising.

Within the context of trade dispute arbitration as an element of forum choice, the general view of both state and non-state actors is that this has not been accorded much weight by Kenya, primarily because Kenya has not been involved in any serious trade disagreements that have required formal arbitration. Misunderstandings which have arisen in the past have been on bilateral/regional trades with regard to specific commodities and applicable tariffs. For instance, in early 2009 Uganda and Tanzania complained that Kenya was imposing non-tariff barriers such as the banning of four-axle trucks, the introduction of new conformity assessment instructions for milk powder and the alleged deliberate delaying of imports at ports and border points in violation of EAC and COMESA guidelines (Wambi, 2009). However, such disagreements have been handled amicably at or below the ministerial level. Both state and non-state actors contend that a discussion on forum choice is critical in the case of serious trade disputes requiring arbitration.

5   Conclusion

A number of state and non-state actors engage in trade policy-making in Kenya. Within the framework of the state, MoT has the mandate to deal with all trade policy issues. The MoT appreciates the importance of consultative mechanisms to ensure stakeholder participation and broad-based ownership of trade policies, but it faces several challenges in its discharge of trade policy-making and implementation mandate. These include inadequate budget and technical expertise, the absence of an institutionalized mechanism to enhance coordination between the MoT and the MEAC and weak internal coordination within the MoT, especially between those units dealing with the WTO and EPA negotiations. Similarly, there is a lack of coordination more widely among the ministries and agencies involved in trade policy development.

Private sector actors interact with government through peak bodies, which have been influential in several areas of trade policy, including in relation to price decontrols, the removal of quantitative restrictions, export promotion and the removal/reduction of import duties. Participation of the private sector in trade policy-making in Kenya can be improved through better balancing of the interests of all members, particularly by the broad-based umbrella organizations such as KEPSA and KNCCI, more organized and sustained lobbying and the improvement of their capacity for technical analysis and advocacy.

Civil society organizations, through their research and analysis, briefs, conferences, seminars and meetings with trade negotiators, have become increasingly influential in trade negotiations. Civil society organizations in Kenya consider trade policy an important area for engagement not just for economic reasons, but also for social, political and equity considerations. Like the private sector, however, the effectiveness of CSOs could be improved by greater technical expertise and capacity building the development of closer relationships with the private sector on selected issues where their interests coincide.

Overall, there is a general perception among NSAs in trade policy-making that notwithstanding the government-initiated consultation mechanisms, the actual influence of NSAs in trade policies has so far been low, though growing. This is because the participation of NSAs is mainly confined to providing information to government officials, but there is no legal or accountability mechanism to guarantee incorporation of the views of NSAs in the trade policies. All the same, participation of NSAs in Kenya's trade policy-making is beginning to acquire a measure of acceptance and, therefore, legitimacy. Despite the constraints outlined in this chapter, the degree of participation turned out to be higher than we hypothesized before embarking on the fieldwork. However, the actual impact of the participation by NSAs is difficult to determine, which is not unique to trade policy in Kenya, or for that matter, in many other countries.

Further, the NSAs in Kenya are yet to acquire a sense of power in the consultations, and government is sometimes reluctant to engage with them, in part because most NSAs lack the experience and the expertise necessary to manage the process of popular participation as well as the experience, skills and knowledge to engage with the state on complex issues of policy. Non-state actors are viewed by the government as being haphazard and uncoordinated, and as being unable to provide legitimate participation as anticipated in the trade agreements. Under the circumstances, the government may be inclined to engage only NSAs viewed as friendly to their policies.

References

Republic of Kenya 2008. *Economic Survey*, Government Printer, Nairobi.
  2009. *Economic Survey*, Government Printer, Nairobi.
Wambi, M. 2009. '*Milk Trade War Spills Over Uganda and Kenya*', available at: http://ipsnews.net/news.asp?idnews=46078, 3.11.09.

ANNEX

Key persons interviewed

Noah Chune, Research Economist, Central Organization of Trade Unions.
Kathrine Githinji, Senior Trade Development Officer, Ministry of Trade.
Louiza Kabiru, Programme Officer, Kenya Human Rights Commission.
Walter Kamau, Trade Officer, Kenya Association of Manufacturers.
Peter Kasango, Deputy Chief Economist, Ministry of East African Community.
James Maina, Chief Economist, Ministry of Planning.
Martin Masinde, Research Economist, Kenya Revenue Authority.
Joshua Matunga, Senior Trade Development Officer, KEPLOTRADE.
Robert Ndubi, Programme Officer, EcoNews Africa.
Dominic Nyambane, Chief Economist, Ministry of Finance.
Collins Odote, Programme Officer, Friedrich Ebert Stiftung.

Asha Okendo, Programme Officer, Consumer Unit Trust.

Miriam Omolo, Programme Officer, Institute of Economic Affairs.

Patrick Omuse, Trade Development Officer, Kenya National Chamber of Commerce and Industry.

Christopher Onyango, Policy Analyst, Kenya Institute for Public Policy Research and Analysis.

Nixon Otieno, Policy Research Coordinator, Action Aid.

Titus Waithaka, Policy Analyst, Federation of Kenya Employers.

Anthony Wanjohi, Programme Officer, Kenya Private Sector Alliance.

Angela Wauye, Food Security Programme Coordinator, Action Aid.

9

South Africa

PETER DRAPER, TSIDISO DISENYANA
AND GILBERTO BIACUANA[1]

1 Introduction

Trade policy-making is a complex affair. In all countries a host of factors influence the outcome, with the mix varying according to domestic circumstances and the relationship of the country concerned with the global economy. As the introductory chapter of this book attests, strictly state-centric explanations regarding how trade policy decisions are made are no longer sufficient in a world where international trade negotiations increasingly impinge on domestic policies. Therefore, a nuanced understanding of how trade policy is made is required, and must interrogate the roles of non-state actors (NSAs), institutions and ideas, and their interactions with each other, in shaping preferences and policy.

This chapter explores those issues in the context of South Africa. Section 2 provides a brief historical overview of South Africa's trade policy history; section 3 reviews the broad patterns of the country's external trade. From this history and structural analysis it is clear that the early preference for liberalization in the post-1990 period has recently given way to a more defensive approach to trade policy and negotiations, which are now regarded as subordinate to sector-based industrial policy. This shift reflects a broader shift within the African National Congress-led tripartite alliance concerning the role of liberalization in economic policy; in other words, the ideological basis for trade policy shifted in the early years of this decade in response to perceived shortcomings of the liberal model. However, as section 4 charts, the institutional arrangements within the state have not really changed much. Furthermore, as section 5 elaborates, the executive branch retained its dominance of the trade policy-making

[1] Respectively, head, deputy head and economist, Development through Trade project at the South African Institute of International Affairs. Research assistance from Cézanne Samuel is gratefully acknowledged.

process throughout this period in relation to NSAs in particular. In other words, the ideological shift in trade policy has not yet been matched by institutional changes through which particular interests are expressed.

Section 6 constitutes the empirical foundation for this chapter, based as it is on interviews with selected NSAs concerning their interests and preferences for preferential trade agreements (PTAs) versus the World Trade Organization (WTO). Our overall conclusions are:

(1) that no clear preference is discernible regarding forum choice;
(2) that the institutional structures through which trade policy is mediated have little bearing on forum choice;
(3) that the influence NSAs can exert is not discernibly different in different forums; and
(4) that the executive branch of government continues to exert its dominant influence over trade negotiations in both forums.

Overall we find that the key driver for all trade negotiations, regardless of the forum chosen, is executive preferences; in other words, the state-centric explanation for trade policy-making holds in the South African case. This is nuanced by the apparent influence that some NSAs, particularly in business and the trade unions, exercise over the content of those negotiations. The institutional mechanisms via which those interest-based preferences are expressed, particularly the National Economic Development and Labour Council, are therefore of substantial importance in explaining the course that particular negotiations take, but do not seem to have much bearing on the matter of forum choice.

2   Historical overview and context of South Africa's trade policy

Despite having been a founding member of the General Agreement on Tariffs and Trade (GATT), South Africa is a relatively new actor on the global stage. Much of the apartheid government's participation in the GATT was framed within the import-substitution industrialization (ISI) development strategy widely pursued at the time. Viewed from the apartheid government's perspective, it faced substantial security threats in the form of mounting economic isolation and regional insurgencies. Within this 'siege mentality' these threats were compounded by decolonization in the region and associated emergence of 'hostile' states on the frontier.[2]

---

[2] In truth the apartheid state was much more of a threat to its neighbours than vice versa.

Therefore, the ISI model extended to the establishment of strategic industries with military and security considerations paramount. Accordingly,
openness to trade was not really on the agenda, even though the ruling
party realized – in the face of mounting domestic economic problems in
the late 1970s and 1980s – that export orientation and associated openness were becoming imperative (Bell 1997). Consequently, South Africa's
conduct in the GATT could best be characterized as defensive.

This framework altered in crucial respects in the late 1980s as moves
towards a political settlement gathered pace. A new consensus-seeking
bargaining structure was established in the form of the National Economic
Forum (NEF) as the liberation movement began to absorb the implications of the unfolding Uruguay Round. The NEF grouped key players in
business, the unions and the liberation movement. Unfortunately, the
history of this period has not been written, consequently little is known
about the bargains struck there. However, this period was marked by deep
thinking on trade and industrial policy matters, particularly on the part
of the liberation movement (Joffe *et al.* 1993; Macro Economic Research
Group 1993). This took place at a time of great political and institutional
ferment in the country, placing enormous demands on those involved in
the process and locking the future government into far-reaching commitments at the same time as it sought to restructure the apartheid state.

In the Uruguay Round, South Africa committed to a major overhaul
(simplification and liberalization) of its complex tariff regime, and signed
up to the Single Undertaking (i.e., the whole package). Special and differential treatment (SDT) did not play a role during this period owing to the
fact that the apartheid government considered South Africa to be a developed country in the GATT context and more generally. Underpinning
South Africa's commitments and participation in the Uruguay Round
was the strong need to overcome the isolation of the 1980s and the need to
promote economic competitiveness in a context of economic stagnation.

International competitiveness and reintegration into the global
economy became crucial pillars of the African National Congress
(ANC) government's policy, as it turned its back on more statist forms
of economic policy in the wake of the first rand crisis in 1996 (Cassim
and Zarenda 2004). This culminated in more rapid liberalization of
tariffs than required in terms of South Africa's GATT bindings.[3] Bell

---

[3] However, it was accompanied by a dramatic increase in the use of anti-dumping as an
instrument of protection, although countervailing duties and safeguards have hardly
been employed.

speculates that this may have been made possible through an implicit bargain struck between the powerful trade union federation, the Congress of South African Trade Unions (COSATU), which played such a critical role in the political transition, and the ANC (Cassim and Zarenda 2004).[4] This envisaged COSATU's acquiescence in the tariff liberalization strategy in return for which they were rewarded through the institutionalization of the structured bargaining model – pioneered by the NEF – in the form of the National Economic Development and Labour Council (NEDLAC). NEDLAC continues to play an important role in the formulation of negotiating positions for trade negotiations (discussed below).

Given that the Uruguay Round was complete when the ANC came to power in 1994, the trade liberalization trajectory turned to bilateral and regional tracks. Unilateral trade liberalization has not been seriously on the agenda since. Rather, adjustments to the most favoured nation (MFN) tariff regime have been left to the Doha Round of multilateral trade negotiations. Here the South African Department of Trade and Industry (DTI) is fighting a rearguard action to stave off potentially major tariff reductions consequent upon formula-driven processes. Underpinning this is a newfound belief in 'strategic industrial policy', a process being driven primarily by the political left in the governing ANC-led alliance. Overall though, their most important objective in the Doha Round remains to resolve the agricultural subsidies puzzle first, before moving onto other areas. Therefore, the G20 developing country alliance on agriculture was a natural one. South Africa is also a member of the Cairns Group, with its market access focus. That is important, but hardly critical, to South Africa's export trajectory, accounting for a small proportion (approximately 10%) of the country's export basket, while agriculture constitutes a small proportion of GDP. Of greater importance is securing access to markets for South Africa's intermediate manufacturing exports. Strangely, South Africa has not been active in seeking liberalization of services sectors in African markets notwithstanding its evident advantages; the reasons for this are to be found in its political relations with Africa and an evident lack of capacity in both government and business to pursue this agenda (Draper, Khumalo and Stern 2008).

---

[4] They do not draw a firm conclusion though. However, they point to the powerful influence of 'Washington Consensus' policies in South Africa's 'great economic debate' of this period.

After the first democratic elections in 1994 relations with the European Union were high on the agenda, given the preponderance of EU markets in South Africa's export basket. When the new government realized that the European Union was not going to grant it full access to Lomé preferences it opted instead to negotiate a comprehensive agreement covering trade, aid and political cooperation.[5] After six years of difficult negotiations the final agreement covered 'substantially all trade' and was asymmetrical in two respects: EU markets were opened first, and to approximately 95% of South African exports versus 86% in return (Bertelsman-Scott, Mills and Sidiropoulos 2000). This experience, and the new government's policy trajectory in support of developing countries, constituted a substantive shift from the previous government's general approach to trade negotiations.

The process of negotiations (Bilal and Laporte 2004) turned out to be divisive, notably the European Union's decision not to include South Africa's customs union partners in its negotiating mandate. Furthermore, many African, Caribbean and Pacific (ACP) states were concerned about the precedent this agreement set for the future of their relations with the European Union – correctly as it turned out given the unfolding economic partnership agreement (EPAs) negotiations taking place under the Cotonou Convention. Those negotiations, in turn, have proved to be particularly divisive, splitting the southern African region and the Southern African Customs Union (SACU) particularly, as South Africa's SACU partners have found themselves caught between an intransigent DTI and an insistent European Union threatening the maintenance of their preferential access to EU markets (Draper and Erasmus 2008).

The second pillar of the regional/bilateral strategy was negotiations with the countries of the Southern African Development Community (SADC) to form a free trade area (FTA). Approximately one-third of South Africa's manufacturing exports go to SADC countries, hence, locking in market access was a key motivation. Once again, these negotiations proved to be divisive, given the presence in the region of the Community of Southern and Eastern African States (COMESA) and associated overlap in memberships. South Africa's decision to opt for SADC over COMESA was widely resented by many countries in the region, which came to the view that the South African government simply wanted to work with a

---

[5] Signed in October 1999, this was known as the Trade, Development and Cooperation Agreement.

grouping it could dominate.[6] This experience, coupled with the South African government's subsequent support for launching the new round of multilateral negotiations at Doha – notwithstanding generalized resistance in the Africa Group, the estrangement of South Africa's customs union partners in the EU negotiations and now the EPAs, has bequeathed a legacy of mistrust of the South African government's intentions in the region.

At the dawn of the new millennium a third pillar of South Africa's bilateral/regional strategy opened up: that of PTA negotiations with key partners. This is broadly guided by the DTI's 'Global Economic Strategy' (Ismail, Draper and Carim 2000), and is divided into two tracks: first, the United States, the European Free Trade Area (EFTA) and Mercado Commun del Sul (MERCOSUR); second, India, China and Nigeria.

Track one has been underway for some ten years now. The MERCOSUR negotiations commenced in 1999 and seem set to conclude imminently, while the EFTA negotiations were completed in 2006, but the deal still has to be ratified (Draper and Khumalo 2009). Negotiations with the United States ran into serious difficulties and were ultimately suspended in April 2006 (Draper 2004; Draper and Soko 2004; Draper and Khumalo 2007). This reflected serious differences between South Africa and the United States concerning trade liberalization in general and the United States' 'WTO-plus' approach to trade negotiations and inflexible negotiating template. To some extent it also reflects the South African government's desire, in common with Brazil, to pursue strong alliances with key developing countries in order to balance US power.

Track two has only just commenced with the first round of preferential trade negotiations between SACU and India commencing in August 2009. Negotiations with China are on the backburner for the foreseeable future owing to concerns on the South African side over labour-intensive industries particularly and in the light of the newly minted industrial policy (Department of Trade and Industry 2007; Draper and Alves, 2007).[7] For those same reasons these negotiations are not likely to bear fruit for a

---

[6] The DTI points out that there is more to this choice than meets the eye, notably the plethora of regional integration arrangements in eastern and southern Africa and the need to promote regional coherence. Critics retort that South Africa's choice to join SADC and not COMESA compounded this problem.

[7] Essentially, the NIPF favours a particular interpretation of the east Asian industrialization experience, notably the 'revisionist' perspective in which that industrialization is seen as having been driven by state intervention through activist industrial policies. This perspective finds particular favour within the ANC's alliance partners – COSATU and the SACP – and in the ideological left of the ANC itself.

long time to come; indeed, it would be true to say that the DTI has backed off from trade liberalizing deals, whether in the WTO or regionally and bilaterally, in favour of pursuing state-led industrialization strategies within which trade policy is regarded as a sub-set of industrial policy.

Finally, it is important to note that trade negotiations in South Africa have become increasingly intertwined with foreign policy. In the multilateral system, for example, the foreign policy imperative revolves around how to mesh South Africa's economic interests with the often conflicting economic interests of the Africa Group given that, according to erstwhile Department of Foreign Affairs (now called the Department of International Relations and Cooperation – see section 4), resolving Africa's problems is the central foreign policy terrain for South Africa. These dynamics inevitably narrow the space for discussion on trade policy on its own merits, as distinct from trade negotiations. It is too early to tell whether this foreign policy lineage will persist in the Zuma Administration – it was closely associated with the Mbeki Administration – but it is likely that Africa will occupy a central place in the post-Mbeki ANC government.

3   Patterns of trade

Here we consider various aspects of South Africa's merchandise trade with the world. First we review the country's aggregate trade with the world; second, we analyse trade with the world by major product category; finally, we analyse South Africa's major trade partners.

3.1   Aggregate trade flows between South Africa and the world

Table 9.1 shows South Africa's total trade with the world from 1996 to 2007. Total trade during this period amounted to US$917.4 billion. Total imports (US$466.4 billion) during this period were marginally higher than total exports (US$451.0 billion). Hence, South Africa's accumulated trade deficit from 1996 to 2007 was about US$15.4 billion (Draper and Freytag 2008). The compounded annual growth rate (CAGR) in exports and imports between 1996 and 2007 was 8% and 10%, respectively. According to Edwards and Lawrence (2006), trade policy in the 1990s has been able to increase imports through reducing input costs and increasing profitability of domestic sales. However, high and opaque import tariffs seriously impede export growth. This has been worsened by the lagging process of structural transformation of the South African economy (Hausmann and Klinger 2006). Edwards and Lawrence argue

Table 9.1 *South Africa's aggregate trade with the world, 1996–2007*

Year	Exports (US$ billion)	Growth (%)	Imports (US$ billion)	Growth (%)
1996	26.6		26.4	
1997	28.3	6.5	27.7	5.0
1998	26.0	−8.3	26.0	−6.3
1999	26.9	3.5	24.1	−7.4
2000	30.2	12.1	27.0	12.2
2001	26.5	−12.1	24.9	−7.6
2002	26.8	1.2	26.0	4.5
2003	34.6	29	34.1	30.9
2004	45.7	31.9	47.4	39.0
2005	51.8	13.3	54.9	15.9
2006	58.1	12.2	68.4	24.5
2007	69.5	19.7	79.5	16.3
Total	451.0		466.4	
CAGR	8%		10%	

Source: SAIIA's calculations from World Trade Atlas data.

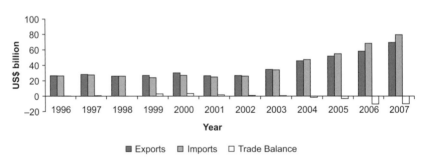

Figure 9.1   Evolution of South Africa's trade with the world, 1996–2007

that additional trade liberalization should be part of a strategy to enhance South Africa's export diversification.

Figure 9.1 shows the evolution of South Africa's trade with the world between 1996 and 2007. As shown, South Africa's exports and imports have exhibited a persistent upward trend since 1996. However, since 2004 imports have grown faster than exports and consequently the country's trade balance has been in deficit since then (see Table 9.2).

Table 9.2 *South Africa's trade flow to the world, 1996–2006*

Year	Exports (US$ billion)	Imports (US$ billion)	Trade balance (US$ billion)
1996	26.6	26.4	0.2
1997	28.3	27.7	0.6
1998	26.0	26.0	0.0
1999	26.9	24.1	2.8
2000	30.2	27.0	3.2
2001	26.5	24.9	1.6
2002	26.8	26.0	0.8
2003	34.6	34.1	0.5
2004	45.7	47.4	−1.7
2005	51.8	54.9	−3.2
2006	58.1	68.4	−10.3
2007	69.5	79.5	−10.0

Source: SAIIA's calculations from World Trade Atlas data.

3.2 Structure of South Africa's trade with the world

Table 9.3 shows the top ten product categories that South Africa exported to and imported from the world in 2007. The top ten export categories accounted for about 95% of the total value of exports in 2007. South Africa's exports are predominantly composed of commodities, which broadly conforms to the African pattern. Precious stones and metals, base metals and machinery combined accounted for about 61.2% of total exports. However, South Africa differs from the African pattern in the machinery and transport equipment categories. Under these categories, South Africa exports advanced manufactured goods mainly consisting of motor cars and components. On the other hand, South Africa's top ten imports in 2007 accounted for 88.7% of the value of imports. During the same period, about 57.2% of the total value of imports comprised machinery, mineral products and transport equipment.

Figures 9.2 and 9.3 show a very broad disaggregation, breaking down South Africa's trade with the world into four broad categories. The beginning (1996) and end points (2007) of the sample allow us to see how South Africa's trade with the world has evolved over the period, albeit in a very rudimentary way. Figure 9.2 indicates that between 1996

Table 9.3 *South Africa's trade with the world: top ten products, HS2, 2007*

Products	Total exports (US$ billion)	Total exports (%)	Products	Total imports (US$ billion)	Total imports (%)
Precious stones and metals	18.9	27.1	Machinery	20.4	25.6
Base metals	12.6	18.2	Mineral products	15.5	19.5
Mineral products	11.1	15.9	Transport equipment	9.6	12.0
Machinery	7.5	10.8	Chemical products	6.4	8.1
Transport equipment	6.2	8.9	Spec class/parts for motorized vehicles	5.7	7.2
Chemical products	3.8	5.5	Base metals	4.2	5.3
Food, beverages and tobacco	2.0	2.8	Plastic products	2.9	3.7
Vegetable products	1.8	2.6	Specialized equipment	2.1	2.7
Paper products	1.2	1.8	Textiles and clothing	2.0	2.6
Plastic products	1.0	1.4	Food, beverages and tobacco	1.6	2.0
Total	69.5	95.0	Total	79.5	88.7

Source: SAIIA's calculations from World Trade Atlas data.

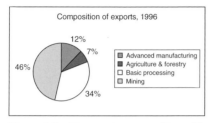

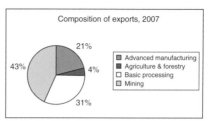

Figure 9.2 Changes in composition of South Africa's exports, 1996–2007

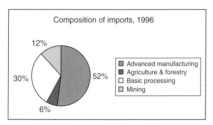

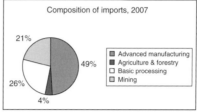

Figure 9.3 Changes in composition of South Africa's imports, 1996–2007

and 2007 South Africa's exports to the world have remained fairly stable, with the majority of exports consisting of mining and basic processing. However, during the same period, exports of advanced manufacturing have almost doubled, whereas agriculture and forestry exports decreased by almost half of the total. These changes probably reflect the structural changes that are taking place in South Africa's economy, where exports of manufactures are becoming more important over time. The top ten exports in the advanced manufacturing category accounted for about 57% of total exports in this category and comprised mainly of car parts and accessories and passenger vehicles. The top ten exports in the agriculture and forestry category accounted for 54% of total exports in this category, and mainly comprised horticultural fruits and wood chips. Figure 9.3 above indicates that the composition of South Africa's imports remained fairly stable. However, the imports of mining products have almost doubled.

3.3 South Africa's principal trade partners

Tables 9.4 and 9.5 show South Africa's top ten export and import markets from 2003 to 2007. Over the five years export and import markets have not changed much. South Africa's top ten export destinations accounted

Table 9.4 *Top ten export markets (all products), 2003–7*

2003			2004			2005
Market	US$ billion	Share (%)	Market	US$ billion	Share (%)	Market
EU 27	10.91	31.5	EU 27	14.61	32.0	EU 27
Unallocated	4.62	13.3	Unallocated	5.36	11.7	Japan
USA	3.28	9.5	USA	4.64	10.2	USA
Japan	2.73	7.9	Japan	4.12	9.0	Unallocated
China	0.88	2.5	Taiwan	1.36	3.0	Australia
Zimbabwe	0.87	2.5	Switzerland	1.13	2.5	China
Australia	0.76	2.2	Australia	1.09	2.4	Switzerland
Mozambique	0.75	2.2	China	1.02	2.2	Zimbabwe
Taiwan	0.66	1.9	Zimbabwe	0.96	2.1	India
Switzerland	0.60	1.7	Mozambique	0.79	1.7	Mozambique
Total	26.05	75.2	Total	35.06	76.8	Total

Source: SAIIA's calculations from World Trade Atlas data.

for about 75.1% of the country's total exports. The European Union, the United States and Japan are the most important export destinations, although China has moved up the list in recent years. Together, these countries accounted for about 51.2% of the value of South Africa's total exports in 2007.

In the same year, the top ten import sources accounted for about 75.6% of South Africa's total imports. The analysis shows that the European Union, China, the United States and Japan are South Africa's major sources of imports. Together, these countries accounted for 58.7% of South Africa's total imports in 2007.

4   Government in trade policy

It is important to note that transforming the apartheid state through rebuilding its institutions has been a tough proposition in general. These difficulties are reflected in the trade policy-making sphere.

In South Africa the executive branch is solely responsible for trade policy formulation and negotiating international trade agreements. There are approximately seven state actors which directly and indirectly participate in the trade policy process in South Africa. These

		2006			2007		
US$ billion	Share (%)	Market	US$ billion	Share (%)	Market	US$ billion	Share (%)
16.86	32.6	EU 27	18.51	31.9	EU 27	20.98	30.2
5.20	10.0	Japan	6.09	10.5	United States	7.44	10.7
4.91	9.5	USA	6.05	10.4	Japan	7.13	10.3
4.50	8.7	Unallocated	5.24	9.0	Unallocated	5.73	8.2
1.52	2.9	China	2.07	3.6	China	3.96	5.7
1.37	2.7	Switzerland	1.71	2.9	Switzerland	1.50	2.2
1.23	2.4	Australia	1.32	2.3	Zambia	1.42	2.0
1.17	2.3	Zambia	1.18	2.0	Australia	1.41	2.0
1.15	2.2	Zimbabwe	1.09	1.9	India	1.34	1.9
1.00	1.9	South Korea	1.01	1.7	Mozambique	1.27	1.8
38.92	75.2	Total	44.26	76.2	Total	52.20	75.1

include the DTI, the Department of International Relations and Cooperation (DIRCO), the Department of Justice, the Department of Agriculture, the National Treasury, the Presidency and parliament. The roles and responsibilities of these institutions are briefly described below:

4.1   Department of Trade and Industry

The DTI is the lead department in the formulation and implementation of trade policy. It has a range of institutions at its disposal: notably, the International Trade and Economic Development Division (ITED); the International Trade Administration Commission (ITAC); and Trade and Investment South Africa (TISA). ITED is solely responsible for trade policy formulation and negotiating bilateral and multilateral trade agreements; ITAC is tasked with the administration of trade policy and has three specialist units covering customs tariff investigations, trade remedies and import and export control; and TISA specializes in the promotion of South African exports and inward investment. In practice, ITED plays the central role in trade policy formulation.

Table 9.5 *Top ten import markets (all products), 2003–7*

2003			2004			2005
Market	US$ billion	Share (%)	Market	US$ billion	Share (%)	Market
EU 27	14.8	43.4	EU 27	19.3	40.7	EU 27
USA	3.3	9.7	USA	4.0	8.5	China
Japan	2.4	7.1	China	3.6	7.5	USA
China	2.2	6.4	Japan	3.2	6.8	Japan
Saudi Arabia	2.0	5.8	Saudi Arabia	2.6	5.6	Saudi Arabia
Iran	1.2	3.6	Iran	2.4	5.0	Iran
Australia	0.8	2.4	Australia	1.1	2.4	South Korea
Brazil	0.7	2.1	South Korea	1.0	2.1	Brazil
Taiwan	0.6	1.8	Brazil	1.0	2.1	Australia
South Korea	0.6	1.6	Nigeria	0.8	1.7	India
Total	28.6	83.8	Total	39.0	82.4	Total

Source: SAIIA's calculations from World Trade Atlas data.

4.2   Department of International Relations and Cooperation

The DICO's role is restricted to advising the DTI negotiators on the content of specific negotiations, particularly from the foreign policy perspective, and reviewing agreements for their consistency with South Africa's international obligations. The DICO retains an interest in the political impact that trade negotiations have on South Africa's bilateral and regional relations.

4.3   Department of Justice

The Department of Justice reviews trade agreements for their consistency with the constitution. This is a relatively perfunctory role with no real power associated with it.

4.4   National Department of Agriculture, Forestry and Fisheries

The Agriculture component of this new department is an important actor in trade policy formulation. This particularly applies in the regional context, where agriculture is a central concern to most SADC states. The old

			2006				2007	
US$ billion	Share (%)	Market	US$ billion	Share (%)	Market		US$ billion	Share (%)
20.9	38.1	EU 27	23.7	34.6	EU 27		26.8	33.7
4.9	9.0	China	6.9	10.1	China		8.5	10.7
4.3	7.8	USA	5.2	7.6	USA		6.1	7.7
3.7	6.8	Japan	4.5	6.5	Japan		5.2	6.6
3.0	5.5	Saudi Arabia	3.6	5.3	Saudi Arabia		3.6	4.5
2.2	4.1	Iran	2.7	3.9	Iran		2.9	3.7
1.4	2.6	South Korea	1.7	2.6	South Korea		1.8	2.2
1.3	2.4	India	1.6	2.4	India		1.8	2.2
1.1	2.1	Australia	1.4	2.1	Nigeria		1.8	2.2
1.1	2.0	Brazil	1.4	2.0	Brazil		1.7	2.1
44.2	80.4	Total	52.7	77.0	Total		60.2	75.6

Department of Agriculture was the best organized department in the trade sphere. It will take into its new institutional setting a well established consultative mechanism in the form of the Agricultural Trade Forum, which brings department officials and industry players together on a regular basis to discuss trade negotiations. The forum plays a critical role in formulating positions on agricultural trade: the bedrock of any trade agreement. The department also has long-established linkages with university-based research organizations, particularly agricultural economists at the universities of Pretoria, the Free State and Stellenbosch.

4.5   National Treasury

The National Treasury theoretically plays an important role in maintaining pressure on the DTI and other specialized departments for ongoing liberalization. In practice, it hasn't really played this role, rather deferring to the DTI's active trade negotiations agenda.[8] The National Treasury has a

---

[8] Apparently, the DTI has argued that it should not give away bargaining chips through unilateral trade reform, saving these rather for its extensive negotiations agenda.

broader interest in trade matters – especially within the African context – given the linkages between trade and debt. This is a persistent theme in the Treasury's international economic diplomacy. Another area of potential interest is international currency alignments and their implications for trade policy and negotiations. Finally, the Treasury is very engaged in analyses and debates concerning South Africa's current account deficit and associated demands for protection and industrial policy. However, until the Treasury builds sufficient capacity to seriously take these issues on it is not likely to be a serious player in the trade agenda.

4.6   Presidency

The Presidency is increasingly active in trying to coordinate activities between various departments through the 'cluster' system. This groups key ministries together in a high-level effort to coordinate policy initiatives among them. Two clusters are relevant to international trade negotiations: the economics and investment cluster, focusing on domestic economic policy coordination; and the International Relations, Peace and Security (IRPS) cluster, covering all external engagements including trade negotiations. The Presidency's role in economic policy formulation is likely to be significantly boosted in the wake of the recent general elections through the establishment of a dedicated Planning Commission. Ironically, the Commission is headed by Trevor Manuel, the former Finance Minister, who is anathema to those on the left of the tripartite alliance in COSATU and the South African Communist Party (SACP), who pushed for its establishment. While its precise mandate is not clear, the emerging consensus seems to be that it will focus on long-range planning as distinct from shorter-term intra-government coordination, which is ostensibly to be left to the new Department of Economic Development (see below) (Manuel 2009). The extent to which the Commission might take an interest in trade policy matters, and the direction it would pursue if so, remains to be seen.

4.7   Department of Economic Development

This is an entirely new ministry, established in May 2009. Its precise mandate is not clear, particularly its likely relationship with the National Treasury which has played a coordinating function in the past (Patel 2009). The Economic Development Ministry seems to have its political origins in COSATU and the SACP, which have pushed for greater coordination within government over economic development policy. Since Mr

Manuel was appointed to head the Planning Commission (originally proposed by the SACP) a veteran trade unionist and long-time secretary general of the Clothing and Textiles Workers Union was appointed Minister of Economic Development. As SACTWU secretary general, Mr Patel, the new minister, actively and successfully lobbied for imposition of import quotas on Chinese textiles and clothing products and is known to be sceptical of trade liberalization. To the extent that his new department will have influence over trade policy, it is likely that he will impel it towards the interventionist industrial policy approach described above. In this regard he was instrumental in negotiating the NEDLAC (see section 5) accord on a framework response to the global economic crisis (Government of South Africa 2009), which contains decidedly protectionist language.

4.8 Parliament

Parliament plays a role in approving international trade agreements, depending on the nature of the agreement.[9] This is an important component of the negotiation process, as failure to ratify could completely undermine carefully constructed international trade treaties. Presumably, parliament could refuse to ratify a trade agreement, but in practice this has not been tested. Yet from the standpoint of promoting effectiveness and transparency in the trade policy process, parliament could be doing much more.

4.9 Southern African Customs Union

South Africa's trade strategy now has to take serious cognisance of partners in the Southern African Customs Union (SACU),[10] as the new SACU agreement came into force in July 2004. This agreement is of historic significance in that it commits South Africa to effectively ceding sovereignty over trade policy formulation and implementation to new supranational

[9] The constitution, specifically section 231, is ambiguous on it. For example, section 231(3) identifies four kinds of agreement not requiring parliament's approval, leaving a fifth category requiring it. But precisely what fits into the fifth category is not stated. Furthermore, in the new SACU Agreement (see below), Article 41 provides for the parties to negotiate annexes which will cover many legal issues. However, in South Africa's case the Executive will probably not be required to submit the annexes to parliament as they will be considered 'subordinate legislation' (section 239 of the constitution) – which does not require parliament's approval. Altogether the legal issues at play here are complex and have not been tested in the courts, hence, the lack of clarity.

[10] Botswana, Lesotho, Namibia and Swaziland (the BLNS).

institutions, which have yet to be established. In essence, all decisions over tariffs and trade remedies will be taken at the SACU level by a council of ministers,[11] advised in turn by a new SACU tariff body and a commission of senior officials. State actors (in South Africa's case ITAC) will merely provide recommendations to the supranational structures on the basis of investigations the former conduct. Any disputes will be resolved by binding decisions taken by *ad hoc* tribunals, which raises interesting questions should the decisions not go South Africa's way. This tension is at the heart of current problems concerning SACU's future, since the new Minister of Trade and Industry and his backers favouring interventionist industrial policy wish to retain maximum trade policy space for South Africa. If the SACU agreement holds and endures, then the use of tariffs as an instrument of industrial policy may be substantially curtailed.

SACU has been fully involved in all current and future bilateral and regional negotiations, as required by Article 31 of the new SACU Agreement. This is a clear break from historical practice whereby South Africa decided all tariff matters unilaterally, albeit these exceptions do not seem to have translated into WTO negotiations yet where South Africa seems to invoke SACU in the NAMA 11 without real consultation. Furthermore, section 8 of the new SACU Agreement outlines a range of policy areas on which the partners are required to coordinate policy. Interestingly, South Africa's negotiations with the United States, and now with the European Union in the context of EPAs, brought home the need to coordinate internally prior to entering into demanding external negotiations.

Notwithstanding these dynamics it remains to be seen to what extent the BLNS will grasp the nettle and use this new framework to constrain South Africa's freedom of action. As noted above, currently there is a split in SACU concerning the EPA negotiations, and concerns on all sides that SACU may split. Partly this situation results from Botswana, Lesotho and Swaziland breaking ranks with South Africa and Namibia – substantially owing to the fear of losing preferential access to the EU market – and signing the interim EPA. How this situation plays out in the months ahead will have great bearing on SACU's future and, therefore, South Africa's trade policy future.

---

[11] Historically finance ministers constituted the Council given the dominance of revenue issues in SACU. Now both trade and finance ministers participate in the council and trade ministers schedule additional focused meetings on broader economic and trade issues.

5 Key non-state actors

There are nine NSAs that play a critical role in trade policy-making in South Africa. Their roles and responsibilities are briefly discussed below (see Table 9.6). Our interviews (see the Annex) extended beyond this group.

5.1 African National Congress

The ANC is the dominant political force in South Africa. Through its Economic Transformation Committee (ETC) key broad policy decisions concerning the economy are taken. The ETC has several sub-committees, one of which covers trade matters and is chaired by the current Minister of Trade and Industry. The work of this committee provides the basis for tripartite alliance negotiations over economic policy.

5.2 Congress of South African Trade Unions

The Congress of South African Trade Unions has long voiced its objections to what it regards as the damage arising from South Africa's liberal trade policy stance in the 1990s. Consequently, they have been key drivers of the current push for industrial policy, and for tempering trade liberalization, if not reversing it. Recently COSATU established its own rather secretive 'panel of progressive economists' comprising twenty members, which has released a ten-point action plan for the economy and, as far as global integration is concerned, takes a negative view.[12]

5.3 Business Unity South Africa

Business Unity South Africa (BUSA) represents South African business across various economic sectors on economic policy issues that affect it domestically and globally. The institution has recently played an influential role in trade policy processes and negotiations. It is essentially a federation of organized business federations, structured along sectoral lines.

---

[12] For more on this see SAIIA's project page on the balance of payments, which contains an exchange of views between one COSATU panel member and the SAIIA trade team, plus the original newspaper articles where COSATU's views were put forward, available at: www.saiia.org.za/index.php?option=com_content&view=article&id=856:south-africas-balance-of-payments-trade-policy-and-the-global-financial-crisis&catid=83:dttp-development-through-trade-projects&Itemid=205.

Table 9.6 NSAs involved in trade policy-making

Name	Policy interest	Constituencies served	Source of funding	International affiliates	Active trade negotiations
NEDLAC	Trade policy in its entirety	Business, labour and community-based organizations	Government, mainly Department of Labour	International Association of Economic and Social Councils and similar institutions and various institutions on the continent	Active in all the trade negotiations
Steel and Engineering Industries Federation of South Africa (SEIFSA)	Representing exporters' interests in the formulation of trade policies and participation in associate organizations	2,300 companies, engineering firms and producers involved in commercial metal and engineering works	Funded solely by membership fees	No international affiliates	Not directly involved but does make representations through BUSA
AgriSA	Trade policy in its entirety	Commercial agriculture	Membership fees and some rental income	International Federation of Agricultural Producers and Southern African Confederation of African Unions	Active in almost all the trade negotiations as agriculture is an integral part of the negotiations
BUSA	Trade policy in its entirety	Represents the interests of business	Membership fees	International Organization of Employers, Business and Industry Advisory Committee to the OECD, SADC Employers Group, Pan African Confederation	Active in all the trade negotiations

Organisation	Focus	Constituency	Funding	Affiliates	Activities
Creamer Media	Their journals address a number of issues including trade policies, sectoral tariffs and unfair trade practices	Stakeholders of the manufacturing, mining and banking sectors but also public companies and government departments	Advertisements and subscriptions	No international affiliates	Actively monitoring and providing coverage of numerous trade negotiations
Danie Jordaan	South Africa's tariff policy, industrial policy	Independent consultant	Consulting fees	No national or international affiliates but occasionally partners with consultants on certain assignments	WTO Trade Policy Review Team, WTO Dispute Settlement Panel, South African negotiation team at Uruguay Round, tariff liberalization and rules of origin negotiations under the TDCA. Through NEDLAC: SADC FTA, EU EFTA, and MERCOSUR negotiations
Textile Federation (Texfed)	Trade-related research	Textile industry	Membership fees	International Textile Federation	Textile Federation has participated in policy inputs (and technical assistance) for the Uruguay Round of negotiations, SADC, EFTA and the TDCA
NALEDI	Macro-economic policy and framework	Serve the interests of the poor	COSATU, Oxfam Novib (Holland), PBC and DBSA to name a few	No international affiliates	NALEDI has participated in the NEDLAC process from COSATU

Table 9.6 (*cont.*)

Name	Policy interest	Constituencies served	Source of funding	International affiliates	Active trade negotiations
Aids Law Project	Intellectual property, trade in services in the health sector and access to healthcare services	Serve the broader public interest	A combination of philanthropic and foreign donors, Department of Trade and Industry also subsidizes some of their activities	The Aids Law Project has no formal affiliates but does have a close working relationship with international, regional and domestic affiliates	The Aids Law Project has not been directly involved in any trade negotiations. They did make some presentations at NEDLAC with regards to intellectual property rights
Institute for Global Dialogue (IDG)	Numerous trade-related issues and policy debates	Government and politicians	Endowment from the German government	**They have no national or international affiliates *per se*, but operate within many networks as part of a progressive epistemic community**	The IDG has not been actively involved in trade negotiations, however, they are involved indirectly through technical support on issues in the WTO, EPAs and of course involvement in NEDLAC
Southern African Stainless Steel Development Association (SASSDA)	Steel imports and to a certain degree exports	Manufacturers of primary products, the raw form of steel after the extraction of minerals, and producers of tertiary and	Membership fees	International Stainless Steel Federation	SASSDA has not been actively involved in trade negotiations. This is because as an organization they have avoided lobbying the government due to the potential conflict between their members

COSATU	Impact that trade policy and negotiations have on job security for the workers in South Africa	secondary products, the refined steel products The entire labour force	Affiliates who pay membership dues	No international affiliates	Active in all the trade negotiations
Economic Justice Network	Debt and finance, aid for trade, trade and development, EPAs, food security, SADC policy advocacy	Churches – Christian voice in economic issues	Church of Sweden and Norwegian Church Aid	Our world is not for sale, World Council of Churches, Church of Churches, SADC Council of NGOs, Norwegian Church Aid, Africa Trade Network, Southern and Eastern Trade Information Negotiation Institute	Participated in the 5th WTO Ministerial Conference in Cancun and organized a meeting between Southern Africa countries with NGOs on the EPAs
Trade and industrial policy strategies	Regional integration, trade flows and tariff analysis, services, research infrastructure (data) and capacity-building	Policy-makers in South Africa and the region	IDRC and Government	Informal affiliates including ESRF, BIDPA, Mauritius University, NEPRU, Mozambican government officials, Dar es Salaam University, Zambia University, Malawi University, UNECA (Southern Africa), World Bank (Madagascar), SADC Secretariat, Trade Hub, GTAP and individual international researchers	Involvement largely indirectly through research outputs. Have been involved directly in the SADC–EU EPAs negotiations. Key role included analysis of tariffs data for member states.

Table 9.6 (*cont.*)

Name	Policy interest	Constituencies served	Source of funding	International affiliates	Active trade negotiations
Tralac	Trade policy, legal and regulatory issues	Government officials and the private sector	Consulting fees, SECO, Swiss Department of Economic Development, DFID, DANIDA	World Trade Organization, academic researchers, regional secretariats, ITC, ICTSD and IISD	Indirectly on regional trade agenda – training, capacity-building, technical analysis and dissemination of research outputs to negotiators
UCT School of Economics	Labour and trade flow impact assessments, poverty, market structures and trade reform	No particular constituencies – independent academic research	Consulting fees	Harvard's Kennedy School of Economics (Center for International Development), International research associates and World Bank	Indirectly through trade negotiations-related capacity-building
UCT Graduate School of Business	International trade, business, emerging markets, globalization, regional trade agreements, public–private partnerships, trade and business linkages, and trade reform	SMMEs, export promotion agencies, DTI, NGOs, aid organizations, private sector	Consulting fees	Evian Group, Centre for the Study of Globalization and Regionalization, BIDPA, Georgetown University, Turfs University, Warwick University, Individual academic researchers	Indirectly providing advice and lobbying using the public platform, e.g., Africa group at the WTO – preparation of briefings

The Trade Committee adopts a very sector-focused view, with not much space being accorded to economy-wide perspectives. We interviewed a few of the sector organizations affiliated to BUSA.

5.4 National Economic Development and Labour Council

The National Economic Development and Labour Council (NEDLAC) brings government, business, labour and civil society together on a national level to discuss and try to reach consensus on issues of social and economic policy. The institution plays an important role in the formulation of negotiating positions for trade negotiations, although the nature of that role is open to question. It does not negotiate itself; rather, its role is confined to providing a forum for negotiations.

5.5 Trade and Industrial Policy Strategies

Trade and Industrial Policy Strategies (TIPS) conducts essentially quantitative studies of trade flows and associated tariff structures to support various negotiations. It is increasingly active on the sector strategy front. Furthermore, through its network of university-based researchers it is well-placed to harness high-level knowledge to drive the broader trade policy debate. Historically it was established to support the DTI analytically, a role it continues to fulfil.

5.6 South African Institute of International Affairs

The South African Institute of International Affairs (SAIIA), through its Development through Trade Programme, conducts independent research on various aspects of trade policy, including regional integration and new generation issues such as services and investment. The institution has a huge media profile in South Africa. SAIIA's trade policy input is facilitated through, among other channels, the production of publications, dissemination of information in the form of opinion pieces, interviews, roundtables and the like, all targeted at state and non-state actors participating in trade policy processes.

5.7 Trade Law Centre for Southern Africa

The Trade Law Centre for Southern Africa (TRALAC) is essentially a regional institute with an extensive network. It works quite closely with various regional governments and institutions. It also conducts courses on various aspects of trade law, and consequently plays an active role in capacity-building. It has conducted some work for the DTI, and regularly produces briefings and reports and conducts public seminars on various trade topics.

5.8 Institute for Global Dialogue

The Institute for Global Dialogue (IGD) is a think-tank aligned to the ANC, and primarily covers foreign policy issues. It recently established a trade programme covering the multilateral and regional terrains. It has close links to COSATU and the ANC,[13] and is an active promoter of industrial policy.

5.9 Treatment Action Campaign

The Treatment Action Campaign (TAC) is particularly concerned with intellectual property rights provisions in bilateral negotiations with developed countries, especially the United States. Until recently they had an adversarial relationship with government, notably the Health Department, owing to their vigorous (and ultimately successful) challenges to the government's AIDS treatment strategy. This history of activism is evident in their approach to the trade debate, where they are particularly interested in the pharmaceutical sector, access to medicines and issues pertaining to intellectual property rights.

6 Findings

A process of interviews with state and non-state actors was conducted between April and May 2009. Two different set of questionnaires were designed for this purpose – one targeted at state actors, the other at non-state actors. A total of twenty-four interviews were conducted, comprising six state actors and eighteen NSAs. The findings from these interviews are discussed below.

6.1 State actors in trade policy-making

Among state actors, there was a consensus that the DTI provides leadership on trade policy formulation and trade negotiations in general.

---

[13] It was established by the ANC in 1994.

Politically, there is an agreement that policy decisions are to some degree taken jointly by the DTI and the Presidency. Based on interactions with representatives from the DTI, parliament and the Department of International Relations and Cooperation, the formal intra-government regional trade negotiations forum assumes first priority. This is based on the notion that the centrepiece of South Africa's foreign policy is based on an 'African Agenda'. However, there is a view that the WTO provides a platform for a fair level playing field (in relative terms) as developing countries can negotiate on more equal terms with developed countries than at the bilateral level. South Africa also sees its involvement in the WTO as a platform from which to influence world trade issues. The taxing time and energy expended on multilateral negotiations is viewed as another reason why bilateral and regional forums are preferred to multilateral forums. This view was shared notably by interviewees at the National Treasury, ITAC, the DTI and the NDA.

According to interviewees, the question of which forum in which to negotiate and manage trade relations is largely driven by South Africa's political and economic interests, though some of the decisions are inextricably linked with the commitments made by the country when it acceded to joining the WTO. Other respondents view the recent lack of political will to engage in bilateral negotiations, especially with the United States and the European Union (through the EPAs), as based on the perceived costs of liberalization, such as loss of employment in uncompetitive sectors.

All state actors interviewed concur that consultation processes (both inter-department and with external stakeholders) are not consistent. Regional trade negotiations issues are more often dealt with through NEDLAC processes than WTO issues. State actors also agree that parliament should have oversight responsibility on trade policy and trade negotiations. Beyond rectifying and approving trade deals, what 'oversight responsibility' entails is not so clear. State actors also attest that there is a need for a structured coordination mechanism with, and capacity-building for, parliamentarians on trade issues. Parliamentarians interviewed concurred with these views and asserted that it is the duty of trade policymakers and negotiators to brief parliament before and after negotiations.

Whereas the DTI largely makes use of NEDLAC processes for NSAs' participation in trade policy and negotiations, the Department of Agriculture engages NSAs through the Agriculture Trade Forum (ATF).[14]

---

[14] It comprises government, industry (commercial and emerging farmers), labour, the Land Bank and provincial agricultural departments. It provides input into trade negotiations irrespective of the forum.

Parliament is also of the view that public hearings on trade negotiations should be considered. Interviewees argued that the consultation processes do not discriminate among NSAs and/or whether negotiations are multilateral or regional. However, the actors have divergent reasons for engaging with NSAs in trade policy-making. For example, the most important reason the DTI, DIRC and the Presidency engage with NSAs in trade policy-making is to satisfy public policy requirements, whereas the key reasons for the Department of Agriculture, ITAC and National Treasury are to promote transparency and to seek technical advice.

State actors concur that NSAs have influenced negotiating positions. However, the actors differ on the level of influence. For example, the Department of Agriculture believes that NSAs have substantial influence, whereas the DTI believes that the level of influence has been moderate to high, depending on sectoral interests and how vocal the industry is. Furthermore, sectoral interests also play a role in the attitudes towards alternative forums, be it preference to the WTO, South–South PTAs, and North–South PTAs.

6.2   Non-state actors in trade policy-making

Non-state actors in South Africa have been active in trade policy formulation for a number of years. The engagement on trade policy-making is usually through NEDLAC, an institution where government, labour, business and other civil society groups come together to try to reach a consensus on trade policy matters. Other forums for trade policy influence include the ATF and the Industry Forum (IF).[15] Non-state actors fund their activities from membership subscriptions, royalties and, in some cases, donor finance. The general consensus among interviewees is that avoiding funding from the South African government maintains the impartiality of most NSAs and avoids conflicts of interest.[16]

---

[15] The Industry Forum (IF) is a formal consultative structure chaired by the director general of the Department of Trade and Industry. The IF meets four to five times a year and it comprises all industrial sectors, provincial governments and commerce. The IF discusses matters relating to economic development, industrial and trade policy (including regional integration and the WTO).

[16] It should be noted that in certain parts of government donor funding is viewed with a degree of suspicion as an avenue for influencing South African government positions. This may explain the government unwillingness to engage with some NSAs where this reticence manifests.

Sometimes NSAs form coalitions in order to lobby government on similar interests and coordination is usually on an *ad hoc* basis. For example, the Textile Federation mentioned that at times it forms coalitions with labour to take a defensive position against certain imports. Where coordination is formalized it happens through meetings or workshops. The motor vehicle industry, for example, has about six council meetings a year. Some NSAs are also affiliated to international organizations, such as the SADC Council of Non-government Organizations, Africa Trade Network, the Evian Group and the Harvard Group among others. Most of the affiliation centres on research collaboration, training, capacity-building and data support. However, among our sample those NSAs with international affiliates do not receive advice on trade policy matters, rather on industry-related technical matters. For example, the motor vehicle and stainless steel industries are affiliated to international industry associations through which they get technical advice, such as standards, and share data. Domestically, most of the NSAs interviewed do not have affiliates. However, they maintain coalitions focused mainly on research collaboration and information sharing.

Areas of trade policy interest for business interests vary from defensive to offensive. Among our sample group these include market access into developed countries, job losses as a result of import competition and intellectual property rights as they relate to access to medicines for the poor. Other non-business NSAs' trade policy interests cover, *inter alia*, market structures, legal and regulatory issues, emerging markets, regional integration, services liberalization, debt and finance, food security and aid for trade among other issues.

Trade negotiations that our NSA sample group have been involved in include the SADC FTA, the EU EPAs, SACU–MERCOSUR FTA, SACU–EFTA and the failed SACU–US FTA. While some NSAs participated directly in these negotiations, others were indirectly involved through research input, capacity-building and technical analysis. The general consensus is that views of NSAs are taken seriously by government. In lobbying government on trade policy matters NSAs generally see multilateral and regional trade negotiations as being equally important; in other words, NSAs accord both negotiating forums the same level of importance.

However, most interviewees concurred that there is a substantial difference in the space offered to NSAs to influence trade policy between the two forums. In the multilateral context the government consults widely and the engagement is more transparent. This is because multilateral negotiations are externally driven and have a predetermined agenda. Hence, the multilateral negotiations are seen as being less influenced by political considerations. Domestic consultations with NSAs concerning the WTO negotiations are conducted through NEDLAC, the ATF and the IF.

In the preferential context, most interviewees concurred that negotiations are not transparent and there is no clear structure for consulting NSAs. However, some business groups, mostly those well established, reported that there was no difference in the space they were offered, which could indicate the differences in government interactions with various industries. Consultation opportunities, when available, are *ad hoc* in nature. Hence, preferential negotiations relative to the WTO are more influenced by political considerations and the delicate nature of these negotiations. During the survey NSAs cited the import quota imposed by the DTI on Chinese clothing and textiles as an example of a decision that was taken by government without proper consultation with relevant stakeholders, particularly via NEDLAC. Some NSAs hinted at the role that ambitious negotiators might take: sometimes a particular deal is rushed through in order for the negotiator to appear to be nimble and subsequently rise in the ranks in the department.

The general perception among NSAs is that the South African government has shifted its attention from the Doha Round to PTA forums. Nonetheless, according to our NSA interviewees the government remains committed to multilateral negotiations. The shift to PTAs is substantially influenced by the deadlock in the Doha Round.

As illustrated in Figure 9.4 about 33% of our sample NSA group seek to influence trade policy through self-initiated lobbying. Meetings organized by government are the second most important way in which our sample NSAs seek to influence policy (28%). Published materials, other means and public campaigns are the least utilized ways of influencing policy. As shown in Figure 9.5 about 39% of NSAs interviewed seek to influence government officials and 22% seek to influence ministers/vice ministers. About 17% of NSAs surveyed seek to influence public opinion; the same proportion also seeks to influence legislators. Legislators are not an important point of influence for most NSAs interviewed, reflecting the dominant view that legislators have limited knowledge about trade policy matters. Concerning our sample group where meetings have been held with the Trade Portfolio Committee at parliament, they have been organized on an *ad hoc* basis and initiated by NSAs.

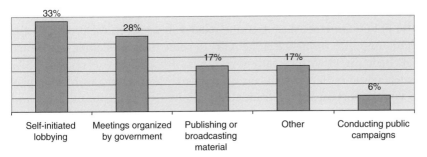

Figure 9.4 Ways in which NSAs seek to influence trade policy

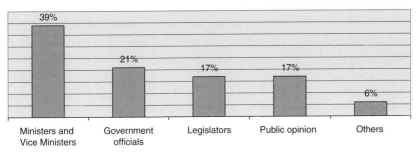

Figure 9.5 Policy-makers that NSAs seek to influence.

While these findings are clearly not definitive they do reinforce the analytical point made in section 4 that the executive dominates the process. Within this, NSA interviewees concur that government takes their policy inputs seriously. Other NSAs pointed out that invitations to government meetings and events show that government is receptive of their inputs, and the fact that the government reciprocates this gesture by attending events organized by NSAs. Though the extent of influence is not measurable, some NSAs argued that processes such as NEDLAC and the Harvard Group usually force an agenda for policy introspection. BUSA, for example, said it was successful in influencing South Africa's position with regard to non-agricultural market access (NAMA) negotiations at the WTO.[17] TIPS pointed out that 80% of the tariffs it recommended under the SACU-MERCOSUR PTA negotiations were implemented.

---

[17] BUSA's position with regard to NAMA negations at NEDLAC has been defensive and other constituencies represented at NEDLAC share BUSA's position. There are no diverging views with regards to NAMA at NEDLAC.

The point of policy influence for our NSA sample is the DTI, through the ITED. On trade negotiations related to agricultural products, the point of policy influence is the ATF. In some instances, policy influence has been direct with certain government officials. In this regard, NSAs interviewed indicated that certain personalities within government play a very important role in trade negotiations. The Minister of Trade and Industry and the Chief Trade Negotiator were cited as having a strong interest in trade policy matters. Many key people in the various industries indicated that they have established relationships over time with the Minister of Trade and Industry and the Chief Trade Negotiator. As such, they are more approachable and are familiar with the issues that industry faces which creates a mutual understanding based on trust.

The general consensus view in our NSA sample is that there are significant outcome differences in lobbying effectiveness between multilateral and preferential negotiations. This is because there are more consultation opportunities offered in the multilateral context than in preferential negotiations.

In conclusion, most NSAs interviewed are of the view that South Africa has adequate structures for trade policy consultation especially with regard to multilateral negotiations, albeit that structures for consultation on preferential negotiations could be improved. Central to the latter is transparency to avoid political interference. Nonetheless, several improvements were suggested. Regarding the effectiveness of NEDLAC there were calls for government to include more community constituencies, such as gender equity groups, consumer groups, youth, and professional associations, such as engineers and chartered accountants. The idea is that this would make NEDLAC more inclusive, although we are sceptical regarding the contribution some of these groups could make to trade policy. There was also a suggestion to increase the consultation period that is offered to NSAs at NEDLAC; this reflected the general view that the time offered for consultation is generally too short.

7   Conclusion

The South African case has its own specificities. In our overall judgement the state retains a dominant role in the process of trade policy-making, with specific reference to trade negotiations in particular. This is a function of South Africa's political process, and cannot be understood without reference to the electoral dominance of the ANC and the institutional arrangements through which this is expressed, particularly the centrality of the executive branch of central government in relation to parliament and second tier (provinces and municipalities) structures. Not surprisingly, therefore, the issue of forum choice is primarily determined by the executive branch of government. Non-state actors, particularly from business and labour, are influential at the level of detail in influencing the content of negotiations, but not the issue of forum choice.

Given the electoral dominance of the ANC it is unlikely that this situation will change in the foreseeable future unless the balance of forces within the dominant party changes decisively in favour of greater heterogeneity in trade policy-making. This is not an unlikely scenario, as our analysis of the key institutions within the executive and their relationship to current political dynamics attests. At that point it is possible that NSAs, to the extent that they have preferences for one particular negotiating forum over another, could exert greater influence over forum choice. However, within the ANC and its alliance partners there is a consensus on the need for the state to lead development (African National Congress 2009); therefore, that seems a rather distant proposition.

References

African National Congress 2009. *2009 Manifesto Policy Framework: Working Together we can do More.*

Bell, T. 1997. 'Trade Policy', in J. Michie and V. Padayachee (eds.), *The Political Economy of South Africa's Transition*. London: Dryden Press.

Bertelsman-Scott, T., Mills, G. and Sidiropoulos, E. 2000. 'The EU–SA Agreement: South Africa, Southern Africa, and the European Union', South African Institute of International Affairs, Johannesburg.

Bilal, S. and Laporte, G. 2004. *'How Did David Prepare to Talk to Goliath? South Africa's experience of trade negotiations with the EU'*, ECDPM, available at: www.ecdpm.org.

Cassim, R. and Zarenda, H. 2004. 'South Africa's Trade Policy Paradigm', in E. Sidiropoulos (ed.), *Apartheid Past, Renaissance Future – South Africa's Foreign Policy: 1994–2004*. Johannesburg: South African Institute of International Affairs.

Department of Trade and Industry 2007. *'National Industrial Policy Framework'*, Pretoria, South Africa.

Draper, P. 2004. 'The SACU–US FTA: In Search of a Contract Zone', The Exporter (Business Day supplement), June.

Draper, P. and Alves, P. 2007. 'Déja Vu? *The Department of Trade and Industry's National Industrial Policy Framework*', Occasional Paper No. 2, Business Leadership, Johannesburg, South Africa.

Draper, P. and Erasmus, G. 2008. 'Fragments of Trade', *Mail and Guardian*, 11 April.

Draper, P. and Freytag, A. 2008. '*South Africa's Current Account Deficit: Are Proposed Cures Worse than the Disease?*', Trade Policy Report No. 25, South African Institute of International Affairs, Johannesburg, South Africa.

Draper, P. and Khumalo, N. 2007. 'One Size Doesn't Fit All: Deal-Breaker Issues in the Failed US–SACU Free Trade Negotiations', South African Institute of International Affairs, Johannesburg.

2009. 'European Free Trade Association – Southern African Customs Union Free Trade Agreement', in S. Lester and B. Mercurio (eds.), *Bilateral and Regional Trade Agreements–Case-Studies*. Cambridge University Press.

Draper, P. and Soko, M. 2004. 'US Trade Strategy After Cancun: Implications, and Prospects for the SACU–US FTA', SAIIA Trade Policy Report No. 4, South African Institute of International Affairs, Johannesburg.

Draper, P., Khumalo, N. and Stern, M. 2008. 'Why isn't South Africa more Proactive in International Services Negotiations?', in J. Marchetti and M. Roy (eds.), *Opening Markets for Trade in Services; Countries and Sectors in Bilateral and WTO Negotiations*. Cambridge University Press.

Edwards, L. and Lawrence, R. 2006. '*South African Trade Policy Matters: Trade Performance and Trade Policy*', CID Working Paper No. 135, Harvard University, Cambridge, MA.

Government of South Africa 2009. '*Framework for South Africa's Response to the International Economic Crisis*', Pretoria, South Africa.

Hausmann, R. and Klinger, B. 2006. '*South Africa's Export Predicament*', CID Working Paper No. 129, Harvard University, Cambridge, MA.

Ismail, F., Draper, P. and Carim, X. 2000. '*South Africa's Global Economic Strategy: A Policy Framework and Key Elements*', International Trade and Economic Development Division, Department of Trade and Industry.

Joffe A., Kaplan D., Kaplinsky R. and Lewis D. 1993. 'Meeting the Global Challenge: A Framework for Industrial Revival in South Africa', in P. H. Baker, A. Boraine and W. Krafchik (eds.), *South Africa and the World Economy in the 1990s*. Cape Town: David Philip.

Macro-economic Research Group 1993. '*Making Democracy Work: A Framework for Macro-economic Policy in South Africa*', Centre for Development Studies, Bellville, South Africa.

Manuel, T. A. 2009. *Address by the Minister in the Presidency: National Planning Commission on the Presidency's Budget Vote debate*, 24 June.

Patel, E. 2009. *Speech by Minister of Economic Development, Debate on the Trade and Industry Budget*, Vote 32, 30 June.

ANNEX

List of interviewees

State actors

Department of Agriculture
Department of International Relations and Cooperation
Department of Trade and Industry
International Trade Administration Commission
National Treasury
Parliament, Trade and Industry Portfolio Committee

NSAs

Economic Justice Network
Institute of Global Dialogue
National Association of Automotive Manufacturers of South Africa
National Economic Development and Labour Council
National Labour and Economic Development Institute
Southern Africa Stainless Steel Development Association
Steel and Engineering Industries Federation of Southern Africa

Textile Federation

Trade and Industrial Policy Strategies
Trade Law Centre of Southern Africa
University of Cape Town, Graduate School of Business
University of Cape Town, School of Economics

10

The influence of international non-state actors in multilateral and preferential trade agreements: a question of forum shopping?

MARIA PEREZ-ESTEVE[1]

1 Introduction

This chapter examines the influence that non-state actors (NSAs) seek to exert on trade policy formulation at the WTO multilateral level and at the national governmental level. The analysis focuses on international NSAs that have a substantial presence in Geneva, either because they are based there or because they seek to engage on a regularized basis with the WTO. The main objectives of this chapter are to explore how these NSAs seek to influence trade policy development, both at the WTO and the national level, especially in relation to the question of forum choice: that is, the relative benefits of negotiating multilaterally or preferentially. It also investigates whether those NSAs involved in trade policy-making consider the WTO versus PTAs as a form of 'forum-shopping' to pursue their particular agendas, interests and objectives.

The analysis focuses on three main categories of NSAs: namely, business organizations, trade unions, and civil society organizations (CSOs). Research for this chapter has been largely gathered through surveys[2] and

---

[1] This paper has been written in the personal capacity of the author and does not represent the views of the WTO members or Secretariat.

[2] Two different sets of surveys were circulated among NSAs. Seventeen responded to the first one, including 3D→Trade–Human Rights–Equitable Economy, Centre du Commerce International pour le Développement (CECIDE), Centre for Socio-Eco-Nomic Development (CSEND), Consumer Unity & Trust Society (CUTS), EcoLomics International, Friedrich Ebert Stiftung (FES), Geneva Social Observatory (GSO), IDEAS Centre, Institute for Agriculture and Trade Policy (IATP), International Centre for Trade and Sustainable Development (ICTSD), International Chamber of Commerce (ICC), International Institute for Sustainable Development (IISD), International Trade Union Confederation (ITUC), Stiching Oxfam International, Quaker United Nations Office (QUNO), The Evian Group, and the World Council of Churches (WCC). Seven completed

was complemented, in some cases, with structured interviews with a number of Geneva-based NSA representatives.[3]

The structure of the chapter is as follows. Section 2 describes how NSAs seek to influence trade policy formulation at both the multilateral and national governmental level. It also examines how NSAs seek to exert influence from the perspective of their aims and interests. Section 3 looks at the influence that NSAs aim to exert on trade policy formulation at the multilateral and national governmental level in relation to the negotiation of PTAs, and tries to determine whether this can be considered a form of 'forum shopping'. Section 4 puts forth the study's main findings and conclusions.

2   Non-state actors and trade policy formulation at the WTO and national level

2.1   Aims and interests

This section outlines the aims and interests of NSAs that seek to influence trade policy formulation at the WTO and national level. It also explores how NSAs seek to exert their influence. The analysis covers the three main types of NSAs: business organizations, trade unions and CSOs.

2.1.1   Business organizations

Business organizations have been by far the most active in seeking to influence trade policy formulation at the multilateral level since the establishment of the General Agreement on Tariffs and Trade (GATT) in 1947. From the early years of GATT until the end of the 1980s, relations with business organizations were virtually non-existent except for informal and *ad hoc* relations with a few, including the International Chamber of Commerce (ICC). One reason for this is that GATT dealt almost exclusively with tariff negotiations (Hoekman and Kostecki 2001; WTO 2007). However, during the Uruguay Round negotiations (1986–94), and since the creation of the WTO in 1995, as the reach of the multilateral trading system has expanded to new areas, so has the number and range of business organizations seeking to influence trade policy formulation at the WTO.

---

the second one, including 3D→Trade–Human Rights–Equitable Economy, CUTS, FES, IDEAS Centre, Stiching Oxfam International, The Evian Group and the ITUC.

[3] The interviews were undertaken with Geneva-based representatives from Stiching Oxfam International, CUTS and FES.

This section looks at how two business organizations that engage on a regularized basis with the WTO, namely, the ICC and the Evian Group at the International Institute for Management Development (IMD), seek to press their aims and interests at the multilateral and national level, in particular within the context of preferential trade agreement (PTA) negotiations.

The ICC has been the most active international business organization seeking to influence trade policy formulation at the multilateral level since the early GATT years. Founded in 1919, it is the global business association and the only representative body that speaks with authority on behalf of enterprises from all sectors in every part of the world. Today it represents thousands of member companies and associations from over 130 countries. National committees in the world's major capitals coordinate with their membership to address the concerns of the business community and to convey to their governments the business views formulated by the ICC. Business leaders and experts drawn from the ICC membership establish the business stance on broad issues of trade and investment policy, as well as on vital technical and sectoral subjects. These include financial services, information technologies, telecommunications, marketing ethics, the environment, transportation, competition law and intellectual property among others.

Since it was established in 1995, the Evian Group at IMD seeks to influence trade policy formulation at the WTO. It is an international coalition of corporate, government and opinion leaders, committed to fostering an open, inclusive, equitable and sustainable global market economy in a rules-based multilateral framework. The Evian Group considers that international trade and investment has the potential to unite people through greater mutual understanding and common interests across countries, continents, cultures and generations. It argues that a market economy, founded on responsible capitalism, combining the critical role of government in providing public goods, a strong ethical base of good governance and free enterprise are the best means for generating growth, employment, empowerment and enrichment in terms of both wealth and welfare. Although global in its outlook and outreach, the Evian Group focuses on four key regions: Europe, the Arab Region, Greater China and South Asia. Its activities are aimed at building confidence and creating knowledge among its members, stakeholders and constituents; establishing vision and direction by formulating agendas for action; enhancing global business leadership and business statesmanship; influencing policy-makers; diffusing its ideas and intellectual capital as widely as possible; and preparing the next generation of industry, government and opinion leaders.

The ICC and the Evian Group seek to influence trade policy formulation, mainly to question the way trade policy is designed and administered, to ensure it is inclusive and engaging and to propose policy solutions. In addition, the Evian Group tries to influence trade policy formulation as a means of opening up space for public argumentation.

Both organizations seek to influence the WTO by participating in major WTO activities such as the annual Public Forum, ministerial conferences and significant meetings organized by the Secretariat as well as WTO-related meetings and roundtables planned by relevant stakeholders all over the world. They try to exert influence through expressions of support for a strengthened multilateral rules-based system and an ambitious and successful conclusion to the Doha Round in press releases, communiqués addressed to government officials, letters to the director general and trade ministers, roundtable meetings, petitions, policy advocacy to governments, pamphlets, research and education. They also try to influence public opinion through global campaigning, education and advocacy based on research and analysis undertaken at the international level. They allot great importance to the creation of 'experts' or expertise on relevant trade issues to present to decision-makers as an effective means of influencing trade policy formulation at the WTO.

Concerning the current Doha Round negotiations, the ICC supports governments' efforts to ensure a successful conclusion of the Round, and feeds business views into the development of multilateral trade policies on issues that directly affect business operations. The ICC also provides business input to the United Nations (UN) and other intergovernmental bodies, both at the international and regional level. In addition, it seeks to influence at the national level trade policy-making through its national committees. For example, the ICC mobilizes business support for the New Partnership for Africa's Development and organizes regular regional conferences focusing on the concerns of business in Africa, Asia, the Arab world and Latin America. The Evian Group is heavily involved in the organization of roundtables with leading institutions around the world, including policy-makers, international business decision-makers and opinion leaders in order to join forces, networks and complement strengths and interests on current key themes. An example of this is the launch of the Open World Initiative (OWI) for preserving, fostering and developing the idealism of an open world economy and society for the decades ahead. In the area of research and analysis they have released a number of studies on trade and regionalism.

Both organizations emphasize the importance of the rules-based multilateral trading system as an engine of economic growth and of new and meaningful trade opportunities through the reduction of trade barriers in both developed and developing countries. Their aim is to arrive at increased market opportunities in target markets as a result of current ongoing negotiations. They see the importance of the WTO as guardian against protectionism, particularly within the context of the current economic crisis. They also have a high interest in safeguarding and strengthening the WTO's dispute settlement mechanism to ensure that when formal adjudications become unavoidable, decisions are implemented fully and expeditiously, thus minimizing instances of retaliation.

Both organizations have a close interest in negotiations to liberalize trade in agriculture, industrial products and services. In addition, they have a strong interest in the negotiation of rules in areas such as anti-dumping, intellectual property measures, investment, government procurement and competition policy among others. In relation to trade facilitation, their principal aim is the creation of new rules to simplify and speed up the movement, transit, clearance and release of goods, with particular benefits for small- to medium-sized enterprises (WTO 2008).

When asked to identify issues that they considered they had been successful in influencing at the multilateral level, the ICC indicated its role in putting trade facilitation on the agenda of the 1996 WTO Ministerial Conference in Singapore, attributing their effectiveness to their policy advocacy to governments. The Evian Group indicated that it had been instrumental in influencing discussions on agriculture, the Doha Development Agenda, trade and environment and trade and migration, primarily through presentations in the annual WTO Public Forum and communiqués to government officials.

The ICC also seeks to influence trade policy at the national level, particularly within the context of PTA negotiations. Influence is exercised primarily by lobbying government officials through its national committees or business associates to push for the inclusion of their particular aims and interests in these negotiations. The degree of participation and consultation at the national governmental level differs from one country to another and the degree of involvement varies. When national consultative mechanisms for trade policy formulation are set up by governments, business organizations are the most frequently consulted for technical advice, information and commercial intelligence, and their input is genuinely considered and sought after.

2.1.2 Trade unions

Trade unions have sought to influence trade policy at the multilateral level since the GATT years. In particular, from the Tokyo Round (1973–9) onwards, trade unions have sought to make the violation of workers' rights as a cost-cutting method made illegal at GATT, and have pressed for the establishment of a working group on that issue. At the 1986 GATT Ministerial Meeting which launched the Uruguay Round, the proposal was raised but it was not taken up, and labour rights remained absent from the GATT agenda during the negotiations. The establishment of the WTO in 1995 provided the labour movement with an effective international organization with legally enforceable rulings in which to lobby for core labour standards to be included in all WTO agreements (He and Murphy 2007). At the first WTO ministerial conference, held in Singapore in 1996, trade union activists lobbied members to push for the inclusion of workers' rights on the WTO work programme. At the meeting, many WTO members opposed to mixing trade policy discussions with labour standards concluded that labour issues were a topic to be dealt with at the International Labour Organization (ILO) not the WTO. Although the proposed core labour standards clause failed to be adopted, namely, because of opposition from developing countries, the subject was mentioned in the final ministerial declaration. This issue has returned to the fore at subsequent WTO ministerial meetings.

The International Trade Union Confederation (ITUC) is the principal trade union organization, examined in this chapter, that engages on a regularized basis with the WTO, and that seeks to influence trade policy formulation at the WTO multilateral level.[4] Its primary aim is the promotion and defence of workers' rights and interests through international cooperation between trade unions, global campaigning and advocacy within the major global institutions. Its goals are to better the conditions of work and life of working women and men and their families, and to strive for human rights, social justice, gender equality, peace, freedom and democracy. The ITUC has three regional organizations: the Asia–Pacific Regional Organization (ITUC-AP); the African Regional Organization (ITUC-AF); and the Americas Regional Organization (TUCA). The ITUC also cooperates closely with the European Trade Union Confederation,

---

[4] Its predecessor, the International Confederation of Free Trade Unions (ICFTU), was created in 1949 and the World Confederation of Labour (WCL) was founded in 1920. In 2006, the ITUC was established out of the merger of the ICFTU and the WCL ending their existence as independent organizations.

including through the Pan-European Regional Council, which was created in March 2007. The ITUC has close relations with the Global Union
Federations and the Trade Union Advisory Committee to the OECD
(TUAC), working together through the Global Unions Council. It also
works closely with the ILO and maintains contacts with several other UN
specialized agencies. The ITUC has offices in Amman, Geneva, Moscow,
New York, Sarajevo, Vilnius and Washington, DC. Its influence and reach
across the world is indisputable, with over 175 million members in 311
affiliated organizations in 155 countries and territories (2009 figures).

The ITUC's goals in influencing trade policy making are to question
the way trade policy is designed and administered; to participate in the
trade policy agenda setting on issues of relevance to them; to ensure that
the agenda is inclusive and engaging; and to propose policy solutions.

In particular, the ITUC seeks to ensure that WTO agreements promote
decent work, development and employment, and that they enhance social
protection and social dialogue. The ITUC is also keen to see the WTO
address labour standards violations relating to trade and production for
exports and to engage further with other organizations at the multilateral
level, including the ILO. It believes that trade must not undermine the
bargaining power of workers and governments, and also that the WTO
could play an effective role in addressing the trade–labour relationship.
Moreover, the ITUC considers that there should be a place where social
and employment issues can be raised legitimately in the WTO without
concerns of protectionism, for example, in a committee or work programme on trade and decent work (WTO 2008).

The ITUC seeks to exert its influence primarily at the WTO, through
lobbying Geneva-based delegates as well as capital-based officials and
by persuading public opinion. At the national level, it engages with the
Geneva-based delegations as well as national officials either directly or
through their national affiliates, but always in coordination with them.
Trade union participation and consultation at the national governmental level differs from one country to another, and the degree of involvement varies. Examples of a high degree of trade union participation at
the national level are present in Latin America, particularly in the coordination for MERCOSUR, in South Africa, in the Caricom region, in the
European Union and in the United States. Other trade unions are consulted by their governments only on an *ad hoc* basis, as is the case in the
Andean and Central American countries, and some are not consulted
at all, as in the case of Serbia and many West African countries (GURN
2005). Most consultations are limited to labour issues or labour-related

issues, such as in India where trade unions were consulted concerning 'social clause' proposals only, but do not have any access to information on the GATS commitments the government has tabled. Others are consulted on a broader range of issues.

The ITUC also seeks to influence multilateral trade policy through research and analysis. For example, since 1997 the ITUC has prepared reports coinciding with every Trade Policy Review (TPR) of WTO members that look at the record of adherence to the core ILO conventions subscribed to by the country examined. In addition, the ITUC's work on trade and labour standards includes regular policy statements to the WTO with comments on investment, services and development, as well as other areas of the organization's activities. It also exerts considerable influence through global campaigning and advocacy undertaken at the international level for the rights of workers, both at the workplace and in broader society. The ITUC works to initiate and coordinate at the international level campaigns in which national trade unions are involved. It believes that grassroots participation of workers in campaigns aimed at improving their lives is essential, as well as ensuring that they have a clear public message that mobilizes citizens. This is achieved by preparing support materials, coordinating actions and participating in international events, including WTO, G8 meetings and the World Social Forum among others.

The ITUC also works with its Global Unions partners to promote effective rules governing the behaviour of private business. In this, it is promoting the development of an international framework for social dialogue and collective bargaining, and effective systems of corporate governance that hold management accountable for the social impact of business activities.

With regard to the Doha Round, the ITUC has focused on negotiations in services and non-agricultural market access (NAMA). In services, the ITUC is concerned about the potential impact of the negotiations on employment, access to services for the poor and the protection of public services and public sector workers. The ITUC has coordinated the 'NAMA 11' trade union group and the Latin American trade union group (together with TUCA), which call for tariff reductions to take into account tariff lines that are sensitive to current and future employment, and for a broader and more strategic approach that allows for an active industrial development policy. They also seek to ensure that developing countries are able to preserve policy space. For example, the ITUC launched a major campaign in 2005 against the current NAMA proposals, and a resolution was adopted at the ITUC General Council in 2007, which called for action by affiliates. This call resulted in lobbying from some developed country trade unions in support of their developing country counterparts. The campaign also calls for an impact assessment of the Doha Round, especially the NAMA negotiations. Its work also focuses on the agreement on Trade-Related Aspects of Intellectual Property (TRIPs), and access to medicine, negotiations related to the temporary movement of people (Mode 4 of the General Agreement on Trade in Services (GATS)) and protection of workers' rights and non-discrimination, development issues and ensuring that the Doha Round results in a fair deal for developing countries.

When asked to identify issues they considered they had been successful in influencing at the multilateral level, the ITUC nominated the NAMA negotiations, Mode 4 negotiations, public services, attention for employment issues, TRIPs and public heath and the Singapore issues. Their influence was exercised primarily through trade union statements and declarations on specific issues, active lobbying, research, media advocacy, alliances with other groups and participation in meetings and conferences to advocate positions. Advocacy at the multilateral level was primarily directed at the WTO director general, ambassadors and ministers during ministerial gatherings. At the regional level, advocacy was undertaken in regional meetings and forums.

In terms of national trade policy-making, the ITUC works through its affiliates upon request by assisting them to lobby governments, ministers and persuade public opinion. The ITUC helps them to coordinate their work, provides advice, information, training and research. Affiliate organizations determine their individual aims and interests and also undertake most of the lobbying themselves at the national and WTO multilateral level during major events, including ministerial conferences. If the issues are of general concern to the whole trade union movement, the ITUC will lobby in Geneva and if needed at the national level, especially if they are requested to do so by their affiliates and always in coordination with them.

With regard to PTA negotiations the ITUC has a particular focus on those involving the United States, the European Union (such as the economic partnership agreements (EPAs)) and the members of the Association of Southeast Asian Nations (ASEAN) countries. Affiliates in developing countries are particularly concerned about the negative economic impacts of such agreements. Influence at the national governmental level is always exerted in coordination with national affiliates based on their aims and interests. Their main objective is to ensure a strong protection of workers' rights in these agreements and to ensure policy space for developing countries in particular to ensure development in general and industrial growth in particular.

2.1.3   Civil society organizations

Civil society organizations' interest in influencing multilateral trade policy formulation became apparent during the end of the 1980s and early 1990s as the Uruguay Round (1986–94) negotiations were intensifying. During this period a number of organizations concerned with environment and development issues began to take an interest in the activities of GATT. This interest rapidly turned into disapproval by the time the GATT dispute settlement panel in the case *United States – Restrictions on Imports of Tuna* issued its decision in the summer of 1991.[5] In addition to the substantive environmental concerns raised, the panel process itself was criticized for lacking transparency and for being closed to the public. Environmental activists argued that important decisions about the environment were being taken by faceless bureaucrats, in a secretive organization that was managed by a club of rich countries without adequate participation and input – including the popular claim of a 'democratic deficit' in global governance and at the WTO (O'Brien *et al.* 2000; Barton *et al.* 2006). As a result, CSOs' interest in GATT at the time was mostly limited to criticism and calls for greater transparency and openness.

The period spanning the creation of the WTO in 1995 to the protests in Seattle in 1999 was characterized by CSOs' growing discontent and mounting criticism as the WTO's reach expanded to new areas such as intellectual property, services, environment and development (WTO 2007). While CSOs were largely absent from multilateral trade negotiations during the Uruguay Round, the situation gradually started to change in the second half of the 1990s, with their interest peaking between 2000 and 2003, when a number of CSOs established a presence in Geneva. These comprise human rights associations, public health advocates, development-based organizations, faith-based groups, consumer protection groups, farmers' cooperatives, women's groups, sustainable development-based organizations or pro-development groups among others.

---

[5] Principally, the panel ruled that a conservation law that was being enforced unilaterally and extraterritorially by the United States violated GATT rules. This ruling created an outcry among environmentalists and placed GATT on the black list of environmental organizations worldwide.

These organizations include, 3D→Trade–Human Rights–Equitable Economy, Centre du Commerce International pour le Développement (CECIDE), Centre for Socio-Eco-Nomic Development (CSEND), Consumer Unity & Trust Society (CUTS), EcoLomics International, Friedrich Ebert Stiftung (FES), Geneva Social Observatory (GSO), IDEAS Centre, Institute for Agriculture and Trade Policy (IATP), International Centre for Trade and Sustainable Development (ICTSD), International Institute for Sustainable Development (IISD), Oxfam International, Quaker United Nations Office (QUNO) and the World Council of Churches (WCC). Increasing activity among CSOs on WTO issues (Charnovitz 2000; Zahrnt 2008), along with their long-standing efforts in a number of areas, have been successful in influencing the agenda-setting at the WTO, including negotiations (Hoekman and Kostecki 2001; WTO 2007, 2008). For instance, the CSOs campaign against enforcing TRIPs to ensure access to essential HIV/AIDS medicines succeeded in producing normative and substantive changes in policy outcomes (Sell and Prakash 2004), such as the decision ultimately taken by WTO members at the Hong Kong Ministerial Conference in December 2005 to amend the TRIPs Agreement by incorporating the agreement reached in August 2003 on the use of compulsory licences by developing countries without manufacturing capacity, allowing them to access life-sustaining medicines in national emergencies more easily, but without undermining the property rights regime (WTO 2008).

All the CSOs examined in this chapter seek to influence trade policy formulation at the multilateral level in one way or another from the perspective of their aims and interests. These range from environmentalists to pro-development activists, farmers' groups, human rights and public health advocates and consumer protection groups to name a few. A common objective underlying the work of many CSOs is to ensure that sustainable development is taken into consideration in trade policy-making along with economic considerations. Their main reasons for seeking to influence trade policy formulation at the multilateral level are to ensure it is inclusive and engaging, to propose policy solutions and to open up space for public debate.

In relation to WTO negotiations, many CSOs argue that they have not delivered on the pro-development reform that was originally promised when the Doha Development Round was launched in 2001. For instance, Oxfam claims that the Doha Round has failed to live up to its promise of rebalancing trade rules in favour of the poor and has turned into a market access negotiation in which developing countries are being asked to make disproportionate concessions. In particular, it claims that the United States and other rich countries have offered largely illusory reforms, while demanding in return real and risky concessions from developing countries, such as greater market openings without adequate flexibility and safeguards (Oxfam 2009). Oxfam also argues that trade policy should seek to expand opportunities for poor people to gain a greater share of the benefits of trade. In addition, a number of CSOs consider that the current economic crisis presents a necessity as well as an opportunity for a real reform of the multilateral trading system (WTO 2010).

The single most important mechanism for exerting their influence on trade policy formulation at the WTO is through lobbying governments, both Geneva-based delegates and government officials at the national level, either directly, through their national offices or local CSOs based in the capitals. Their efforts are pursued by working in dense networks, linking national organizations in their networks to exchange information on common problems and actual and potential solutions in their respective areas of expertise. These networks can be informal and *ad hoc*, issue-specific and formal, or multi-issue coalitions and of varying membership. They may be surprisingly spontaneous or the result of long-lasting alliances. These networks, together with government networks, characterize a new world order in which information is exchanged and activities are coordinated across national borders to deal with global problems (Slaughter 2004) which, in turn, has confirmed CSOs as important players in global value creation and governance (Teegen *et al.* 2004).

An example of a successful CSO network is the one established during the 1990s when a number of organizations came together under the umbrella concept of sustainable development. One common characteristic of these networks today is that much of their work is carried out through the Internet. As a result, networks of CSOs work at the global level linking national and international CSOs as they increasingly exchange information and coordinate activities to influence multilateral trade policy formulation at the WTO.

Another means for CSOs to exercise their influence, particularly in the last decade, is through partnering with governments – principally from developing countries. In this regard, CSOs often provide governments with expertise, training and policy advice at different levels. Examples of this successful contribution of ideas can be found in several of the topics on the negotiating agenda of the Doha Round, subjects for which NSAs have fought long and hard, including the issue of intellectual property rights and access to medicines, the reduction of agricultural subsidies in developed countries, the lowering of environmentally-harmful fisheries subsidies, the trade-opening in environmental goods and services and ensuring greater compatibility between WTO rules and multilateral environmental agreements (MEAs).

On all of these issues WTO members partnered with specialized organizations that had developed particular expertise that contributed towards pushing these issues onto the WTO agenda. In order to develop this knowledge civil society organizations pursue the creation of expertise through research and analysis that feed into the different programmes and activities in the areas of interest to them. For example, ICTSD has developed particular programmes on a number of issues including agriculture, Aid for Trade, dispute settlement and legal aspects of international trade, climate change, trade and sustainable energy, environment and natural resources, intellectual property and a programme on trade in services, labour mobility and sustainable development; IISD has put forth programmes on Sustainable Markets and Responsible Trade (SMART), aimed at understanding and progressively removing the obstacles to sustainable production through the wide use of standards, and on Trade and Climate Change; and IATP's Trade Information Project staff is in daily contact with CSOs and government representatives in relation to several projects they have launched including the Biodiversity and Intellectual Property Project and the Trade and Agriculture Project. Civil society organizations have also influenced government positions and the rule-making process at the WTO through participation in the official delegations of members, either from their country of origin or from another for attendance at ministerial conferences and in WTO councils and committees.

Civil society organizations also try to influence trade policy formulation at the WTO by engaging in public campaigns that support their aims and interests. For instance, in 2002 Oxfam launched its 'Big Noise' worldwide petition calling for governments to help end unfair trade practices, and its 'Make Trade Fair' campaign[6] in 2003 to promote trade justice and fair trade among governments, institutions and multinational

---

[6] Oxfam's 'Make Trade Fair' campaign has eighteen global partners, including Consumers International (CI), Consumer Unity & Trust Society (CUTS), European Fair Trade Association (EFTA), Fairtrade Labelling Organizations International (FLO), Friends of the Earth International (FoEI), The Institute for Agriculture and Trade Policy (IATP), International Council on Human Rights Policy (ICHRP), International Commission of Jurists (ICJ), International Centre for Trade and Sustainable Development (ICTSD), International Federation for Alternative Trade (IFAT), International Society for Human Rights (ISHR), International Union of Food (IUF), Network of European World Shops

corporations. Its Geneva office has led Oxfam's advocacy and campaigning work on the WTO to achieve a pro-development outcome in the Doha Round negotiations.

In addition, many of these CSOs seek to influence policy formulation at the national level by trying to influence the position of governments in PTA negotiations. In this regard, they either engage directly with Geneva-based delegates or capital-based officials or through their country offices or national affiliates. If they do not have national affiliates they often form alliances with local organizations that try to influence national trade policy-making. Examples of CSOs that seek to influence trade policy-making at the national level include the Consumer Unity & Trust Society (CUTS) International, Oxfam International and FES.

Civil society organizations are also active in the consultative mechanisms established by governments. Some governments legitimately recognize the importance of having inclusive and participatory trade policy-making processes to increase transparency and to promote greater participation, which are considered essential to enhance the legitimacy of these processes (Ostry 2002; Hocking and McGuire 2004; Wolfe and Helmer 2007). Others simply establish them as a means for maintaining social cohesion and contributing towards preserving broad support for trade liberalization in response to the growing demands from CSOs to participate in trade policy-making as the trade agenda has expanded to include subjects of particular interest to them. In some cases, governments have put in place new processes for consulting CSOs on trade policy matters, while in others, CSOs have been invited to participate in existing consultation mechanisms along with business and industry groups.

The opening up of this space, particularly since the late 1990s, has allowed CSOs to be more visible and assertive. However, CSOs identify a number of shortcomings with regard to these consultation mechanisms set up by governments that call into question their effectiveness as a serious manner of influencing trade policy formulation. First, they often lack a clear legal mandate that requires governments to consider the analysis and advice provided by CSOs and thus they often remain a forum for dialogue only. Second, the coverage of issues is often less than comprehensive and some stakeholders are not represented at all, such as parliamentarians and small businesses. Third, the meeting of these consultative mechanisms hardly ever function regularly.

(NEWS!), Third World Network (TWN), Third World Network Africa (TWN Africa), World Organisation Against Torture (OMCT) and the World Wide Fund for Nature (WWF).

As a result, there is a perception among CSOs that these consultative mechanisms lack predictability and function on an *ad hoc* basis, and that they exist only because national governments need to comply with the transparency and public policy requirements involved in trade policy-making. For example, CUTS has actively participated in the national consultative process set up by the Department of Commerce in India. However, it recognizes that its influence is limited because they are not invited to participate in this consultative process on a permanent basis. Their goal is to form part of the group of stakeholders that are permanently consulted along with business organizations and industry chambers.

The FES seeks to exert influence on trade policy formulation at the national level through activities that provide a platform to foster dialogue between relevant stakeholders, primarily CSOs, trade union organizations, parliamentarians, academics and government officials. To this end, they organize consultations, dialogue seminars, technical workshops and other activities at the national level to discuss trade policy issues with relevant NSAs, other interested stakeholders and government officials. For example, FES seeks to exert influence on the new EPAs negotiated between the West African Region and the European Union by supporting the participation of relevant stakeholders in the negotiation process. The complexity of the issues, the variety of interests in the region and the technical details have posed serious obstacles to the effective participation of many key actors (FES 2009). In order to overcome these difficulties, FES worked with twenty experts from ten countries, all closely involved with the EPA negotiations and the issues surrounding them, to map out what the likely consequences of different negotiated results might be for the future development of the region.

The Consumer Unity & Trust Society also seeks to exert influence on trade policy formulation at the national level through the creation of National Reference Groups (NRGs) of relevant stakeholders, including other CSOs, within the framework of the Fostering Equity and Accountability in the Trading System (FEATS) Project. These NRGs range from twenty to fifty relevant stakeholders depending on the size of the project. For example, in the three-year project aimed at improving ownership through inclusive trade policy-making processes in Kenya, Malawi, Tanzania, Uganda and Zambia, CUTS works with approximately fifty-five partners in Kenya alone. According to CUTS, the research emanating from this project shows that a number of initiatives that have been undertaken by the governments in the project countries to open the trade policy-making process to a larger group of stakeholders, including relevant government ministries and agencies, the private sector, CSOs and research institutions, include formal consultative mechanisms, primarily, and the relevant stakeholders are aware of these efforts and eager to play an active role in trade policy-making. However, their improved and effective participation in the trade policy-making process entails the enhanced capacity of all stakeholders, improved and regularized use of the consultative mechanisms and the promotion of a culture of dialogue among the relevant stakeholders (CUTS 2009).

Oxfam also tries to influence national trade policy-making by lobbying government officials and engaging in advocacy and media campaigns. At the national level, Oxfam relies on their national offices or affiliates that partner with local CSOs trying to influence national trade policy. The agenda focuses on issues related to the local national trade agenda and PTAs. When partnering with local organizations, Oxfam carefully evaluates whether the common aims and interests warrant their association with organizations with whom they might not necessarily share the same views on all issues.

2.2   The influence of non-state actors on trade policy formulation

This section presents the main trade-related issues that the NSAs surveyed indicated being most interested in (see Figure 10.1). It then looks at the success of NSAs in influencing trade policy formulation at the WTO multilateral level and at the national governmental level from the perspective of their aims and interests (see Figure 10.2). This section concludes that the majority of the NSAs surveyed indicate a preference for seeking to influence trade policy formulation at the WTO multilateral level and rate their success in influencing the negotiations at the WTO highest. A large number of NSAs believe that their views and preferences are shaped through their own policy positions and preferences based on research and analysis, while others indicate that they are shaped principally through interactions with the WTO, national governments and NSAs, and some consider that they are formed through a combination of both.

The main issues that these organizations identified as being of major interest to them are presented in Figure 10.1. Out of the twenty-four options provided, trade and environment was identified as the single most important issue, followed by trade and development, trade in services, agriculture and food security/food aid, all of which are rated equally in terms of significance. Intellectual property issues, including TRIPs and access to medicines, are the sixth issue rated in importance. Research and analysis, NAMA, investment, labour and least-developed countries

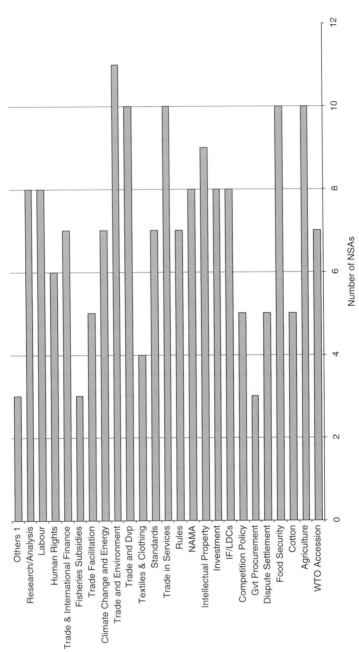

Figure 10.1 NSAs' particular areas of interest as they relate to trade policy

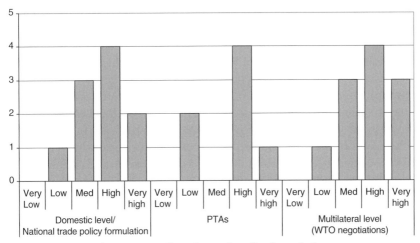

Figure 10.2   NSAs' success in influencing trade policy formulation

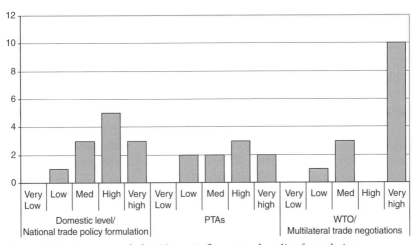

Figure 10.3   Forum sought by NSAs to influence trade policy formulation

(LDCs) issues, such as the integrated framework, followed in importance and were all rated equally. The issues that score lowest in terms of import-ance were government procurement, textiles and clothing and fisheries subsidies.[7] Chemicals and wastes and energy/low carbon policies were cited as important issues under the 'others' category.

---

[7] The low rating assigned to fisheries subsidies can be explained by the fact that Geneva-based CSOs are not actively devoting huge amounts of resources to this issue, which for

The NSAs examined in this chapter rate their success in influencing trade policy formulation at the multilateral level highest, followed closely by their achievements at the national governmental level. Their influence on trade policy formulation in PTAs scores lowest. The majority of them indicated a preference for pursuing their goals and interests at the WTO through multilateral negotiations rather than through PTAs. They argue that the decision-making process within the WTO favours the diverse interests of developing countries in a more coherent way than in PTAs, where a lot of pressure ends up falling on the weakest participant. They also consider the negotiation of PTAs as being more secretive and thus limiting the ability to reach an interested audience. Furthermore, they note that the administration of multiple PTAs at the global level has become very complex and that a multilateral framework is likely to be more comprehensive.

In addition, most of them value the way in which a multilateral approach binds all members and includes important issues such as agricultural subsidies and rules which are often not part of PTA negotiations. They also argue that developing countries are better able to preserve policy space in the WTO multilateral negotiations than in PTAs. A number of NSAs also consider that PTAs divert the interests and limited government resources and expertise available in developing countries for negotiating trade agreements away from the multilateral trade negotiations. Some argue that PTAs end up dividing the interests of WTO members in the long run. Lastly, a number of NSAs noted that their primary interest in multilateral negotiations was due to the expertise and contacts, in both the WTO Secretariat and the Geneva-based delegations, that they had acquired as a result of their Geneva location.

The majority of the NSAs surveyed indicated that their views and preferences are shaped through their own policy positions, and are based on research and analysis. A number of them noted that they were shaped mostly through interactions with the WTO, national governments and other NSAs, and some indicated that they were shaped through a combination of both. In relation to this matter, the Evian Group indicated that they have strong policy positions, but are open to dialogue. Oxfam noted that they have their own policy positions and preferences fully shaped, but also certainly consider and evaluate other positions in order to consider scenarios that will help to determine their final positions.

years has been dealt with successfully by WWF and OCEANA, neither of which have a presence in Geneva.

Friedrich Ebert Stiftung and CUTS noted that their views and preferences are shaped through their interactions with the WTO, national governments and other NSAs. The ITUC bases its policy positions and preferences on its analysis of the impacts of different negotiation texts tabled at the WTO.

3   Non-state actors, the World Trade Organization and preferential trade agreements: a question of forum shopping?

This section looks at the issue of forum choice and whether there are significant differences in NSAs' approach towards influencing policy outcomes at the multilateral level or within the context of PTAs. It also seeks to determine whether NSAs involved in trade policy-making consider the WTO versus PTAs as a form of 'forum shopping' (Busch 2007) to pursue their particular agendas, interests and objectives. The analysis once again covers the three main types of NSAs: business organizations, trade unions and CSOs.

The majority of the NSAs surveyed indicated that their choice of forum for seeking to influence trade policy formulation is the WTO, giving it a very high importance (see Figure 10.3). Influencing trade policy formulation at the national level is rated second, while seeking to influence PTAs is rated lowest, with only six out of the seventeen NSAs surveyed considering PTAs as being of high or very high importance.

3.1   Business organizations

Although business organizations have an undisputable interest in seeking to influence the rules for multilateral trade, it is clear that companies cannot wait indefinitely for the Doha Round negotiations to conclude, so they adjust their interests and aims, in particular in the short term, to changing situations and opportunities. These include prospects obtainable within the context of PTAs. In this manner, as long as the Doha Round continues to stall, business organizations will focus more and more on PTAs as an alternative means of pursuing trade liberalization in line with their particular aims and interests.

When asked if there are significant differences in their approach towards influencing policy outcomes at the multilateral level or within the context of PTAs, the Evian Group and the ICC stated that the approaches are, indeed, different. This difference results primarily from the fact that the number of actors in PTAs is more limited and that there are generally fewer issues to deal with. Both the Evian Group and the ICC have a normative preference for seeking to influence trade policy formulation at the WTO. They both acknowledge that there are a number of issues that can be resolved only at the multilateral level, for example, the reduction of subsidies in agriculture and global rules. However, the ICC also recognizes that multilateral trade rules require adjustments at the national level, which is why the ICC engages at the national level through its national committees or business associates.

According to the Evian Group, the assumption in the academic literature that export-oriented business interests prefer to pursue their interests at the WTO through multilateral negotiations rather than through PTAs may have been correct in the past, but is no longer the case today. They note that business by and large, especially big business, is 'turned off' by the snail's pace of WTO multilateral negotiations and has become increasingly disengaged. Although they may not have a strategic preference for seeking to influence PTAs, at least they are moving. They note that a distinction should be made between the aims and interests of multinational corporations (MNCs) and those of small and medium enterprises (SMEs). Although transaction costs in PTAs may be significantly higher, they argue that MNCs have deep enough pockets to absorb the costs.

In terms of forum choice for settling disputes, business organizations favour the WTO where the rules apply to all members who are subject to binding dispute settlement procedures. This is of great importance to business groups that seek to introduce multilateral disciplines on a variety of subjects, including competition and investment policies to name two.

3.2   Trade unions

The ITUC did not clearly express a preference for seeking to pursue its interests at the WTO through multilateral negotiations, but it did indicate a normative preference for the multilateral regulatory framework over the bilateral one and outlined a number of particular concerns they have with the negotiation of PTAs, such as the difficulty of following the details of these negotiations, the lack of transparency that surround them and the lack of consultation with trade unions on many of them. The ITUC also recognizes that labour standards and clauses on labour standards are only included in a number of bilateral PTAs, in particular those involving the United States. Therefore, from that point of view the ITUC acknowledges that seeking to influence bilateral PTAs is preferable. However, the

ITUC considers that on balance labour clauses in bilateral PTAs do not serve their purpose, and are often included in exchange for far-reaching commitments by developing countries in terms of market access and investment which the ITUC considers have adverse effects on developing country economies. In that sense, the ITUC expressed a preference for trying to influence WTO multilateral negotiations where development outcomes or the specific interests of developing countries are better taken care of and where commitments are not so far-reaching.

When asked if there are significant differences in their approach towards influencing policy outcomes at the multilateral level or within the context of PTAs, the ITUC indicated that the approach is similar, but the impacts are more severe in PTAs where they focus on the inclusion of social chapters, which are not part of the WTO negotiations.

In terms of forum choice for dispute settlement, the ITUC favours the WTO multilateral level where the rules apply to all members, who are subject to binding dispute settlement procedures. This is particularly of interest to trade union organizations that seek to introduce multilateral disciplines on labour standards and worker's rights.

3.3   Civil society organizations

The CSOs surveyed expressed a normative preference for seeking to influence trade policy formulation at the WTO, because they favour the multilateral regulatory framework over the bilateral one. Civil society organizations generally consider that developing countries are better off negotiating within a multilateral framework. They tend to see PTAs, both bilateral and regional free trade agreements (FTAs), in particular those involving the richer countries (the countries of the European Union and the United States) as a means of forging new markets for their goods and services in the absence of a new multilateral trade deal. They condemn the effects of these PTAs which they argue are devastating for the constituencies they represent, particularly small-scale farmers, indigenous people and women.

According to many of them, the vast majority of PTAs are typically written to benefit industrialized farms and pharmaceutical corporations, with little consideration given to development needs in poor countries with high levels of poverty and inequality. In addition, many CSOs denounce the provisions in PTAs that go beyond WTO commitments, in particular, in the areas of services, investment, government procurement, intellectual property and competition policy. For a number of these organizations influencing PTAs is not a priority *per se*, but they do seek to exercise influence depending on how it connects with their specific goals and interests. A number of CSOs indicated a high interest in seeking to influence the EU EPAs, including Oxfam International, FES, CUTS and the ICTSD. They have been working on developing expertise in the area of regional trade agreements for some time now. For example, Oxfam is working to defeat those PTAs they consider to be a threat to people's rights to livelihoods, local development and access to medicines. Oxfam's campaign against the signing of the EPAs is a good example. Oxfam also tried to exert influence on the North America Free Trade Agreement (NAFTA) negotiations by establishing a presence in Mexico and working with local national CSOs. In addition, during the Central American Free Trade Agreement (DR-CAFTA) negotiations, Oxfam led a campaign to influence the negotiations with support from their partners based in Central America.

Friedrich Ebert Stiftung indicated that their degree of involvement in trying to influence the negotiation of PTAs depends on the priorities of their country offices. To date, FES has focused on the EPA negotiations and various regional agreements in Asia and Latin America. Consumer Unity & Trust Society International noted that although seeking to influence PTAs is not a priority they are undertaking a 'back of the envelope' analysis of all the PTAs in which India is engaged. This analysis is sent to the government on a monthly basis along with a set of advocacy messages, including warning messages from the consumers' perspective. Sometimes the government strongly disagrees with the contents of the monthly dossier, but generally speaking those that read it consider it useful. This dossier is perceived as the position of 'others' versus that of the Indian government negotiators.

When asked if there are significant differences in approach to influencing trade policy outcomes according to whether the context is multilateral or regional the responses of the CSOs surveyed varied. Consumer Unity & Trust Society International indicated no significant difference in their approach and noted that research-based advocacy is more effective at the multilateral level because the decision-making process is more inclusive and the process is based on substance rather than politics. In contrast, decisions taken within the context of PTAs are often not based on economic rational but politics. Oxfam noted that their approach in seeking to influence trade policy outcomes in multilateral or regional contexts was, indeed, different given that the number of actors and issues covered varied depending on the situation. Finally, according to FES, the differences in approach to influencing trade policy outcomes does not depend on whether the context is multilateral or regional but rests on the interaction with decision-makers. Indeed, FES argues that the effectiveness of the different instruments for seeking to influence trade policy outcomes, such as publications, dialogue, seminars and workshops, depends on the interactions with decision-makers. The closer the relationship with them, the more influence is possible. This criterion, in their view, is more important than the differentiation between the multilateral and regional context.

In conclusion, although the majority of the CSOs have a normative preference for the WTO over PTAs as a choice of forum for influencing trade policy formulation based on their aims and interests, they also seek to influence the negotiation of PTAs at the same time, in particular those that involve the European Union and the United States, as well as the EU's EPAs. In response to the question of whether there are significant differences in approach to influencing trade policy outcomes according to whether the context is multilateral or regional the responses of the CSOs varied.

4   Conclusions

The key issue investigated in this chapter is how international NSAs seek to influence trade policy development, both at the WTO and the national level, especially in relation to the question of forum choice: that is, the relative benefits of negotiating multilaterally or preferentially.

The international NSAs examined here, whether they represent business, trade unions or a wide variety of CSOs, have a strong preference for seeking to influence multilateral trade negotiations at the WTO rather than PTAs. This is not surprising given their focus on the WTO, their Geneva location and the expertise they have developed, as well as their contacts with the Geneva-based delegations, the WTO Secretariat and other NSAs.

The majority of NSAs expressed a normative preference for seeking to influence the WTO negotiations versus PTAs for a number of different reasons. First, they favour the multilateral regulatory framework over the bilateral one, because they consider that developing countries' interests are better taken care of in the WTO as they lack the economic and political power to pursue their demands effectively elsewhere. A second reason that explains the NSA preference for seeking to influence the WTO negotiations as opposed to PTAs rests with the multilateralist orientation that many of the international NSAs established in Geneva have across a whole range of international issues, ranging from human rights, to environmental protection, pro-development policies, climate change and so on. Third, the preference for seeking to influence the WTO negotiations also lies in the advantages that result from having established a presence in Geneva in terms of networking and coalition-building with like-minded actors that also seek to influence the WTO negotiations. Fourth, one might speculate that a number of NSAs established a presence in Geneva to try and influence trade negotiations at the WTO, because they consider the multilateral framework a better vehicle for advancing the interests of the constituencies they represent reflecting a relative lack of success experienced in influencing trade policy-making at the national level.

Finally, long-established NSAs in Geneva, including the ICC and the ITUC, as well as some of the CSOs such as Oxfam, are likely to prefer the multilateral framework on account of the recognition they accord to the role that the WTO plays as a system of justiciable rules versus a framework that will deliver market access. In this regard, the main interest of NSAs is to rebalance the multilateral trade rules in favour of the developing countries, particularly in agriculture, as well as the inclusion of global rules in other areas of interest to them, such as trade facilitation, competition policy, investment and labour issues. For instance, the allegation made by Oxfam that the Doha Round had primarily become a market access negotiation rather than an opportunity to rebalance decades of unfair trade rules in agriculture would appear to support this claim. However, further research would be needed to substantiate this argument further.

Another key question investigated here was whether the NSAs involved in trade policy-making consider choosing between multilateral and regional venues as 'forum shopping' in pursuit of particular agendas, interests and objectives. This question turned out to be quite complex as the NSAs covered here did not consider these alternative venues as mutually exclusive. One important aspect to take into consideration in the discussion on 'forum shopping' is the aspect of forum choice as it relates to the enforcement of trade agreements through dispute settlement. In this regard, the NSAs surveyed indicated a preference for the WTO as a forum for settling disputes and expressed interest in safeguarding and strengthening the WTO's dispute settlement mechanism. More needs to be known, however, on how NSAs view this issue and position themselves to influence governments on the choice between PTAs and the WTO to settle disputes.

Although the majority of the NSAs have a normative preference for seeking to influence trade policy at the WTO, a number of them also seek to influence trade policy-making in PTAs concurrently, particularly through their national affiliates. To a certain extent, the slow pace of the Doha Round has prompted NSAs to focus on the negotiation of PTAs where things are actually moving. This is particularly true with regard to PTAs in which trade unions and CSOs expressed concerns about developing countries being at a disadvantage because of power asymmetries, such as in PTA negotiations involving the European Union and the United States, and also the EU's EPAs.

References

Barton, J. H., Goldstein, J. L., Josling, T. E. and Steinberg, R. H. 2006. *The Evolution of the Trade Regime: Politics, Law, and Economics of the GATT and the WTO*. Princeton University Press.

Busch, M. L. 2007. 'Overlapping Institutions, Forum Shopping, and Dispute Settlement in International Trade', *International Organization* **61**: 735–61.

Charnovitz, S. 2000. 'Opening the WTO to Nongovernmental Interests', *Fordham International Law Review* **24**, 1/2: 173–216.

Consumer Unity & Trust Society International (CUTS) 2009. *Improving Ownership through Inclusive Trade Policy Making Processes: Lessons from Africa*. Jaipur Printers P. Ltd.

Friedrich Ebert Stiftung (FES) 2009. *The Cotonou Scenarios: Negotiations on the Economic Partnership Agreement (EPA) between the European Union and West Africa*. Cotonou: Editions COPEF.

Global Union Research Network (GURN) 2005. '*Report of the Online Discussion on Bilateral and Regional Trade Agreements*'.

He, B. and Murphy, H. 2007. 'Global Social Justice at the WTO? The Role of NGOs in Constructing Global Social Contracts', *International Affairs* **83**, 4: 707–27.

Hocking, B. and McGuire, S. (eds.) 2004. *Trade Politic*. London: Routledge.

Hoekman, M. and Kostecki, M. 2001. *The Political Economy of the World Trading System*. New York: Oxford University Press.

O'Brien, R., Goetz, A. M., Scholte, J. A. and Williams, M. 2000. *Contesting Global Governance: Multilateral Institutions and Global Social Movements*. Cambridge University Press.

Ostry, S. 2002. 'Preface', '*The Trade Policy-Making Process: Level One of the Two-Level Game: Country Studies in the Western Hemisphere*', INTAL-ITD-STA (Inter-American Development Bank), Occasional Paper No. 13, Institute for the Integration of Latin America and the Caribbean and the Inter-American Developmental Bank, Buenos Aires, pp. i–iv.

Oxfam 2009. 'Empty Promises, What Happened to "Development" in the WTO's Doha Round?', *Oxfam Briefing Paper, No. 131*, 16 July.

Sell, S. and Prakash, A. 2004. 'Using Ideas Strategically: The Contest Between Business and NGO Networks in Intellectual Property Rights', *International Studies Quarterly* **48**, 1: 143–75.

Slaughter, A. 2004. *A New World Order*. Princeton University Press.

Teegen, H., Doh, J. and Vachani, S. 2004. 'The Importance of Nongovernmental Organizations (NGOs) in Global Governance and Value Creation: An International Business Research Agenda', *Journal of International Business Studies* **35**: 463–83.

Wolfe, R. and Helmer, J. 2007. 'Trade Policy Begins at Home: Information and Consultation in the Trade Policy Process', in M. Halle and R. Wolfe (eds.), *Process Matters: Sustainable Development and Domestic Trade Transparency*. Winnipeg: International Institute for Sustainable Development, pp. 1–19.

World Trade Organization (WTO) 2007. *World Trade Report – Six Decades of Multilateral Trade Cooperation: What Have we Learned?* Geneva: WTO.

    2008. *How Can the WTO Help Harness Globalization?* 2007 WTO Public Forum, Geneva: WTO.

    2009. *Trading into the Future*. 2008 WTO Public Forum, Geneva: WTO.

    2010. *Global Problems, Global Solutions: Towards Better Global Governance*. 2009 WTO Public Forum, Geneva: WTO.

Zahrnt, V. 2008. 'Domestic Constituents and the Formulation of WTO Negotiating Positions: What the Delegates Say', *World Trade Review* 7, 2: 393–421

Main findings and conclusions

ANN CAPLING AND PATRICK LOW

1 Introduction

One of the most pressing issues confronting the multilateral trade system today is the rapid proliferation of preferential trade agreements (PTAs). Much has been written about why governments might choose to negotiate preferentially or multilaterally, but this literature has been written almost exclusively from the perspective of governments. We know very little about how non-state actors (NSAs) view the issue of forum choice, or how they position themselves to influence choices by governments about whether to emphasize PTAs or the World Trade Organization (WTO). The case studies in this book have sought to address these issues through interviews with state and non-state actors involved in trade policy-making in eight countries.

This chapter briefly summarizes the main findings from the case studies and distils a set of conclusions that we consider to be of general applicability. This summary does poor justice to the wealth of analysis and detail contained in the individual case studies, and thus it is very far from being a substitute for reading the individual studies. Nonetheless, some clear patterns have emerged from the case studies which allow us to make some more general observations about trade policy-making and forum choice. We have divided the main findings into three sections, each dealing with a particular aspect of the domestic trade policy-making process. Section 2 concerns the way governments organize themselves and fashion national priorities when formulating trade policy. Section 3 focuses on mechanisms that governments use for consulting with NSAs and the attitudes underlying this interaction. Section 4 deals with NSAs themselves and how they perceive their interests and go about their business. In discussing these various aspects of domestic policy-making, we shall draw illustratively but not exhaustively from the case studies. Section 5 contains the conclusions.

2   State actors

2.1   Institutional and organizational aspects
of trade policy-making

As trade policy at both the multilateral and preferential level has grown in complexity and embraced an ever widening set of issues, in most case study countries more attention has been paid to policy formulation by a growing set of governmental actors. This has led to a diffusion of power and influence within the executive branch, diluting what in many cases was more or less a monopoly of decision-making prerogatives held by the trade and/or foreign affairs ministries, and in some cases with the involvement of finance ministries. Moreover, in many, but not all, countries in our sample the legislative branch of government has also become more engaged and influential. This has been both a source of opportunity and frustration for NSAs active in trying to influence policy – an opportunity to focus more directly on particular issues and sometimes make common cause with particular branches of government, including the legislature, and a greater challenge in terms of the ability to be heard on the broader canvas of a country's overall policy stance. A growing tendency towards diversified, bottom–up as opposed to top–down policy-making in many countries leads to a more diffuse and nuanced process, which in our country case studies is probably more apparent in preferential than multilateral negotiations.

With the exception of Chile and Thailand, in our case study countries, the lead role for trade policy-making and trade negotiations has been located in an economic ministry. In a minority of cases, the lead agency is a ministry of trade that does not carry functional responsibilities for industry policy (e.g., Kenya and Indonesia). But more typically, the lead agency for trade policy is also responsible for the manufacturing sector and industrial development more broadly (e.g., Colombia, Jordan and South Africa). In most of these cases, concerns about 'bureaucratic capture' has seen departments of agriculture actively seek to exercise influence in trade policy-making, due to a perception that the trade interests of agricultural producers (both defensive and offensive) will take a back seat to the interests of manufacturers.

The exceptions are both noteworthy. In Chile, the trade agency (DIRECON) is located within the Ministry of Foreign Affairs, rather than in an economic department. Perhaps this is reflective of the relatively open nature of Chile's economy, which may have weakened the traditional relationship between trade policy and industry policy that has existed in many developing countries. The Thai case is different, as the trade policy function effectively became centralized in the office of the prime minister during the period of the Thaksin regime.

What is clear in all our case studies is that the nature of the contemporary trade policy agenda demands a high level of inter-agency coordination. In Chile, for example, DIRECON works with a wide variety of agencies on different aspects of the trade negotiations. Kenya's Ministry of Trade is the lead agency, but all economic policy ministries, the Ministry of East African Community and a number of parastatal organizations are also involved. In Mexico, the Ministry of the Economy is in charge of trade negotiations and plays a key role in policy formulation, but power is shared with ministries responsible for agriculture, foreign affairs, finance, home affairs and with the Central Bank. A similar pattern exists in Indonesia and South Africa. Prior to the Thaksin government, Thailand had well developed processes for inter-agency cooperation on trade policy.

Rivalrous relationships obviously develop among different government agencies in the process of policy formulation, so the quality of ministerial leadership and the organization and structure processes become important determinants of the degree of coherence and clarity of national policy. Chile, Colombia, Mexico and Kenya have relatively formalized and well-coordinated procedures that in themselves have led to a fairly clear and unified articulation of national positions. South Africa's process has been similar to these, but there may be growing agency rivalry between the Department of Trade and Industry and the new Department of Economic Development in the future as the country moves towards a more interventionist trade policy stance. Jordan's structure is centralized from the outset, with a Council of Ministers determining trade policy directions and with the Ministry of Industry and Trade acting primarily as an agency of implementation. This requires far less inter-agency coordination than is typical in the other case study countries. In Thailand, the picture appears to be one of fairly well articulated and diffused decision-making before the Thaksin period, which was characterized by a high degree of centralization. There has been a return to a more diffused approach in the post-Thaksin period, but with a certain degree of inter-ministerial friction.

The Indonesian case study argues that a weak trade ministry combined with a lack of adequate inter-agency coordination is an impediment to effective trade policy formulation, informed more by competition for influence and protectionist privileges than an over-arching conception of the national interest. This fragmentation of the policy process is also likely to make it much more difficult for NSAs to press their demands effectively.

It is also important to note that the absence of a clearly defined national stance may be more apparent in some of the other case study countries as well when it comes to multilateral negotiations, where these are 'price takers' rather than 'price makers' in the global context. This distinction refers to the notion that in contrast to a regional setting, individual countries view the WTO as a setting in which they wield little influence in relation to agenda formation or outcome, and therefore positions are more fluid or initially less well defined. In practice this perceived degree of powerlessness may be diluted through coalitional activity and groups of smaller players have certainly influenced outcomes in the WTO. Nevertheless, this is a matter of degree and even if there is coalitional activity, individual governments would have less authority over positions taken than were they to be purely national in formulation.

As noted in Chapter 1, the constitutional rules that determine which branch of government has authority over trade policy, the nature of legislative processes and the extent to which societal groups can influence legislators have an impact on trade policy outcomes. On the face of it, one might expect engagement by the legislative branch of government to afford greater legitimacy, and perhaps coherence, to domestic trade policy-making. But whether this is so also depends on the nature, workings and quality of the legislature. The overall trend in the case study countries appears to be one of increased involvement by the legislative branch. This is particularly true in the case of the Latin American countries where legislatures have a formal role in the ratification of trade agreements. In Chile, while the executive has the power to make trade agreements, the Congress has the authority to accept or reject such agreements without amendment. The same is true in Colombia, where the president would veto a trade agreement only in cases where the legislature amended a trade agreement that had been negotiated by the executive. In Mexico, the executive branch is required to report upon and justify decisions to enter into trade negotiations and to keep the Senate informed throughout the process. The Senate is also required to approve trade agreements.

Notwithstanding the relatively robust role for these legislatures in the passage of trade agreements, legislative interest in trade policy matters has not been consistent across the board or across time. The Colombian legislature was particularly active in the lively national debate over a free trade agreement with the United States, and the executive went to considerable lengths to directly involve Congress members in the process. In Mexico, the legislative branch has become increasingly active in overseeing the establishment of trade agreements. By contrast, the Chilean legislature has generally adopted a passive position in relation to trade agreements, with the exception of the debate on the trade relationship to be negotiated with MERCOSUR. The passivity is probably explained by the large measure of agreement in Chile regarding the advantages of open trade.

The story is somewhat different in Africa and East Asia. In Kenya and South Africa, the constitutional powers of the legislatures with regard to trade policy-making are unclear and largely untested. This state of affairs reflects the British constitutional tradition where the power to conduct foreign relations, including treaty-making, is exercised by the executive branch without the parliament's consent. In South Africa, the constitution was changed in the 1990s to require constitutional approval of treaties, but this new parliamentary role has not yet been asserted in relation to trade agreements. More generally, there is a relative lack of engagement on trade policy matters in the Kenyan, South African and Jordanian parliaments. However, in the case of Kenya and South Africa this is likely to change in the future.

In Indonesia, the executive branch holds the authority to draw up trade agreements, and while the legislature has the authority to act on such agreements, in practice it has been little engaged. In Thailand, trade agreements were also the prerogative of the executive, but the 2007 constitution established a significant legislative role in trade policy formulation. Parliament has to approve both the initiation of negotiations leading to a trade agreement and the adoption of such an agreement.

Generally speaking, we can see that the role of parliaments in relation to trade agreements has recently evolved in response to the changing nature of trade agreements that are more likely now to embrace regulatory arrangements and policies that were formally considered to be the exclusive preserve of domestic policy. Notions of democratic legitimacy, the importance of ensuring that international commitments are supported by those whom they affect and the need to maintain social cohesion have all led to a greater role for parliaments in trade agreements.

2.2   Government attitudes towards forum choice

The choice of the negotiating context – that is, the option between selecting a unilateral approach to trade policy-making, or negotiating preferentially or multilaterally – is not always an open one. Many developing countries have opted for unilateral trade-opening over the years, suggesting a primary focus on the domestic economic consequences of freer trade rather than on access to foreign markets. Implicit in the unilateral option is also a lack of concern about reciprocity, which is doubtless more typical of smaller countries without terms of trade concerns or the conviction that they are large enough to attract reciprocal action from their trading partners. If countries are significantly different in size, larger ones will be more reluctant to negotiate with smaller ones if they are required to exchange obligations upon which third parties can free-ride. These factors likely explain small countries' relative lack of interest in trade-opening via the multilateral as opposed to the preferential route, and will also make a unilateral approach relatively more attractive.

Countries that are price-takers in a global setting are far less likely to choose whether or not to enter into a multilateral negotiation. They may regard multilateral negotiations as exogenous occurrences which call for some sort of engagement on their part, but they would probably hold out little hope of exerting much influence over the negotiating agenda. Efforts to influence the multilateral agenda are much more likely to involve coalitional activity with like-minded countries than would be the case with preferential negotiations, suggesting at least in some instances a different and less domestically-based process of decision-making.

Preferential and multilateral options are not perfect substitutes for at least three other reasons. First, the two venues rarely offer the same coverage or depth of commitment. Preferential agreements tend to go further in terms of market-opening commitments, with free trade often being the ultimate objective for a significant part of total trade. The WTO's market-opening aspirations tend to be more modest. On the other hand, with a few exceptions, PTAs often have less well-developed structures of rules than the WTO and they may rely on WTO dispute settlement procedures.

Second, the interests that prompt action in trade negotiations may be highly influential in the choice of venue. As discussed in Chapter 1, a wider range of quite distinct economic, political and political economy motivations may be behind preferential negotiations compared with multilateral ones, especially in countries like the those in our sample. This would limit a genuine choice between venues. These distinct motivations are strongly evident in our case study countries. With few exceptions, countries had a strong interest in negotiating PTAs with their most important trade partners for commercial or defensive reasons – often to protect existing levels of market access in the face of other PTAs. In some cases, foreign policy reasons were also an important factor. Indeed, the majority of the case study countries had negotiated, or tried to negotiate, a PTA with the United States. There is also a strong regional story that emerges in Latin America, Africa and Southeast Asia, which is partly determined by trade patterns and economic inter-dependencies, but may also be motivated by considerations of regional solidarity.

Third, there may be some very particular issues that can be effectively negotiated only at the multilateral level. The case of production subsidies is often cited as an example, where it is impossible to discriminate among foreign markets. It is possible to imagine other examples, such as negotiations aimed at addressing truly global spillovers or externalities, such as climate damage and financial regulation. Concerns about free-riding and burden sharing may be sufficiently intense to push countries to eschew preferential venues for such international cooperation.

Even if preferential and multilateral venues are not perfect substitutes, it is instructive to see where state and non-state actors place their priorities and how much effort they expend on multilateral negotiations compared with preferential ones. Virtually all the countries in our sample have engaged in some degree of unilateral trade-opening at some stage in the last two or three decades. More interesting from our perspective, however, is how they have balanced preferential and multilateral interests.

Chile has been highly active in negotiating PTAs, although for policy autonomy reasons it has avoided full engagement in MERCOSUR or Andean integration efforts. The government's rationale for relying on preferential agreements embodies several elements. One is to secure greater market access and another to diversify its trading partners. A third reason is essentially defensive: to make sure that Chile is among the countries with the best possible market access to as many markets as possible – something that most favoured nation (MFN) opening does not provide to the same degree. Chile has nevertheless remained active in the WTO, particularly in areas where preferential arrangements tend to fall short, such as fishery subsidies and anti-dumping disciplines.

Colombia has also been active in PTA negotiations, dedicating the bulk of its negotiating resources to these endeavours. Interviewees in the Colombia study – state and non-state actors alike – maintained that in the final analysis the multilateral option was the optimum one from a systemic perspective, although the ability to influence outcomes was far less in that venue, and called for more coalitional activity. Moreover, multilateral outcomes tended to be somewhat incomplete, slow and more remote from immediate interests. Forum choice was seen as largely exogenous.

Mexico has emphasized PTAs in much the same way as Chile since the NAFTA negotiations which began in the early 1990s. Reliance on PTAs was a logical continuation following the unilateral liberalization that characterized Mexican trade policy in the 1980s. Since the major decisions about the direction of Mexican trade policy had already been taken in unilateral and preferential contexts, the WTO did not entail hard decisions in relation to market opening. In this sense, the question of forum choice was moot. Mexico has nevertheless remained active in the WTO, and articulated interests in areas where a multilateral forum provides a better context than a preferential one. More recently, the momentum of trade-opening has been slowed by public opposition, based on the conviction that much has already been done and insistence by NSAs and elements of the legislature on reciprocity from trading partners.

An interesting issue in the Mexican case involves the use of dispute settlement mechanisms, where in certain instances a choice of forum is possible. Private parties can bring disputes against governments under the North American Free Trade Agreement (NAFTA), but since this is not a possibility under the WTO it is of less interest in the present context. However, NAFTA allows state-to-state disputes to be brought either under its own provisions or to the WTO. The WTO has been the preferred venue. This is partly because agreement was elusive on the procedural aspects of the NAFTA arrangements, but more substantively because the WTO allowed the participation of third parties and gave wider exposure to the issues at stake. This is an important finding in that it emphasizes the distinction between the WTO as a vehicle for trade opening and as a system of justiciable trade rules – a distinction to which we shall return in due course.

Indonesia embraces a three-pronged strategy focusing on multilateral, regional and bilateral approaches, although the last of these has been a more recent part of the country's trade policy focus. The case study reports a sense that it is an administrative challenge to run a comprehensive trade policy strategy on all fronts. Unlike the NSAs (see section 4 below), government attitudes have tended to become more questioning of the multilateral approach, the concern stemming both from the way some issues appear to be framed in terms of the interests of developed countries and the slow pace of progress.

In Thailand, the Thaksin government had a strong preference for bilateral PTAs, and the centralization of trade policy-making which resulted in the temporary eclipse of the established inter-ministerial processes meant that there was limited engagement in multilateral negotiations. This has to some extent been reversed in the post-Thaksin period, but the dramatic politicization of trade policy in the context of a much more far-reaching political struggle, combined with NSA opposition to further trade-opening, has left trade policy and questions about forum choice in something of a limbo.

Jordan has pursued a fairly active PTA agenda in recent years and is a relative newcomer to the multilateral world, having only joined the WTO in 2000. While views varied among government officials as to the preferred negotiating forum, there is a broadly shared view that the question of forum choice has never really been posited, since the matter is regarded as entirely exogenous from a trade policy perspective. Moreover, the centralized locus for trade policy-making has not encouraged much debate on trade policy options.

Since the demise of the apartheid regime and the assumption of power by the African National Congress (ANC) in 1994, trade policy in South Africa has focused mainly on PTAs. The motivation has been to secure improved market access, but more recently foreign policy factors have played a role, particularly in trade relations with other parts of Africa. In both cases, regional arrangements have better suited the policy purpose at hand. Interestingly, however, South Africa does not exclude the WTO as an important trade policy forum where it believes it can exert some influence. This may well be in part because of South Africa's economic predominance on a large part of the African continent. The WTO is perceived as a fairer playing field, particularly in dealings with large trade partners such as the United States and the European Union, although there are reservations about the WTO in terms of the time and effort required to secure results.

Kenya's early trade policy focus was on regional arrangements involving immediately neighbouring countries. This was followed by a period when unilateral liberalization played an important role. Much of Kenya's current trade policy focus is on regional agreements. The country participates fairly actively in the WTO, but to a degree defensively and often in the context of coalitions. This reflects the challenges for a small country of exerting influence in a global setting. Overall, the government seeks to work in both preferential and multilateral contexts, but does not see the WTO as an important forum for consolidating trade liberalization.

Table 11.1 below is an eloquent statement of why the WTO cannot match either unilateral trade action or PTAs when it comes to market opening. With the exception of Kenya and Thailand, the case study countries have bound all, or almost all, of their tariffs in the WTO. But a comparison of the bound rates and the applied rates reveals in every case that a substantial margin for manoeuvre exists, allowing countries to raise their tariffs to considerably higher rates than those applied before a WTO

Table 11.1 *Bound and applied tariff rates in case study countries, 2008*

	Share of tariff bound (%)	Simple average bound rate (%)	Simple average MFN applied rate (%)
Chile	100	25	6
Colombia	100	43	13
Indonesia	97	37	7
Jordan	100	14	11
Kenya	15	96	13
Mexico	100	36	13
South Africa	97	19	8
Thailand	75	29	11

Source: ITC, UNCTAD, WTO: World Tariff Profiles 2009.

market access obligation kicks in. These are average rates not weighted by trade, and the disaggregated story might be a little modified in the case of particular tariff lines, but the overall picture does not change. Moreover, when preferential trade is taken into account, the simple average applied MFN rate is an overstatement of the actual level of protection. In short, the WTO by and large is not regarded by the case study countries, and doubtless many like them, as a place to define constraining market access obligations.

3 Government mechanisms for consulting non-state actors

3.1 The evolution of consultation processes

As already noted, concerted efforts to systematize consultation mechanisms involving NSAs are a recent phenomenon in most of the case study countries. Mexico was a forerunner in this process, with the business sector being consulted in the context of the GATT accession negotiations in the mid-1980s, a process that became more formal and structured in the NAFTA negotiations in the early 1990s. In Chile, a consultative process with business started in the 1990s, and evolved to include labour as well. Non-state actors became involved in such consultations towards the end of the 1990s in the context of the free trade agreement (FTA) with Canada. In Colombia, structured and inclusive consultation mechanisms were established in the context of the bilateral negotiations with the United States and subsequently extended to all PTA negotiations.

In South Africa, the National Economic Development and Labour Council was established by the ANC government as the principal forum to bring together government, business, labour and civil society organizations (CSOs). Several other consultative bodies also exist. Kenya's formal consultative processes began in 2003 with the establishment of the multi-stakeholder National Committee on the WTO (NCWTO). Previously, the government had links with the private sector through business associations, and the NCWTO was established in response to pressure from CSOs. A number of other institutional consultative mechanisms have also been established to deal with particular aspects of trade policy formulation and especially the negotiation of PTAs. In Jordan, the role of NSAs in trade negotiations remains limited, but is gradually taking form. Many NSAs are partly organized and funded by the state itself.

Indonesia's efforts to engage with NSAs began with the establishment of a democratic government. Formal consultation mechanisms were eliminated during the Thaksin period in Thailand, and the public perception that positions were being stitched up by the government and big business contributed significantly to the politicization of trade policy.

3.2 Differential treatment between business non-state actors and civil society organizations

As noted in Chapter 1, previous studies have found that trade policy consultative mechanisms have tended to privilege business actors above CSOs. Our study confirms this finding, and differentiated treatment between business NSAs and CSOs is a feature of consultative processes in the majority of case study countries. For instance, the polarized nature of NAFTA debate in Mexico – where business came to the table with specific commercial objectives, while CSOs had more general issues pertaining to principles and political positions and 'all or nothing' demands – entailed very different interactions with government. The Mexican pattern was characteristic of Chile in earlier times, although attempts have been made recently to be more inclusive of CSOs. This pattern is also discernible in Indonesia, Thailand (especially during the Thaksin period) and Kenya. In Kenya, the government sometimes works with CSOs under pressure from other governments and international agencies. Mindful of the domestic political sensitivities involved in the FTA negotiation with the United States, the Colombian government attempted to be more inclusive of a very broad range of NSAs and the public at large in terms of disseminating information and providing consultative forums.

South Africa may be something of an outlier with regard to the relative treatment of business NSAs and CSOs, since the original institutional structure set up for consultations was inclusive. But generally speaking, there was differentiated treatment of business and CSOs in our case study countries, with some CSOs seeing their involvement as largely tokenistic, a view that was backed by the Geneva-based CSOs interviewed for this project (see Chapter 10). Of course, a challenge inevitably arises for governments when they consider consultative processes with groups that are opposed to an intended course of action, sometimes implacably so. This leaves limited room for meaningful exchange, and it is not surprising that this results in differential treatment. Nevertheless, it would seem that some governments have tried harder than others to be inclusive, although not necessarily with materially different results.

3.3   Motivations for government consultation processes with non-state actors

Case study authors asked governments why they consulted with NSAs. In the majority of cases, the most important reason given was because of the need to acquire technical advice, information and/or commercial intelligence from their interlocutors. These findings are consistent with the literature that argues that trade policy-making is not an exclusively state-centric process, that governments lack the internal research capacity and knowledge that is crucial for the determination of negotiation positions and, in turn, that the business sector and CSOs also rely on governments and the authority of the state to help them pursue their goals. Respondents in most cases also identified public policy requirements as an important reason for consultations. From these responses, it did not necessarily follow that the consultations were merely *pro forma* superficial encounters, as in most cases respondents also identified the role of consultations in promoting transparency and engendering support. In other words, there was an appreciation among government officials of the importance of increasing transparency and promoting participation so as to promote broad support for trade policy and trade negotiations, maintain social cohesion and promote the legitimacy of these processes. The one major exception to this was the case of Thailand, due to the lack of consultation processes in the Thaksin period and the fact that since then there has been little PTA activity. Were such activity to re-ignite, however, consultation processes would doubtless be important, as would the role of the legislature under the new constitution.

A final issue to consider in relation to consultation mechanisms is how far the substance of the negotiations and the negotiating forum themselves are determinants of the nature of consultation processes. In virtually all the case study countries with active NSA sectors, many businesses and CSOs will typically focus on the issues of particular interest to them. Only CSOs with an over-arching agenda – most typically an anti-trade one – will seek to play a role in all aspects of a negotiation. The latter are obviously harder for governments to deal with, and consultations involving them, if they are more than *pro forma*, are likely to emphasize 'big picture' issues over the substance of prospective deals.

3.4   *The influence of subject matter and forum choice on consultation processes*

What about the influence of the issues at hand on the choice between preferential and multilateral venues for negotiations? Chile, Colombia, Jordan, Kenya, South Africa and Thailand have all developed more active consultation mechanisms in the context of PTAs than for the WTO. Indonesia, as a relative newcomer to PTAs, does not have well-developed consultation mechanisms for these kinds of negotiations and they tend to be more of an *ad hoc* nature. Virtually all the countries in the sample have mechanisms for WTO consultations, and an interesting question is why they receive less attention. Several reasons for this emerge in the studies. First, the WTO is seen as more remote and slower-moving, with less frequent negotiating episodes about which to be concerned. Second, the perception in 'price-taker' countries is that there is limited scope for influencing outcomes in the WTO, unless issues at hand are particularly important and engender coalitional activity. Third, the WTO is a less important venue when it comes to market opening, since most developing countries do not define their actual market access policies or international obligations in the WTO. Instead, the true conditions of market access are typically a combination of unilateral decisions and PTA commitments. Thus, it is more likely that PTA negotiations will involve deeper commitments across a broader range of areas (especially in a bilateral negotiation with a developed country partner), and therefore that the stakes are likely to be higher for both opponents and supporters of an agreement. A fourth reason that does not really emerge from the case studies but that is worth considering, is whether the WTO rule-making function is not fully valued by NSAs, or is not regarded by governments as being of much concern to NSAs. This would be the case if their view was that small countries play little part in shaping the rules, or if the rules are taken for granted as a public good supplied by others but available as needed. These questions will be taken up again in the conclusion.

As has been noted earlier, in several of the case study countries there is awareness that certain market access issues, such as production subsidies in agriculture and fisheries, do require a multilateral approach. A good example of this is the case of fish subsidy negotiations in the Doha Round, where the Latin American base of OCEANA, a CSO dedicated to preserving fish stocks, is located in Chile, and where the predominant view is that this is a WTO and not a preferential issue.

4   The interests and attitudes of non-state actors

4.1   The wide array of non-state actor interests

In most case study countries there is a broad array of interest groups, often more diversified on the CSO than on the business side. But among business groups some clearly wish to limit trade opening in their sectors, while others want to exchange domestic market-opening for better market access opportunities abroad and also for lower cost inputs into their production processes. Similar to business in terms of specific economic interests are labour and farmer groups. Among the CSOs, there are sometimes differences between environmental and development groups, but these differences do not always reduce to those who wish to see less trade and those who wish to see more. Within the broad category we refer to as CSOs there is a wide range of issue groups. At a certain level of generality, many of these groups can make common cause, but detail will tend to divide them more. Among the CSO community are those interested in various aspects of intellectual property, public health advocates, consumer protection groups, environmentalists, developmentalists, anti-poverty groups, academics and so on.

Consistent with earlier studies, in several of the case studies the point was made that the CSOs are frequently less well prepared, less technically adept and more poorly funded than business interest groups. This would tend to be reflected in less nuanced positions and would make constructive engagement with government more difficult for them. This, in turn, feeds into the preferred choices of avenue for influencing government.

4.2 Avenues for influencing governments

While earlier studies have described the various ways that governments seek to engage NSA stakeholders in trade policy-making, their focus on government-initiated consultation exercises excludes analysis of the other avenues that NSAs might pursue for the purpose of influencing government. Indeed, much of the literature seems to assume that governments have fixed preferences and they seek to engage NSA participation for the primary purpose of mobilizing support for state preferences. Thus, one of the objectives of our study was to gain a better understanding of how NSAs try to influence the development of trade policy and who they seek to influence.

In Colombia, Indonesia, Thailand and Mexico a clear pattern emerges. Those that have closer positions to the government and who favour in some measure the completion of negotiations prefer direct contact with government officials and/or ministers. They are far less likely to mount public campaigns than NSAs who do not share the government's vision of the national interest. In these countries, groups who eschew trade-opening or who feel that their particular public policy concerns are receiving inadequate attention will mount public campaigns. Public campaigns are designed to garner support for their cause and attract political attention. They are also undoubtedly useful for fund-raising purposes, but whether they are as effective as direct dialogue is another matter. In Thailand, the TradeWatch campaign against PTAs proved very successful, although this was in a highly charged political atmosphere where fundamental political changes were afoot. In other instances, public campaigns by special interest groups have probably been less successful, but it is not easy to identify the counterfactual in terms of what outcomes would have looked like.

In Chile, most NSAs seem to prefer direct interaction with the government, a fact likely explained by the relatively broad pro-trade consensus in that country. In Jordan, many NSAs are at least in part government-sponsored, suggesting a degree of control over positions taken as well as the ability to access government officials and political figures. There are some CSOs, however, who engage in public campaigns. In South Africa, only a minority of NSAs seek to appeal directly to the public. The inclusiveness of South Africa's initial setup for consultations probably accounts for the prevalence of direct contact with government. In the case of Kenya, the majority of NSAs seek to influence outcomes through contacts with government. Public campaigns are less preferred and this is in part because of a certain degree of government intolerance of campaigns and demonstrations.

It is noteworthy that legislators are seen as less important than government officials and ministers as interlocutors. In the South African case this was attributed to the perception that parliamentarians are relatively lacking in knowledge about trade issues. This is probably applicable to most cases given the relatively low levels of involvement of legislators in the negotiation of trade agreements, with the exception of controversial negotiations.

4.3   Non-state actor views regarding the choice of forum for negotiations

We have already discussed the reality that preferential and multilateral settings for negotiations are not perfect substitutes, although at the margin the degree of emphasis placed on each of the options will make a difference to trade policy outcomes. Thus, an important question for this study is what NSAs think about different forums – that is, the choice between preferential and multilateral approaches – for negotiations and how they might have influenced the choice of forum. Indeed, we are not aware of any other empirical studies that have investigated this question. The findings of this study are preliminary, but telling.

The conviction that the WTO is too remote and too big for effective direct influence to be exerted pervades much, but not all, NSA thinking. And this is reinforced by the sense that what happens in the WTO is less important to their interests than the outcomes of PTA negotiations. Relatively minor exceptions to this thinking are found with respect to specific issues of an essentially multilateral nature and in cases where NSAs are engaged in international activity through affiliated or subsidiary arrangements involving multi-country non-state organizations (see below).

Chile, with its twenty or more PTAs, and Mexico, with its dozen, have both moved close to free trade across the board. Getting there was almost exclusively through a combination of unilateral- and PTA-driven trade-opening episodes. This is why NSAs have been so active preferentially and relatively disengaged at the WTO, at least in terms of market-opening negotiations. Both countries have been active to a degree in rules-related negotiations, reflecting a sophisticated and well-informed understanding that their trade interests – be they offensive or defensive – are not entirely covered through their PTA networks. That realization appears less well developed in other case studies, and may also be less true in terms of their current trade interests.

The Colombia case study reports limited comprehension or connection among NSAs in relation to the WTO, which was considered to be remote and hard to influence. Nevertheless, it is notable that both the government and many NSAs regard the WTO as a better option in a systemic sense. There was some criticism in interviews of the fact that the business sector had not engaged more with the WTO agenda.

Indonesian NSA attitudes offer a particularly interesting take on the issue of forum choice. For the most part, NSAs have a preference for multilateral negotiations, in part because of a longer history of engagement and less PTA activity than in many other countries. There is some suggestion that international donors and development agencies have encouraged a pro-WTO stance. In addition, the WTO is seen as more protective of developing country interests, especially when it comes to PTAs involving a bilateral agreement with a developed country. Another way of seeing this is in terms of a preference for less active trade policies and less market opening – something the WTO delivers more effectively than PTAs.

In Thailand, NSAs have been traditionally hostile to the GATT/WTO, which has been seen as a rich country club careless of developing country interests. This attitude is also supported by a lack of enthusiasm among many NSAs for more open trade. The Thaksin period entirely eclipsed any subtleties that might have existed in NSA thinking about the relative merits of preferential and multilateral approaches to international trade relations. Thaksin's interest in PTAs provoked overwhelming popular opposition to trade in general. Since the failure of the Thailand–US FTA and the removal of Thaksin from power, trade policy has been in a holding pattern. If the Doha Round were to make progress or other PTAs appeared on the horizon, it may be that CSO opposition to trade agreements might be softened, since a non-trivial part of the original objections concerned process. That being said, Thai NSAs are firmly opposed to bilateral PTAs because they are seen as a form of domination and subjugation by developed countries. They are more ambivalent, and potentially more receptive, to regional PTAs out of a sense of Asian/developing world solidarity.

In the case of Jordan, there has been very little NSA engagement on the multilateral front. In common with the government in South Africa, South African NSAs believe that the WTO is important and that influence upon it can be exerted. They probably consider PTAs and the WTO of similar importance, but of relevance in somewhat different contexts.

As suggested earlier, a favourable attitude towards the WTO may also reflect defensive interests when it comes to North–South trade relationships. Finally, in the case of Kenya, NSAs do not appear to have strong preferences as between certain PTAs and the WTO, although they have fewer opportunities for activism in the case of the WTO. Most reservations among the NSAs in relation to trade agreements concern the economic partnership agreements (EPAs) with the European Union.

4.4 National non-state actors and their relationships with international non-state actors

Many NSAs in the case study countries have links of one sort or another with international NSAs, especially in the CSO community. In some of the countries, including South Africa, Thailand and possibly Jordan, international links seem to focus more on information, research collaboration, training and capacity-building, rather than entailing a direct effort to influence national policy positions. In other cases, such as Kenya, Mexico, Chile, Colombia and Indonesia, international NSAs may also be active in policy formulation in collaboration with their national counterparts. In some of these countries, governments will also depend on international NSAs for technical support of various kinds and perhaps policy advice.

Chapter 10 analysed the interests and preferences of Geneva-based NSAs that were involved in trade policy-making and that had national affiliates or worked with other NSAs based in national jurisdictions. Without exception and irrespective of whether they represented business, trade unions or a wide variety of CSOs in areas such as the environment, development, consumers and public health, these NSAs had a strong preference for multilateral trade negotiations. This finding is not altogether surprising given their Geneva base, which implies a significant investment of expertise and resources in WTO-related matters, but it is somewhat at odds with the views of many of the national NSAs that were interviewed for the country case studies.

Many of these had connections with governments and NSAs in our case study countries, and among the Geneva-based NSAs those representing trade unions and CSOs sought to influence the positions adopted by governments and national NSAs in the negotiation of PTAs. This was especially true in relation to PTAs, where there were concerns about developing countries being at a disadvantage due to power asymmetries, for instance, in negotiations that involved the United States or the European Union, and also the EU's EPAs. By contrast, the Geneva-based business organizations placed very little emphasis on trying to influence PTA negotiations.

The results of these kinds of interaction are not easy to identify in a systematic way. Much depends on whether international NSAs are seen as supporters of broad-based efforts to empower countries to participate more effectively in international negotiations, or whether they are regarded as partisan supporters of positions regarded as minoritarian. But what is striking is that the strong preference for multilateralism that was evident among the Geneva-based business organizations was not manifested by national business organizations interviewed for the country case studies.

5   Conclusions

The world of trade policy has evolved dramatically in at least three senses in the last few decades. First, many more countries are engaged in trade today than thirty years ago. Second, the range of issues covered under the rubric of trade and trade-related negotiations has expanded enormously as economies have become more intertwined in a globalizing world. Third, the architecture for trade cooperation has changed, with an explosion of PTAs involving almost every trading nation. This last development in particular has raised important systemic questions about the respective roles for preferential and multilateral trade cooperation under the WTO.

Literature on all the above issues has burgeoned over the years, and in many instances has provided useful insights and better understanding. An issue that has been a lesser subject of focus, however, is the domestic side of trade policy-making – particularly in developing countries – and in this connection the role of NSAs in influencing the process of trade policy formulation. The case studies on eight countries in this volume have been prepared by trade specialists from the countries concerned, often by individuals directly involved in the policy processes they analyse.

In comparing these authoritative accounts of how governments go about formulating negotiating positions in a domestic setting, how and why they consult with NSAs in this process and how the NSAs themselves participate, it is very clear there is much that is specific to individual countries. A wealth of different experiences are recounted in the chapters, demonstrating how the specificities of the context matter and what the risk would be of generalized over-simplifications. The studies have also shown how the complexity of trade policy formulation processes has grown, as well as the diversity of interests among stakeholders. Policy-making power has become more diffuse, coherence among different government authorities more elusive and the need for securing legitimacy from a broader public more pressing.

Despite the miscellany of individual national experiences, certain similarities are discernible among the issues arising in each of the case studies. Consultation mechanisms involving NSAs came to most of the countries quite recently. Governments have generally found it easier to interact with business than CSOs, whose interests may be antithetical to those being pursued by governments. While several government representatives said in interviews that a reason for consulting was to meet public policy obligations and satisfy a public relations imperative, many also pointed to beneficial spin-offs from doing so, including the acquisition of knowledge and information, the promotion of transparency and a better understanding of different views.

In almost all the case study countries where NSAs had become more prominent, they had demonstrated a wide range of differences and object-ives, and with the exception of the special situation in Thailand, showed little inclination to establish common cause against governments. This lack of cohesion and common purpose has facilitated the politics of NSA consultative processes from the perspective of governments. To the extent that positions taken by individual NSAs, and especially CSOs, represent minority views there is no interest on any side to forge coalitions. On the other hand, if governments are perceived to rely on 'divide and rule' tactics as a means of neutralizing opposition to their trade policy objectives they may risk a dilution of their legitimacy in the eyes of the public at large. The participation of internationally connected and influenced NSAs in domestic policy formulation processes may have caused some disquiet on the part of certain governments, but in other cases it seems that the international connections served purposes other than policy-making, such as research and training.

5.1   Forum choice

A key issue investigated in this study was the influence of NSAs on government decisions on whether to negotiate preferentially or multilaterally. This turned out to be a fairly complex question. In the first place, the choice sometimes simply did not exist as these alternative negotiating forums are not substitutes. Differences in emphasis, context and negotiating content influenced forum choice in important ways. More often than not the preferential and multilateral venues would be characterized as complements not substitutes, although this does not detract from the reality that a government can signal priorities and preferences in terms of venue choice in all sorts of ways. Several governments in the sample countries emphasized the price-taking character of their engagement at the global level, arguing that their scope for influencing outcomes, or even choosing whether or not to participate in negotiations, was circumscribed by their size. They also considered that the WTO was remote and slow in doing business.

The argument that occurrences in the WTO are exogenous and entirely isolated from influence on the part of the case study countries is almost certainly an over-statement, not least because of the scope for coalitional activity which has become more commonplace in WTO deliberations in recent years. This argument could serve another purpose. If countries are too unimportant to influence outcomes, then they cannot be reasonably expected to contribute to any public good characteristics that may be embodied in the WTO. It is clear that most developing countries do not see the WTO as an interesting venue for negotiating trade-opening – which in any event is not a public good in the strict sense – and there are arguably good reasons for such a position. But this does leave open the question of whether the contribution of a system of rules to the gains from trade should simply be enjoyed as a public good supplied by others. In effect, the observation reported in several of the case studies that the rules were seen as tilted in favour of rich countries suggests a case for engagement on that front. Several of the governments of case study countries appear to acknowledge this as, despite their reliance on PTAs for defining much of their trade policy, they remain active in WTO negotiations on rules. Moreover, in at least one case study country there appeared to be a firm sentiment in favour of the WTO as the preferred forum, notwithstanding the challenges of doing business there.

As far as the NSAs are concerned, similar reactions to those of governments were discernible. The WTO was seen as remote and difficult to influence, even if it was a natural venue for certain issues that needed a multilateral approach. There were some interesting nuances in CSO attitudes. On the one hand, the WTO was seen as an attractive venue because it achieved less in terms of trade-opening than PTAs. On the other hand, there was a certain feeling that the rules were written to give preference to developed country interests.

5.2   Are there lessons for the WTO?

For the most part, the case studies did not convey the impression that natural antipathy and competition characterized the relationship between preferentialism and multilateralism. But the WTO was widely perceived as being of less relevance than PTAs in mapping out domestic trade policy. This was largely true of governments as well as NSAs, although all parties acknowledged that there existed a unique set of issues, particularly those involving subsidies or large global externalities that needed multilateral attentions.

What was perhaps surprising in most of the underlying discourse in the case studies about trade policy formulation and negotiation, and the role of NSAs therein, focused on market access issues, or, in other words, on trade liberalization. This was not always made explicit, but there was little discussion about the dual role of international agreements: that of modifying the conditions of competition (trade-opening) and that of setting rules subject to formal enforcement.

As we have already observed, the WTO is generally not seen by our case study countries as the place to define constraining market access obligations. There are a variety of reasons why this situation is unlikely to change. This brings us back to the point already made about the more valuable role that the WTO plays as a system of justiciable rules. The results of this study suggest that this point is poorly appreciated, even though in some cases stakeholders expressed reservations about the neutrality of the WTO rules. If there were any lessons for the WTO from this study, they would be, first, to encourage debate about the core functions of the WTO. Second, it seems that more work needs to be done in raising awareness of the value of global rules in a world of multiple venues for defining trade policy against the background of a distinction between the changes in competition brought about by reducing trade barriers, and the stability afforded by minimum justiciable standards of policy conduct. Third, the assumption that rules are exogenously determined by a few major trading powers should be revisited and tested against an alternative scenario where rule-making is a process for generating global public goods in which a broad range of trading partners can participate.

INDEX